Prospectus.

THE

SCOTTISH NATION;

OR THE

SURNAMES, FAMILIES, LITERATURE, HONOURS,

AND

Biographical History of the People of Scotland.

BY WILLIAM ANDERSON,

SECRETARY OF THE SCOTTISH LITERARY INSTITUTE.

In announcing, under a comprehensively national title, the Work now offered to the public attention and support, it is assumed that the various information it contains is so illustrative of the Scottish nation, and of the origin and constitution of modern Scottish society, as to justify the adoption for it of a designation so conspicuous. Of any other country, it is true, an account of its surnames, families, and honours, would cast little or no light over the constitution of the society existing therein. Such an account would probably tell next to nothing of the earlier races out of which society was formed, because, in the case of any other nation, whatever might elsewhere be found to illustrate that part of its history, few indications in the names now borne by individuals or families, or in its titles of honour, will be found to mark the tribes or institutions whence they sprung, or to be otherwise identified with the commencement of its national history. This is a result to be found in Scotland alone; not uniformly, indeed, nor always without admixture of doubt, but certainly in a greater degree than in any other kingdom or state.

Modern Scottish society, and Scottish nationality in its proper sense, may be said to have come into existence together. Hereditary monarchy, hereditary surnames, families, and honours, hitherto unknown among its peoples, were *their* common instruments for consolidation, for conservation, and for progress. To the Cumbrian, the Pict, the Scot, Norwegian, Dane, or Saxon, who, at various times and in various degrees, were spread over its soil, these distinctions were exceptional and comparatively unknown.

In the early part of the twelfth century, the greater part of the country now constituting Scotland was in a state little better than that of chaos, and worse than that of anarchy. The arrival of a new people of polished manners, military discipline, and Christian zeal, by giving new institutions and for a time a new language to this incongruous mass, created a nation and a nationality, yet without a so-called revolution or even a change of dynasty. The new race, whose presence was so beneficially felt in Scotland, came through England, yet were not of it. They were the Normans,—a people of the same original stock as many of the tribes above referred to, but refined and instructed by familiarity with the institutions of the South.

This new order of things, however, might have attained to no permanence, or even if permanent, to no historic significance—at least in the sense which our title assumes—had not the silent but ceaseless immigration of the new race continued without interruption for nearly two centuries, in the course of which they identified their fortunes with those of a dynasty which, although sprung from an elder settlement of the population, was led by sympathy, education, and the necessities of their position, to cherish, enrich, and lean upon this new people for the preservation of their crown and prerogatives, and to cement their union by numerous family alliances. A revolution, which placed first one and then another family of the new race upon the throne of Scotland, completed the solidarity of the social union of races in Scotland, while it prevented fresh admixtures of foreign blood; and lastly and chiefly the practice of bestowing hereditary surnames and honours, and of holding all lands from the Crown, which obtained generally throughout this period, and found a permanent and faithful record in charters and other public deeds, many of which are still in existence, insured to Scotland the integrity and continuity of its social annals.

The *surnames* traceable to immigrant Norman chiefs, or to the lands bestowed upon their retainers, constitute by far the greater portion of those peculiar and pertaining to vast numbers of individuals forming modern Scottish society. Under those derived from lands, not a few Danish and Norwegian names are to be found, which, in like manner as those of Celtic and Norman origin referring to personal or local distinctives, are to be recognised by their composition; yet, while of this latter class, even in the remote North we find in the names Fraser, Grant, Cameron, and others, undeniable proofs, notwithstanding their present use of the Celtic tongue, of a Norman or French immigration, the composition of the southern population is singularly manifested when the distinctive of an individual of the more ancient lineage is *there*, as in the case of a Fleming or an Inglis, expressed by the simple name of Scott. An account of the origin or of the original holders of these surnames of the forefathers of the present Scottish people, cannot fail to be highly interesting to all classes at the present day.

But, a mere explanation of the origin of *surnames* alone would lack completeness unless accompanied with some account of the families by which they were borne,—of the distribution of those families over the country,—

of their subdivision into new families,—and of the distinguished individuals who sustained their reputation and promoted their influence: and such an account it is one of the objects of this Work to supply. 'THE SCOTTISH NATION' professes to present the succession, the affiliations and alliances, and the leading incidents in the history of the families whose surnames have obtained distinction and influence throughout Scotland since the reign of Malcolm Canmore.

The ancient *baronies* of Scotland, associated as they were with hereditary jurisdictions only short of regal, had all a significancy in that country unequalled in any others where the feudal regime obtained. The holders of these *honours* were regarded as heads of its name as well as of their vassals; and to promote the honour of the one as well as the welfare of the other was their business and their strength. An account of these *honours* is an account of the territorial supremacy of a name and of a family, among the members of which the lands under the jurisdiction of their heads were in course of time parcelled out.

A history of Scottish *titles* is a necessary supplement to that of families, and a key to many of the social and political incidents in that kingdom as well as in the history and fortunes of its families. Such a history forms, therefore, another and it is hoped a valuable topic of the present Work.

Immeasurably beyond all these social facts in importance, although greatly illustrated by the lights they furnish, the biographies of its distinguished natives become, when properly treated, the topic which illustrates and shows forth in its strength and peculiarities 'THE SCOTTISH NATION.' The poorest country in Europe, occupied by a hardy race trained to military exercises, struggling for centuries to maintain their national independence, and ever contending for mastery amongst themselves, Scotland has beheld her sons loving and honouring the country that gave them birth with a high and pure patriotism; and clinging to each other with a proverbial partiality, yet not alone on account of their common relationship, but also for those qualities of endurance, energy, and intelligence which their common struggles and even social feuds drew forth and incorporated as it were with the national character. At a comparatively early period she sent forth many of her sons to obtain distinction and honours in other lands; and when more peaceful times had arrived and milder institutions obtained, she saw them launch into the arts of civil life, for which their hereditary qualities, animated by the lessons of a simple but sincere piety, had well prepared them, and assert for themselves a front rank among the leaders of mind and intellect in Europe, in numbers altogether unexampled in the social development of other nations. Of such men is Scotland's pride and glory, and their lives and deeds constitute the truest account of the Scottish nation.

In its *general biography* the present work embraces a wider range than is contemplated in any of those specially devoted to that subject, comprising many names not to be met with in history, yet of men whose skill, genius, or labours have added to the comfort, the knowledge, or the happiness of mankind. Not a few names, moreover, that have long been borne down by undeserved obloquy have been restored to their proper position; while others, upheld by misstatement or exaggeration at an undue elevation, have been placed on a lower pedestal. In all cases the truth has been stated, without reference to party feelings or sectarian misrepresentations.

In the department of *literature* great attention has been bestowed upon the articles relating to men distinguished by their writings. By appending the titles and dates of their works, and sometimes when these were numerous, classifying the subjects treated of, easy reference is combined with great economy of space. In a word, as respects the productions of its literary characters, 'THE SCOTTISH NATION' becomes as it were a *Bibliotheca Scottica* corrected and brought down to the present day.

To the student of Scottish history the value of the assistance furnished by a work of the character of 'THE SCOTTISH NATION' need not be dwelt upon. In the accounts given of every family or title of antiquity and note, numerous indirect and incidental lights are thrown upon its pages. The direct additional matter it supplies, is, however, perhaps of still more importance. In this as well as in many other points, it will be found a more accurate and complete exhibition of the Earlier History of Scotland than any that has yet been presented to the public. It may give some idea of the care and research bestowed upon this work when it is stated that already the author has been ten years occupied in its composition and correction.

'THE SCOTTISH NATION' will be richly embellished with Autographs, Seals, Genealogical and Titular tables, and other illustrative objects, as also with Portraits on wood and steel, all taken from original or other authentic sources, and executed in the first style of art.

A National Gallery of Scottish Portraits has long been pointed out as a desideratum, and learned societies have recently brought the matter strongly before the public. In the care taken to make the Portrait illustrations authentic and numerous in a degree far beyond those in any collection heretofore presented to the world, the Publishers anticipate that the first exhibition of a NATIONAL PORTRAIT GALLERY worthy of the name will be found in the pages of 'THE SCOTTISH NATION.'

CONDITIONS OF PUBLICATION.

1. THE SCOTTISH NATION will be issued in Parts at Two Shillings and Sixpence each. Each Part will contain one hundred and twelve pages of Letter-press, and (besides various woodcuts) one illustrative Engraving on Steel.

2. The work will be completed in Twenty Parts. It will form Three handsome Volumes uniform with the Publishers' "Faiths of the World." Any surplus parts beyond the number of Twenty will be supplied to Subscribers gratis.

3. The Publishers being pledged to complete the Publication on the terms and in the manner above detailed, will hold each Subscriber bound on his part to take and pay for the work as it appears. No abatement or discount will be allowed to any party.

A. FULLARTON AND CO.,

STEAD'S PLACE, LEITH WALK, EDINBURGH, AND 73 NEWGATE STREET, LONDON.

RECOMMENDATIONS OF "THE SCOTTISH NATION."

FROM "THE CRITIC." (London Weekly Literary Journal).

THIS is the First Part of a highly interesting and important new work on Scotland. Its editor is well known as an able and laborious man of letters, and its object is to supply a complete account of the surnames, titles, baronies, literature, and general biography of Caledonia, from the earliest period to the present time. It is arranged in alphabetical order, after the fashion of an encyclopædia, and is to be richly embellished with autographs, seals, genealogical and titular tables, and also with portraits on wood or steel, all taken from original or other authentic sources. Peculiar attention is to be paid to the history of Scottish literature, and its editor promises that "as respects the productions of its literary characters, the 'Scottish Nation' is to be a 'Bibliotheca Scotica' corrected and brought down to the present day." The author has been ten years employed in its preparation.

Such was the plan proposed, and the first part, now in our hands, enables us in some measure to judge of its execution. That seems to us to be exceedingly creditable to Mr. Anderson's taste and learning. The portrait prefixed to this part is that of brave old George Buchanan, with his ample brow, his thoughtful, peering, and somewhat peevish eyes, and his noble flowing beard. All our readers are familiar with the portrait of the same worthy which has for forty-two years frowned from the title-page of Maga. This in the "Scottish Nation" is somewhat different, and has on the whole a more agreeable expression. To this succeeds a table of the Earldom of Athol, forming the first of a series of the "Ancient Earldoms of Scotland." Coming then to the letterpress, we find interesting, well-written, and comprehensive accounts, under the letter A, of Dr. Arthur Abercrombie, the celebrated Edinburgh physician, with a medallion likeness; of Sir Ralph Abercrombie, the hero of Aboukir, with some spirited woodcuts; of the eccentric Dr. Abernethy (whose name and family were Scotch, although some maintain that he was born in Londonderry, Ireland); of Dr. Adair, of Bath (by the way, he was an acquaintance of Robert Burns, and married Charlotte Hamilton—one of Burns's loves, and to whom he addressed his last song :

> " Fairest maid on Devon's banks,
> Crystal Devon, winding Devon, &c.);"

of Dr. Adam, the great scholar, author of " Roman Antiquities," with a woodcut; of Robert Ainslie, another friend and correspondent of Burns; of the four Dukes of Albany who figure so prominently in the early history of Scotland, with portraits of them all; and of Alexanders the first, second, and third, the Kings of Scotland, whose lives, like those of the Albanies, are given *in extenso*. Besides these, there are a number of subordinate characters, more or less briefly outlined and characterized. The first part closes with a full and interesting biography of Sir William Alexander, first Earl of Stirling, the eminent poet and statesman, styled by Drummond of Hawthornden "that most excellent spirit and earliest gem of the North." This remarkable man, besides figuring boldly in the chequered history of his country, and identifying himself with the early planting of Nova Scotia, was the author of various poetical productions of merit, such as his four " Monarchick Tragedies," his " Doomsday," the " Parænesis to Prince Henry," and the first book of an intended heroic poem entitled " Jonathan"—works which called forth in his own age the praise of Drummond and Michael Drayton, and in the next century that of Addison himself.

Altogether, if the rest of the parts of this truly national work be as carefully compiled as the first, it must be a very valuable addition to the stores of Scottish biographical literature.

FROM "THE BOOKSELLER" (London monthly periodical issued for the guidance of the Trade).

THE 'Scottish Nation,' a work recently commenced by Messrs. Fullarton of Edinburgh, promises to be one of the most valuable historical and biographical works ever produced in that country. Under surnames and local titles, it gives a history of the families, and of all the illustrious individuals who have borne them; and where they have figured in literary history, a list of their works is given. As an original work it is remarkably cheap. Taken as a whole, the 'Scottish Nation' is a work that Scotland's sons may be proud of.

FROM THE "SCOTTISH PRESS." (Edinburgh.)

THIS work proposes to illustrate the surnames, families, literature, honours, and biographical history of the people of Scotland. Its literary execution has been committed to Mr. Anderson, the distinguished Secretary of the Scottish Literary Institute, who in a well-written Prospectus states the general features, importance, and facilities for the compilation of such a work. Peculiar and rare qualifications are needed,—the author has to be deeply read in antiquarian and genealogical lore, he must also possess a correct taste and sound judgment, else he would be found giving a prominence, which popular feeling would neither approve nor ratify, to names and matters of heraldic or septish interest, to the exclusion of information relating to men and measures, places and things, about which living men are eager to know whatever authentic history can disclose.

We have looked carefully through the First Part of this great national work, and can honestly bear our testimony to the able and scholarly manner in which it is compiled. Much curious and interesting information is given of men whose names are household words, and of others less known whom it is good to know. The labour of verifying dates and circumstances must have been immense, and autographs, seals, coins, and other illustrative objects are made to render up their historical lessons. Characteristic portraits and landscapes on wood and steel lend charms and vividness to the narrative. The book craft has been accomplished by the eminent firm of publishers whose name is on the title page with proverbial success, and the price is something fabulous in the walk of cheap literature. Nothing can repay Messrs. Fullarton & Co. but a circulation which we will not venture to estimate, but which we hope may requite the enterprise.

FROM THE "MORNING JOURNAL." (Glasgow.)

THESE (Parts 1 and 2) are the first instalments of what promises to be a most valuable contribution to the antiquities, the literature, and the general and family histories of Scotland. Of late years we have had various collections of the lives of eminent Scotsmen, but the design of the present publication—and its execution thus far seems thoroughly adequate to the conception —is more wide, comprehensive, and elaborate in its research and details, than any that has hitherto appeared. When finished, it will be a most valuable repository of individual and family history—a work of reference to which every Scotsman who wishes to learn the origin and antecedents of the family whose surname he bears, may turn with every confidence of obtaining satisfactory information. Like the vesture of the Celt, the texture of Scottish society is composed of various, but, on the whole, harmoniously blended elements. To unravel the various threads, and trace them to their respective sources, must be a labour of no small difficulty; but, judging from the sample of the work before us, we should say that Mr. Anderson must have qualified himself in no ordinary measure by study and research for the task. In the prospectus, he informs us that he has already been ten years engaged on the composition and correction of the work. The illustrations are at once beautiful, appropriate, and profuse. There are portraits on steel, finely engraved, of George Buchanan the historian, and of Dr. Chalmers, with engravings on wood of various personages, and of objects of antiquarian interest—old buildings, old medals, and old seals, &c., with a coloured table of the genealogical shields, and the armorial bearings of the Athol family. Altogether, if these parts may be taken as an earnest of the style in which the work is to be carried out, it will, when completed, reflect equal credit upon the erudition and literary talent of the author and upon the professional enterprise and the artistic resources of the publishers—a firm which has long been known for the superiority of its publications. We have very little doubt, indeed, that "The Scottish Nation" will meet with a favourable reception from the Scottish people—a people who have ever been peculiarly alive to the interests and the honours of their "kith and kin."

FROM THE "GLASGOW CITIZEN."

"THE SCOTTISH NATION," of which this is the second part, is a work which, when finished, will present a complete gallery of the "Scots Worthies," ancient and modern. One excellent feature in this work is the great mass of historical notes furnished concerning many of the great historical names and estates in the kingdom of Scotland. Written in a plain, understandable style, the biographies are enriched with the latest and fullest information regarding the various characters under consideration. Another good feature in this work is the graphic and authentic portraits and sketches which embellish and illustrate its pages.

FROM THE "CALEDONIAN MERCURY." (Edinburgh.)

"THIS is the first part of a work designed to be thoroughly national. Its aim is to get at the root of the Scottish nation, and, step by step upwards, to develop the goodly stems, branches, buds, blossoms, and fruits of our numerous and varied genealogical trees. More than any other country in the world Scotland is essentially and intensely national. She asserts everywhere her unity, her individuality, her independence, her "nain sel;" she claims to be read and comprehended by the intermingled light of what she was and what she is—what she has ever been, and what she has not ceased to be; she points to the registries of her proud ancestral names, to the recorded glories of thousands of her great families, to the crowded niches in the temple of fame occupied by children's children through long lines of unextinguishable generations; and she has no fear as to a comparison with other nations either as respects her present self, or those that, bearing her image, have "gone before." There is ample material in our public libraries, and throughout our private families, to invest a work like the present with high national interest, and Mr. Anderson is the man to bring it out, gather together its numerous facts and incidents, classify and arrange its multitudinous details, and work the whole into a narrative scrupulously accurate and symmetrically exact. His previous studies qualify him peculiarly for the task; and the standing he has taken in literature, by the numerous interesting and able works that have proceeded from his pen, is itself a sufficient guarantee that he will not fail to do his work well.

The biographies, which form so large a portion of the work, judging from those in this first part, are ably and impartially written. They are to include all Scotsmen of eminence, from the earliest period to the present time. The work is also to be profusely illustrated with portraits, woodcuts, heraldic tables, seals, coins, &c. The present part contains, with a variety of woodcuts, a steel portrait of George Buchanan, and a heraldic table of the Earldom and Dukedom of Athol—both capitally executed; indeed the style in which the work is being brought out is quite superior, the publishers having apparently, in paper, typography, and engravings, resolved to secure to it that which it claims to merit—a standard reputation and a truly national character.

FROM THE "GLASGOW COMMONWEALTH."

OF the value of such a work the reader will have no difficulty in forming a high estimate, but few will reflect on the vast amount of labour and research which alone could render an undertaking of this kind even tolerably complete. The learned author must have given years of untiring industry to the elaboration of this Bibliotheca Scotica, and by the care which everywhere appears in those parts already published, he has worthily earned the gratitude of all true Scotsmen. His labour is one of elucidation, not merely that of the annalist. He does not content himself with telling the story, but with an amount of conscientious research that indicates a due regard to the dignity of his subject, and to the paramount value of accuracy, he has endeavoured to assemble together all the collateral elements that could throw light on the records of the Scottish names that figure in Scottish history. The succession, the affiliations and alliances, and the leading incidents in the history of the families whose surnames have obtained distinction and influence throughout Scotland since the days of Malcolm Canmore, are combined with notices of the honours, jurisdictions, titles, and literature of the country, and these again are farther illustrated by autographs, seals, genealogical and titular tables, and by portraits on wood and steel, "all taken from original or other authentic sources, and executed in the first style of art." The author further assures us that in the department of literature great attention has been bestowed upon the articles relating to men distinguished by their writings. By appending the titles and dates of their works, and sometimes, when these were numerous, classifying the subjects treated of, easy reference is combined with economy of space. Of this truly national work we can safely say that, wherever there is a Scottish man, he will here find a fund of interesting information which will teach him to regard the work as a peculiar treasure. Scotsmen all over the world will here meet on common ground to pay a willing tribute to the glories of the past.

FROM THE "DUMFRIES HERALD."

MR. ANDERSON conveys his information fully, precisely, and neatly—the best praise that can be given to books of this class. The portrait of George Buchanan, prefixed to the work, is a very fine one, and the various other illustrations in the Part are clearly and beautifully executed. We trust the work will be as popular as it is useful.

FROM THE "ABERDEEN JOURNAL."

THE idea of this work is a comprehensive one. Taking a wider sweep than history, it adds several other elements, all, in the case of Scotland, having an important bearing on its progress. Thus, not one, but several lights—history, archæology, genealogy, &c.—are made to converge on the past; and the story of our country is told in that of the men who have given her a name above that of many nations. The title will impart an idea of the design of the work; and instead of giving any further statement, which would indeed scarce convey a full and accurate conception on the point, we prefer the easier and better course of simply recommending the work itself to our readers. Of Mr. Anderson's literary qualifications, as well as his learning and impartiality, we have no doubt. . . . . Altogether the work is one of great interest to Scotsmen.

GEORGE BUCHANAN

G Buchanan

THE

SCOTTISH NATION

OR THE

SURNAMES, FAMILIES, LITERATURE, HONOURS,

AND

BIOGRAPHICAL HISTORY

OF THE

PEOPLE OF SCOTLAND

VOLUME A

William Anderson

Secretary of the Scottish Literary Institute

HERITAGE BOOKS
2013

HERITAGE BOOKS

AN IMPRINT OF HERITAGE BOOKS, INC.

Books, CDs, and more—Worldwide

For our listing of thousands of titles see our website
at
www.HeritageBooks.com

A Facsimile Reprint
Published 2013 by
HERITAGE BOOKS, INC.
Publishing Division
5810 Ruatan Street
Berwyn Heights, Md. 20740

Originally published 1876
A. Fullarton & Co.
44 South Bridge, Edinburgh; and
73 Newgate Street, London

International Standard Book Numbers
Paperbound: 978-0-7884-0245-6
Clothbound: 978-0-7884-6888-9

THOMAS CHALMERS D.D. LL.D.

Thomas Chalmers

A. Fullarton & Co. London & Edinburgh.

I.

Campbell, Lord of Lochow.—Family of Argyle.

GREAT ANCESTOR ON FEMALE SIDE.

Diarmid O'Dwin, Lord of Lochow.—Clan Campbell styled from him *Siol Diarmid.*

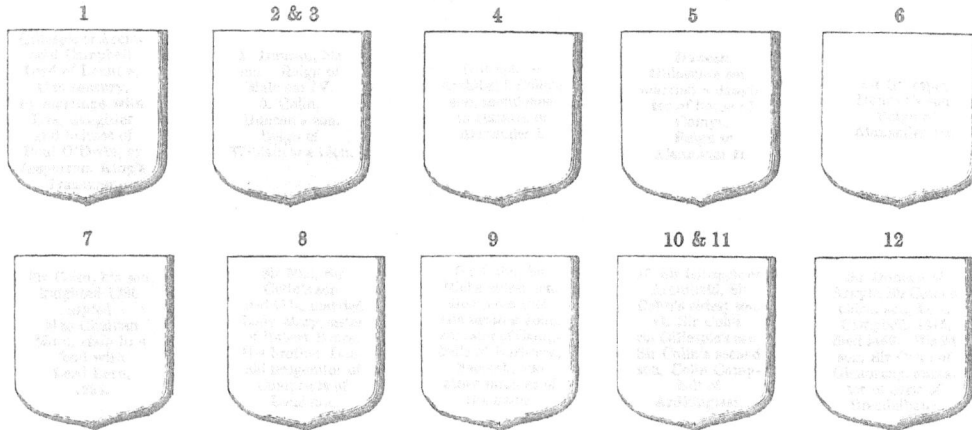

Earls of Argyle.

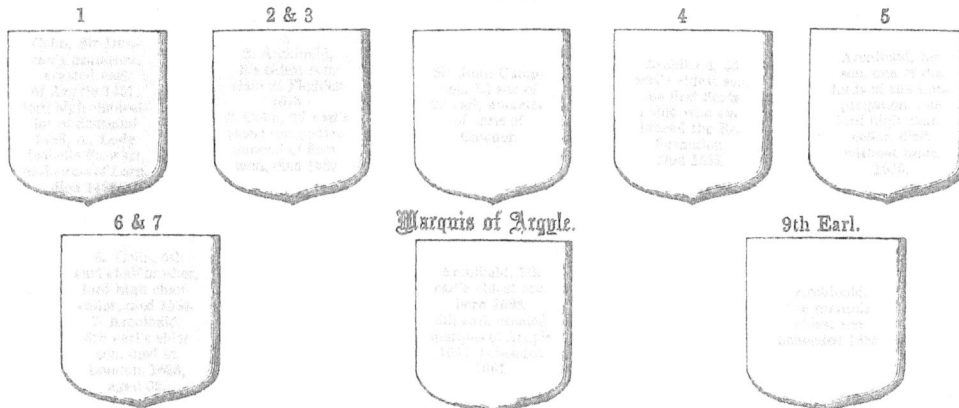

Marquis of Argyle.   9th Earl.

Dukes of Argyle.

ARMS OF CAMPBELL, DUKE OF ARGYLE.

Quarterings:—1. and 4. for the name of Campbell. 2. and 3 for lordship of Lorn. Behind the shield the two great badges of great master of the household and high justiciary of Scotland.

THE

SCOTTISH NATION.

ABERCORN.

ABERCORN, Marquis of, a peerage held by a branch of the Hamilton family, descended from Lord Claud Hamilton, third son of James, second earl of Arran and first duke of Chatelherault. Lord Claud, who was distinguished for his zealous and steady attachment to Mary Queen of Scots, was created a peer by her son, James VI., 29th July 1587, by the title of Lord Paisley. He died in 1622, aged 78. He married Margaret, only daughter of George, sixth Lord Seton, and had by her one daughter, Margaret, married to William, first marquis of Douglas, and four sons, of whom James, the eldest, was created Baron Abercorn, 5th April 1603, and, on 10th July 1606, advanced to the dignity of earl of Abercorn, baron of Paisley, Hamilton, Mountcastle, and Kilpatrick. Having zealously promoted the scheme known in history as the plantation of Ulster—formed on his accession to the English throne, by King James I. for the pacification and colonization of the north of Ireland—the earl of Abercorn was by letter from James to the lord-deputy called to the parliament of Ireland, in 1613, and 20th May 1615, was appointed of the council of the province of Munster, and had a large grant of lands in the barony of Strabane, county Tyrone. The earl died 16th March 1618, and, in his lifetime, his son James was created, 18th October 1616, a peer of Ireland, by the title of Baron Strabane; which peerage he resigned in favour of his brother Claud 11th November 1633. He succeeded as 2d earl of Abercorn, on the death of his son, George. third earl, the male line failed in the eldest branch, and the titles devolved on Claud, fifth Lord Strabane, grandson of Claud, second Lord Strabane. Claud, fourth earl of Abercorn, adhered to James VII. at the Revolution, and was at the siege of Londonderry. After the defeat of the Boyne, he embarked for France, but was killed on the voyage in 1690. His brother, Charles, fifth earl, gave in his adhesion to King William's government, and died in June 1701 without surviving issue. The titles devolved on James, descended from the Hon. Sir George Hamilton, fourth son of the first earl. James, sixth earl of Abercorn, was created baron of Mountcastle and viscount of Strabane, 9th September 1701. John James Hamilton, 9th earl of Abercorn, was advanced to the dignity of a peer of Great Britain, 1st Oct. 1790, by the title of marquis of Abercorn, and dying 27th January 1818, was succeeded by his grandson James. The head of this family is the heir male of the noble and illustrious house of Hamilton. The

ABERCROMBIE.

estate of Abercorn, from which the title is derived, is in Linlithgowshire, and formerly belonged to Sir John the Graham, the 'fides Achates' of Wallace, who fell in the battle of Falkirk in 1298. The name is derived from *Aber*, beyond, and *Corn*, a corruption of Carron.

ABERCROMBIE, or ABERCROMBY, a surname derived from a barony of that name in Fifeshire, erected in a district originally named Abercrombie, *aber* meaning beyond, and *crombie*, the crook, in allusion to the bend or crook of Fifeness. The parish, until recently called St. Monance, and now Abercromby, was known by the name of Abercrom*bie* so far back as 1174. The Abercrombies of that ilk were esteemed the chiefs of the name until the seventeenth century, when that line became extinct, and Abercromby of Birkenbog, in Banffshire, became the head of the clan of Abercromby. In 1637 Alexander Abercromby of Birkenbog was created a baronet of Scotland and Nova Scotia, and distinguished himself as a royalist during the civil wars. The baronetcy is still in the family.

ABERCROMBIE, Baron, an extinct peerage, bestowed by Charles I., by letters patent dated at Carisbrooke castle 12th December 1647, on Sir James Sandilands of St. Monance, or Abercrombie, in Fife, descended from James Sandilands belonging to the noble house of Torphichen. In 1649 Lord Abercrombie disposed of his property in Fife, including St. Monance, and the castle of Newark, to Lieutenant-general David Lesly, who took his title of Lord Newark from thence. Lord Abercrombie married Lady Agnes Carnegie, second daughter of David, first earl of Southesk, and by her he had a son, James, second Lord Abercrombie, who dying without issue in 1681, the title became extinct.

ABERCROMBY, of Aboukir and Tullibody, Baron, a title in the peerage of the United Kingdom, conferred in 1801 on Mary Anne, widow of the celebrated Sir Ralph Abercromby, immediately after her husband's death at the battle of Alexandria, with remainder to the heirs male of the deceased general. Baroness Abercromby died in 1821, and was succeeded by her eldest son, George, a barrister at law, first baron. On his death in 1843, Colonel George Ralph Abercromby, his son, born in 1800, became second baron. The latter died in 1852, when his son, George Ralph Campbell

Abercromby, born in 1838, became third baron. See ABER-CROMBY, SIR RALPH.

ABERCROMBIE, JOHN, M.D., an eminent physician, and moral and religious writer, was born in Aberdeen, 12th October, 1780. His father was minister of the East church of that city. After having completed his literary education in his native city, he was sent to the university of Edinburgh, to prosecute his studies for the medical profession. The celebrated Dr. Alexander Munro was at that time professor of anatomy and surgery there, and the subject of this memoir attended his lectures.

In 1803, being then twenty-three years of age, Dr. Abercrombie began to practise as a physician in Edinburgh. He soon acquired a high reputation, and became extensively known to his professional brethren through the medium of his contributions to the 'Medical and Surgical Journal.' On the death of the celebrated Dr. Gregory in 1821, Dr. Abercrombie at once took his place as a consulting physician. He was also named physician to the king for Scotland, an appointment which, though merely honorary and nominal, is usually conferred on the physician of greatest eminence at the time of a vacancy. He subsequently held, till his death, the office of physician to George Heriot's Hospital. In 1828, he published a treatise on the 'Diseases of the Brain and Nervous System,' and soon after an essay on those of the 'Abdominal Organs,' both of which rank high among professional publications. In 1830 he appeared as an author in a branch of literature entirely different, and one involving the treatment of subjects in the highest department of philosophy and metaphysical speculation, having published in that year his able work, in 8vo, on the 'Intellectual Powers.' In 1833 he produced a work of a similar kind, on 'The Philosophy of the Moral Feelings,' also in 8vo. In 1832, during the prevalence of the cholera, he had published a medical tract entitled 'Suggestions on the Character and Treatment of Malignant Cholera.' In 1834 he published a pamphlet entitled 'Observations on the Moral Condition of the Lower Orders in Edinburgh.' The same year appeared an address delivered by him at the Fiftieth Anniversary of the Destitute Sick Society, Edinburgh. He was also the author of Essays on the 'Elements of Sacred Truth,' and on the 'Harmony of Christian Faith and Character;' besides other writings which have been comprised in a small volume entitled 'Essays and Tracts.' Of writings so well known, and so very highly esteemed, as proved by a circulation extending, as it did in some, even to an eighteenth edition, it were useless to speak in praise either of their literary or far higher merits. But, distinguished as he was, both professionally and as a writer in the highest departments of philosophy, it was not exclusively to his great fame in either respect, or in both, that he owed his wide influence throughout the community in which he lived. His name ever stood associated with the guidance of every important enterprise, whether religious or benevolent,—somehow he provided leisure to bestow the patronage of his attendance and his deliberative wisdom on many of the institutions of Edinburgh, and, with a munificence which has been rarely equalled, ministered of his substance to the upholding of them all. He valued money so little, that he often declined to receive it, even when the offerer urged it, as most justly his own His diligence and application were so great that whoever entered his study found him intent at work. Did they see him travelling in his carriage, they could perceive he was busy there. [*Obituary notice in Witness newspaper.*]

In 1834 the university of Oxford conferred upon him the degree of M.D., which he had long previously obtained from the university of Edinburgh. In 1835 he was chosen by the students lord rector of Marischal college, Aberdeen. Dr. Abercrombie died suddenly at Edinburgh, from rupture of an artery in the region of the heart, on the 14th of November, 1844. Distinguished alike as a physician, an author, a benefactor of the poor, and a sincere Christian, his loss was universally lamented. He was buried in the West churchyard, Edinburgh, where a monument with a medallion has been erected to his memory, the former bearing the following inscription :—" In memory of John Abercrombie, M.D., Edin. and Oxon., Fellow of the Royal colleges of Physicians and Surgeons, Edinburgh, Vice-president of the Royal Society of Edinburgh, and first Physician to the

Queen in Scotland, born xii. Oct. MDCCLXXX. From a life very early devoted to the service of God, occupied in the most assiduous labours, and distinguished not more by professional eminence than by personal worth and by successful authorship on the principles of Christian morals and philosophy, it pleased God to translate him suddenly to the life everlasting xiv. Nov. MDCCCXLIV." Annexed is a copy of the medallion, which embodies as true a likeness of Dr. Abercrombie as stone or wood can convey.

The procession at his funeral was one of the largest ever seen in Edinburgh. It was joined by the members both of the Royal College of Physicians, and the Royal College of Surgeons, as well as by the Free Church presbytery of Edinburgh and the commission of the General Assembly of the Free Church, and by many professional brethren from a distance. Dr. Abercrombie married in 1808 Agnes, only child of David Wardlaw, Esq., of Netherbeath in Fifeshire, and had eight daughters, one of whom died at the age of four. Seven daughters survived him, the eldest of whom became the second wife of the Rev. John Bruce, minister of Free St. Andrew's church, Edinburgh, in whose congregation Dr. Abercrombie was an elder, and who preached his funeral sermon, which

was afterwards published. The estate of Netherbeath descended to Mrs. Bruce.

The following is a list of Dr. Abercrombie's publications:

Diseases of the Brain and Nervous System, 8vo, 1828.
Diseases of the Abdominal Organs, 8vo, 1829.
The Intellectual Powers, 8vo, 1830.
Suggestions on the Character and Treatment of Malignant Cholera, 8vo, 1832.
The Philosophy of the Moral Feelings, 8vo, 1833.
Observations on the Moral Condition of the Lower Orders in Edinburgh, 8vo, 1834.
Address delivered at the Fiftieth Anniversary of the Destitute Sick Society, Edinburgh, 1835.
Mental Culture, 18mo, being the Address delivered to the students of Marischal College when he was elected Lord Rector of that university, 1835.
The Harmony of Scripture Faith and Character, 18mo, 1836.
Think on these Things, 18mo, 1839.
Messiah our Example, 18mo, 1841.
The Contest and the Armour, 18mo, 1841.
The Elements of Sacred Truth, 18mo, 1844.
Essays and Tracts, including the two last works and some other writings on similar subjects, 8vo, 1844, 1847.

ABERCROMBIE, JOHN, conjectured by Dempster, in his *Hist. Eccl. Scot.*, to have been a Benedictine monk, was the author of two energetic treatises in defence of the Church of Rome against the principles of the Reformers, entitled 'Veritatis Defensio,' and 'Hæresis Confusio.' He flourished about the middle of the sixteenth century.

ABERCROMBIE, PATRICK, physician and historian, third son of Alexander Abercrombie of Fetterneir, Aberdeenshire, a branch of the Birkenbog family of that name, was born at Forfar in 1656, and took his medical degrees at St. Andrews in 1685. His elder brother, Francis Abercrombie of Fetterneir, on his marriage with Anna, Baroness Sempill, was, in July 1685, created by James VII. Lord Glassford, under the singular restriction of being limited for his own life. After leaving the university, Patrick travelled on the continent, and on his return to England, embracing the Roman Catholic religion, he was appointed physician to James VII.; but at the Revolution was deprived of his office, and for some years lived abroad. Returning to his native country, he afterwards devoted himself to the study of national antiquities. In 1707 he gave to the world a translation of M. Beauge's rare French work, 'L'Histoire de la Guerre d'Ecosse,' 1556, under the title of 'The Campaigns in Scotland in 1548 and 1549,' which was reprinted in the original by Mr. Smythe of Methven for the Bannatyne Club, in 1829, with a preface containing an account of Abercrombie's translation. His great work, however, is 'The Martial Achievements of the Scots nation, and of such Scotsmen as have signalized themselves by the Sword,' in two volumes folio, the first published in 1711, and the second in 1715. He also wrote the 'Memoirs of the family of Abercrombie.' Dr. Abercrombie died in poor circumstances in 1716; some authorities say 1720, and others 1726. The following is a list of his works.

The Advantages of the Act of Security, compared with those of the intended Union; founded on the Revolution Principles, published by Mr. Daniel De Foe. Edin. 1707, 4to.

A Vindication of the same, against Mr. De Foe. Edin. 1707, 4to.

The History of the Campaigns 1548 and 1549, between the Scots and the French on the one side, and the English and their foreign auxiliaries on the other. From the French of Beauge, with a Preface, showing the Advantages which Scotland received by the Ancient League with France, and the mutual assistance given by each kingdom to the other. Edin. 1707, 8vo.

The Martial Achievements of the Scots nation, being an Account of the Lives, Characters, and Memorable Actions of such Scotsmen as have signalized themselves by the Sword, at home and abroad. Edin. 1711-1715. 2 vols. fol.

ABERCROMBIE, JOHN, an eminent horticulturist, and author of several horticultural works, was the son of a respectable gardener near Edinburgh, where he was born about the year 1726. In his eighteenth year he went to London, and obtained employment in the royal gardens. His first work, 'The Gardener's Calendar,' was published as the production of Mr. Mawe, gardener to the duke of Leeds, who received twenty guineas for the use of his name, which was then well-known. The success of that work was so complete, that Abercrombie put his own name to all his future publications; among which may be mentioned, 'The Universal Dictionary of Gardening and Botany,' 4to, 'The Gardener's Vade Mecum,' and other popular productions. He died at Somerstown, London, in 1806, aged 80. A list of his works is subjoined.

The Universal Gardener and Botanist, or a General Dictionary of Gardening and Botany, exhibiting, in Botanical Arrangement, according to the Linnæan system, every Tree, Shrub, and Herbaceous Plant that merit Culture, &c. Lond. 1778, 4to.

The Garden Mushroom, its Nature and Cultivation, exhibiting full and plain directions for producing this desirable plant in perfection and plenty. Lond. 1779, 8vo. New edition enlarged, 1802, 12mo.

The British Fruit Garden, and Art of Pruning; comprising the most approved Methods of Planting and raising every useful Fruit Tree and Fruit-bearing Shrub. Lond. 1779, 8vo.

The Complete Forcing Gardener, for the thorough Practical Management of the Kitchen Garden, raising all early crops in Hot-beds, and forcing early Fruit, &c. Lond. 1781, 12mo.

The Complete Wall-tree Pruner, &c. Lond. 1783, 12mo.

The Propagation and Botanical Arrangement of Plants and Trees, useful and ornamental. Lond. 1785, 2 vols. 12mo.

The Gardener's Pocket Dictionary, or a Systematical Arrangement of Trees, Herbs, Flowers, and Fruits, agreeable to the Linnæan Method, with their Latin and English names, their Uses, Propagation, Culture, &c. Lond. 1786, 3 vols. 12mo.

Daily Assistant in the Modern Practice of English Gardening for every Month in the Year, on an entire new plan. Lond. 1789, 12mo.

The Universal Gardener's Kalendar, and System of Practical Gardening. Lond. 1789, 12mo; 1808, 8vo.

The Complete Kitchen Gardener and Hot-bed Forcer, with the thorough Practical Management of Hot-houses, Fire-walls, &c. Lond. 1789, 12mo.

The Gardener's Vade-mecum, or Companion of General Gardening; a Descriptive Display of the Plants, Flowers, Shrubs, Trees, Fruits, and general Culture. Lond. 1789, 8vo.

The Hot-house Gardener, or the general Culture of the Pine Apple, and the Methods of forcing early Grapes, Peaches, Nectarines, and other choice Fruits in Hot-houses, Vineries, Fruit-houses, Hot-walls, with Directions for raising Melons and early Strawberries, &c. Plates. Lond. 1789, 8vo.

The Gardener's Pocket Journal and Annual Register, in a concise Monthly Display of all Practical Works of General Gardening throughout the year. Lond. 1791, 12mo; 1814, 12mo.

———

It has been already stated, in giving the origin of the name, (see page 1,) that in the 17th century, Abercromby of Birkenbog in Banffshire, became the chief of the name of Abercromby. Alexander Abercromby of Birkenbog was grand falconer in Scotland to King Charles I. In 1636 his eldest son, Alexander, was created a baronet of Nova Scotia, and took an active part against King Charles in the civil wars of that period. From the pedigree of the family it appears that Sir Alexander Abercromby of Birkenbog, the first baronet, had two sons. The eldest, James, succeeded his father. Alexander, the second son, succeeded his cousin George Abercromby of Skeith, in the estate of Tullibody, in Clackmannanshire, formerly a possession of the earls of Stirling. This Alexander was the grandfather of the celebrated military commander, Sir Ralph Abercromby, and the second of the name of Abercromby who possessed Tullibody. The most eminent of this family were General Sir Ralph Abercromby; and his two brothers, Alexander, Lord Abercromby, a judge of the court of session; and General Sir Robert Abercromby, K.C.B.; of all three notices are here given.

ABERCROMBY, SIR RALPH, K.B., a distinguished general, was the eldest son of George Abercromby, of Tullibody, in Clackmannanshire, by Mary, daughter of Ralph Dundas, Esq. of Manor. His father was born in 1705, passed advocate in 1728, and died June 8, 1800, at the advanced age of ninety-five, being the oldest member of the college of justice. He was one of the early patrons of David Allan, the celebrated painter, by whose aid, as mentioned in the life of that artist, the latter was enabled to proceed to Rome and to prosecute his studies there for sixteen years. His son Ralph was born on the 7th of October, 1734, in the old mansion of Menstrie, then the ordinary residence of his parents, near the village of that name which lies at the southern base of the Ochil hills, on the boundary between the parish of Alloa in Clackmannanshire, and the Perthshire part of the parish of Logie. The day of his birth has not been inserted in the session books of the parish of Logie, but the following is an extract from the register of his baptism: " A. D. 1734, October 26th, Bap. Ralph, lawful son to George Abercromby, younger of Tullibody, and Mary Dundas his lady." Menstrie house, in which he was born, possesses a double interest from its having been, in the beginning of the seventeenth century, the property and residence of Sir William Alexander, the poet, afterwards created earl of Stirling. Although not now inhabited by any of the Abercromby family, it is still entire, and is pointed out to strangers as the birthplace of Sir Ralph Abercromby. A woodcut representation of it is here given.

After the usual course of study, young Abercromby entered the army in 1756, as a cornet in the 3d regiment of dragoon guards. His commission is dated 23d March of that year. In February 1760 he obtained a lieutenancy in the same regiment; in April 1762 he was promoted to a company in the 3d regiment of horse. In 1770 he became major, and in 1773, lieutenant-colonel. In 1780 he was included in the list of brevet colonels, and in 1781 he was appointed colonel of the 103d, or King's Irish infantry. This newly raised regiment was reduced at the peace in 1783, when Colonel Abercromby was placed on half-pay. In September 1787 he became major-general. In 1788, in which year he resided in George's Square, Edinburgh, he obtained the command of the 69th regiment of foot. He was afterwards removed to the 6th regiment, from that to the 5th, and in November 1797 to the 7th regiment of dragoons.

He first served in the seven years' war, and acquired great knowledge and military experience in that service, before he had an opportunity of distinguishing himself, which afterwards, when the opportunity came, enabled him to be the first British general to give a check to the French in the first revolutionary war. He has often been confounded with the General Abercrombie who commanded the troops against the French at Crown Point and Ticonderoga in America in 1758, but Sir Ralph at that period was only a cornet of dragoons, and notwithstanding the mistake into which some of his biographers have fallen, it is certain that he never was in America.

In the year 1774, when lieutenant-colonel, he had been elected member of parliament for Clackmannanshire, which county he continued to represent till the next election in 1780, but never made any figure in parliament.

On the commencement of the war with France in 1792, he was employed in Flanders and Holland, with the local rank of lieutenant-general, and in the campaigns of 1793 and 1794 he served under the duke of York, when he gave many proofs of his skill, vigilance, and intrepidity. He commanded the advanced guard during the action on the heights of Cateau, April 16, 1794. On this occasion he captured 35 pieces of cannon, and took prisoner Chapuy the French general. In the despatches of the duke of York his ability and courage were twice mentioned with special commendation. In the succeeding October he received a wound at Nimeguen, and upon him and General Dundas devolved the arduous duty of conducting the retreat through Holland in the severe winter which followed. It has been remarked that the talents, as well as the temper, of a commander are put to as severe a test in conducting a retreat as in achieving a victory. This was well illustrated in the case of General Abercromby. The guards and the sick were committed to his care; and in the disastrous march from Deventer to Oldensaal the hardships sustained by those under his charge were such as the most consummate skill and judgment were almost inadequate to alleviate, while the feelings experienced by the commander himself were painful in the extreme. Harassed in the rear by a victorious enemy, upwards of fifty thousand strong, obliged to conduct his troops with a rapidity beyond their strength, through bad roads, in the most inclement part of a winter more than usually severe,—the sick being placed in open waggons, as no others could be procured,—and finding it impossible to procure shelter for his soldiers in the midst of the drifting snow and heavy falls of sleet and rain, the anguish he felt at seeing their numbers daily diminishing from the effects of cold, fatigue, and hunger, can scarcely be described. About the end of March 1795, the British army, which during the retreat had sometimes to halt, face and fight the enemy, arrived at Bremen in a very reduced state, and thence embarked for England. The judgment, patience, humanity, and perseverance shown by General Abercromby in this calamitous retreat were equal to the occasion, and received due acknowledgment.

In the autumn of 1795 General Abercromby was appointed to succeed Sir Charles Grey, as commander-in-chief of the troops employed against the French in the West Indies. Previous to his arrival, the French revolutionary army had made considerable exertions to recover their losses in that quarter. They retook the islands of Guadaloupe and St. Lucia, made good their landing on Martinique, and hoisted the tricolour on several forts in the islands of St. Vincent, Grenada, and Marie Galante; besides seizing the property of the rich emigrants who had fled thither from France, to the amount of 1,800 millions of livres. The expedition under General Abercromby was unfortunately prevented from sailing until after the equinox, and several transports were lost in endeavouring to clear the Channel. The remainder of the fleet reached the West Indies in safety, and by the month of March 1796 the troops were in a condition for active duty. A detachment of the army under Sir John Moore, was sent against the island of St. Lucia, which was speedily captured, though the attack on this island was attended with peculiar difficulties from the intricate nature of the country. A new road was made for the heavy cannon, and on the 26th of May 1796, the garrison surrendered. St. Vincent was next subdued; and thence the commander-in-chief proceeded to Grenada, where the fierce and enterprising Fedon was at the head of a body of insurgents prepared to oppose the British. After the arrival of General Abercromby, however, hostilities were speedily brought to a termination; and on the 19th of June, full possession was obtained of every post in the island, and the haughty chief Fedon, with his troops, was reduced to unconditional submission. The British also became masters of the Dutch colonies on the coast of Guiana, namely Demerara, Essequibo, and Berbice.

Early in the following year (1797) the general sailed, with a considerable fleet of ships of war and transports, against the Spanish island of Trinidad, and on the 16th of February approached the fortifications of Gaspar Grande, under cover of which a Spanish squadron, consisting of four sail of the line and a frigate, were found lying at anchor. On perceiving the approach of the British, the Spanish fleet retired farther into the bay. General Abercromby made arrangements for attacking the town and ships of war early in the following morning. Dreading the impending conflict, the Spaniards set fire to their own ships, and retired to a different part of the island. On the following day the British troops landed, and soon after the whole colony submitted to General Abercromby.

After an unsuccessful attack on the Spanish island of Puerto Rico, the general returned to

England the same year (1797) and was received with every demonstration of public respect and honour. In his absence he had been made a knight of the Bath and presented to the colonelcy of the Scots Greys. On his return he was appointed governor of the Isle of Wight, and was afterwards invested with the lucrative governments of Forts George and Augustus. The same year he was raised to the rank of lieutenant-general, which he had hitherto held only locally.

In 1798 Sir Ralph was appointed commander-in-chief of the forces in Ireland, where the insurrectionary spirit, inflamed by promises of assistance from France, was every day assuming a more serious form and threatening to break out into open rebellion. Soon after his arrival, finding that the disorderly conduct of some of the British troops had but too much tended to increase the spirit of insubordination and discontent that prevailed, he issued a proclamation, in which he lamented and reproved the excesses and irregularities into which they had fallen, and which, to use his own words, "had rendered them more formidable to their friends than to their enemies," and declared his firm determination to punish, with exemplary severity, any similar outrage of which they might be guilty in future. He did not long retain his command in Ireland. The inconveniences arising from the delegation of the highest civil and military authority to different persons, had been felt to occasion much perplexity and confusion in the management of public affairs, at that season of agitation and alarm, and finding the service, under such circumstances, disagreeable, Sir Ralph resigned the command, and the Marquis Cornwallis, on becoming lord-lieutenant of Ireland, was appointed his successor.

Sir Ralph was next nominated commander-in-chief of the forces in Scotland; and for a short interval, the cares of his military duties were agreeably blended with the endearments of his kindred and the society of his early friends. During his residence in Edinburgh at this time, the military spirit that generally prevailed rendered the occurrence of reviews extremely popular among the inhabitants. The accompanying woodcut represents Sir Ralph in the act of giving the word of command to the troops.

It was at this period that the Lochiel Highlanders were inspected at Falkirk by General Vyse, one of the major-generals of the staff in Scotland, under Sir Ralph Abercromby, who was present at the inspection. Cameron, the chief of Lochiel, married Sir Ralph's eldest daughter Anne. The regiment was ostensibly composed of Camerons, but there were enrolled in its ranks, not only lowlanders, but even Englishmen and Irishmen. Some laughable attempts at fraud in endeavouring to pass inspection are related, but unless actually disabled, few objections were made, although Scotsmen in general found a preference. "Where are you from?" said General Vyse to a strange-looking fellow, who was evidently an Irishman, although he endeavoured to make believe that he was Scotch. "From Falkirk, yir honour, this morning," was the ready answer. His language betraying him, the general demanded to know how he came over. "Sure I didn't come in a wheelbarrow!" The rising choler of the inspecting officer was speedily soothed by the milder tact of Sir Ralph, who, seeing the man a fit recruit, laughed heartily, and he was passed. On this occasion Sir Ralph, during his stay in Falkirk, took up his residence with the son of his late father's gardener at Tullibody, Mr. James Walker, a merchant in the town, and long known for his agricultural skill, as "the Stirlingshire Farmer." Sir Ralph delighted, after dinner, to recall the incidents of their boyhood, when he and Mr. Walker, with their brothers, were at school together. He had previously shown the attachment of former days to a younger brother of Mr. Walker, during the struggle for liberty between America and the mother country. These kindly and benevolent traits, it has been well remarked, easily explain why Sir Ralph Abercromby was personally so dear to all who knew him.—[*Kay's Edinburgh Portraits.*]

In the autumn of 1799 he was selected to take the chief command of the expedition sent out to Holland, for the purpose of restoring the prince of Orange to the stadtholdership, from which he had been driven by the French. In this expedition the British were at the outset successful. On the 27th of August the British troops disembarked near the Helder point, but were almost immediately attacked by General Daendells; after a contest, which lasted from day-dawn till about five in the afternoon, the Dutch were defeated, and retired, leaving the British in possession of a ridge of sand hills which stretched along the coast from south to north. Sir Ralph Abercromby resolved to attack the Helder next morning, but the enemy withdrew during the night, in consequence of which thirteen ships of war and three Indiamen, together with the arsenal and naval magazine, fell into the possession of the British. Admiral Mitchell, who commanded the British fleet, immediately offered battle to the fleet of the Batavian republic lying in the Texel, but the Dutch sailors refusing to fight against those who were combating for the rights of the prince of Orange, the whole fleet, consisting of twelve sail of the line, surrendered to the British admiral. This encouraging event, however, did not put an end to the struggle. The mass of the Dutch people held sentiments very different from those of the sailors, and they refused to receive the British as their deliverers from the yoke of France. On the morning of the 10th of September the Dutch and French forces attacked the position of the British, which extended from Petten on the German ocean

to Oude-Sluys on the Zuyder-Zee. The onset was made with the utmost bravery, but the enemy were repulsed with the loss of a thousand men. From the want of numbers, however, Sir Ralph Abercromby was unable to follow up this advantage, until the duke of York arrived as commander-in-chief, with a reinforcement of Russians, Batavians, and Dutch volunteers, which augmented the allied army to nearly thirty-six thousand men. Sir Ralph now served as second in command.

On the morning of the 19th September the army under the duke of York commenced an attack on the enemy's positions on the heights of Camperdown, which was successful. The Russian troops, under General Hermann, made themselves masters of Bergen, but beginning to pillage too soon, the enemy rallied, and attacked them with so much impetuosity that they were driven from the town in all directions. The British were in consequence compelled to abandon the positions they had stormed, and to fall back upon their former station. Another attack was made on the 2d of October. The conflict lasted the whole day, and the enemy abandoned their positions during the night. On this occasion Sir Ralph Abercromby had two horses shot under him. Sir John Moore was twice wounded severely, and reluctantly carried off the field, while the marquis of Huntly (the last duke of Gordon) who, at the head of the 92d regiment, eminently distinguished himself, received a wound from a ball in the shoulder. The Dutch and French troops had taken up another strong position between Benerwych and the Zuyder-Zee, from which it was resolved to dislodge them before they could obtain reinforcements. A day of sanguinary fighting ensued, which continued without intermission till ten o'clock at night amid deluges of rain. The French republican general, Brune, having been reinforced with six thousand additional men, and the ground which he occupied being found to be impregnable, the duke of York resolved upon a retreat. A convention was accordingly concluded with General Brune, by which the British troops were allowed to embark for England.

In June 1800 Sir Ralph was appointed to the command of the troops, then quartered in the island of Minorca, which had been sent out upon a secret expedition to the Mediterranean. On the 22d of that month he arrived at Minorca, and on the 23d the troops were embarked, and sailed for Leghorn. They arrived there on the 9th of July, but in consequence of an armistice having been concluded between the French and the Austrians, they did not land there; but while part of the troops proceeded to Malta, the remainder returned to Minorca. On the 26th of July Sir Ralph arrived again at that island, where he remained till the 30th of August, when the troops were again embarked; and on the 14th September the fleet, which consisted of upwards of two hundred sail, under the command of Admiral Lord Keith, came to anchor off Europa point in the bay of Gibraltar. After taking in water at Teutan, the fleet, on the 3d of October, arrived off Cadiz, where it was intended to disembark the troops, and orders were accordingly issued for the purpose, but a flag of truce was sent from the shore, and some negotiations took place between the commanders, in consequence of which the orders for landing were countermanded. After thus threatening Cadiz, and sailing about apparently without any distinct destination, orders were at last received from England, for part of the troops to proceed to Portugal, and the remainder to Malta, where they arrived about the middle of November. The latter portion afterwards formed part of the forces employed in the expedition to Egypt, with the view of driving the French out of that country. The sailing backwards and forwards of the fleet for so many months, seemingly without any definite aim, so far from being indicative of want of design or weakness in the councils of the government at home, as was believed and said at the time, was no doubt intended to deceive the French as to the real object and destination of the expedition.

From Malta the fleet, with Sir Ralph Abercromby and the troops on board, sailed on the 20th December, taking with them 500 Maltese recruits, designed to act as pioneers. On the 1st of January 1801, it rendezvoused in the bay of Marmorice, on the coast of Caramania, where it remained till the 23d of February, on which day, to the number of 175 sail, it weighed anchor again; and on the 1st of March, it came in sight of the coast of Egypt. On the following morning the fleet anchored in Aboukir bay, in the very place where, a few years before, Admiral Nelson had added so signally to the naval triumphs of Great Britain.

This was undoubtedly the most glorious period of Sir Ralph Abercromby's career. "All minds," says a contemporary historian, "were now anxiously directed towards Egypt. It was a novel and interesting spectacle to contemplate the two most powerful nations of Europe contending in Africa for the possession of Asia. Not only to England and France, but the whole civilized world, the issue of this contest was of the utmost importance. With respect to England, the difficulties to be surmounted were proportioned to the magnitude of the object. The vizier, with his usual irresolution, yet debated on the propriety of co-operation, while the captain bashaw, who was at Constantinople, with part of his fleet, inclined to treat with the enemy. The English taking the unpopular side, that of the government, still less was to be hoped from the countenance and support of the people, whom the French had long flattered with the idea of freedom and independence. It remained, also, to justify the breach of faith so speciously attributed to this nation in the treaty of El Arish. These were serious obstacles to the progress of the expedition in Egypt; but they were not the only obstacles. The expedition had to contend with an army habituated to the country, respected at least, if not beloved, by the inhabitants, and flushed with reputation and success; an army inured to danger; aware of the importance of Egypt to their government; determined to defend the possession of it; and encouraged in this determination, no less by the assurance of speedily receiving effectual succours, than by the promise of reward, and the love of glory."

The violence of the wind, from the 1st to the 7th of March, rendered a landing impracticable; but the weather becoming calmer on the 7th, that day was spent in reconnoitring the shore; a service in which Sir Sidney Smith displayed great skill and activity.

In the meantime Bonaparte had sent naval and military reinforcements from Europe, and the delay in the disembarkation of the British troops caused by the state of the weather, enabled the French to make all necessary preparations to receive them. Two thousand five hundred of the latter were strongly intrenched on the sand hills near the shore, and formed, in a concave figure, opposite the British ships. The main body of the French army was stationed at and near Alexandria, within a few miles. At two o'clock on the morning of the 8th, the British troops began to assemble in the boats, their fire-locks between their knees. A rocket from the admiral's ship gave the signal; and when all was ready, the boats, containing five thousand men, pulled in towards the shore, a distance of about five miles. The silence was broken only by the sullen dip of the oars. As soon as the boats came within reach, a most tremendous fire was opened upon them from fifteen pieces of artillery placed on the ridge of sand hills in front, besides the guns of Aboukir castle and the musketry of 2,500 men. These completely swept the sea, and the falling of the balls and shot is compared, by a contemporary writer, to the falling of a violent hail-storm on the water. Two boats were sunk with all on board of them. Each man had belts loaded with three days' provisions, and a cartouch-box with sixty rounds of ball cartridge. It was nine o'clock when the rest reached land; and the French, who had poured down in thousands to the beach, and even attacked the British in the boats, were ready to receive them at the bayonet's point. It was now that their commander reaped the advantage of his precautionary discipline. While anchored in the bay of Marmorice, he had caused the troops to practise all the manœuvres of landing; so that, disembarkation having become familiar to them, on reaching the shore, they leaped from the boats, formed into line, mounted the heights, in the face of the enemy's fire, without returning a shot, charged with the bayonet the enemy stationed on the summit, put them to flight, and seized their cannon. In this service the 23d and 40th regiments, which first reached the shore, particularly distinguished themselves; while the seamen, harnessing themselves to the field artillery with ropes, drew them on shore, and replied to the incessant roar of the hostile cannon with repeated and tri-

umphant cheers. In vain did the enemy endeavour to rally his troops; in vain did a body of cavalry charge suddenly on the guards at the moment of their debarkation. The French gave way at all points, maintaining, as they retreated, a scattered and inefficient fire. The boats returned to the ships for the remaining part of the army, and before noon the landing was effected. It not being deemed expedient, however, to bring on shore the camp stores; the commander-in-chief and the troops, after having advanced three miles into the country, alike slept in huts made of the date-tree branches.

The next day the troops were employed in searching for water, in which they happily succeeded; and the castle of Aboukir refusing to surrender, two regiments were ordered to blockade it. On the 13th, Sir Ralph, desirous of forcing the heights near Alexandria, on which a body of French, amounting to 6,000 men, was posted, marched his army to the attack.

After a severe contest, the French were compelled to retire to the heights of Necopolis, which formed the principal defence of Alexandria. Anxious to follow up the victory, by driving the enemy from his new position, Sir Ralph ordered forward the reserve under Sir John Moore, and the second line under General Hutchinson, to attack the heights, which were found to be commanded by the guns of the fort. As they advanced into the open plain, they were exposed to a most destructive fire, from which they had no shelter; and having ascertained that the heights, if taken, could not be retained, the attempt was abandoned, and the British army retired, with considerable loss, to the position which was soon to be the theatre of Sir Ralph's last victory;—that, namely, from which the enemy had been driven, comprising a front of more than half-a-mile in extent, with their right to the sea, and their left to the canal of Alexandria and Lake Maadie, thus cutting off all communication with the city, except by way of the desert. The loss of the British, on that unfortunate day, in killed and wounded, was upwards of 1,000, and General Abercromby himself, on this occasion, had a very narrow escape. His horse being shot under him, he became surrounded by the enemy's cavalry, and was rescued only by the devoted intrepidity of the 19th regiment. After the 13th, Aboukir castle, which had hitherto been only blockaded, was besieged, and on the 18th the garrison surrendered. The annexed woodcut represents the general viewing the army encamped on the plains of Egypt, a short time before his lamented death.

It is very characteristic of him, and though the glass at his eye may indicate that age had begun to affect his sight, the erectness of his figure shows that, notwithstanding his long and active career, advancing years and the hard services in which he had been engaged, had left their traces but lightly on his frame.

The French commander-in-chief, General Menou, having arrived from Cairo, with a reinforcement of 9,000 men, early on the morning of the 21st of March, was fought the decisive battle of Alexandria, in which, after a sanguinary and protracted struggle, the British were victorious, General Menou being obliged to retreat with a loss of between three and four thousand men, including many officers, and three generals killed. The loss of the British was also heavy, and this was the last field of the victor, for here Sir Ralph Abercromby received his death-wound.

Meaning to surprise the British, the French commander attacked their position between three and four o'clock in the morning, with his whole force, amounting to about twelve thousand men. The action was commenced by a feigned attack on the left, while the main strength of the enemy was directed against the right wing of the British army. They advanced in columns, shouting "Vive la France!" "Vive la Republique!" but they were received with steady coolness by the British troops, who, warned the previous evening, by an Arab chief, of the intentions of the French general, were in battle array by three o'clock, and prepared to receive the onset of the enemy. The contest continued with various success until eight o'clock, when General Menou, finding that all his efforts were fruitless, ordered a retreat, and from the want of cavalry on the part of the British, the French effected their escape to Alexandria, in good order.

On the first alarm, Sir Ralph Abercromby, blending the coolness and experience of age with the ardour and activity of youth, repaired on horseback to the right, and exposed himself to all the dangers of the field. During the battle he rode about in all parts, cheering and animating his men, and while it was still dark he got among the enemy, who had already broken the front line and fallen into the rear. Unable to distinguish the French soldiers from his own, he was only extricated from his dangerous situation by the valour of his troops. To the first British soldier who came up to him he said, "Soldier! if you know me, don't name me." Soon after, two French dragoons rode furiously at him, and attempted to lead him away prisoner. Sir Ralph, however, would not yield; one of his assailants made a thrust at his breast, and passed his sword with great force under the general's arm. Although severely bruised by a blow from the sword-guard, Sir Ralph, with the vigour and strength of arm for which he was distinguished, seized the Frenchman's weapon, and after a short struggle, wrested it from his hand, and turned to oppose his remaining adversary, who, at that instant, was shot dead by a corporal of the 42d, who had witnessed the danger of his commander, and ran up to his assistance; on which the other dragoon retired.

Although Sir Ralph, early in the action, had been wounded in the thigh by a musket ball, he treated the wound as a trifle, and continued to move about, and give his orders with his characteristic promptitude and clearness. On the retreat of the enemy he fainted from pain and the loss of blood. His magnanimous conduct, both during the battle and after it, is thus detailed by

the late General David Stewart, of Garth, who was an eye-witness to it. After describing Sir Ralph's rencontre with the French dragoons, he continues: "Some time after the general attempted to alight from his horse; a soldier of the Highlanders, seeing that he had some difficulty in dismounting, assisted him, and asked if he should follow him with the horse. He answered, that he would not require him any more that day. While all this was passing, no officer was near him. The first officer he met was Sir Sidney Smith; and observing that his sword was broken, the general presented him with the trophy he had gained. He betrayed no symptom of personal pain, nor relaxed a moment the intense interest he took in the state of the field; nor was it perceived that he was wounded, till he was joined by some of the staff, who observed the blood trickling down his thigh. Even during the interval from the time of his being wounded, and the last charge of cavalry, he walked with a firm and steady step along the line of the Highlanders and General Stuart's brigade, to the position of the guards in the centre of the line, where, from its elevated situation, he had a full view of the whole field of battle. Here he remained, regardless of the wound, giving his orders so much in his usual manner, that the officers who came to receive them perceived nothing that indicated either pain or anxiety. These officers afterwards could not sufficiently express their astonishment, when they came to learn the state in which he was, and the pain which he must have suffered from the nature of his wound. A musket ball had entered his groin, and lodged deep in the hip joint; the ball was even so firmly fixed in the hip joint that it required considerable force to extract it after his death. My respectable friend, Dr. Alexander Robertson, the surgeon who attended him, assured me that nothing could exceed his surprise and admiration at the calmness of his heroic patient. With a wound in such a part, connected with and bearing on every part of his body, it is a matter of surprise how he could move at all, and nothing but the most intense interest in the fate of his army, the issue of the battle, and the honour of the British name, could have inspired and sustained such resolution. As soon as the impulse ceased in the assurance of victory, he yielded to exhausted nature, acknowledged that he required some rest, and lay down on a little sand hill close to the battery."

From the field of victory he was removed on a litter, feeble and faint, on board the admiral's flag ship, 'the Foudroyant,' where every effort was made by the medical gentlemen of the fleet and the army to extract the ball, but without effect. During a week that he lingered in great bodily suffering, he continued to exercise the same vigilance over the condition and prospects of his army as he had manifested while at its head. His son, Lieutenant-colonel Abercromby, attended him from day to day, and regularly received his instructions, as if no serious accident had befallen him. Throughout the evening of the 27th, he became more than usually restless, and complained of excessive languor, and an increased degree of thirst; next day mortification supervened, and in the evening he expired; thus closing his glorious career, on the 28th March 1801, in the 68th year of his age.

In the despatches sent home with an account of his death by General (afterwards Lord) Hutchinson, who succeeded him in the command, the latter says: " We have sustained an irreparable loss in the person of our never-sufficiently-to-be-lamented commander-in-chief, Sir Ralph Abercromby, who was mortally wounded in the action, and died on the 28th of March. I believe he was wounded early, but he concealed his situation from those about him, and continued in the field giving his orders with that coolness and perspicuity which had ever marked his character, till long after the action was over, when he fainted through weakness and loss of blood. Were it permitted for a soldier to regret any one who has fallen in the service of his country, I might be excused for lamenting him more than any other person; but it is some consolation to those who tenderly loved him, that, as his life was honourable, so was his death glorious. His memory will be recorded in the annals of his country, will be sacred to every British soldier, and embalmed in the recollection of a grateful posterity." His remains were conveyed, (in compliance with his own request,) to Malta, and interred in the Commandery of the Grand Master, beneath the castle of St. Elmo. A monument was erected to his memory in St. Paul's Cathedral, parliament having voted a sum of money for the purpose. His widow was created Baroness Abercromby of Aboukir and Tullibody, with remainder to the heirs-male of the deceased general; and, in support of the dignity, a pension of £2,000 a-year was granted to her, and to the two next succeeding heirs-male.

Sir Ralph Abercromby possessed, in a high degree, some of the best qualities of a general, and his coolness, decision, and intrepidity, were the theme of general praise. As a country gentleman, also, his character stood very high, being described as " the friend of the destitute poor, the patron of useful knowledge, and the promoter of education among the meanest of his cottagers." His studies were of so general a nature that it is stated in Stirling's edition of Nimmo's History of Stirlingshire, that when called to the continent in 1793, he had been daily attending the lectures of the late Dr. Hardy, regius professor of church history in the university of Edinburgh.

To Sir Ralph's patronage many who would otherwise have passed their lives in obscurity, owed their being placed in situations where they had opportunities of advancement and distinction; among the rest was the late Major-general Sir William Morison, K.C.B., one of the many able officers whom the East India Company's service has produced. His father, Mr. Morison of Greenfield, Clackmannanshire, was a land surveyor in Alloa in the county of Stirling, who was well known to most of the gentlemen in that neighbourhood, and was in particular employed by Sir Ralph Abercromby. When Sir Ralph was going abroad on foreign service, he had occasion to consult Mr. Morison, the father, about one of his farms, and was particularly pleased with the accuracy and clearness of the plan and its references, which he submitted to him. On being asked who drew them up, Mr. Morison told Sir Ralph that it was done by his son, and the general immediately said that he should like to have the whole of his estate mapped in the same manner, so that, when away from home, he might be able, by reference, to correspond about any point that occurred. The maps were made by young Morison, who waited on

Sir Ralph to explain them, and the veteran general, who was a great judge of character, instantly perceived the value of the self-taught youth. He made inquiries as to his views and prospects, and finding that he was anxious to go to India, he procured for him a cadetship, in the year 1800. From the outset the young man justified Sir Ralph's estimate of his abilities, and he so applied his faculties to military science, that his attainments raised him to a high rank in the Indian army, and he died 15th May 1851, a major-general in the East India Company's service, a knight commander of the Bath, and member of parliament for Clackmannanshire and Kinross-shire.

Sir Ralph married Mary Anne, daughter of John Menzies, Esq., of Fernton, Perthshire, and left four sons, namely, George, a barrister at law, who succeeded his mother on her death in 1821, as Lord Abercromby, and died in 1843; Sir John, a major-general, and G.C.B., who died unmarried in 1817; James, also a barrister, returned, with Francis Jeffrey, Esq., (subsequently a lord of session,) as one of the members of parliament for the city of Edinburgh at the first election under the Reform act, afterwards Speaker of the House of Commons, created Lord Dunfermline in 1839; and Alexander, a colonel in the army; with three daughters; Anne, married to Donald Cameron, Esq. of Lochiel, died in 1858, leaving a son, Ralph, second Lord Dunfermline; she died in 1844; Mary, died unmarried in 1825; and Catherine, wife of Thomas Buchanan, Esq., in the service of the East India Company; she died in 1841.

ABERCROMBY, ALEXANDER, an eminent lawyer and occasional essayist, was born October 15, 1745. He was the second son of George Abercromby of Tullibody, and the brother of Sir Ralph. He received his education at the university of Edinburgh, and was admitted a member of the faculty of advocates in 1766. He distinguished himself at the bar, and in 1780, after being sheriff of Stirlingshire, he became one of the depute-advocates. He was raised to the bench in May 1792, when he assumed the title of Lord Abercromby. In December of the same year, he was made a lord of justiciary. He was one of the originators of the 'Mirror,' a periodical published

at Edinburgh in 1779 and following year, to which he contributed eleven papers. He also furnished nine papers to the 'Lounger,' a work of a similar kind, published in 1785 and 1786. He caught a cold, while attending his duty on the northern circuit in the spring of 1795, from which he never recovered, and died on the 17th of November of that year, at Exmouth, in Devonshire, where he had gone on account of his health. A short tribute to his memory was written by his friend, Henry Mackenzie, for the Royal Society of Edinburgh.—*Haig and Brunton's Senators of the College of Justice.*

ABERCROMBY, SIR ROBERT, the youngest brother of Sir Ralph Abercromby, was a general in the army, a knight of the Bath, and at one period the governor of Bombay and commander-in-chief of the forces in India. He was afterwards for thirty years governor of the castle of Edinburgh. When the late Mr. Robert Haldane, the brother of Mr. James Alexander Haldane, determined upon selling his estates, and devoting himself to the diffusion of the gospel in India, Sir Robert Abercromby, whose niece Mr. J. A. Haldane had married, purchased from him his beautiful and romantic estate of Airthrey, in Stirlingshire, and was succeeded by his nephew, Lord Abercromby, the son of his elder brother, Sir Ralph. Sir Robert died in 1827.

ABERDEEN, earldom of, a peerage possessed by a branch of the ancient family of Gordon. In 1644, Sir John Gordon of Haddo was beheaded at Edinburgh, for his adherence to the cause of Charles I. After the Restoration, Sir John Gordon, his eldest son, was restored to the baronetage which had been bestowed on his father in 1642, and to the estates of the family. He was succeeded by his brother George, who was lord high chancellor of Scotland in 1682, and the same year was created Earl of Aberdeen, Viscount Formartine, Baron Haddo, Methlic, Tarves, and Kellie. In 1814 the fourth earl of Aberdeen was created Viscount Gordon of Aberdeen, in the peerage of the United Kingdom. See GORDON, p. 323.

ABERNETHY—(beyond the Nethy)—a surname derived from a barony of that name in Lower Strathearn, Perthshire, which was possessed in the reign of William I. by Orme, the son of Hugh, who was styled Abbot of Abernethy, and whose decendants assumed the name of Abernethy. In 1288 Sir William de Abernethy, the first of the family styled of Saltoun, and Sir Patrick de Abernethy, lay in wait for Duncan earl of Fife, one of the regents of the kingdom during the minority of Margaret of Norway, at Potpollock, and murdered him. William was seized by Sir Andrew Moray of Bothwell and condemned to perpetual imprisonment, and Patrick fled into France and died there. [*Fordun.*] His nephew, Alexander de Abernethy, in 1308, along with Robert de Keith,

Adam de Gordon, and other leading barons, were sureties to Edward for the good behaviour of William de Lambyrton, bishop of St. Andrews. [*Rymer's Fœdera*, tome iii. p. 82.] The same individual was appointed by Edward warden of the country between the Forth and the mountains of Scotland, 15th June, 1310. [*Ibid.* tome iii. p. 211.] His eldest daughter Margaret was married to John Stewart, earl of Angus, who got with her the barony of Abernethy, the superiority of which is still possessed by the family of Douglas, (now Hamilton,) as representatives of the earl of Angus. To the famous letter to the Pope, drawn up by the barons of Scotland at the parliament of Aberbrothic 6th April, 1320, appears the name of William de Abernethy, lord of Saltoun. He was the son of the first Sir William de Abernethy of Saltoun. His son, also named Sir William, appears in the list of noble persons who fought at the battle of Halidon hill, 19th July, 1333, [*Hailes' Annals*, vol. ii. p. 307,] from which disastrous field he appears to have escaped. He had from David II. a grant of the lands of Rothiemay in Aberdeenshire. George Abernethy of Saltoun, his son, was taken prisoner at the fatal fight of Durham, 17th Oct., 1346. At the battle of Harlaw 24th July 1411, William Abernethy, son and heir to the Lord Saltoun, was one of the principal leaders, and was slain. But although he is called "the worthy Lord Saltone," and of his death it is said in the popular ballad,

"And on the other side war lost
Into the field that dismal day,
Chief men of worth of mickle cost,
To be lamented sair for aye,
The lord Saltoune of Rothiemay,
A man of micht and mickle main,
Great dolour was for his decay
That sae unhappily was slain;"

yet the peerage was not conferred upon the family till 28th June, 1445,— 34 years later,— in the person of Laurence Abernethy of Saltoun and Rothiemay, created Baron Saltoun of Abernethy, and as the said William Abernethy predeceased his father, he was called " the Lord Saltone" only by courtesy. This Laurence Abernethy of Saltoun and Rothiemay, first Lord Saltoun, was the twelfth in descent from Orm the founder of the family. Margaret, the eldest daughter of the seventh Lord Saltoun, married Sir Alexander Fraser of Philorth in Aberdeenshire, and their son, Sir Alexander Fraser, became the tenth Lord Saltoun, and his descendants succeeded to the title. The brother of his mother, John, eighth Lord Saltoun, sold the estate of Rothiemay. The family of Abernethy is now represented by the Frasers of Philorth, lords Saltoun.—See SALTOUN.—The parish and village of Abernethy are of great antiquity. The latter was at one period the capital of the Pictish kings. It is named by various English writers and by Fordoun as the place where Malcolm Canmore concluded a peace with William the Conqueror in 1072, delivered to him hostages, and did homage to him for the lands which he held in England. But although now a mean village, "it would appear," says Dr. Jamieson, "that it was a royal residence in the reign of one of the Pictish princes who bore the name of Nethan or Nectan. The Pictish chronicle has ascribed the foundation of Abernethy to Nethan I., in the third year of his reign, corresponding with A.D. 458. The Register of St. Andrews, with greater probability, gives it to Nethan II. about the year 600." We find that while the church of Abernethy was granted by William I. in 1178, to his foundation of the abbey of Aberbrothock, Orme, abbot of Abernethy, granted the half of the tithes of the property of himself and his heirs to the same institution. The other half belonged to the Culdees, as in ancient times Abernethy was a principal seat of the Culdees, who had a university at Abernethy, which in 1273 was turned into a priory of canons regular of St. Augustine. It is a burgh of barony, and has a charter from Archibald, earl of Angus, lord of Abernethy, dated November 29, 1628. The title of Lord Abernethy was conferred on the earl of Angus when created marquis of Douglas in 1633, and is now one of the inferior titles of the duke of Hamilton as representative and chief of the illustrious house of Douglas.—See HAMILTON.

ABERNETHY, JOHN, an eminent physician of London, was born in 1763 or 1764, at Abernethy in Perthshire, it is believed; although Londonderry in Ireland is also mentioned as his birth-place. When very young, his parents removed to London, where he was apprenticed to the late Mr. (afterwards Sir) Charles Blick, surgeon of St. Bartholomew's Hospital. He was the pupil and friend of the celebrated John Hunter. In 1780, on being elected assistant-surgeon to St. Bartholomew's, he began to give lectures in the hospital on anatomy and surgery. On the death of Sir Charles Blick he succeeded him as surgeon to the Hospital. In 1793 he published 'Surgical and Physiological Essays.' In 1804 appeared 'Surgical Observations,' volume first, relating to tumours, and two years afterwards, volume second, treating principally of the digestive organs. Having been elected anatomical lecturer to the Royal College of Surgeons, he published in 1814 the subject of his first two lectures, under the title of ' An Enquiry into Mr. Hunter's Theory of Life,' elucidatory of his old master's opinions of the vital processes. In 1809 appeared his 'Surgical Observations on the Constitutional Origin and Treatment of Local Diseases, and on Aneurisms,' in which are detailed his memorable cases of tying the iliac artery for aneurism; a bold and successful operation, which at once established his reputation. He was the author of several other popular medical works. In chemistry, we owe to him in conjunction with Mr. Howard, brother of the duke of Norfolk, the discovery of the "fulminating mercury," the force of which, as an explosive power, is greater than that of gunpowder. He died on the 20th of April, 1831, at his house at Enfield. Many amusing anecdotes are related of his eccentricities. He attributed most complaints to the disordered state of the stomach, and his chief remedies were exercise and regulation of the diet. Once he prescribed a skipping rope to a female hypochondriac patient of the upper ranks; and at another time, as a cure for gout, he advised an indolent and luxurious citizen to "live upon sixpence a-day, and earn it." In spite of the bluntness of his manner, however, he was very benevolent, and often not only gratuitously visited persons whose poverty prevented them from coming to him, but even sometimes supplied their wants from his own purse. The following is the account given of the abrupt and unceremonious but truly characteristic manner in which he obtained his wife. The name of the lady is not given. "While attending a lady for several weeks, he observed those admirable qualifications in her daughter, which he truly esteemed to be calculated to make the marriage state happy. Accordingly, on a Saturday, when taking leave of his patient, he addressed her to the following purport :—' You are now so well that I need not see you after Monday next, when I shall come and pay you my farewell visit. But, in the meantime, I wish you and your daughter seriously to consider the proposal I am now about to make. It is abrupt and unceremonious, I am aware; but the excessive occupation of my time by my professional duties affords me no leisure to accomplish what I desire by the more ordinary course of attention and solicitation. My annual receipts amount to £——, and I can settle £—— on my wife (mentioning the sums): my character is generally known to the public, so that you may readily ascertain what it is. I have seen in your daughter a tender and affectionate child, an assiduous and careful nurse, and a gentle and ladylike member of a family; such a person must be all that a husband could covet, and I offer my hand and fortune for her acceptance. On Monday, when I call, I shall expect your determination; for I really have not time for the routine of courtship.' In this humour, the lady was wooed and won; and the union proved fortunate in every respect."—*Annual Obituary*, 1832.

The following is a list of his works:

Surgical and Physiological Essays. Lond. 1793-7, 8vo.

Surgical Observations, containing a Classification of Tumours, with Cases to illustrate the History of each Species. Lond. 1804, 8vo.

Surgical Observations, part second, containing an Account of the Disorders of the Health in general, and of the Digestive Organs in particular. Observations on the Diseases of the Urethra, and Observations relative to the Treatment of one Species of the Nævi Maternæ. Lond. 1806, 8vo. Lond. 1816, 8vo.

Surgical Observations on the Constitutional Origin and Treatment of Local Diseases; and on Aneurisms. Lond. 1809, 8vo. 3d edit. 1813, 8vo.

Surgical Observations, part second, containing Observations on the Origin and Treatment of Pseudo-syphilitic Diseases, and on Diseases of the Urethra. Lond. 1810, 8vo.

Surgical Observations on Injuries of the Head, and other Miscellaneous Subjects. Lond. 1810, 8vo.

An Inquiry into the Probability and Rationality of Mr Hunter's Theory of Life, being the Subject of the first two Anatomical Lectures before the Royal College of Surgeons. Lond. 1814, 8vo.

The Introductory Lecture for the year 1815, exhibiting some of Mr. Hunter's Opinions respecting Diseases; delivered before Royal College of Surgeons, London. Lond. 1815, 8vo.

Surgical Works, a new edit. 1815, 2 vols. 8vo.

Physiological Lectures, 1817.

ABOYNE, Earl of, a title belonging to a branch of the Gordon family, derived from the parish of Aboyne in Aberdeenshire. On the death of the last duke of Gordon in 1836, when that dukedom became extinct, the title of earl of Aboyne merged in that of marquis of Huntly. See HUNTLY.

ABTHANE, a title which occurs in Scottish history, and which appears peculiar to Scotland, as no trace of it has been found in any other country. It is a Thanedom or proprietorship of land held of the crown, and in the possession of an abbot. Like a Thanedom also, it is the title of a Saxon proprietor, that is, a proprietor under the Saxon laws, holding direct of the crown, and is therefore exactly equivalent to that of a Norman baron. Three Abthainries only have been as yet traced in Scotland, viz. those of Dull, Kilmichael, and Madderty; the two former in Athol, the latter in Strathearn. Mr. Skene, whose investigations supply the foregoing information, seems to have established that all these three were created between the years 1098 and 1124,—that is, between the accession of Edgar to the throne and that of David I.; that they were all held in connection with the Culdee monks of Dunkeld; that they must have been in possession of an abbot of that monastery; and that the party who then held that dignity, and in whose favour they were created, was Ethelred, youngest son of Malcolm III., who consequently had obtained them from one of his brothers, Edgar or Alexander, the then reigning monarchs of Scotland. The fact of the possession of these and other lands in Athol by the then reigning family of Scotland, is one of the many circumstances adduced by this gentleman to demonstrate the descent of Malcolm III., and after him a long line of Scottish kings, from the ancient Maormors of Athol, one of the many facts illustrative of early Scottish history for which we are indebted to his careful investigations and ingenious inductions. See ATHOL, EARLS OF. On the death of Ethelred, these lands again reverted to the crown. In various charters so recent as the reign of David II. they are described as the "abthanes of Dull" of "Kilmichael," &c. The second family whose chief obtained the earldom of Lennox appears by an entry in an early history of the Drummonds to have been previously the hereditary baillies of the abthainries of Dull, and on the promotion of its head to that dignity, that baillierie passed to a younger branch or cadet of it according to Celtic usage.— *Skene on the Origin of the Highlanders*, vol. ii. pp. 129—137, 152, 153.

ACHAIUS, or ACHAYUS, or EOCHY, the son of King Ethwin, or Ewen, succeeded to the crown of Scotland in 788, upon the death of Solvatius, or Selvach. Before his accession to the throne, he lived familiarly with the nobles, and was well acquainted with the causes of their mutual feuds. It was, therefore, the first act of his reign to reconcile the chiefs with one another, and check the turbulent spirit which their animosities had engendered. No sooner had he succeeded in thus reconciling his subjects, than he was called upon to take measures to repel an aggression of the predatory Irish. A number of banditti from Ireland, who infested the district of Kintyre, in the west of Scotland, having been completely routed by the inhabitants, the Irish nation was highly exasperated, and resolved to revenge the injury done to them. Achaius despatched an ambassador to soften their rage, but before he had time to return from his fruitless mission, an immense number of Irish plundered and laid waste the island of Isla. These depredators were all drowned when returning home with their spoil, and such was the terror which this calamity inspired into the Irish, that they immediately sued for peace, which was generously granted them by the king of Scotland. A short time after the conclusion of this treaty, the emperor Charlemagne sent an ambassador to Achaius, requesting the Scots king to enter into a strict alliance with him against the English, who, in the language of the envoy, "shamefully filled both sea and land with their piracies, and bloody invasions." After much hesitation and debate among the king's counsellors, the alliance was unanimously agreed to, and Achaius sent his brother William, along with Clement, John Scotus, Raban, and Alcuin, a native of the north of England, four of the most learned men then in Scotland, together with an army of four thousand men, to accompany the French ambassador to Paris, where the alliance was concluded, on terms very favourable to the Scots. In order to perpetuate the remembrance of this event, Achaius added to the arms of Scotland a double field sowed with lilies. After assisting Hungus, king of the Picts, to repel an aggression of Athelstane, king of the West Saxons, Achaius spent the rest of his reign in com-

plete tranquillity, and died in 819, distinguished for his piety and wisdom.—*Brewster's Edin. Encyc.*

ADAIR, JAMES MAKITTRICK, physician and medical writer, for several years practised at Bath. He was a native of Scotland, but neither the date nor the place of his birth is known. He was noted for extreme irritability of temper, and among other persons with whom he had a dispute was the eccentric Philip Thicknesse, in the dedication to whose memoirs is given an account of one of his last quarrels. He afterwards went to Antigua, and became physician to the commander-in-chief and the colonial troops, and one of the judges of the court of king's bench and common pleas in that island. He was the author of several medical tracts on regimen, the materia medica, &c., as also of a pamphlet against the abolition of the slave trade. He died 24th April 1802, at Harrowgate, at an advanced age.

The following is a list of Dr. Adair's works:—

Medical Cautions for the Consideration of Invalids, more especially of those who resort to Bath. Lond. 1786, 8vo. Second edit. greatly enlarged, 1787, 8vo.

A Philosophical and Medical Sketch of the Natural History of the Human Body and Mind, with an Essay on the Difficulties of attaining Medical Knowledge. Lond. 1787, 8vo.

Essays on Fashionable Diseases; the Dangerous Effects of Hot and Crowded Rooms; the Clothing of Invalids; Lady and Gentlemen Doctors; and on Quacks and Quackery. Lond. 1789, 8vo.

Essay on a Non-Descript, or Newly Invented Disease; its Nature, Causes, and Means of Relief, with some very important Observations on the Powerful and most Surprising Effects of Animal Magnetism, in the Cure of the said Disease. Lond. 1790, 8vo.

Anecdotes of the Life, Adventures, and Vindication of a Medical Character, metaphorically Defunct. By Benjamin Goosequill. Lond. 1790, 8vo, with regard to his own Life and Character.

A Candid Inquiry into the Truth of Certain Charges of the Dangerous Consequences of the Suttonian or Cooling Regimen under Inoculation for the Small Pox; with some remarks on a Successful Method used some years ago in Hungary, in the case of Natural Small Pox. Lond. 1790, 8vo.

Two Sermons; the first addressed to Seamen, the second to British West India Slaves, by a Physician, (Dr. A.); to which are subjoined, Remarks on Female Infidelity, and a Plan of Platonic Matrimony, by which that Evil may be Lessened or totally Prevented, by F. G. 1791, 8vo.

An Essay on Regimen. Air, 1799, 8vo.

Unanswerable Arguments against the Abolition of the Slave Trade, with a Defence of the Proprietors of the British Sugar Colonies. Lond. 1790, 8vo.

An Essay on Diet and Regimen, as indispensable to the Recovery and Preservation of Firm Health, especially to Indolent, Studious, Delicate, and Invalid; with appropriate Cases. Lond. 1804, 8vo.

Observations on Regimen and Preparation under Inoculation, and on the Treatment of the Natural Small Pox in the West Indies; with Strictures on the Suttonian Practice. Med. Com. viii. p. 211, 1782.

Hints respecting Stimulants, Astringents, Anodynes, Cicuta, Vermafuga, Nausativa, Fixed Air, Arsenicum Album, &c. Ib. ix. p. 206.

Remarks on Alumen Rupium, and several other Articles of the Materia Medica. Ib. x. p. 233.

Three Cases of Pthisis Pulmonalis, treated by Cuprum Vitriolatum and Conium Maculatum, two of which terminated favourably. Med. Com. xvii. p. 473, 1792.

Case of Inflammatory Constipation of the Bowels, successfully treated. Mem. Med. ii. p. 236, 1789.

ADAM, a surname belonging to a family of some antiquity in Scotland. Duncan Adam, son of Alexander Adam, lived in the reign of Robert the Bruce, and had four sons, Robert, John, Reginald, and Duncan, from whom all the Adams, Adamsons, and Adies in Scotland, are descended. [*Burke's Landed Gentry.*] From the youngest son, Duncan Adam, who accompanied James, Lord Douglas, in his expedition to Spain on his way to the Holy Land, with the heart of King Robert, is stated to have descended, JOHN ADAM, who was slain at Flodden in 1513. His son CHARLES ADAM was seated at Fanno, in Forfarshire, and his descendant in the fourth degree, ARCHIBALD ADAM, of Fanno, sold his patrimonial lands in the time of Charles I., and acquired those of Queensmanour in the same county. His great-grandson, JOHN ADAM, married Helen Cranstoun, of the family of Lord Cranstoun, by whom he left one son, WILLIAM ADAM, an eminent architect, who purchased several estates, particularly that of Blair, in the county of Kinross, where he built a house and village, which he named Maryburgh. He married Mary, daughter of William Robertson, Esq. of Gladney, and, with other issue, had JOHN ADAM, his heir (the father of the Right Hon. WILLIAM ADAM, Lord Chief Commissioner of the Jury Court in Scotland, the subject of a subsequent biography), and ROBERT and JAMES ADAM, the celebrated architects, of both of whom notices are here given:—

ADAM, ROBERT, a celebrated architect, was born at Kirkaldy in 1728. He was the second son of Mr. William Adam of Maryburgh, who, like his father, was also an architect, and who designed Hopetoun house, the Edinburgh Royal Infirmary, and other buildings. After studying at the university of Edinburgh, Robert, in 1754, proceeded to the continent, and resided three years in Italy, studying his art. From the splendid monuments of antiquity which that country presents to the traveller, he imbibed that scientific style of design by which all his works are distinguished. But it was only from fragments that he was enabled to form his taste, the ravages of time and the hands of barbarians having united for the destruction of those noble specimens of ancient architecture, the ruins of which only remain to attest their former grandeur and magnificence. With the intention

of viewing a more complete monument of ancient splendour than any he had seen, accompanied by M. Clerisseau, a French artist, and two expert draughtsmen, in July 1757 he sailed from Venice to Spalatro in Dalmatia, to inspect the remains of the palace to which the emperor Dioclesian retired from the cares of government. They found the palace much defaced; but as its remains still exhibited the nature of the structure, they proceeded to a minute examination of its various parts. Their labours, however, were immediately interrupted by the interference of the government of Venice, from a suspicion that they were making plans of the fortifications. Fortunately, General Græme, commander-in-chief of the Venetian forces, interposed; and, being seconded by Count Antonio Marcovich, they were soon allowed to prosecute their designs. In 1762, on his return to England, he was appointed architect to the king, an office which he resigned six years afterwards, on being elected M.P. for the county of Kinross. In 1764 he published, in one volume folio, a splendid work, containing seventy-one engravings and descriptions of the ruins of the palace of Dioclesian at Spalatro, and of some other buildings. In 1773 he and his brother James, also an eminent architect, brought out 'The Works of R. and J. Adam,' in numbers, consisting of plans and elevations of buildings in England and Scotland, erected or designed, among which are the Register House and the University of Edinburgh, and the Glasgow Royal Infirmary, in Scotland, and Sion House, Caen-Wood, Luton Park House, and some edifices at Whitehall, in England.

Mr. Adam died 3d March, 1792, by the bursting of a blood-vessel, and was buried in Westminster Abbey. The year before his death he designed no less than eight public buildings and twenty-five private ones. His genius extended itself beyond the decorations of buildings, to various branches of manufacture; and besides the improvements which he introduced into the architecture of the country, he displayed great skill and taste in his numerous drawings in landscape. —*Annual Register*, vol. xxxiv.—*Scots Mag.* 1803.

Of the Register House at Edinburgh it is remarked by Telford, in his contribution on Civil

Architecture to the Edinburgh Encyclopedia, that "only a part of this masterly plan has been executed, but even this composes an apparently complete building. The original design as given in the works of R. and J. Adam, has in the centre a magnificent circular saloon, covered and lighted by a dome. This saloon is surrounded by small apartments, and the whole of these are enclosed by buildings in the shape of a parallelogram, by which ingenious contrivance access to all the apartments and an effective lighting of the whole is perfectly accomplished. Even as it is, this building, both internally and externally, reflects great credit on the architect, and from the chasteness of the details, it is evident that the external features have been the result of much attention. A greater degree of magnificence," he adds, "might have been obtained by keeping the basement of the principal front lower, by adding to the magnitude of the order," and by a few modifications of other details.

Among the private edifices pertaining to Scotland connected with the name of Robert Adam, are, Hopetoun House, on the south bank of the estuary of the Forth, to which magnificent edifice he added the graceful wings; Melville Castle, on the banks of the Esk near Lasswade, which was by his ingenuity rendered a magnificent and appropriate feature in that part of the kingdom; Culzean Castle, on a bold promontory on the coast of Ayrshire, where, with his usual fertility of invention, the same architect has rendered this seat of the marquis of Ailsa a just resemblance of a Roman villa as described by Pliny; and last, but not least, Gosford House in East Lothian, perhaps the most extensive and superb of modern Scottish structures, built by the earl of Wemyss from one of his designs. Of Sion House, the mansion of the duke of Northumberland, in the Strand, London, the chief features of novelty are in the style of Spalatra and the Pantheon at Rome, but the interior arrangements are in every respect as good as can well be imagined. Luton park in Bedfordshire, the seat of the marquis of Bute, is the most original of all his works, and although not in all respects the happiest, may be considered—the façade especially—as designed in his best manner.

ADAM, James, the brother of the preceding, held, at one period, the office of architect to his majesty George III. He was the designer of Portland Place, one of the noblest streets in London, and died on the 17th October, 1794. From the two brothers the Adelphi Buildings in the Strand derive their name, being their joint work.

ADAM, William, Right Hon., nephew of the two foregoing gentlemen, lord chief commissioner of the jury court in Scotland, on its first introduction there for the trial of civil causes, the son of John Adam of Blair Adam, and his wife Jean, the daughter of John Ramsay, Esq., was born 21st July 1751, O.S. He was educated at Edinburgh, Glasgow, and Oxford, and in 1773 was admitted a member of the faculty of Advocates, but never practised at the Scottish bar. In 1774 he was chosen M.P. for Gatton; in 1780 for Stranraer, &c.; in 1784 for the Elgin burghs; and in 1790 for Ross-shire. At the close of Lord North's administration in 1782, in consequence of some family losses he became a barrister-at-law. In 1794 he retired from parliament to devote himself to his profession. In 1802 he was appointed counsel for the East India Company, and in 1806 chancellor of the duchy of Cornwall. In the same year he was returned M.P. for Kincardineshire, and in 1807, being elected both for that county and for Kinross-shire, he preferred to sit for the former. In 1811 he again vacated his seat for his professional duties. Being now generally esteemed a sound lawyer his practice increased, and he was consulted by the prince of Wales, the duke of York, and many of the nobility. In the course of his parliamentary career, in consequence of something that occurred in a discussion during the first American war, he fought a duel with the late Mr. Fox, which happily ended without bloodshed, when the latter jocularly remarked, that had his antagonist not loaded his pistol with government powder, he would have been shot. Mr. Adam generally opposed the politics of Mr. Pitt. In 1814 he submitted to government the plan for trying civil causes by jury in Scotland. In 1815 he was made a privy councillor, and was appointed one of the barons of the Scottish exchequer, chiefly with the view of enabling him to introduce and establish the new system of trial by jury in civil cases.

In 1816 an act of parliament was obtained, instituting a separate jury court in Scotland, in which he was appointed lord chief commissioner, with two of the judges of the court of session as his colleagues. He accordingly relinquished his situation in the exchequer, and continued to apply his energies to the duties of the jury court, overcoming, by his patience, zeal, and urbanity, the many obstacles opposed to the success of such an institution. In 1830, when sufficiently organized, the jury court was, by another act, transferred to the court of session, and on taking his seat on the bench of the latter for the first time, addresses were presented to him from the Faculty of Advocates, the Society of Writers to the Signet, and the Solicitors before the Supreme Courts, thanking him for the important benefits which the introduction of trial by jury in civil cases had conferred on the country. In 1833 he retired from the bench; and died at his house in Charlotte Square, Edinburgh, on the 17th February 1839, in the 89th year of his age.

After his appointment to the presidency of the jury court, he spent a great part of his time at his paternal seat in Kinross-shire. "Here," says Lockhart, in his Life of Scott, "about Midsummer 1816, he received a visit from his near relation William Clerk, Adam Fergusson, his hereditary friend and especial favourite, and their lifelong intimate, Scott. They remained with him for two or three days, in the course of which they were all so much delighted with their host, and he with them, that it was resolved to re-assemble the party with a few additions, at the same season of every following year. This was the origin of the Blair-Adam club, the regular members of which were in number nine; viz., the four already named, —the chief commissioner's son, Admiral Sir Charles Adam; his son-in-law, the late Mr. Anstruther Thomson of Charleton, in Fifeshire; Mr. Thomas Thomson, the deputy register of Scotland; his brother, the Rev. John Thomson, minister of Duddingstone, one of the first landscape painters of his time; and the Right Hon. Sir Samuel Shepherd, who became chief baron of the court of exchequer in Scotland, shortly after the third anniversary of this brotherhood. They usually contrived to meet on a Friday; spent the

Saturday in a ride to some scene of historical interest within an easy distance; enjoyed a quiet Sunday at home,—'duly attending divine worship at the Kirk of Cleish (not Cleishbotham)'—gave Monday morning to another antiquarian excursion, and returned to Edinburgh in time for the courts of Tuesday. From 1816 to 1831 inclusive, Sir Walter was a constant attendant at these meetings." It was during one of these visits to Blair-Adam that the idea of 'The Abbot' had first arisen in Scott's mind, and it was at his suggestion that the chief commissioner commenced a little book on the improvements which had taken place on his estate, which, under the title of 'Blair-Adam, from 1733 to 1834,' was privately printed for his own family and intimate friends. "It was," says the Judge, "on a fine Sunday, lying on the grassy summit of Bennarty, above its craggy brow, that Sir Walter said, looking first at the flat expanse of Kinross-shire (on the south side of the Ochils), and then at the space which Blair-Adam fills between the hill of Drumglow (the highest of the Cleish hills) and the valley of Lochore—'What an extraordinary thing it is, that here to the north so little appears to have been done, when there are so many proprietors to work upon it; and to the south, here is a district of country entirely made by the efforts of one family, in three generations, and one of them amongst us in the full enjoyment of what has been done by his two predecessors and himself! Blair-Adam, as I have always heard, had a wild, uncomely, and unhospitable appearance, before its improvements were begun. It would be most curious to record in writing its original state, and trace its gradual progress to its present condition.'" Lockhart adds, "upon this suggestion, enforced by the approbation of the other members present, the president of the Blair-Adam club commenced arranging the materials for what constitutes a most instructive as well as entertaining history of the agricultural and arboricultural progress of his domains in the course of a hundred years, under his grandfather, his father (the celebrated architect), and himself. And Sir Walter had only suggested to his friend of Kinross-shire what he was resolved to put into practice with regard to his own improvements on Tweedside; for he began at precisely the same period to keep a regular journal of all his rural transactions, under the title of 'Sylva Abbotsfordiensis.'" (See *Lockhart's Life of Scott*, chapter 50.)

Mr. Adam was a personal friend of George IV., and at one period held a confidential office in the royal household at Carlton House, when the latter was prince regent. He married in 1777 a daughter of the tenth Lord Elphinstone, and had a family of several sons: viz. John, long at the head of the council in India, who died in 1825; Admiral Sir Charles, M.P., one of the lords of admiralty, and governor of Greenwich Hospital; died in 1854; William George, an eminent king's counsel, afterwards accountant-general in the court of Chancery, who died 16th May 1839, three months after his father; and the Right Hon. General Sir Frederick, who distinguished himself in the Peninsular war, held a command at Waterloo, where he was wounded, was afterwards high commissioner of the Ionian islands, and subsequently governor of Madras; died 17th August 1853. A younger son died abroad.

ADAM, ALEXANDER, an eminent scholar, and author of a standard work on 'Roman Antiquities,' was born at Coats of Burgie, in the parish of Rafford, county of Elgin, on the 24th June, 1741. (*Coates* or *Cots*, meaning a house or enclosure for sheep.) His parents, who rented a small farm, were in humble circumstances; and, like many of his countrymen who have afterwards raised themselves to distinction, he received the first part of his education at the parish school. His constant application to his book induced his father to have him taught Latin. Before he was sixteen, he had borrowed, from a clergyman in the neighbourhood, a copy of Livy in the small Elzevir edition, and we are told used to read it before daybreak, during the mornings of winter, by the light of splinters of bogwood dug out of an adjoining moss, not having an opportunity of doing so at any other period of the day. In 1757 he endeavoured, but without success, to obtain a bursary or exhibition at King's college, Aberdeen. In 1758, a relative of his mother, the Rev. Mr. Watson, one of the ministers of the Canongate, Edinburgh, advised him to remove to that city, "provided he was prepared to endure every hardship for a season;" and hardships of a severe na-

ture he did endure, but nothing could deter him from the pursuit of knowledge. Through Mr. Watson's influence he obtained free admission to the lectures of the different professors, with, of course, access to the college library; and while attending the classes, it appears that all his income was only the sum of one guinea per quarter, which he received from Mr. Alan Maconochie, afterwards Lord Meadowbank, for being his tutor. At this time he lodged in a small room at Restalrig, for which he paid fourpence a-week. His breakfast consisted of oatmeal porridge with small beer, and his dinner was often no more than a penny loaf and a drink of water. After about eighteen months of close study, at the early age of nineteen he was fortunate in being elected, on a comparative trial of candidates, head master of Watson's Hospital, where he continued to improve himself in classical knowledge, by a careful perusal of the best authors. Three years afterwards he resigned this office, on becoming private tutor to the son of Mr. Kincaid, subsequently lord provost of Edinburgh. In April 1765 he was, by that gentleman's influence, appointed assistant to Mr. Matheson, rector of the high school, whose increasing infirmities compelled him to retire, on a small annuity, paid principally from the class-fees; and on the 8th June 1768 he succeeded him as rector. He now devoted himself assiduously to the duties of his school, and to those literary and classical researches for which he was so peculiarly qualified. To him the high school of Edinburgh owes much of its reputation, and is entirely indebted for the introduction of Greek, which he effected in 1772, in spite of the opposition of the Senatus Academicus of the university, who, considering it an encroachment on the Greek chair, presented a petition and remonstrance against it to the town council, but without success. Having introduced into his class a new Latin grammar of his own compiling, and recommended its adoption in the other classes, instead of Ruddiman's which had been heretofore in use, a dispute arose between him and the under masters, and the matter was referred by the magistrates of Edinburgh, the patrons of the school, to Dr. Robertson, the historian, principal of the university, who decided in favour of Ruddiman's. The magistrates, in consequence, issued an order in 1786 prohibiting the use of any other grammar of the Latin language; but this, and a subsequent order to the same effect, Dr. Adam disregarded, and continued to use his own rules, without being further interfered with. In 1772 he had published the work in question, under the title of 'The Principles of Latin and English Grammar;' the chief object of which was to combine the study of English and Latin grammar, so that they might illustrate each other, in order to avoid the inconvenience to pupils of learning Latin from a Latin grammar, before they understood the language. One of the most active opponents of the new grammar was Dr. Gilbert Stuart, who was related to Ruddiman, and who inserted several squibs in the papers of the day against Adam and his work, to the author's great annoyance.

In 1780 the degree of LL.D. was conferred upon Mr. Adam by the college of Edinburgh, chiefly at the suggestion of Principal Robertson; and before his death, he had the satisfaction of seeing his grammar adopted in his own seminary. Among the more celebrated of his pupils was Sir Walter Scott, who joined the rector's class at the high school in 1782. It was from Dr. Adam, he says, that he first learned the value of the knowledge he had till then considered only as a burdensome task. As he gained some distinction by his poetical versions from Horace and Virgil, the rector took much notice of Scott, and when he began afterwards to be celebrated in the literary world, Dr. Adam never failed to remind him of his obligations to him. "The good old Doctor," says Sir Walter, "plumed himself upon the success of his scholars in life, all of which he never failed (and often justly) to claim as the creation, or at least the fruits, of his early instructions. He remembered the fate of every boy at his school, during the fifty years he had superintended it, and always traced their success or misfortunes, entirely to their attention or negligence when under his care." One of the under-masters at the high school, a person of the name of William Nicol, the hero of Burns' famous drinking song of "O Willie brew'd a peck o' maut," is said to have been encouraged by the magistrates of Edinburgh to insult the person and authority of Dr. Adam, at the time of the famous dispute with him about his grammar.

"This man," says Sir Walter Scott, "was an excellent classical scholar, and an admirable convivial humorist (which latter quality recommended him to the friendship of Burns); but worthless, drunken, and inhumanly cruel to the boys under his charge. He carried his feud against the rector within an inch of assassination, for he waylaid, and knocked him down in the dark," one night in the High School Wynd. The rector's scholars, at the instigation of the future author of Waverley, took a schoolboy's revenge. Exasperated at the outrage, the next time that Nicol went to teach the rector's class, they resolved on humbling him. "The task," says Mr. James Mitchell, Sir Walter's tutor at this time, "which the class had prescribed to them was that passage in the Æneid of Virgil, where the queen of Carthage interrogates the court as to the stranger that had come to her habitation—

'Quis novus hic hospes successit sedibus nostris?'

Master Walter having taken a piece of paper, inscribed upon it these words, substituting *vanus* for *novus*, and pinned it to the tail of the master's coat, and turned him into ridicule by raising the laugh of the whole school against him." [*Lockhart's Life of Scott.*]

Dr. Adam's principal work was the 'Roman Antiquities,' or, an account of the manners and customs of the Romans, published in 1791, which was translated into various foreign languages, and which is now used as a class-book in many of the English schools. For this work he got £600. In 1794 appeared his 'Summary of Geography and History,' in one thick volume of 900 pages, having increased to this size from a small treatise on the same subject, printed, for the use of his pupils, in 1784. The least popular of his works is the 'Classical Biography,' published in 1800; and the last of his laborious and useful compilations was an abridged Latin Dictionary, entitled 'Lexicon Linguæ Latinæ Compendiarum,' 8vo., which was published in 1805, and intended for the use of schools. Dr. Adam's books are valuable auxiliaries to the student, from the mass of useful and classical information which they contain. He had commenced a larger dictionary than the one published, but did not live to complete it.

Having been seized in the high school with an apoplectic attack, he was conducted home, and put to bed, where he languished for five days, and, as death was approaching, fancying himself, during the wanderings of his mind, with his pupils, he said, "But it grows dark, boys, you may go!" and almost immediately expired, on the 18th of December, 1809, at the age of 68. Possessed of an ardent and independent mind, and liberal in the extreme in politics, he took a great interest in the progress of the French Revolution, believing it to be the cause of liberty, and even went so far as to introduce political matters into his school, for which he was much censured at the time, and that by many of his friends; but after the first excitement had passed away, he soon regained the respect even of those who had been most embittered against him. He was universally regretted, and the magistrates of Edinburgh honoured his memory by a public funeral. His portrait by Raeburn, taken shortly before his death at the desire of some of his old pupils, was placed in the library of the high school. Annexed is a woodcut of it.

"His features," says his biographer, "were regular and manly, and he was above the middle size." He was twice married, and left a widow, two daughters, and a son. One of his daughters married a Dr. Prout, and at one time resided in Sackville Street, London. His son, Dr. Adam, for many years resided in Edinburgh.—*Henderson's Life of Dr. Adam; Edin. Monthly Mag.* 1810.

The following is a list of his works:

The Principles of Latin and English Grammar. Edin. 1772, 8vo. 7th Edit. improved, 1809, 12mo.

A Summary of Geography and History, both Ancient and Modern, designed chiefly to unite the Study of Classical Learning with that of General Knowledge Edin. 1784, 8vo. 1794, 8vo. 1809, 8vo.

Roman Antiquities, or an Account of the Manners and Customs of the Romans, their Government, Laws, Religion, &c. Edin. 1791, 8vo. 2d edit. enlarged. 1792, 8vo. 1807, 8vo.

Geographical Index, containing the Latin Names of the principal Countries, Cities, Rivers, and Mountains, mentioned in the Greek and Roman Classics, with the Modern Names subjoined; also, the Latin Names of the Inhabitants, being a Summary of the Ancient and Modern Geography. Edin. 1795, 8vo.

Classical Biography; exhibiting alphabetically the proper Names, with a short Account of the several Deities, Heroes, &c. mentioned in the ancient Classic Authors; and a more particular Description of the most Distinguished Characters among the Romans, the whole being interspersed with Occasional Explanations of Words and Phrases, designed chiefly to contribute to the Illustration of the Latin Classics. Edin. 1800, 8vo.

Dictionary of the Latin Tongue. Edin. 1805, 8vo. 2d edit. greatly improved and enlarged. Edin. 1815, 8vo.

ADAM, ROBERT, the Rev., B.A. author of 'The Religious World Displayed,' was born in the parish of Udny, Aberdeenshire, of poor but respectable parents, about the year 1770. He was educated and took his degree of M.A. at Aberdeen. He was afterwards sent, by some persons interested in his welfare, to St. Edmund Hall, Oxford, where he took the degree of bachelor of arts. Subsequently he was ordained deacon and priest by Dr. Beilby Porteus, bishop of London. About the year 1801 he was appointed assistant to Dr. Abernethy Drummond of Hawthornden, titular bishop of Glasgow, whom he succeeded as minister of Blackfriars' Wynd episcopal chapel, Edinburgh. He was also chaplain to the earl of Kellie. In 1809 he published an elaborate and comprehensive work in three volumes, entitled 'The Religious World Displayed, or a View of the Four Grand Systems of Religion, Judaism, Paganism, Christianity, and Mahomedanism, and of the Various Denominations, Sects, and Parties in the Christian World; to which is subjoined, a View of Deism and Atheism ;' which he inscribed to the memory of Bishop Drummond, formerly senior minister of his congregation. He was subsequently appointed to a church in the Danish island of St. Croix, where he was much annoyed by the Danish authorities, and ultimately ordered to leave the island. His conduct met with the full approbation of our own government, and he proceeded to Denmark to procure redress, which it appears he never obtained. After his return from Copenhagen to London, he accompanied the newly appointed bishop of Barbadoes to the West Indies in 1825, and was appointed interim pastor of the island of Tobago, where he died on the 2d July 1826.

ADAM, Scotus, one of the doctors of the Sorbonne, and a canon regular of the order of Premonstratenses, flourished in the twelfth century. He was born in Scotland, and educated in the monastery of Lindisfarne, or Holy Island, in the county of Durham. He afterwards went to Paris and taught school divinity in the Sorbonne. In his latter years he became one of " the monks of Melrose." He afterwards retired to the Abbey of Durham, where he wrote the Lives of St. Columbanus, and of some other monks of the sixth century, and also of David I. king of Scotland. He died in 1195. His works were printed at Antwerp in folio, in 1659 —*Biog. Dic.*

ADAMSON, Henry, a poet of the seventeenth century, was the son of James Adamson, dean of guild in Perth in 1600, the year of the Gowrie conspiracy, and provost of that city in 1610 and 1611. He was educated for the church, and is stated to have been a good classical scholar. He wrote some Latin poems which are described as being far above mediocrity. In 1638 he published a poem, in 4to, entitled 'Muses Threnodie, or Mirthful Mournings on the Death of Mr. Gall, with a description of Perth, and an account of the Gowry conspiracy,' &c. He was honoured with the approbation of Drummond of Hawthornden, and appears, from the complimentary verses prefixed to his poems, to have been much respected for his talents and worth. It was at the request of Drummond that Adamson published his 'Muses Threnodie,' after having resisted the solicitations of his friends to print it. The letter which the poet of Hawthornden wrote to him on the occasion, is dated Edin-

burgh, 12th July 1637. It was inserted in the introductory address to the reader, prefixed to the first edition, and contains the following passage: " Happie hath Perth been in such a citizen, not so other townes of this kingdome, by want of so diligent a searcher and preserver of their fame from oblivion. Some Muses, neither to themselves nor to others, do good, nor delighting nor instructing. Yours inform both, and longer to conceal them, will be, to wrong your Perth of her due honours, who deserveth no less of you than that she should be thus blazoned and registrate to posterity, and to defraud yourself of a monument which, after you have left this transitory world, shall keep your name and memory to after times. This shall be preserved by the towne of Perth, for her own sake first, and after for yours; for to her it hath been no little glory that she hath brought forth such a citizen, so eminent in love to her, so dear to the Muses." Adamson died unmarried in 1639. A new edition of his poem was published in 1774, with illustrative notes, by James Cant, in 2 vols. 12mo. The book is now scarce.—*Campbell's Introduction to the History of Poetry in Scotland.*

ADAMSON, Patrick, an eminent prelate and Latin poet, was born at Perth, March 15, 1537. His parents are said to have been poor, but he received a sufficiently liberal education, first at the grammar school of his native town, and afterwards at the university of St. Andrews, where he studied philosophy, and took his degree of master of arts. His name first appears in the diaries and church records of the period, not as Adamson, but under the varieties of Constaine, Cousting, Constan, Constant, and Constantine. [See *Bannatyne's Journal*, p. 323; *James Melville's Diary*, pp. 25 and 42; *Calderwood*, vol. ii. p. 46; and *The Booke of the Universall Kirk of Scotland*, pp. 2 and 23.] His biographers state that on quitting the university he became a schoolmaster at a village in Fife, but on the meeting of the first General Assembly, in December 1560, he was, under the name of Patrick Constan, among those who were appointed in St. Andrews, " for ministering and teaching." [*Calderwood*, vol. ii. p. 46.] Under the same name he was, in 1563, minister of Ceres, in Fife, and was appointed a commissioner " to plant kirks from Dee to Ethan." [*Ibid.* p. 245.] In the seventh General Assembly, held at Edinburgh in June 1564, he preferred a request to be allowed to pass to France and other countries, " for aug menting of his knowledge for a time ;" but the Assembly unanimously refused his application, and ordained that he should not leave his congregation, " without speciall licence of the haill kirk." [*Booke of the Universall Kirk of Scotland*, p. 23.] Early in 1566, on the invitation of Sir James Makgill of Rankeillor, clerk-register, he accompanied his eldest son, as tutor, to France, where the latter was going to study the civil law, on which occasion he appears to have demitted himself of the office of the ministry. On the 19th of June of that year, Mary queen of Scots was delivered of a prince, afterwards James the Sixth, on which occasion Constant or Adamson, then at Paris, wrote a Latin poem, styling the royal infant " Prince of Scotland, England, France, and Ireland," which so offended the French government that he was imprisoned for six months. Queen Mary herself, and several of the nobility, interceded for his liberation. On regaining his freedom he proceeded with his pupil to the universities of Poitiers and Padua, where he applied himself to the study of the civil and canon laws. On their return from Italy, they visited Geneva ; and here, from his intercourse with Beza, he imbibed the Calvinistic doctrines of theology. Some time before their return to Scotland they revisited Paris. As well-known Protestants, however, they found it dangerous to remain in the capital, and retired to Bourges, where Constant concealed himself for seven months in an inn, the master of which, an old man 70 years of age, was, for harbouring heretics, thrown from the roof of his own house and killed on the spot. In this sepulchre, as he called it, he employed his time in composing a Latin poetical version of the Book of Job, and in writing in the same language a piece called the Tragedy of Herod—the latter of which has never been published. Before leaving France he was bold enough to publish a Latin translation of the Confession of Faith, for which he obtained great credit.

At what period Constant returned to Scotland does not appear, but it must have been previous to 5th March 1571, for the Assembly which met at Edinburgh at that time earnestly desired him,

in consideration of the lack of ministers, to re-enter the ministry. He craved time till next Assembly, which met on 6th August thereafter, to which he sent a written answer, complying with their request. He had previously married the daughter of a lawyer.

On the election of Mr. John Douglas, rector of the university of St. Andrews, to the archbishopric of that diocese, on the 8th of February 1572, Constant is mentioned as having preached a sermon, and John Knox the discourse before the installation. [*Bannatyne.*] On this occasion he was not, as afterwards alleged by his enemies, a candidate for that see. Most of his biographers represent him to have been in France at the period of the massacre of St. Bartholomew, which occurred on the 24th August of this year (1572), but he had certainly returned to Scotland more than a year before that event, and no mention is made of a second visit to that country. Constant appears at this time to have enjoyed the friendship of Andrew Melville and of many of the ministers of Edinburgh. He had been appointed minister of Paisley, and through his influence with the regent Morton the valuable living of Govan, near Glasgow, was in the year 1575 annexed to the university of that city, " the only good thing," says the spiteful James Melville, " he or Morton were ever known to have done." [*Diary*, p. 42.] In the same year he was named one of the commissioners of the General Assembly, for settling the polity and jurisdiction of the church, which, at that period of ecclesiastical transition, was episcopalian in its spirit and form, although the supreme authority in spiritual matters was placed in the General Assembly. About this time he appears to have dropped the name of Constant, as he is ever afterwards called Adamson by contemporary writers.

In the course of 1576 Adamson was nominated, with John Row and David Lindsay, to report the proceedings of the commissioners to the regent Morton, who appointed him one of his chaplains. In the same year, on the death of Douglas, archbishop of St. Andrews, Adamson, on the presentation and recommendation of Morton, was advanced to the vacant archbishopric. His elevation to the archiepiscopal see became the origin of all his misfortunes. The General Assembly, having generally acceded to the new views which Melville introduced from Geneva as to the Presbyterian form of government for the church, sought to impose limitations on his powers, which were contrary to the previous usage of the church and to the laws of the kingdom; to which restrictions, however, Adamson from the outset and even before his installation declared, when questioned by that court, that he would not submit. From the period of his instalment, therefore, he was engaged, for several years, in almost perpetual altercation with the General Assembly. "Adamson," says Bishop Keith, "did not receive, for what we know, any ecclesiastical consecration." This, however, is incorrect. From the acts of the General Assembly threatening proceedings against his inaugurators, the chapter of St. Andrews, we infer that he was installed by a form of consecration similar to that of his predecessor; which, as formally settled by the General Assembly with reference to that ceremony, was the same as that of the superintendents, and of which Bannatyne details the formula, (p. 321).

In the General Assembly, which met at Edinburgh in April, 1577, Adamson was cited to answer before some commissioners who had been appointed to examine him; and, in the interim, it was ordered that he should be discharged from exercising his episcopal functions "till he should be admitted by the Assembly." [*Calderwood's History*, vol. iii. p. 379.] The same year he published a translation of the Catechism of Calvin in Latin verse, for the use of the young prince (James VI.), which was much commended in England, France, and the Netherlands, where he was already well known by his translation of the Confession of Faith. In 1578 he was induced to submit himself to the General Assembly, but this did not long secure his tranquillity; for in the year following he was exposed to fresh troubles. In the record of the 38th General Assembly, which met at Stirling, 11 June 1578, as printed in 'The Booke of the Universall Kirk of Scotland,' there are five pages blank, supposed, as marked in an old hand on the copy transcribed, "to be pairt of that which was torn out by Adamson B. of St. Andrews." Some after blanks are also pointed out. [*B. of Universall Kirk*, pp. 180, 183, 203, 207, 338, foot-

notes.] This, however, is as likely to have been done by another. The General Assembly which met at Edinburgh 7th July 1579, summoned him to answer to five several charges, three of which were for voting in parliament without a commission from the Assembly, for giving collation of the vicarage of Bolton, and for opposing the policy of the church in his place in parliament. Finding it expedient to retire for a time to the castle of St. Andrews, where he lived, as James Melville expresses it, "like a tod in his hole," he was, in the year 1582, attacked with a grievous chronic distemper, from which, as he could get no relief from his physicians, he had recourse to a simple remedy, administered by an old woman named Alison Pearson, which completely cured him. His enemies now accused him of dealing with a witch, and applying to an emissary of the devil for means whereby to save his life. The old woman herself was committed to the castle of St. Andrews for execution, but by the connivance of the archbishop she contrived to make her escape. Four years thereafter, however, she was again apprehended, and burnt for witchcraft.

In the year 1583, King James visited St. Andrews, when Archbishop Adamson preached before him with great approbation. In his sermon, he inveighed, as Calderwood expresses it, against the Presbyterian clergy, the lords reformers, and all their proceedings. [*Calderwood's History*, vol. iii. p. 716.] The doctrines which the archbishop avowed on this occasion recommended him to the favour of the king, who sent him as his ambassador to the court of Queen Elizabeth, where his object was twofold, namely, to recommend the king his master to the nobility and gentry of England, and to obtain support to the tottering cause of episcopacy in Scotland. His eloquent sermons and address attracted such numerous auditories, and excited such a high idea of the young king, that Queen Elizabeth's jealousy was kindled, and she prohibited him from preaching while he remained in England. In 1584 he was recalled, and on his return to Edinburgh, he exerted himself strenuously in support of King James' views in favour of episcopacy. He sat in the parliament held at Edinburgh in the month of August of that year, and concurred in several laws which were enacted for establishing the king's supremacy in ecclesiastical matters. In the following year he was appointed to vindicate these acts of parliament, and his apology is inserted in Holinshed's English Chronicle. Mr. James Melville gives a full copy of what he styles "a Bull which the archbishop of St. Andrews got of the king as supreme governor of the kirk, whereby he has power and authority to use his archiepiscopal office within the kirk and his diocese." [*Diary*, p. 132.]

In April 1586, the provincial synod of Fife met at St. Andrews, when Mr. James Melville, as moderator of the previous meeting, preached the opening sermon, in the course of which he denounced the archbishop to his face, and demanded that he should be cut off, for having devised and procured the passing of the late acts of parliament in 1584, which were subversive of the Presbyterian discipline. In his defence Adamson said that the acts were none of his devising, although they had his support as good and lawful statutes. He then declined the jurisdiction of the court, and appealed from it to the king and parliament, but nevertheless was formally excommunicated by the synod. In return, he next day ordered Mr. Samuel Cunningham, one of his servants, to pronounce the archiepiscopal excommunication against Andrew Melville, James Melville, and others, with Andrew Hunter, minister of Carnbee, who had denounced the anathema of the synod against the archbishop. The proceedings of the synod being manifestly informal, the General Assembly, which met at Edinburgh in the following month, annulled the sentence of excommunication against him, and reponed him to the same position which he had held before the meeting of the provincial synod of Fife. The Melvilles being summoned before the king for their conduct in this harsh and vindictive transaction, were ordered to confine themselves, Andrew to his native place during the king's will, and James to his college. [*Melville's Diary*, p. 165.] The archbishop, besides his usual clerical duties, was required to teach public lessons in Latin within the Old college, and the whole university commanded to attend the same. [*Ibid.* p. 166.] As archbishop of St. Andrews he was *ex officio* chancellor of the university.

About the end of June 1587, M. Du Bartas, the famous French poet, being in Scotland as ambassador from the king of Navarre, afterwards Henry IV. of France, accompanied King James to St. Andrews. His majesty, desirous of hearing a lecture from Mr. Andrew Melville, principal of St. Mary's college, gave him an hour's notice of his wish. Melville endeavoured to excuse himself, but his majesty insisting, he delivered an extempore discourse, upon the government of the church of Christ, when he refuted the whole acts of parliament which had been passed against the presbyterian discipline. On the following day an entertainment was given by the archbishop to the king and the French envoy, when Adamson took occasion to pronounce a lecture, to counteract that of Melville, his principal topics being the preeminence of bishops and the supremacy of kings. Melville was present and took notes, and had no sooner returned to his college than he caused the bell to be rung, and an intimation to be conveyed to the king that he intended to deliver another lecture after an interval of two hours. On this occasion, besides the king, Du Bartas and Adamson were present. Avoiding all formal reference to the previous speech of the archbishop, Melville dexterously quoted from popish books, which he had brought with him, all his leading positions and arguments in favour of episcopacy. When he had shown them to be plain popery, he proceeded to refute them with such force of reason that Adamson remained silent, although he had previously requested permission from the king to defend his own doctrines. The king, however, spoke for him, and after making some learned and scholastic distinctions, he concluded with commanding them all to respect and obey the archbishop. The whole of this narrative, however, rests upon the authority of James Melville, which, besides being that of a prejudiced opponent, is unfortunately in other matters relative to Adamson found to be opposed to facts recorded in the proceedings of the Church.

By the act of annexation passed in 1587 the see of St. Andrews, with all the other church benefices in the kingdom, was annexed to the crown. The revenues of the archbishopric were thereafter bestowed on the duke of Lennox, by James VI., excepting only a small pittance, reserved for the subsistence of Archbishop Adamson. In the following year he was exposed to a fresh prosecution by the church, having been summoned for having, contrary to an inhibition of the presbytery of Edinburgh, married the Catholic earl of Huntly to the king's cousin, the sister of the duke of Lennox, without requiring the earl to subscribe the Confession of Faith, although he had already subscribed certain articles which were required of him previous to the proclamation of the bans. Adamson on this occasion appeared by his procurator, Mr. Thomas Wilson, (very likely his son-in-law,) who produced a testimonial of his sickness, subscribed by the doctor who attended him and two bailies, but the memorial was not admitted as sufficient. The presbytery of St. Andrews proceeded against him in absence, deprived him of all office in the church, and threatened him with excommunication. The Assembly ratified the sentence of the presbytery, and for this and other alleged crimes he was deposed and again excommunicated.

In the beginning of 1589 he published the Lamentations of Jeremiah, in Latin verse, which he dedicated to the king in an address, complaining of the harsh treatment he had received. The same year he also published a Latin poetical translation of the Apocalypse, and addressed a copy of Latin verses to his majesty, deploring his distress. The unfortunate prelate had at one period stood so high in the royal favour that James had condescended to compose a sonnet in commendation of his paraphrase of the Book of Job; but times were altered, and the king paid no attention to his appeals. In his need Adamson is said to have addressed a letter to his former opponent, Mr. Andrew Melville, with whom he at one period lived on terms of good neighbourhood, but opposite views in church government had long not only driven them asunder, but rendered them bitter antagonists. On receipt of his letter containing the sad disclosure of his destitute situation, Melville hastened to pay the archbishop a visit, and besides procuring contributions on his behalf from his brethren of the presbytery of St. Andrews, continued for several months to support him from his own private purse. Reduced by poverty and disease, the unfortunate prelate, in the year 1591, sent to the Presbytery of St. Andrews a paper expressive of his regret at the course he had pursued, and desiring to be restored into the church. This is not the same paper which afterwards appeared under the title of 'The Recantation of Maister Patrick Adamsone,' and which was published as a pamphlet in 1598. Some of the Episcopal writers are disposed to deny the genuineness of the latter, and it is to be regretted that the proofs of its genuineness are not more complete. Adamson died on the 19th February 1592, and his death was speedily followed by the restoration of the presbyterian form of church government in Scotland. A collection of his Latin poetical translations from the Scriptures was published in a quarto volume in London in 1619, with his Life by his son-in-law, Thomas Wilson, an advocate, under the title of *Poemata Sacra*. Several of his other poems are to be found in the *Deliciæ Poetarum Scotorum*, tome i., and in the *Poetarum Scotorum Musæ Sacræ*, tome ii.

Adamson's character has been much traduced by contemporary writers, but by none more so than by Robert Semple, a minor poet of that day, who wrote a gross and scurrilous work professing to be his life, which he styled 'A Legend of the Bischop of St. Androis' Life.' It is thought that this 'legend' had an effect on the king's mind unfavourable to Adamson, but he fell more into disgrace with his majesty after having been "put to the horn," in 1587, and "denounced rebel," for withholding their stipends from several ministers in his diocese, and "for not furnishing of two gallons of wine to the communion."

The following address to his departing soul, written by Adamson in Latin poetry, in which he so much excelled, is, says Dr. Irving, "as much superior to that of Adrian as Christianity is superior to Paganism :"

O anima! assiduis vitæ jactata procellis,
Exilii, pertæsa gravis, nunc lubrica, tempus
Regna tibi, et mundi invisas contemnere sordes:
Quippe parens rerum cæco te corpore clemens
Evocat, et verbi crucifixi gratia, cœli
Pandit iter, patrioque beatam limine sistet.
Progenies Jovæ, quo te cœlestis origo
Invitat, felix perge, æternumque quiesce.
Exuviæ carnis, cognato in pulvere vocem
Angelicam expectent, sonitu quo putro cadaver
Exiliet redivivum, et totum me tibi reddet.

Ecce beata dies! nos agni dextera ligno
Fulgentes crucis, et radiantes sanguine vivo
Excipiet: quam firma illic, quam certa capesses
Gaudia, felices inter novus incola cives!
Alme Deus! Deus alme! et non effabile numen!
Ad te unum et trinum, moribundo pectore anhelo.

Besides the poems and translations already mentioned, Archbishop Adamson wrote many things which were never published, among which may be mentioned Six books on the Hebrew Republic, various translations of the Prophets into Latin verse, Prelections on St. Paul's Epistles to Timothy, various apological and funeral orations, and a very candid history of his own times.

The following is a list of his published works:

Catechismus Latino Carmine Redditus, et in libros quatuor digestus. Edin. 1581, 12mo.

Poëmata Sacra, cum aliis Opusculis, et cum Vita ejus; a T. Voluseno. Lond. 1619, 4to.

De Sacro Pastoris Munere Tractatus: cum Vita Auctoris, per Th. Volusenum. Lond. 1619, 4to. 8vo.

Refutatio Libelli de Regimine Ecclesiæ Scoticanæ. Lond. 1620, 8vo.

Adamsoni Vita et Palinodia. 1620, 4to.

Genethliacon Jacobi VI. Regis Scotiæ, Angliæ I. Carmine. Amst. 1637, 8vo. Inter Poët. Scot. vol. i. p. 13.

Recantation of Mr. Patrick Adamson, sometime Archbishop of St. Andrews in Scotlande. To which is added, his Life in Latin. 1598, 8vo.

Sermons. 1623, 8vo.

———

AGNEW, the name of an ancient family in Wigtonshire, the head of which was constable of the castle of Lochnaw, and hereditary sheriff of that county. See LOCHNAW.

AIDAN, the greatest of all the kings of the Scots of Dalriad, a kingdom which formed what is now Argyleshire, was the son of Gabran, or Gavran, and succeeded to the throne in 575, on the death of his cousin, Conal I. He reigned twenty-four years, according to the celebrated *Duan*, a Gaelic poem supposed to have been written by the court-bard of Malcolm the third; or thirty-four by the old lists. Duncan the son of Conal seems to have contested the kingdom with him, but he was defeated and slain in battle at a place called Loro in Kintyre. Pinkerton thinks that the *Duan* dates the commencement of his reign from his unction as king, which Columba long deferred, having a preference for Aidan's brother Eogenan or Eugain. The *Duan* calls him "Aidan of the extended territories," and he certainly carried the Dalriadic power to a height from which it ever after declined, till Kenneth II. ascended the Pictish throne, in

836, and united the Picts and the Scots. In 579 the battle of Ouc against Aidan is mentioned in the annals of Ulster, and in 581 the battle of Manan, (O'Flaherty says, the Isle of Mann,) in which he was victor. He also conquered in the battle of Miathorum, or Lethrigh, in 589. In the following year he was at the famous council of Drumkeat in the diocese of Derry in Ulster, consisting of kings, peers, and clergy, summoned by Aid, king of Ireland, in which council Aidan procured the remission of all homage due by the kings of Dalriad to those of Ireland. In 594 Aidan's brother Eugain died. In 603, Aidan, who is styled by Bede, "the king of the Scots who inhabited Britain," marched against Ethelfrid, king of Northumbria, "with an immense and strong army," but was conquered, and fled with a few. "Forasmuch as," says Bede, "in the most famous place which is called Degsastone, almost all his army was cut to pieces: In which fight also Theobold, brother of Ethelfrid, with all that army which he himself commanded, was killed." The place where this disastrous battle was fought is now unknown, but it is conjectured by Bishop Gibson to have been Dalston near Carlisle, or as Bishop Nicolson supposes, Dawston near Jedburgh. Aidan died in 605, in Kintyre, at an advanced age, and was buried at Kilcheran, where no king was ever buried before. If the date of his death be correct, he reigned just thirty years. He was succeeded by his son Achy, or Achaius, or Eochoid-buidhe (Eochy the yellow) who reigned for seventeen years. Another son, Conan, was drowned in 622. He had several younger sons. His brother Brandubius was king of Leinster.—See *Pinkerton's Enquiry*, vol. 2. page 113, and *Ritson's Annals of the Caledonians, Picts, and Scots*, vol. 2, page 39.

AIDAN, bishop of Lindisfarne, or Holy Island, in the seventh century, was originally a monk in the monastery of Iona, and is said by some to have been a native of Ireland. By his zeal, a large portion of the northern part of England was converted to Christianity. In 634, when Oswald became king of the Angli of Northumberland, he sent to Scotland for a missionary, to instruct his subjects in the doctrines and duties of Christianity. Aidan was accordingly consecrated a bishop, and sent to the court of Oswald, and by his advice, the episcopal see was removed from York, where it had been fixed by Gregory the Great, to Lindisfarne, a peninsula adjoining the Northumbrian coast, by a narrow isthmus, called also Holy Island, because it was chiefly inhabited by monks. Here Aidan exercised an extensive jurisdiction, and preached the gospel with great success; deriving encouragement and assistance in his labour from the condescending services of the king himself. On Oswald being killed in battle, Aidan continued to govern the church of Northumberland under his successors, Oswin and Oswy, who reigned jointly. The following extraordinary instance of the bishop's liberality to the poor is related. Having received a present from King Oswin of a fine horse and rich housings, he met with a beggar, and dismounting, gave him the horse thus caparisoned. When the king expressed some displeasure at this singular act of humanity, and the slight put upon his favour, Aidan quaintly but forcibly asked, "Which do you value most, the son of a mare, or the son of God?"—the king fell upon his knees and entreated the bishop's forgiveness. The death of Oswin so much affected him, that he survived him only twelve days, and died in August 1651. He was buried in the church of Lindisfarne.

AIKMAN, a surname, being the same as *Oakman.* An oak tree was carried in the arms of persons of this surname, and the family of Aikman of Cairney had for crest an oak tree proper.

AIKMAN, WILLIAM, an eminent painter, the son of William Aikman of Cairney, advocate, by Margaret, third sister of Sir John Clerk, of Pennycuik, Baronet, was born 24th October 1682. He was intended by his father for the law, but the bent of his own mind early led him to painting as a profession. In 1707, after selling off his paternal estate, he went to Rome, were he spent three years in studying the great masters, and returned to his native country in 1712, having also visited Constantinople and Smyrna. At first his manner was cold, but it afterwards became soft and easy. He was particularly happy in giving graceful airs and genteel likenesses to the ladies whose portraits he painted. In 1723, being patronized by John, duke of Argyle, he was induced to settle as a portrait-painter in London, where he further

improved his colouring by the study of Sir Godfrey Kneller's works. His taste and genius introduced him to the acquaintance and friendship of the duke of Devonshire, the earl of Burlington, Sir Robert Walpole, Sir Godfrey Kneller, and others. For the earl of Burlington, he painted a large picture of the royal family, which his death prevented him from finishing. It is now in possession of the duke of Devonshire. Aikman married Marion, daughter of Mr. Lawson of Cairnmuir, county of Peebles, by whom he had an only son, John. He died 4th June, O. S. 1731, in his 49th year. His remains, with those of his son, who predeceased him about six months, were removed to Edinburgh, and interred together in the Greyfriars' churchyard. An epitaph, by his friend Mallet the poet, was inscribed on his tomb. Several of his portraits are in the possession of the dukes of Hamilton, Argyle, Devonshire, and others. He numbered among his friends Allan Ramsay, who wrote a pastoral farewell to him on his departure for London, Somerville, the author of the Chase, and Thomson, the author of the Seasons, who, as well as his friend Mallet, wrote elegiac verses on his death. Mallet's epitaph has been long effaced. Thomson's poem on his death closes with the following lines:

" A friend, when dead, is but remov'd from sight,
　Sunk in the lustre of eternal night;
　And when the parting storms of life are o'er,
　May yet rejoin us on a happier shore.
　As those we love decay, we die in part,
　String after string is severed from the heart,
　Till loosen'd life, at last but breathing clay,
　Without one pang is glad to fall away.
　Unhappy he who latest feels the blow
　Whose eyes have wept o'er every friend laid low;
　Dragg'd ling'ring on from partial death to death,
　Till dying, all he can resign is breath."

Aikman was also intimate with Pope, Swift, Arbuthnot, Gay, and most of the wits of Queen Anne's days. His style bears a close resemblance to that of Kneller. In the duke of Tuscany's collection of the portraits of painters done by their own hands, will be found that of Aikman, in the ducal gallery at Florence.—*Cunningham's Lives of Painters.*

AILSA, marquis of, a title borne by the ancient family of Kennedy, earls of Cassillis, conferred in 1831, and taken from the " craggy ocean pyramid," Ailsa Craig, in the mouth of the frith of Clyde, which is the property of that family. See CASSILLIS, earl of, and KENNEDY.

AINSLIE, ROBERT, writer to the signet, the friend and correspondent of Robert Burns, was born 13th January 1766. He was the eldest son of Mr. Ainslie of Darnchester, residing at Berrywell, near Dunse, the land agent for Lord Douglas in Berwickshire. He served his apprenticeship with Mr. Samuel Mitchelson, in Carrubber's close, Edinburgh, who was a great musical amateur, and in whose house occurred the famous " Haggis scene " described by Smollett in Humphrey Clinker. In the spring of 1787, when he had just completed his twentieth year, Burns being at that time in Edinburgh, he was fortunate enough to make his acquaintance, and in May of that year, he and the poet went upon an excursion together into Berwickshire and Teviotdale, when he introduced Burns at his father's house, and the reception he received from the family is pleasantly referred to, in his gifted companion's memoranda on this tour. In 1789 Ainslie passed writer to the signet. He afterwards visited Burns at Ellisland, when the poet gave him a manuscript copy of *Tam O'Shanter*, which he presented to Sir Walter Scott. He married a lady named Cunningham, the daughter of a colonel in the Scots Brigade in the Dutch service, by whom he had a numerous family, of whom only two daughters survived him. He had two brothers, and one sister, the latter of whom, whose beauty was highly spoken of by Burns, died before him. One of his brothers, Douglas, succeeded his father as land agent; and the other, Sir Whitelaw Ainslie, is known as the author of an elaborate book on the Materia Medica of India, where he for many years held the situation of medical superintendent of the southern division of India, for which work he was knighted by William IV. Mr. Ainslie died on the 11th April 1838. He was the author of two religious little works, 'A Father's Gift to his Children,' and 'Reasons for the Hope that is in Us,' the latter comprising many of the evidences for the truth of Christianity. He was also a contributor to the Edinburgh Magazine, and others of the periodicals, for forty years previous to his death. His disposition was kind and benevolent, his manners affable and frank, and his conversation cheerful and abounding in anecdote. Many of Burns' letters to him will be found in the poet's printed correspondence.—*Obituary at the time.—Personal recollections.*

AIRLIE, earl of, a title possessed by a family of the name of Ogilvy, lineally descended from Gilbert, third son of the first thane of Angus, who fought at the battle of the Standard in 1138, and obtained from William the Lion the lands of Powrie, Ogilvy, and Kyneithin, when, as was customary in those days, he assumed the name of Ogilvy from his barony.

In 1392 Sir Walter Ogilvy of Wester Powrie and Auchterhouse, sheriff of Angus, was slain with sixty of his followers, at Gasklune near Blairgowrie, in endeavouring to repel an incursion of the clan Donnochy, or sons of Duncan (the clan now called Robertson) who had burst down upon the low country from the Grampian mountains.

Among the slain at the battle of Harlaw in 1411, was his eldest son, "the brave lord Ogilvy, of Angus sheriff-principal." See OGILVY, surname of.

Sir Walter Ogilvy, knight, the second son, was in 1425 constituted lord high treasurer of Scotland. In 1430 he became master of the royal household. In the following year he was appointed a commissioner for renewing the truce with England. In 1434 he attended the princess Margaret into France, on her marriage with the dauphin. By an order from the king he erected the tower or fortalice of Eroly or Airly in Forfarshire, into a royal castle. He married Isabel de Durward, heiress of Lintrathen, by whom he acquired that barony. He died in 1440, leaving two sons. From Sir Walter, the younger, sprang the earls of Findlater and Seafield, and the lords of Banff; see BANFF, FINDLATER, and SEAFIELD.

The elder son, Sir John Ogilvy, knight, of Lintrathen, was succeeded by his eldest son Sir James Ogilvy of Airlie, ambassador from Scotland to Denmark in 1491. By James IV. he was created, 28th April of that year, a peer of parliament by the title of lord Ogilvy of Airlie. James, the seventh lord Ogilvy, for his loyalty and faithful services to Charles I., was on the 2d April, 1639, created earl of AIRLIE, ALYTH, and LINTRATHEN. He distinguished himself in the campaigns of the marquis of Montrose, in particular at the battle of Kilsyth in 1645. Nimmo, in his history of Stirlingshire, states, that at the commencement of that engagement, a thousand Highlanders in Montrose's army, without waiting for orders, marched up the hill to attack the enemy. Though displeased with their rashness, Montrose despatched a strong detachment to their assistance, under the command of the earl of Airlie, whose arrival not only preserved this resolute corps from being overpowered by a superior force, but obliged the Covenanters to retreat. This was the most complete victory Montrose ever gained. The loss on his side was small, only seven or eight persons having been slain, three of whom were Ogilvies, relations of the family of Airlie.

James, the second earl, was taken prisoner at Philiphaugh, and sentenced to death, but escaped from the castle of St. Andrews, the night before the day of his intended execution, in the clothes of his sister.

David the third earl had two sons; the eldest, James, lord Ogilvy, having engaged in the rebellion of 1715, was attainted of high treason. He was afterwards pardoned, but, dying without issue, he was succeeded by his brother, John, fourth earl. His son David, lord Ogilvy, joined Prince Charles Edward Stuart, at Edinburgh, in 1745, with six hundred men, chiefly of his own name and family. He also was attainted of high treason, but escaped to France, where he had the command of a Scotch regiment in the service of the French king, called Ogilvy's regiment. Having obtained a free pardon, he returned to Scotland in 1783, and died in 1803.

The title was for some time in abeyance. Walter Ogilvy, Esq. of Airlie, Lord Ogilvy's son, styled the seventh earl, assumed the title in 1812, but it was not restored till May 1826, when his son David was confirmed in it by act of parliament.

Airlie castle, "the bonnie house of Airlie" of Scottish song, once the chief residence of the family, was destroyed, with Forthur, another of their seats, by the marquis of Argyle, in consequence of an order of the committee of estates, in 1640. The place had been regarded as almost impregnable by nature, and had already, under Lord Ogilvy, eldest son of the proprietor, successfully resisted an attack made by the earls of Montrose and Kinghorn, but on the approach of Argyle in 1641, with 5,000 men, the garrison fled, leaving the fortress an easy prey to the Covenanters, who set it on fire, and reduced it to ashes; Argyle himself, according to tradition, having taken a hammer and assisted in the demolition of the doorways and hewing of the stone work, till he was completely fatigued. The modern house of Airlie, erected upon the ruins of the old castle, is a beautiful mansion, most picturesquely situated upon a peninsulated rock, at the point where the river Melgam forms a junction with the Isla. A fragment of the old castle remains, consisting of an old strong gateway and part of a tower.

AIRTH, a dormant earldom in the peerage of Scotland, formerly possessed by a branch of the noble family of Graham, conferred in 1633 on William, seventh earl of Menteith, descended from Sir Patrick Graham of Kincardine, the brother of Sir John the Graham, the faithful companion and "right hand" of Wallace, who was slain at the battle of Falkirk. Sir Patrick had previously fallen at Dunbar. The grandson of the latter, Sir David Graham, styled in a royal charter, witnessed by him in 1360, of Old Montrose, was the ancestor of the dukes of Montrose of the name of Graham. See MONTROSE, dukes of. and GRAHAM, surname of. His only son, Sir Patrick Graham, styled *Dominus* de Dundaff et Kincardine, acted a distinguished part in the reigns of David Bruce and Robert II. The eldest son of the latter, by a second marriage, Sir Patrick Graham of Elieston and Kilpont, married Eupheme, the sole heiress of Prince David Stewart, earl of Strathearn, and acquired that title. He was killed near Crieff in 1413, by the steward of Strathearn, Sir John Drummond, of Concraig. His son Malise was by James I. in Sept. 1427 created earl of Menteith or Monteith in lieu of Strathearn. His descendant and representative William, seventh earl of this line, having attempted to resume the earldom of Strathearn, was by Charles I. deprived both of it and the earldom of Menteith; but to compensate him for the loss, he created him earl of Airth, as already mentioned, with precedence equal to what he had enjoyed as earl of Menteith, in which earldom he was afterwards reinstated. Kilpont was the baronial title of the family. It seems to have been selected as marking their descent from the stem of Kincardine, subsequently Montrose. The tower of Airth, in Stirlingshire, is famous for an assault made upon it by Sir William Wallace, when held by an English garrison, whom he put to the sword. The square tower which makes a part of the present house of Airth, upon the west, is said to be the same in which that bloody exploit was performed. [*Nimmo's History of Stirlingshire—Stirling's edition*, 1817, page 170.] The title of earl of Airth has been dormant since the death of William, second earl of Airth and Menteith in 1694. It was claimed by

Robert Barclay Allardyce, Esq. of Urie and Allardyce, who died in 1855. See MENTEITH.

AITKEN, JOHN, for some time editor of Constable's Miscellany, was born on 25th March 1793, in the village of Camelon, Stirlingshire. His first situation was in the East Lothian bank, and soon after he was sent to the banking office of Mr. Park, Selkirk, brother of Mungo Park the traveller, where he remained for several years. He was afterwards appointed teller in the East Lothian bank, where he had formerly been. He subsequently removed to Edinburgh, and became a bookseller. Having early displayed a predilection for literature, he now resolved to follow the bent of his mind, and commenced editing 'The Cabinet,' an elegant selection of pieces in prose and verse, three volumes of which were published. The taste and judgment evinced in this publication recommended him to Mr. Archibald Constable, as the fittest person to undertake the editorship of his Miscellany; and though for a time the failure of Messrs. Constable and Company postponed the publication, when the work at last appeared, it was under Mr. Aitken's management. On the death of Mr. Constable, he, in conjunction with Mr. Henry Constable and Messrs. Hurst, Chance, and Company, London, purchased the work, and continued editor till 1831, when some new arrangements rendered his retirement necessary. He afterwards became a printer on his own account, with some prospect of success; but having caught cold, which produced erysipelas in the head, he died on the 15th of February 1833, in the 39th year of his age, leaving a widow and four children. Mr. Aitken wrote a few pieces of poetry of uncommon beauty and sensibility; of these, perhaps the most touching is the address to his children, prefixed to the third series of the Cabinet.—*Obituary at the time.*

AITON,—for the origin of the name of Aiton, see AYTON.

AITON, WILLIAM, styled the Scottish Linnæus, was born in 1731, at a village near Hamilton. Going to England in 1754, he was employed as an assistant in the Physic gardens at Chelsea, under Philip Miller, the superintendent, on whose recommendation he was in 1759 appointed head gardener to the Royal botanical garden at Kew, and became a great favourite with George III. In

1783 he obtained also the appointment of superintendent of the pleasure-grounds at Kew. He introduced a number of improvements into the Royal gardens, and formed there one of the best collections of rare exotic plants then known, a catalogue of which, with the title, *Hortus Kewensis,* was published in 1789 in 3 vols. 8vo, containing an enumeration of between five and six thousand species, with thirteen plates. He died in 1793, of a schirrus in the liver, and his son, William Townsend Aiton, was nominated by the king himself his successor.

Mr. Aiton's publications are :

Hortus Kewensis: or a Catalogue of the Plants cultivated in the Royal Botanic Gardens at Kew, illustrated with Engravings. Lond. 1789, 3 vols. 8vo.

New Edition enlarged. Lond. 1810–13, 5 vols. 8vo.

An Epitome of 2d. edit. Lond. 1814, 8vo.

ALBANY, duke of, a title formerly given to a prince of the blood-royal of Scotland,—Albany, Albion, or Albinn, being the ancient Gaelic name of North Britain, and until the time of Cæsar the original appellation of the whole island. The Scottish Highlanders denominate themselves 'Gael Albinn,' or Albinnich, or Albainach. The name Albany is evidently derived from the Pictish word *Alban,* "the superior height," and is now applied to the extensive mountainous district comprising Appin and Glenorchy in Argyleshire, Athol and Breadalbane in Perthshire, and a part of Lochaber in Inverness-shire. The title of duke of Albany was first conferred on the regent Robert, earl of Fife, son of Robert II. Since the Union, it has always been borne by the king's second son, by creation, and was last held, as a secondary title, by the late duke of York, son of George III. The history of Scotland mentions four dukes of Albany who made a figure in their time; whom, in consequence of their relation to the royal family of Scotland, we insert here, rather than under the family name of Stuart.

ALBANY, ROBERT, first duke of, the third son of Robert II. the first of the Stuarts, by his first wife, Elizabeth, daughter of Sir Adam Mure of Rowallan in Ayrshire. He was born in 1339. He obtained the earldom of Menteith by his marriage with Margaret, countess of Menteith, and afterwards in 1371 that of Fife, on the resignation of that earldom into the king's hands in his favour by Isobel, countess of Fife, the widow of his eldest brother Walter, who had died young, without issue. He was accordingly thereafter styled earl of Fife and Menteith. In the years 1371 and 1372, he presided at the courts of redress for settling differences on the marches. In 1383 he was appointed great chamberlain of Scotland, which office he resigned in 1408, in favour of his son

John, earl of Buchan. In 1385, accompanied by the earl of Douglas, and John de Vienne, admiral of France, who was then in Scotland, and a body of French auxiliaries, he marched with an army of 30,000 men towards Roxburgh, at that time in the hands of the English. Proceeding into England they took the castle of Wark in Northumberland, and ravaged the country from Berwick to Newcastle; but on the approach of the duke of Lancaster, they resolved to return to Scotland. On their way back, they sat down before Roxburgh, but were obliged soon to raise the siege. On the invasion of Scotland by the English, the earls of Fife and Douglas, and Archibald lord of Galloway, made an incursion on the west borders, as far as Cockermouth, spoiling the rich country between the Fells of Cumberland and the sea, and returned with several prisoners and abundance of plunder. The talents of the earl of Fife, it is stated, were so highly prized, that the principal youth of Scotland flocked eagerly to his standard. In the summer of 1388, when Douglas invaded England on the east, and fell at Otterbourne, the earl of Fife, with his brother the earl of Strathearn, entered that kingdom on the west, and after passing towards Carlisle, returned by Solway, without sustaining any loss.

In 1389, in consequence of the advanced age of the king his father, and the bodily infirmity of his elder brother, the earl of Carrick, afterwards Robert III., who had been rendered lame in early youth by the kick of a horse, the earl of Fife was, by the three estates of the realm, appointed governor of the kingdom. Desirous of signalizing the commencement of his administration, he raised an army, and advanced against the earl of Nottingham, marshal of England, warden of the east marches, who, after the battle of Otterbourne, had boasted that he hoped to conquer the Scots, even though opposed by a force double his own numbers. On the approach of the regent and the new earl of Douglas, however, instead of giving battle, he posted his men in a secure and inaccessible place, and refused to stand the hazard of a fight; and the Scots army, after waiting half-a-day, with banners displayed in sight of the foe, returned home, wasting and destroying the country. A truce was agreed to the same year, 1389. In

c

April of the following year his father died, and his elder brother John succeeded to the throne, when he took the name of Robert III., that of John being considered inauspicious. The new king, besides being lame, was of a quiet disposition and had no strength of mind, and the management of public affairs was continued in the hands of the earl of Fife. His nephew, however, Prince David, earl of Carrick, conceiving that, as heir-apparent to the crown, he was entitled, in preference to his uncle, to be at the head of the administration, had the address to compel his retirement from the office of governor, and to get himself named regent in his place, under the condition that he should act by the advice of a council, of whom his uncle was the principal. In March 1398 Albany and his nephew Prince David had a meeting at a place called Haudenstank, with John of Gaunt, duke of Lancaster, and other English commissioners, for settling mutual differences; and it is supposed that, on this occasion, Lancaster, from his superior title of duke, claimed some precedence not relished by the prince and his uncle; for this year the first introduction of the ducal title into Scotland took place, the earl of Carrick, the king's son, being created duke of Rothesay, and the earl of Fife, the king's brother, duke of Albany. According to Fordun, these titles were conferred in a solemn council held at Scone, April 28, 1398. In 1400, when Henry IV. of England invaded Scotland, Albany assembled an army to oppose that monarch. Henry took Haddington and Leith, and laid siege to the castle of Edinburgh, at which time William Napier of Wrightshouses was constable of the castle. With the aid of Archibald, earl of Douglas, and the duke of Rothesay, at this time governor of the kingdom, he maintained that important fortress against the whole English army, which was numerous and well appointed. In accordance with the chivalrous custom of the times, Rothesay, who was not wanting in courage, though frequently charged with imprudence, sent King Henry a knightly challenge to meet him where he pleased, with a hundred nobles on each side, and so to determine the quarrel, but the English king was not disposed to give him this advantage, and sent back an equivocating verbal reply. He then sat down with his numerous host before the castle, till cold and rain, and the want of provisions, as the inhabitants had, as usual in those days, taken care to remove every thing that the invaders could lay their hands on from their reach, compelled him to raise the siege and hastily recross the Border, without his visit being productive of much injury either in his progress or retreat. On his part the duke of Albany, whose ambition was equal to his ability, desirous of having the government to himself, permitted the enemy to withdraw without molestation, and obtained much praise from them for his clemency to all who surrendered.

Two years afterwards occurred the tragic death of the duke of Rothesay, which left a dark cloud of suspicion on his uncle's name, and the mystery attendant on which has never been satisfactorily cleared up. The circumstances of his death are related by Boece, who attaches the guilt of murder distinctly to Albany, but the love of the marvellous which is so prominent in this writer as to make even Tytler call him the most apocryphal of Scottish historians, may be supposed to have led him to give a high colouring to his narrative, which the subsequent unpopularity of Albany and the disfavour into which his memory fell with the Scottish court, would not diminish. After mentioning the death of the young duke's mother, Queen Annabella Drummond, his narrative thus proceeds: "Be quhais deith, succedit gret displeseir to hir son, David, duk of Rothesay; for, during hir life, he wes haldin in virtews and honest occupatioun, eftir hir deith, he began to rage in all maner of insolence; and fulyeit virginis, matronis, and nunnis, be his unbridillit lust. At last, King Robert, informit of his young and insolent maneris, send letteris to his brothir, the duk of Albany, to intertene his said son, the duk of Rothesay, and to leir [learn] him honest and civill maneris. The duk of Albany, glaid of thir writtingis, tuk the duk of Rothesay betwixt Dunde and Sanct Androis, and brocht him to Falkland, and inclusit [enclosed] him in the tour thairof, but [without] ony meit or drink. It is said, ane woman, havand commiseratioun on this duk, leit meill fall down throw the loftis of the toure; be quilkis, his life wes certane dayis savit. This woman, fra it wes knawin, wes put to deith. On the same maner, ane othir woman gaif him milk of hir paup, throw ane lang reid; and wes slane with gret cruelte, fra it wes knawin. Than wes the duk destitute of all mortall supplie; and brocht, finalie, to sa miserable and hungry-appetite, that he eit, nocht allanerlie [not only] the filth of the toure quhare he wes, bot his awin fingaris; to his great marterdome. His body wes beryit in Lundoris, and kithit miraklis mony yeris eftir; quhil [till], at last King James the First began to punis his slayeris; and fra that time furth, the miraclis ceissit." The melancholy death of the duke of Rothesay forms one of the most effective incidents in Sir Walter Scott's popular novel of 'The Fair Maid of Perth,' in which the characters of the young prince, of his weak-minded father Robert the Third, and of his uncle the regent duke of Albany, are drawn with great faithfulness and power.

It would appear that the duke of Rothesay, who was of a wild and thoughtless disposition, and little qualified for a charge so important as that of regent of the kingdom, had alienated the affections of all whom he ought to have courted and conciliated. He had in early life been affianced to his own cousin, the beautiful Euphemia de Lindsay, sister of Sir William de Lindsay of Rossie and of David earl of Crawford,—he slighted her for Elizabeth Dunbar, sister of the earl of March and Dunbar, to whom he was solemnly contracted,—and her again for Marjory Douglas daughter of the brave but unfortunate Archibald earl of Douglas surnamed the *Tineman,*—whom he ultimately married. The consequence was the deadly enmity of the earl of March and Sir William Rossie, the latter—in absence of the earl of Crawford in Spain—the representative of the house of Lindsay. More recently he had offended his father-in-law, the earl of Douglas, by personal affronts and neglect of his daughter, and by his shameful debaucheries and vicious courses with other women. He had disgusted and insulted one of his own immediate followers, Sir William Ramorgny, a man of highly polished manners, but of a revengeful heart. He conceived a strong desire to effect the overthrow of Albany, which he was at no pains to conceal, and was guilty of repeated excesses which rendered his being placed under some restraint a matter of necessity.

On his suspension from the office of governor, it was suggested by Sir William Lindsay and Ramorgny to the prince, in order to facilitate his capture, that he should ride to St. Andrews—the bishop of which had just died,—and keep the castle for the king's interest. He set off with a small train, but was intercepted by them, and conveyed a prisoner to the castle. Albany, and his father-in-law Douglas, then at Culross, presently arrived, and after holding a council of the regency, it was decided to transport the unfortunate prince to Falkland, where he was placed under the custody of two individuals called Wright and Selkirk. The rest of the story we have given in the words of Boece. The tale contains matter that is fabulous and untrue as well as revolting and improbable. All the parties named by the tradition as the murderers in chief we know to have died a natural death, except the gallant Douglas, who fell at the battle of Verneuil. If the remains of the prince could have wrought miracles at all, there was no truth therefore in the reason assigned why the faculty had ceased. After a life so dissipated, it is not improbable that the account given by Bower, the continuator of Fordun, may have had foundation, namely, that the young prince really died of dysentery, and to this view of the case the filthy details of Boece would rather seem to give some countenance. It is singular that Wyntoun, the earliest narrator of the event, says nothing whatever of the alleged murder. At the time of his death, he was in his 29th year, having been born in 1373.—See ROTHESAY, duke of.

The mysterious death of the heir to the crown having excited great attention, a parliament met at Edinburgh on the 16th May after, to investigate the matter, when Albany and the earl of Douglas acknowledged having imprisoned the duke of Rothesay, but denied being guilty of his death, attributing it to divine providence. These statements appear to have induced the parliament to declare him innocent of the murder, while at the same time he sought to make himself legally secure by taking out a remission under the great seal for the imprisonment, both for himself and for Douglas. This remission, which is in Latin, was first printed by Lord Hailes, but it does not follow from the concluding remark of his comment, as

Pinkerton says, that he considered the prince as having been murdered; namely, " The duke of Albany and the earl of Douglas obtained a remission in terms as ample as if they had actually murdered the heir apparent." On the capital of the pillar of the old chapel of St. Giles' cathedral at Edinburgh are still to be seen sculptured the arms of Robert duke of Albany, and those of Archibald, fourth earl of Douglas, the father-in-law of Rothesay, the former on the south and the latter on the north side, and the author of 'Memorials of Edinburgh in the Olden Time' infers from this fact that this chapel had been founded and endowed by them, as an expiatory offering for the murder of the duke of Rothesay, and its chaplain probably appointed to say masses for their victim's soul. [*Wilson's Memorials of Edinburgh*, vol. ii. page 168.] The friendship which subsisted between Albany and Douglas seems a more likely reason why their arms should have been thus placed together, than any thing in connection with the death of the young and wilful prince, that could be imputed to either of them.

Soon after the death of Rothesay, Albany, in order to turn the attention of the nation into another channel, gave his consent for the renewal of hostile operations against England. Two Scottish armies were successively marched across the Borders, but both were defeated and dispersed, the first at the battle of Nesbit Moor, fought on the 22d June 1402, and the other at Homeldon hill, on the 14th September of that year, when the celebrated Hotspur gained the victory. In the latter the leaders of the Scots, Murdoch earl of Fife, eldest son of the regent Albany, with the earl of Douglas, his friend and supposed accomplice in the death of Rothesay, and eighty knights, and a crowd of esquires and pages, were taken prisoners, while not only among those slain but in the list of the captives, were many of that party which supported the king and his young son Prince James, against the encroaching power of Albany, whom they believed to be the murderer of his nephew the duke of Rothesay. Soon after the battle of Homeldon, the Percies, who by this time had become dissatisfied with the monarch whom they had placed upon the English throne, began to organize that famous rebellion which terminated

with the defeat and death of Hotspur in the battle of Shrewsbury, in which they were aided by their prisoner the earl of Douglas. As a pretext for assembling an army they pretended an invasion of Scotland, and the duke of Albany, influenced probably by the example and advice of Douglas, and hoping that the kingdom would benefit by their services, readily gave in to their designs At the head of a large army Percy advanced across the Border, but had only marched a few miles into Scotland, when he commanded his forces to halt before the insignificant border-tower of Cocklaws, but the officer commanding the tower having entered into an agreement to capitulate in six weeks if not relieved, the whole English army retired. On receiving information of this, Albany assembled the principal of the nobility, and having explained to them the circumstances, advised an immediate expedition into England. The Scottish barons, who had been amazed at Albany's former lukewarmness and inactivity, when the capital had been invaded by Henry IV. in person and the principal castle of the kingdom was in danger of falling into his hands, were now overwhelmed with astonishment at the sudden blaze of bravery which seemed to animate his breast when a paltry Border fortress was threatened by the English. " All were of opinion," says Bower, " without a single dissentient voice, that, upon so trivial an occasion it would be absurd to peril the welfare of the kingdom; but Albany starting up, and pointing to his page, who held his horse at a little distance; 'You, my lords,' said he, ' may sit still at home; but I vow to God and St. Fillan that I shall be at Cocklaws on the appointed day, though no one but Pate Kinbuck, the boy yonder, should accompany me.'" The warlike resolution of the governor was hailed with great joy. " Never," says the historian, " did men more joyfully proceed to a feast, than they to collect their vassals." At the head of an immense army, Albany advanced to the Borders, but on his march, a messenger from England brought the intelligence of the result of the battle of Shrewsbury and the termination of the rebellion in England. This, however, did not deter him from pushing on to Cocklaws, and surrounding the fortalice with his troops, and after causing it to be proclaimed by a herald that the Percies had been utterly defeated, and so relieved the fortress, he returned, without entering England, with his army, which he immediately disbanded.

In the meantime, the afflicted monarch, Robert III., resolved to send his second son James, then in his eleventh year, to France for greater security; but the vessel in which he sailed having been driven by a storm on the coast of England, was taken by an English cruiser, and the youthful prince, although there was a truce at the time between the two kingdoms, was ungenerously detained a prisoner by Henry IV. for nineteen years.

Robert III. died of a broken heart, 4th April, 1406, and the duke of Albany, in the absence of James, was, by a parliament which met at Perth, confirmed in the regency. He was then approaching his seventieth year, but vigorous, politic, and ambitious as ever. During his regency occurred the famous battle of Harlaw, which was fought in 1411, between his nephew Alexander, earl of Mar, and Donald lord of the Isles, the cause of which was ostensibly the earldom of Ross, to which the lord of the Isles laid claim in right of his wife, but there can be no doubt that this claim and his subsequent invasion of the district of Ross, formed merely a pretext, which was intended to conceal his ulterior views on the throne itself. It appears that the male line of the possessors of this earldom had become extinct, and the succession had devolved upon a female, Euphemia Ross, the wife of Sir Walter Lesley, by whom she had a son, Alexander, who succeeded as earl of Ross, and a daughter, Margaret, married to Donald of the Isles. The countess of Ross, on the death of her husband, married Alexander earl of Buchan, fourth son of King Robert II. Her son by her first marriage, Alexander earl of Ross, married Lady Isabel Stewart, eldest daughter of the regent Albany, and the only issue of this marriage was a daughter, also named Euphemia, countess of Ross, at her father's death. This lady became a nun, and committed the government of her earldom to Albany, with the intention, as it is conjectured, of resigning it in favour of her uncle, John Stewart, earl of Buchan, the second son of the regent. As the countess Euphemia, by be-

coming a nun, was regarded as dead in law, her next heir was her aunt Margaret, the only sister of the deceased Alexander, earl of Ross, and the wife of Donald lord of the Isles. That chieftain accordingly asserted her right to the earldom, and demanded to be put in possession of it. The claim and the demand were both rejected by the regent, "whose principal object," says Skene, "appears to have been to prevent the accession of so extensive a district to the territories of the lord of the Isles, already too powerful for the security of the government, and whose conduct was more actuated by principles of expediency than of justice." [*History of the Highlanders*, vol. ii. p. 72.] Resolved to maintain his claims by force of arms, and show his scorn of the authority of the regent, Donald formed an alliance with Henry IV. of England, and at the head of ten thousand men, which he had raised in the Hebrides and in the earldom of Ross itself, suddenly invaded the district in dispute, by the inhabitants of which he was not opposed, and speedily obtained possession of the earldom. On his arrival at Dingwall, however, he was encountered by Angus Dow Mackay of Farr, or Black Angus, as he was called, at the head of a large body of men from Sutherland. After a fierce attack the Mackays were completely routed, and their leader taken prisoner, while Angus' brother Roderick was killed. Donald took possession of the castle of Dingwall, and seized the island of Sky, contiguous to his own extensive territories. Flushed with success, he now resolved, in accordance with his secret design of overturning the government, to carry into execution a threat he had often made to burn the town of Aberdeen. He ordered the army to assemble at Inverness, and gathering as he proceeded all the men capable of bearing arms to his standard, he swept through Moray without opposition, and penetrated into Aberdeenshire. In Strathbogie, and in the district of Garioch, which belonged to the earl of Mar, he committed great excesses. To arrest his progress, the earl of Mar, the nephew of the regent, and Sir Alexander Ogilvy, the sheriff of Angus, hastily raised as many forces as they could collect in the counties north of the Tay, consisting of most of the retainers of the ancient families of these counties, the Ogilvies, the

Lyons, the Maules, the Carnegies, the Lindsays, the Leslies, the Murrays, the Straitons, the Irvings, the Arbuthnots, the Leiths, the Burnets, and others, led by their respective chiefs. The two armies met at the village of Harlaw, in the parish of Chapel of Garioch, upwards of fifteen miles from Aberdeen. Although the earl of Mar's army was inferior in point of numbers to that of the lord of the Isles, it was composed of Lowland gentlemen, better armed and disciplined than the wild and disorderly hordes that followed Donald, who was assisted by Mackintosh and Maclean, and other Highland chiefs, all bearing the most deadly hatred to their Saxon foes. This memorable battle was fought on the 24th July, 1411, "upon the issue of which," says Skene, "seemed to depend the question of whether the Gaelic or Teutonic part of the population of Scotland were in future to have the supremacy." [*History of the Highlanders*, vol. ii. page 73.] The disastrous result of this battle was one of the greatest misfortunes which had ever happened to the numerous respectable families in Angus and the Mearns. The earl of Mar lost five hundred men, among whom were several gentlemen of distinction. Besides Sir James Scrymgeour, constable of Dundee, Sir Alexander Ogilvy, the sheriff of Angus, with his eldest son, George Ogilvy, Sir Thomas Murray, Sir Robert Maule of Panmure, Sir Alexander Irving of Drum, Sir William Abernethy of Saltoun, Sir Alexander Straiton of Laurieston, Sir Robert Davidson, provost of Aberdeen, and a number of the inhabitants of that city, were among the slain. A gentleman, named Leslie of Balquhain, whose residence was in the neighbourhood of the field of battle, with six of his sons, was killed. On the side of the lord of the Isles nine hundred men were slain, including the chiefs of Maclean and Mackintosh. Neither party gained the victory, and each, on reckoning its loss, considered itself vanquished, but the lord of the Isles felt himself so much weakened that he was compelled to abandon the contest. The earl of Mar and those of his companions who survived were so much exhausted with fatigue that they passed the night on the field of battle, expecting a renewal of the attack next morning, but at daydawn they discovered that Donald and the remains of his force

had retired during the darkness, without molestation, retreating first to Ross, and then to the Isles. Immediately after the battle, the regent, anxious to follow up the check which the Highland force had received, collected an army, and marched to the castle of Dingwall, which he took and garrisoned towards the end of autumn. In the following summer he sent three separate forces to invade the territories of Donald. The haughty lord of the Isles was obliged to relinquish his claims to the earldom of Ross, to make personal submission, and to give hostages for indemnification and for the future observance of peace. The instrument by which the earldom of Ross was resigned by Euphemia the nun in favour of her grandfather is dated in 1415, just four years after the battle of Harlaw. The battle itself, as has been well remarked, "from the ferocity with which it was contested, and the dismal spectacle of civil war and bloodshed exhibited to the country, appears to have made a deep impression on the national mind. It fixed itself in the music and the poetry of Scotland; a march, called 'The Battle of Harlaw,' continued to be a popular air down to the time of Drummond of Hawthornden, and a spirited ballad on the same event is still repeated in our age, describing the meeting of the armies, and the deaths of the chiefs, in no ignoble strain." [*Laing's Early Metrical Tales*, page 229.] For a long time after, it was customary for schoolboys to arrange themselves into opposite parties, and fight the battle of Harlaw over again, for recreation. The ballad of the Battle thus concludes:

There was not, sin' King Kenneth's days,
    Sic strange intestine cruel strife
In Scotlande seen, as ilk man says,
    Where monie likelie lost their life;
    Whilk made divorce tween man and wife,
And monie children fatherless,
    Whilk in this realm has been full rife;
Lord help these lands! our wrangs redress!

In July, on Saint James his evin,
    That four-and-twenty dismal day,
Twelve hundred, ten score, and eleven
    Of years sin' Christ, the soothe to say;
    Men will remember, as they may,
When thus the veritie they knaw;
    And monie a ane will mourne for aye
The brim battle of the Harlaw.

In the year last mentioned, namely 1415, the regent obtained from Henry V. the liberation of his son Murdoch, in exchange for Henry Percy, the son of Hotspur. In 1416 he sent his second son, John earl of Buchan, ambassador to England, to endeavour to procure the release of James I. from the captivity in which he was held by the English monarch. With a strange perversity, the writers of Scottish history have almost unanimously charged the regent Albany with "being in no hurry to obtain the release of his nephew," as Sir Walter Scott gently phrases it—nay, they even go farther, and accuse him of treasonably intriguing with the English king to retain his sovereign in prison, that his own power might not be interrupted; but here is one instance where Albany intrusted his son, the earl of Buchan, one of the bravest and most accomplished knights of his age, with a mission to England to endeavour to procure the liberation of James. In 1417, when King Henry V. was in France, prosecuting his wars there, the regent, with a large army invaded England, and after beginning the siege of Roxburgh, immediately retreated in all haste on learning that an English force, under the dukes of Bedford and Exeter, was on the way to meet him. This was long popularly remembered as the "Foul Raid." In 1419 he despatched his son, the earl of Buchan, with a chosen army of 7,000 men, into France, to assist the dauphin against the English king. Neither this invasion of England, nor this assistance sent to France, would have taken place had Albany desired to keep on those good terms with Henry which implied a mutual understanding as to the retention of James from his kingdom. This son, the earl of Buchan, was the offspring of Albany's second marriage with Muriella, the daughter of Sir William Keith, marshal of Scotland. He was born about 1380. When his father became regent in 1406, after the death of his brother Robert III., he resigned, in favour of his son, the office of great chamberlain. In 1408 Albany, as regent, created him earl of Buchan. Five years afterwards Buchan married Lady Elizabeth, daughter of Archibald earl of Douglas. While engaged on the dauphin's side against the English in France, the earl of Buchan, on the 22d March 1421, defeated the duke of Clarence, the brother

of Henry V., at Baugé in Anjou, and slew him with a battle axe, after he had been pierced with a spear by Sir William Swinton. To recompense this signal victory the dauphin conferred upon him the high office of constable of France. In 1422 he revisited Scotland, with the view of inducing his father-in-law, the earl of Douglas, to join his arms. Douglas consented, and was created duke of Touraine in France by the dauphin. Both Douglas and the earl of Buchan, constable of France, were slain at the battle of Verneuil in Normandy, 17th August 1424. A portrait of this illustrious warrior is given on page 43, at the end of the memoir.

The duke of Albany continued to administer the affairs of the kingdom till his death, which took place at Stirling castle, on the 3d of September 1420, at the age of 81. His body was interred in the Abbey church of Dunfermline. Our historians generally have given a very unfair view of Albany's character. Pinkerton thus depicts it: "His person was tall and majestic; his countenance amiable. Temperance, affability, eloquence, real generosity, apparent benignity, a degree of cool prudence, bordering upon wisdom, may be reckoned among his virtues. But the shades of his vices are deeper; an insatiate ambition, unrelenting cruelty, and its attendant cowardice, or, at least, an absolute defect of military fame, a contempt of the best human affections, a long practice in all the dark paths of art and dissimulation. His administration he studied to recommend, not by promoting the public good, but by sharing the spoils of the monarchy with the nobles, by a patient connivance at their enormities, by a dazzling pomp of expenditure, in the pleasures of the feast, and in the conciliation of magnificence. As fortune preserved his government from any signal unsuccess, so it would be an abuse of terms to bestow upon a wary management which only regarded his own interest the praise of political wisdom." In this same strain all our historians follow one another in their estimate of Albany's character, but I am not disposed to agree with them entirely. Nothing could be wiser or more calculated for the public good, than his resistance to Donald of the Isles, whose object was by the aid of England to destroy the Scottish kingdom to his own aggrandisement; and whatever may be the motives imputed to Albany, or the objects assigned as the moving springs of his administration, surely it cannot be denied that the public good was indeed promoted by his policy, and by his judicious and vigorous measures on all occasions. During his regency justice was regularly administered. He took great care not to lay any taxes on the people, and especially he steadily and successfully opposed the levying of a tax of two pennies on every hearth in the kingdom, which had been proposed in parliament for the purpose of defraying the expense of demolishing Jedburgh castle. "Even in his time," says Sir Walter Scott, "it would seem that the extent of writings used for the transference of property, had become a subject of complaint. When upon this subject, Albany used often to praise the simplicity and beauty of an ancient charter by King Athelstan, a Saxon monarch. It had been granted to the ancient Northumbrian family called Roddam of Roddam, and had fallen into the hands of the Scots on some of their plundering excursions." The duke of Albany, it is quite certain, was one of the most popular and most able governors that the kingdom ever possessed. He enjoyed to a high degree the confidence of both king and nobles, while the people placed the utmost reliance on the justice and firmness of his government. The following is an impression of his seal, taken from the *Diplomata Scotiæ:*

Robert duke of Albany was twice married: first to Margaret, countess of Menteith; and secondly to Muriella, eldest daughter of Sir William Keith, great marischal of Scotland, and had issue by both marriages.—*Douglas' Peerage*, vol. i.—*Pinkerton's History of Scotland*, vol. i. p. 85.

ALBANY, MURDOCH, second duke of, son of the preceding, succeeded him both as duke and regent. At first he bore the title of earl of Fife. He had a grant from Robert III. in the third year of his reign, of a hundred merks sterling annually from the customs of Aberdeen. He was Justiciary of Scotland benorth the Forth, and designed of Kinclevyne when taken prisoner at the battle of Homeldon in 1402. Henry IV. presented him in full parliament on 20th October, and he was allowed to be at large on his parole of honour. By a letter from his father to Henry the Fourth, dated Falkland, June 2, 1405, he seems to have received much kindness from that monarch during his stay in England, as he thanks him for his good treatment of his son Murdoch, and the favourable audience given to Rothesay herald. In 1415 he was exchanged for Henry Percy of Northumberland, the son of Hotspur, who, since the battle of Shrewsbury, had remained in Scotland. He does not appear to have possessed the same degree of energy as his father, but the accounts of him given by our historians are manifestly partial and exaggerated. It is stated that on his father's death in 1419, he assumed the office of governor of Scotland, just as if he had naturally and legitimately succeeded to it as a matter of hereditary right, and that he did not think it necessary even to obtain the sanction of parliament, but supported by the feudal nobility at once usurped the government. This is not likely to have been the conduct of a person of the indolent, incapable, and unambitious character which Duke Murdoch's is universally represented to have been. In the commission preserved in the chapter of Westminster, and of which a copy is given in Anderson's *Diplomata*, No. 64, it is expressly stated that the parties therein named, being the bishop of Glasgow, chancellor of Scotland, James Douglas of Balvany, brother-in-law of Duke Murdoch, the earl of March, the abbot of Balmerinoch and others, empowered to negotiate for the deliverance of James from his captivity in England, were so appointed with the knowledge and by the deliberate council of the three estates of the realm (*ex certa scientia et deliberato concilio trium statuum regni*), which must have been assembled at the time, and probably for the purpose. This document bears date 19th August 1423, and is stated to have been passed in the *third* year of Murdoch's government. As, however, his father died in 1419, it is impossible that it could have been so expressed had he *then* assumed the government; for it would, in that case, have been stated to have been done in the *fourth* and not the *third* year of his regency; and it is but reasonable to infer that the post of governor remained vacant after the death of his father, till it could be legitimately conferred on Murdoch by an act of some parliament, of the proceedings of which, as well as of the one referred to in the commission, no trace is now to be found in history. It is said that Murdoch's conduct as regent created so much dissatisfaction in the nation that some persons refused to accept of the most profitable offices, and others resigned theirs; while the loss of place was accounted a proof of men's honour and integrity. But in the commission referred to, men of the highest rank and character are mentioned as being in possession of some of the chief offices in the kingdom. It is certain, however, that during Murdoch's government, the affections of the people became more intensely fixed upon their absent sovereign; and the greatest desire was manifested for his return; to which Murdoch was induced to accede. A traditionary story, in which we place no faith, is related that he was driven to this by his son Walter having savagely wrung the neck of a favourite falcon which he coveted, on its being refused to him, as Murdoch set out one day to enjoy the recreation of hawking. Provoked by his conduct, the regent said to the youth, "Since thou canst not find in thy heart to obey me, I will bring in another whom both of us shall be forced to obey." Ambassadors being despatched to negociate with the English court, after some delay the duke of Bedford, then protector of England, agreed to deliver up the king of Scotland, on payment of £40,000, within six years by half-yearly payments, hostages be-

ing given for payment of the same. The ambassadors who went to England, to concert measures about the payment of this sum, were the bishops of Aberdeen and Dunblane and Mr. Thomas Myreton. The arrangement for the release of the king was finally adjusted by the Scottish commissioners, who proceeded to London for that purpose, on the 9th of March, 1424. In the following April James returned to Scotland, after having married the Lady Jane Beaufort, a daughter of the earl of Somerset, of the blood royal of England. At his coronation, Murdoch, duke of Albany, as earl of Fife, performed the ceremony of installing the sovereign on the throne, and amidst the rejoicings on the occasion, the king conferred the honour of knighthood on Alexander Stewart, the second son of the duke of Albany, and twenty-four others of his principal nobility and barons. An act had been passed in the first parliament after James' return, ordering the sheriffs to enquire what lands had belonged to the crown during the three preceding reigns, and empowering the king to summon the holders to show their charters. There had, probably, been some demur, which roused James to adopt vigorous measures, and to have recourse to the cruel expedient of cutting off his own cousin and his family as the authors of it. He first ordered the arrest of Walter, eldest son of Murdoch, duke of Albany, the late regent, with that of Malcolm Fleming of Cumbernauld, and Thomas Boyd of Kilmarnock; and in a parliament held at Perth, 25th March 1425, he ordered the arrest of Murdoch himself, his second son, Sir Alexander Stewart, the earls of Douglas, Angus, and March, and twenty other gentlemen of note. His view, it is probable, in arresting so many was to prevent an insurrection. Murdoch was committed a close prisoner to Caerlaverock castle, while his duchess, Isabella, was sent to Tantallan, and the king immediately took possession of Albany's castles of Falkland in Fife, and Doune in Menteith. Immediately after the arrest of the duke of Albany and the other nobles, the king adjourned the parliament for two months. It reassembled in the palace of Stirling, on the 24th of May, when the king presided in person, at the trial of Duke Murdoch, his two sons, and his father-in-law, the aged earl of Lennox. No known record specifies their crime, and our historians have conjectured that the charge was one of high treason, for the alleged usurpation of the government on the part of Albany. Walter Stewart, the eldest son, was first tried, on the 24th of May, and being found guilty was instantly beheaded in front of the castle. On the following day, the duke of Albany, Alexander his second son, and the earl of Lennox, were tried by the same jury, and being convicted were immediately executed. None of the noblemen and others arrested with them were brought to punishment. Seven of them even sat on the jury of twenty-six persons who found the duke and his companions guilty on their trial. Alexander, lord of the Isles, who succeeded Donald, whom Duke Murdoch's father had humbled (see p. 37), was also one of the jury, whose verdict sent him and his sons and his father-in-law to the block. Upon this Alexander of the Isles, the earldom of Ross, with extensive possessions in the Western Islands, was bestowed by James: an impolitic act, which afterwards brought much evil upon the kingdom. The scene of the execution was a rising ground in front of the castle of Stirling, which is still known by the name of the Heading Hill.

"Amongst the people," says Tytler, "the shedding of so much noble blood excited a sympathy and commiseration for which James was not prepared. Albany and his two sons, Walter and Alexander Stewart, were men whose appearance and manners, in a feudal age, were peculiarly fitted to command popularity. Their stature was almost gigantic; their countenances cast in the mould of manly beauty; and their air so dignified and warlike that when the father and the two sons ascended the scaffold, it was impossible to behold the scene without a feeling of involuntary pity and admiration. Behind them came the earl of Lennox, a venerable nobleman in his eightieth year; and, when he laid his head upon the block, and his grey hairs were stained with blood, a thrill of horror ran through the crowd, which, in spite of the respect or terror for the royal name, broke out into expressions of indignation at the unsparing severity of the vengeance." From the place of his execution Duke Murdoch might see in

the distance the fertile territory of Menteith, which formed part of his family estates, and even distinguish the stately castle of Doune, which had been his own vice-regal residence. Of this magnificent edifice the following is a wood-cut.

The title and possessions of the duke of Albany were forfeited, and the latter annexed to the crown. To obtain these was, no doubt, the cause of his death. A contemporary narrative of the murder of King James, preserved in the General Register House, and printed by Pinkerton, represents the general impression to have been that "the kyng did rather that rigorous execucion upon the lordes of his kyne for the covetise of thare possessions and goodes, thane for any rightful cause; althoe he fonde colourabill wayes to serve his intent yn the contrarye." [Pinkerton's Hist. vol. i. p. 463.] The estates of the earl of Lennox, his father-in-law, were allowed to remain unforfeited. Duke Murdoch's marriage to Isabella, the eldest daughter of Duncan, earl of Lennox, who had been left a widower without male issue, took place in 1391. By the marriage contract, it was agreed that should the earl of Lennox marry again, and have an heir male, the latter should marry Duke Murdoch's sister.

The earl did not marry again, and had no heir

male of his body who might fulfil the condition of a marriage with the regent's daughter. Of the marriage of Murdoch and Isabella, four sons were born, Robert, who died early, Walter, Alexander, and James. The latter, who was the fourth son, when his father, grandfather, and two brothers were seized and executed, was the only male member of the family who escaped. Resolving to succour his kindred or avenge their fate, with a body of armed followers, as desperate as himself, he carried fire and sword into the town of Dumbarton, and put to death the king's uncle, John Stewart, called the Red Stewart of Dundonald, with thirty-two others of inferior note. The king pursued him with such determined animosity that he was compelled to fly with his abettor, the bishop of Argyle, to Ireland.—See AVANDALE, lord, p. 169. [*Napier's History of the Partition of the Lennox*, p. 10.] Duke Murdoch's widow was allowed to retain her estates and titles, and to reside till her death upon her earldom of Lennox. She lived in the castle of Inchmurrin on Loch Lomond, the chief messuage of the earldom, and there granted charters to vassals as countess of Lennox. She survived to hear of the assassination of him whose inflexible sentence had cut off her father, her husband, and her two sons. On one of the pillars of St. Giles' church, Edinburgh, are the arms of Isabella, duchess of Albany and countess of Lennox, who, in 1450, founded the collegiate church of Dumbarton and largely endowed other religious foundations. She died about 1460. See LENNOX, family of. [*Douglas' Peerage.—Tytler's Lives of Scottish Worthies, Life of James I.*]

The physical strength and imposing appearance of the descendants of Robert the first duke of Albany have been frequently mentioned by historians. Murdoch's half-brother, the earl of Buchan, constable of France, slain at Verneuil in Normandy, in 1424 (see *ante*, page 39,) of whom a portrait is extant, seems to have possessed all the qualities of his race in this respect. Of this portrait, which was discovered about the middle of the last century by Sir George Seton of Garleton, of the noble family of Winton, in the gallery of M. Fiebet, at his seat near Chambord in France, an engraving is given in Pinkerton's Portrait Gallery. A woodcut of it is annexed.

ALBANY, ALEXANDER, third duke of, was the second son of King James II. His first titles were earl of March and lord of Annandale, but he was about 1456 created duke of Albany, a title which had been forfeited to the crown when Duke Murdoch was beheaded. Having been sent to France to complete his education, he was in 1464, on his voyage homeward from his uncle, the duke of Gueldres, towards Scotland, captured by the English, but soon released, a herald having been sent to England to declare war in case of his being detained. In February 1478 his brother James III., a prince of a weak and irresolute temper, and fond of mean favourites, on the sinister information of some of these. ordered his arrest, and imprisoned him in Edinburgh castle. Soon after, his younger brother, the earl of Mar, was also arrested by the king's orders. Both of these princes were popular with the nobility and people, and had incurred the king's suspicion and the hatred of his favourites. As lord warden of the east frontiers, Albany had besides restrained and disobliged the Homes and Hepburns and others of the Border clans, and in revenge they bribed Cochrane, the king's principal adviser, to set the king against him. Marr was taken out of his bed and sent prisoner to Craigmillar castle, and shortly thereafter, being accused by the king's favourites of consulting with sorcerers and witches to take the king's life, he was sentenced to have a vein in his leg opened, and in a bath to bleed to death, which was executed in the Canongate in 1479. [*Balfour's Annals*, vol. i. p. 203.] Albany was committed prisoner to the castle of Edinburgh, but effected his escape, and proceeded to his castle of Dunbar, from whence, after victualling and providing it with all manner of munitions of war, he sailed for France. [*Ibid.* vol. i. p. 202.] He was forfeited 4th October 1479, and troops were sent to besiege his castle of Dunbar, which soon yielded, the garrison escaping in boats to England. On arriving at Paris, the duke met with an honourable reception from Louis XI. He remained in France till 1482, when he proceeded to England, and entered into an agreement with Edward IV., by which the English king obliged himself to aid him in invading Scotland, and to place him on the throne; in return for which he consented to surrender Berwick, to acknowledge himself the vassal of England, to renounce all alliance with Louis of France, and to marry one of Edward's daughters. In consequence of this Albany assumed the title of king, declaring his brother to be a bastard. An English army amounting to 40,000 men, under the duke of Gloucester, afterwards Richard III., accompanied by Albany, marched to Berwick, and invested that town. The town speedily surrendered, but the castle held out. In the meantime King James having assembled his nobility, marched towards the Borders to meet the enemy. As he lay encamped near Lauder, his nobles, highly exasperated at their sovereign's conduct, headed by Archibald Douglas, earl of Angus, commonly called, after this event, "Bell-the-Cat," after securing the chief favourite Robert Cochrane, burst into the royal tent during the night, and seized the rest of the king's minions, all of whom, with Cochrane, they hanged over the bridge of Lauder. They then carried the king to Edinburgh, and shut him up in the castle, under the care of his uncles the earls of Athol and Buchan. The road to the capital was now open, and the dukes of Gloucester and Albany, with their forces, advanced, in the month

of July, towards Edinburgh. The archbishop of St. Andrews, the bishop of Dunkeld, with Lord Avandale, the chancellor, and the earl of Argyle, hastily collected a small army, and posted themselves at Haddington, to impede the advance of the enemy. At the same time they entered into negociations with Albany, and on the 2d of August a treaty of peace was concluded. Albany engaged to be a true and faithful subject to King James, on his titles and estates, with Dunbar castle, and the possessions of the late earl of Mar, his brother, being restored to him, and the office of king's lieutenant of the realm being conferred on him. Two heralds were commanded to pass to the castle to charge the captain to open the gates and set the king at liberty. In Balfour's Annals of Scotland, (vol. i. p. 207,) it is stated that the duke of Albany and the lord chancellor then governed all the realm, and that with several of the nobility Albany went to Stirling to visit the queen and prince, and after his return he laid siege to Edinburgh castle, which he took, when the king and such servants as were with him were set at liberty. According to Lindsay of Pitscottie, (vol. i. p. 200), the king, on recovering his freedom, "lap on a hackney to ride down to the abbay; but he would not ride forward, till the duik of Albanie his brother lap on behind him; and so they went down the geat to the abbey of Hallyraid hous, quhair they remained ane lang time in great mirrines;" and, as Abercromby adds, he "would needs make him a partner in his bed, and a comrade at his table," that being considered in those days the best proof of a perfect reconciliation. Albany immediately concluded a truce with the duke of Gloucester, and on the 23d of August 1482 surrendered to him the fortress of Berwick, after it had been in possession of the Scots for twenty-one years. Notwithstanding the favour which was now shown to him by the king, Albany, in the following year, engaged in another secret treaty with Edward IV., for depriving his brother of the throne, and securing it to himself. His designs being detected by the nobles, he was obliged to fly to England, having previously placed his castle of Dunbar in the hands of the English. In consequence of this traitorous proceeding, he was formally accused of treason, and summoned to stand his trial; but failing to appear, he was condemned to death as a traitor and to have his estates confiscated. Having assembled a small force, he joined the earl of Douglas, who was likewise an exile in England, and made an inroad into his native country, but was routed near Lochmaben, 22d July 1484, when Douglas was taken prisoner, but Albany escaped by the fleetness of his horse. A truce for three years was then agreed upon between the two countries, and Albany, finding that he could obtain no farther protection in England, retired to France, where he was well received by Charles VIII. He was accidentally killed at Paris in November 1485, by the splinter of a lance, while an onlooker at a tournament between the duke of Orléans and another knight, and, by act of parliament 1st October 1487, all his lands and possessions in Scotland were annexed to the crown. According to the description given of him by an ancient Scottish author, the duke of Albany was well-proportioned, and tall in stature, and comely in his countenance; that is to say, broad-faced, red-nosed, large-eared, and having a very awful countenance when displeased. Like his younger brother, the unfortunate earl of Mar, who was of a milder temper and manners, he excelled in the military exercises of tilting, hunting, hawking, and other personal accomplishments, for which his brother James III. had no taste. He had married first Lady Catherine Sinclair, eldest daughter of William earl of Orkney and Caithness, but a divorce took place, 2d March 1478, on account of propinquity of blood. By her he had one son, Alexander, who was declared illegitimate by act of parliament, 13 November 1516, and who was made bishop of Moray and abbot of Scone, in 1527. He married, secondly, in February 1480, Anne de la Tour, third daughter of Bertrand, Count d'Auvergne and de Bouillon, and by her he had one son, Duke John, the subject of the following notice.— *Douglas' Peerage.—Histories of the Period.*

ALBANY, JOHN, fourth duke of, son of the preceding, was born about 1481. In 1505, he married his cousin, Anne, or Agnes, de la Tour, countess d'Auvergne and de Laurajais, by whom he got large possessions. On the death of James IV., in 1513, his son James V. being then only in his second year, the queen mother was appointed regent of the kingdom, but at a convention of the estates held soon after at Perth, it was agreed, at the urgent suggestion of the venerable Elphinston, bishop of Aberdeen, seconded by the earl of Home, that the duke of Albany, then in France, and who after the infant king was next heir to the throne, should be invited to Scotland to be governor of the kingdom, during James' minority. This election was ratified by a public meeting of the estates held at Edinburgh soon after, and Lyon king at arms, with Sir Patrick Hamilton, was sent to France to notify the appointment to the duke. In the meantime, the sentence of forfeiture which had excluded him from the enjoyment of his rank and estates in Scotland was annulled, and his arrival impatiently looked for by the people, as the queen mother had married the earl of Angus, and, being opposed by the nobility, nothing but anarchy and disorder prevailed in the kingdom. On the 18th May, 1515, the duke arrived at Dumbarton, Balfour says at Ayr, with a squadron of eight ships; and soon after he was installed into the office of regent. "He wes ressaueit," says a chronicler of the period, "with greit honour, and convoyit to Edinburgh with ane greit cumpany, with greit blythnes, and glore, and thair wes constitute and maid governour of this realme; and sone thairefter held ane parliament, and ressauit the homage of the lordis and thre estaittis; quhair thair wes mony things done for the weill of this countrey." His inauguration into the regency was attended with great splendour. A sword was delivered to him, and a crown placed upon his head, while the peers made solemn obeisance. He was declared governor of the kingdom till the king attained the age of eighteen years. The duke took up his residence at Holyrood, and seems to have immediately proceeded with the enlargement of the palace, in continuation of the works which James IV., the late king, had carried on till near the close of his life.

Albany, unfortunately, was ignorant not only of the constitution, the laws and the manners, but even of the language of Scotland. He was in fact more French than Scotch. His mother was a Frenchwoman, and so was his wife. His chief estates were in France, where the greater part of his life had been spent, and his loyalty to the

French king was so undisguised that he constantly styled him master. When it is added to this that his temper was passionate, that every corner of the kingdom was filled with spies and agents in the pay of England, and that the powerful houses of Home and Douglas swayed the faction that were opposed to him, it was hardly to be expected that he would be successful in restoring peace to the country. The infant king and his brother were still under the care of the queen-mother; and a parliament which assembled at Edinburgh, nominated eight lords, four of whom were to be chosen by lot, and from these four the queen-mother was to select three who were to have the charge of the two infant princes. The queen, however, was not disposed to part with her children, and when the peers proceeded to the castle of Edinburgh, to notify to her the commands of parliament, her majesty, who was then no more than twenty-four years of age, and in the full bloom of her beauty, was seen standing under the archway at the entrance, with the little king at her side, holding her hand, while a nurse stood behind with his infant brother, the duke of Ross, in her arms. In a loud voice, and with a dignified air, she desired them to stand and declare what they wanted. They answered that they came in the name of the parliament to receive their sovereign and his brother, on which the queen commanded the warder to drop the portcullis, and this being instantly done, she thus addressed the astonished lords: "I hold this castle by the gift of my late husband, your sovereign, nor shall I yield it to any person whatsoever; but I respect the parliament, and require six days to consider their mandate, for most important is my charge; and my councillors, alas! are now few." Apprehensive, however, that she would not be able to hold the castle of Edinburgh against the forces of the parliament, she soon removed, with the young king and his brother, to Stirling castle. Albany immediately collected an armed force, and proceeded in person to Stirling, where the queen finding her adherents deserting her, was soon obliged to surrender. The young princes were then committed to the care of the earl Marshal and the lords Fleming and Borthwick, while the queen was conducted with every mark of respect to Ed-

inburgh, where she took up her residence in the castle. On the success of the regent, Lord Home, one of the queen's principal adherents, at once commenced to intrigue with England, and concerted measures with Lord Dacre, the English warden, of resistance and revenge. Albany summoned the whole force of the kingdom to the aid of the government, and transmitted proposals to the queen-mother, offering her a complete restoration of all the rights and revenues which she had not forfeited by her marriage, if she would accede to the wishes of the parliament, and renounce all secret correspondence with England. These proposals she indignantly rejected, whereupon Albany proceeded against the insurgents, and took the castle of Home. The queen sent Albany's proposals privately to Lord Dacre, while Home requested the assistance of an English army, and retook the castle of Home. He also secured the strong tower of Blackater, situated within the Scottish border, about five miles from Berwick, to which place the queen immediately fled. The regent followed her with a considerable army, and surprising Home in the house to which he had hastened for refuge, made him prisoner, and committed him to the custody of the earl of Arran, governor of the castle of Edinburgh. Arran disliked Albany and his measures, and was easily persuaded by Home to retire with him to the Borders, where they actively commenced hostilities. Home and his brother were again proclaimed rebels, and Arran was required to surrender himself within fifteen days. At the same time the regent, at the head of a select body of troops, and a small train of artillery, proceeded to invest the castle of Cadzow, near Hamilton, Arran's principal fortress. Arran's mother, who was the daughter of James the Second, at that time resided there, and ordering the gates to be opened, she came out to meet the regent, and as she was his aunt by the father's side, and greatly respected by him, he was easily prevailed upon to listen to her solicitations in favour of her son. Terms of accommodation were soon agreed to, and Arran was allowed to return and resume possession of his estates.

In the meantime Home had fled to England, whither he was soon followed by the queen and her husband Angus. Negotiations for peace between the two countries were set on foot, and Angus, to whom the queen had recently, at Harbottle castle in England, borne a daughter, the Lady Margaret Douglas, the mother of Darnley, husband of Mary Queen of Scots, withdrew from his wife, who lay dangerously ill at Morpeth, and with Home returned into Scotland. They both made their peace with the regent, who restored them to their hereditary possessions, and for a time they abstained from disturbing the government. Queen Margaret on her recovery proceeded to the court of her brother Henry VIII., where she inveighed bitterly against both Angus and Albany, but especially the latter, whom she accused of having poisoned her second son, the duke of Ross, who had died, at Stirling, of one of the many diseases incident to childhood. Henry, anxious to have Arran regent, directed a letter to be written to the three estates of Scotland, commanding them to expel the regent Albany from the kingdom, as, from his being the nearest heir of the throne, he was the most dangerous person to have the charge of the young king, his nephew. The Scottish parliament, which assembled at Edinburgh on the first of July 1516, replied with becoming spirit. They reminded the English king that they themselves had elected Albany to the office of regent, to which he had a right as nearest relative to their infant king, that he had fulfilled its duties with much talent and integrity, and that the person of their infant sovereign was intrusted to the keeping of the same lords to whose care he had been committed by the queen-mother. They concluded by assuring Henry of their determination to resist to the death any attempt to disturb the peace of their country, or to overthrow the existing government. Notwithstanding this spirited reply, the intrigues of Henry's minister, Lord Dacre, soon succeeded in creating distrust and disturbance, and once more reinstating in its strength the English faction in Scotland. On the 23d August Dacre wrote from Kirkoswald to Cardinal Wolsey, informing him that he had in his pay four hundred Scots, whose chief employment was to distract the government of Albany, by exciting popular tumults, encouraging private quarrels, and rekindling the jealousy of the feudal nobility. In Scotland at this time Albany's administration was

rather popular than otherwise. He was "supported," says Tytler, "by the affection and confidence of the middle classes, and the great body of the nation; but their influence was counteracted, and his efforts completely paralysed by the selfish rapacity of the clergy, and the insolent ambition of the aristocracy." A new insurrection soon broke out, headed by the earl of Arran, who associated himself with the earls of Glencairn, Lennox, Mure of Caldwell, and the majority of the noblemen and gentlemen of the west. They met at Glasgow to the number of 12,000 men, and seized on the royal magazines there. Understanding that some French ships, with supplies of arms and ammunition for Albany, had appeared in the Clyde, they sent a body of troops to take possession of them. The vessels, however, had sailed before their arrival, but they seized a quantity of gunpowder and other ammunition which had been landed, and which they conveyed to Glasgow. Lest it might fall into the hands of their enemies the powder was thrown into a drawwell. By a stratagem Arran made himself master of the castle of Dumbarton, and expelled Lord Erskine the governor. In the meantime the regent having collected an army, advanced upon Glasgow, when an accommodation was once more brought about, chiefly through the means of Beaton, archbishop of Glasgow, who was high in favour with the regent. The earl of Home on his part soon violated the conditions on which the regent had consented to pardon him. He renewed his treasonable correspondence with Dacre, and employed bands of marauders to break across the border and ravage the country. Determined to put an end to the anarchy created by the rebellious proceedings of this fierce opposer of his government, the regent allured the earl, who held the office of lord chamberlain, and his brother Alexander, to the court at Holyrood, where they were instantly arrested. They were immediately tried, on a charge of treason, for having excited the late commotions against the regent, of having been accessory to the defeat at Flodden, and being concerned in the assassination of James IV. after the battle. Being found guilty, they were both beheaded, on the 8th of October 1516, and their heads placed above the tolbooth of Edinburgh. Soon after the duke of Albany, in a convention of the estates of the realm held at Edinburgh, was declared heir apparent to the crown.

Anxious to procure assistance from the French king. and to revisit his estates in France, the regent, in the parliament which assembled in November 1516, requested leave of absence for a short period. The parliament accorded an unwilling consent for four months, and in June 1517 he embarked at Dumbarton, leaving the government in the hands of a council, consisting of the archbishops of St. Andrews and Glasgow, the earls of Huntly, Argyle, Angus, and Arran, and carrying with him the eldest sons of many of the great barons as hostages for the peace of the country. To each of the six persons mentioned was assigned the charge of that part of the country contiguous to his own estates, while to a brave and accomplished French knight, whose real name was Anthony D'Arcie, but whose handsome person procured for him the distinguishing title of Seigneur de la Beauté (absurdly called de la Bastie in all our histories) was intrusted the government of the eastern and middle marches, with the command of the important castles of Home and Dunbar. The young king was brought from Stirling to Edinburgh castle, and placed under the charge of Lord Erskine, the earl Marshal, and the lords Borthwick and Ruthven. Fresh tumults broke out on the borders, and the vassals of the late Lord Home, out of revenge at his fate, surprised and murdered the Sieur de la Beauté, who had distinguished himself by the activity and diligence with which he punished and repressed disorder. Sir David Home of Wedderburn, whose wife was the sister of Angus, the husband of the queen-mother, galloped into the town of Dunse, with the head of the unfortunate Frenchman knit to his saddlebow, by the fine long hair which he wore in accordance with the fashion of the age, and after fixing it on the market-cross, took shelter in his strong castle of Edington, on the banks of the Whiteadder. For this outrage the estates of the laird of Wedderburn and his associates were forfeited.

After this the kingdom became a scene of disorder, anarchy, and confusion, the rival factions of Douglas and Hamilton everywhere contending for the mastery. The earl of Arran had been elected by the council of regency their president, and at this time had the chief direction of affairs, but he was, upon all occasions, opposed by the earl of Angus, who still had great influence, and the private animosity which subsisted between these two powerful noblemen kept the country in a continual state of excitement and disturbance. As soon as the queen-mother heard of Albany's departure, she returned to Scotland. Her arrival was at a time of such universal confusion and strife that even Albany himself, unwilling to leave France, wrote to her, advising her that, if she could unite the factions, she should resume the regency. Margaret, however, wished to have the office of regent conferred on her husband, the earl of Angus, to whom she had been lately reconciled, but this neither the council nor the majority of the nobles would agree to. Her jealousy, however, soon caused a fresh quarrel with her husband, and as her brother Henry VIII. took the part of Angus, she forsook the English interests, and entered into a correspondence with the duke of Albany, urging him to return and take the regency once more into his own hands. During Albany's absence the famous street battle at Edinburgh, between the rival factions of the Douglasses and the Hamiltons, commemorated under the name of "Cleanse-the-Causeway," was fought 30th April 1520, the result of which was that the Hamiltons were defeated, and the earl of Angus got possession of the capital.

The next year Albany returned to Scotland after an absence of five years. He arrived in the Gaerloch on the third of December 1521, and was met at Stirling by the queen-mother, accompanied by several lords and gentlemen. It is stated that Margaret, who was very changeable in her affections, and by no means careful of her conduct, received him with transports of joy, and with such familiarity as excited scandalous rumours. Lord Dacre, in a letter to his sovereign, King Henry, says that, not satisfied with being with him during the day, she was closeted the greater part of the night with Albany, taking no heed of appearances. The earl of Arran and others of the nobility hastened to Stirling to welcome his arrival, and on the 9th he entered the capital, accompanied by the queen and the chancellor and a numerous attendance of peers and gentlemen. Proceeding to the castle, he was admitted to an interview with the young king, on which occasion the captain delivered the keys of the fortress into his hands. These the regent laid at the feet of the queen-mother, and she again presented them to Albany, saying that she considered him the person to whose tried fidelity the care of the monarch ought to be intrusted. On the regent's approach the earl of Angus and his party precipitately left the city, and fled to the Border. In a parliament held at Edinburgh, on the 26th day of December, Angus and his adherents were cited to appear before it, to answer for various crimes and misdemeanours, but they paid no attention to the summons, and had already renewed their negotiations with the English king. The regent now endeavoured to reconcile the factions, and to procure a peace with England. But it did not suit the ambitious projects of the English court that Albany should continue at the head of affairs, or that peace and order should be restored to Scotland. Lord Dacre, Henry's unscrupulous agent, in the letters which he wrote to Henry, represented that the life of the young king was in danger, and that his mother was anxious to obtain a divorce from Angus, that she might marry Albany, who, on his nephew's death, would become king. He distributed money among the factious nobles, and did every thing that he could to stir up war between the two countries. Henry, on his part, as he had done once before, addressed a letter to the Scottish estates, demanding the dismissal of Albany, and received a similar answer to the former, being sharply told by the Scottish parliament that they had themselves freely chosen Albany to the regency, and would not dismiss him at the request of his grace, the king of England, or of any other sovereign prince whatever. Upon this Henry, in the spring of 1522, sent the earl of Shrewsbury with a large force to invade Scotland. He advanced as far as Kelso, giving up the country everywhere to havoc and spoliation, until he was encountered and driven back into England, with considerable loss, by the bold borderers of Teviotdale and the Merse. Albany having, with consent of parliament, declared war, and mustered the whole force of the kingdom for an invasion of

England, at the head of eighty thousand men, and with a formidable train of artillery, advanced towards the English borders, and encamped at Annan. The queen-mother at this time, with her characteristic fickleness, had cooled in her attachment to the regent, and not only intrigued with a party of the Scottish nobles to support her views, but betrayed all Albany's secrets and plans to the English warden, Lord Dacre. The regent, ignorant of this, with his large army crossed the borders and advanced to Carlisle. When within five miles of that city Dacre opened negotiations with him, and succeeded in prevailing upon him to agree to a cessation of hostilities for a month, in order that ambassadors might treat for peace. As the English king, then engaged in a war with France, had wisely departed from his demand for Albany's dismissal from the regency, the nobles who had joined in the expedition saw no further cause for continuing in arms, and Albany himself, desirous of peace with England, disbanded his army, and returned to Edinburgh, without striking a blow.

Finding the difficulties of his situation increase, with the view of soliciting assistance from the French king, Albany, in October 1522, retired for the second time to France, after appointing a council of regency, consisting of the earls of Huntly, Arran, and Argyle, to whom he added Gonzolles, a French knight, in whom he had much confidence. He promised to return in ten months on pain of forfeiting his office. During his absence, in the spring of 1523, the English renewed the war by a vast inroad into Scotland. The earl of Surrey, the victor of Flodden, at the head of 10,000 men, broke into the Merse, reduced its places of strength, and advancing to Jedburgh, burnt that town, and left its beautiful abbey a heap of ruins. Lord Dacre, after reducing the castle of Ker of Fernihurst, and taking that celebrated border chief prisoner, sacked and depopulated Kelso and the adjoining villages, while the marquis of Dorset, the warden of the east marches, made an incursion into Teviotdale, giving its villages to the flames, and carrying off its grain and beeves. Albany returned from France in September 1523, with a fleet of eighty-seven small vessels, and a force of four thousand foot, five hun-

D

dred men at arms, a thousand hagbutteers, six hundred horse, and a fine train of artillery, which had been furnished to him by the French. He landed in the island of Arran, Balfour says " at Kerkubright," having eluded the enemy's fleet, which was sent out to intercept him, and immediately proceeded to Edinburgh. The embarrassment of his position at this crisis was greater than ever. He found that the queen-mother was no longer on his side, but deeply engaged in intriguing against him. That fickle, passionate, and unprincipled woman, whose character somewhat resembled that of her imperious brother, Henry VIII., was now as anxious to promote the English interests as she had formerly been the French, and had entered into negotiations with Surrey and Dacre, with the view of recovering the regency to herself. The nobles, though willing to assemble an army for the defence of the Borders, were totally averse to an invasion of England, while they were jealous of the foreign auxiliaries which the regent had brought with him.

The parliament assembled without delay, and a proclamation was issued for a muster of the whole force of the kingdom on the 20th of October. Albany summoned together the principal nobility, and urged them to carry the war into England, to avenge the disastrous defeat at Flodden and the late excesses on the Borders. He had brought with him a large supply of gold from France, and as he liberally dispensed it, he won over some of the more venal of the nobles, and even the queen herself was so charmed by his presents, that she wrote to the earl of Surrey, that unless her brother Henry remitted her more money, she might be induced to abandon the English interest, and co-operate with Albany. On the day appointed a force of about 40,000 men assembled on the Borough-muir near Edinburgh, at the head of which the regent set forward towards the Borders. But never had general commenced an aggressive march under such discouraging circumstances. Most of the leaders who had answered the summons to arm had taken the gold of England, and bound themselves not to cross the Borders, while others, such as Argyle, Huntly, and the master of Forbes, did not appear at all at the muster. The expedition was nationally unpopular, and as the Scots

soldiers did not conceal their dislike of the foreign auxiliaries, indications of disorganization soon became but too evident. Added to this, the season was now far advanced, and much time was lost in dragging the cumbersome artillery over the rude and difficult roads of those days, which had been rendered still more wretched by recent falls of snow and rain. Albany arrived at Melrose on the 28th of October. When he reached the wooden bridge at that place, a large portion of his army refused to cross the Tweed, and those divisions of the troops which had already passed over, turned back, and in spite of all his entreaties and reproaches, recrossed the bridge to the Scottish side. The regent remained in the neighbourhood of Melrose two days, after which he marched down the Tweed, and arrived at Eccles, on the side of the river opposite to Wark. The Scottish army encamped near Coldstream, while Albany lodged in Home castle. He ordered part of the artillery to be conveyed to Berwick, but afterwards he laid siege to Wark castle, chiefly with his foreign troops and artillery. The historian, George Buchanan, who was a volunteer in his army, gives a highly valuable account of his operations in this his last campaign in Scotland. An attempt to storm the castle was bravely met by the garrison, who poured a destructive fire from the ramparts upon the besiegers, and on the approach of night, the latter were compelled to retire. It was proposed, however, to renew the assault next day, but during the night there was a heavy fall of rain and snow, which so flooded the river that all retreat was threatened to be cut off. It was known that the Earl of Surrey was advancing from Alnwick with a formidable force. Under these circumstances Albany, on the 4th of November, withdrew his artillery, and the assaulting party recrossed the Tweed, leaving three hundred killed, mostly Frenchmen, and once more joined the main army. Balfour says that with the latter portion of his troops he had spoiled all Glendale and Northumberland to the walls of Alnwick, and returned with a great booty. [*Annals*, vol. i, page 252.] The regent retired to Eccles, and thence marched rapidly towards Edinburgh, apprehensive all the way of being seized by some of the lords with him, and delivered up to the English.

His retreat had all the appearance of a flight, the disorder of which was increased by a severe snowstorm. On reaching Edinburgh, he assembled a parliament, and ascribed the failure of the expedition to the nobles refusing to march into England, while they, on their part, accused him of being the cause of the disgrace. Notwithstanding the presence of the English army, under Surrey, on the Borders, and the inclemency of the season, some of the peers insisted on his instantly dismissing the foreign auxiliaries. Thus compelled to embark, the French were by a storm driven out of their course, and a considerable number of them were shipwrecked and drowned among the western Isles. Soon after, having obtained three months' leave of absence, Albany, in the end of 1523, retired in disgust and despair to France, after taking an affectionate leave of the young king, then at Stirling, and returned no more to Scotland.

He afterwards, in 1524, attended Francis I. in his unfortunate expedition into Italy; but before the fatal battle of Pavia, fought 24th February 1525, he was detached with part of the French army against Naples. It was the absence of this large portion of his troops, amounting to 16,000 men, which caused Francis to lose the battle, when attacked by the emperor Charles. In 1533 Albany conducted his wife's niece, Catherine de Medici, into France, on her marriage with Henry II. of that kingdom. He was governor of the Bourbonnois, d'Auvergne, de Forest, and de Beaujolais. He died at his castle of Mirefleur, 2d June 1536. By his duchess he had no issue. By Jean Abernethy, a Scotswoman, he had a natural daughter, Eleonora, who, after being legitimated, was in 1547 married at Fontainebleau, in presence of the French king, to the count de Choisy.

This duke of Albany was a man of elegant and graceful manners and high accomplishments, and very gay and sprightly in conversation,—qualities which made him a personal favourite with Francis I. of France, but were little appreciated in Scotland, where his vanity, of which he had a large share, and evident partiality for French officers and confidents, soon disgusted the haughty and rapacious nobility. In Pinkerton's Scottish Gallery, there is a fine portrait, supposed to be that of Albany, of which a woodcut is annexed. It is on the same engraving with one of Queen Margaret

The sign manual autograph "Jehan" underneath, is from the Cotton MSS. B. vi. fol. 170, in the British Museum.

The title of duke of Albany was bestowed in 1540 on Arthur, second son of James V. and his spouse Mary of Guise, a prince who died in 1541. It was afterwards given to Henry Stewart, lord Darnley, or Dernely, by Queen Mary, shortly before their marriage in 1565. Charles I. was created duke of Albany, on his baptism at Dunfermline in 1600, his elder brother Henry, who died in 1612, being duke of Rothesay, the title of the king's eldest son. The following is a fac simile of the autograph and motto of this ill-fated prince, written in an album in the Sloane MSS. No. 3415, as duke of Albany, in 1609, before he had completed the ninth year of his age:

Albany king at arms was one of the secondary heralds in Scotland, when Scotland was an independent kingdom. Prince Charles Edward Stuart, in the latter years of his life, styled himself count of Albany.

ALES, or ALESSE, ALEXANDER, see HAILES, Alexander.

ALEXANDER I., king of Scotland, surnamed the Fierce, from his vigour and impetuous character, has hitherto been represented as the fifth son of Malcolm III., surnamed Canmore, or great head, by

Margaret, daughter of Edward, nephew of Edward the Confessor, king of England, but it is now admitted that Ethelred, who had been believed to be the third, was the youngest son of that marriage, and consequently Alexander was not the fifth but the fourth son of Malcolm and Margaret. It is also placed beyond a doubt that by a previous marriage with Ingibiorge, the widow of Thorfin, a powerful Norwegian earl,—who for thirty years, during the reigns of Alexander's father Malcolm and his predecessor Macbeth, ruled over all Scotland north of the Grampians, and part of the present county of Forfar,—Malcolm had two sons, Duncan, afterwards king of Scotland, and Malcolm, both of whom were alive at the time of his death, so that Alexander was in reality the sixth of the sons of Malcolm Canmore. [See life of Duncan, king of Scotland, *post*.] There is no earlier instance in Scottish history of the name of Alexander having been borne by king or noble, although it afterwards became one of the most common and familiar Christian names in Scotland. Lord Hailes has supposed that it was bestowed in honour of Pope Alexander II. If so, it was given to him after the death of that pontiff, which occurred in the year 1073, as no calculation from family or other events can place the birth of Alexander, of which the precise date is unknown, earlier than about the year 1078.

Alexander was educated with great care, not only in letters but in religious principles, and the solemn injunctions of his excellent mother, on her death-bed, to Turgot, prior of Durham, her confessor and biographer, which have descended to us in his interesting memoir of that good queen, prove how great was her solicitude in the latter respect in regard to all her children. Alexander partook of those vicissitudes of the family, after the death of his father, which are detailed in the lives of his uncle Donald Bane and of his brothers Duncan and Edgar, and which serve to exhibit, in a strong light, the peculiarities of the law of succession to the throne among the Celtic or Pictish races of that age, and they no doubt contributed to form and give a direction to his character and future government, when he became king.

On the death of his brother Edgar, 8th January 1107, Alexander succeeded to the throne, but not to the enjoyment of the same extent of possessions as his predecessor. For the conquest of the *western* portion of the ancient principality of *Cumbria* —a region extending between the Roman walls of Agricola and Antoninus—having sometime previously been effected, by David his younger brother, with an army of Norman chivalry from England, the government of the province was also bestowed upon him, and Edgar, on his death-bed, bequeathed him all those extensive lands in those regions held by him and Malcolm his father which formed the subject of that homage rendered to the Norman conqueror and his son William Rufus so frequently referred to in English history. [*Lord Hailes' Quotations* from English contemporary writers, compared with the narrative of the inquisition into the lands of the see of Glasgow, and existing charters of that epoch.] All Scottish historians, from the fourteenth until within the present century, have concurred in stating that the province of Cumbria corresponded exactly in territory with the present English county of Cumberland, but charters, and Saxon as well as earlier Scottish writers, when correctly understood, leave it beyond doubt that the portion of country so called comprehended the district extending from the Clyde to the Solway, and included all the present Scottish counties of Ayr, Galloway, Wigton, Kirkcudbright, and Dumfries, with perhaps part of Cumberland; the district of Lothian, comprising the three counties which still bear that name; and the shires of Renfrew and Lanark, with part of Lennox now Dumbartonshire. Such distributions of the royal possessions amongst the members of their family were not uncommon with the monarchs of that age.

Whatever were the motives that led to this disjunction from the Scottish crown, it proved a fortunate arrangement for the nation. By the subsequent death of Alexander without issue, and the consequent succession of David to the *northern* throne, the danger of contention between rival families for these possessions, and of their permanent separation from the ancient kingdom, was averted, and a united kingdom was afterwards formed, able, with more or less success, to withstand the powerful neighbouring southern state; which, if it had continued disjoined, would most probably have fallen to it by piecemeal a comparatively easy prey. While, on the one hand, the happy genius of David for government, and for attracting towards himself the love and affection of all classes of people committed to his care, enabled him to introduce amongst them order and civilization, and to combine Saxon law with Norman refinement, as well as the still higher blessing of religious instruction, and while his amiable qualities and the accident of his birth endeared through him the family of Malcolm to the Saxon race, so that nearly four hundred years afterwards an English writer resident in Scotland thus commemorates one of them:

> " Our soverane of Scotland . .
> Quhilk sall be lord and ledar
> Oer broad Brettane all quhair
> As saint Mergarettes air;"
> [Buke of the Howlat, st. xxix, printed for
> the Bannatyne Club.]

the sterner rule of Alexander was made available to keep under the dissatisfied feelings of the warlike tribes of the north, not less averse to that deviation from the ancient rule of succession by which the descendants of Margaret were placed on the throne, than jealous of the innovations of Saxon law and Saxon settlements. It was not, however, to be expected that to this disposition of lands Alexander would at once quietly accede. On the contrary, he at first disputed its validity, and would willingly have annulled it, had he not found that the powerful barons of the province in question, and of the northern English counties, as Gospatrick, Baliol, Bruce, Lindesay, Areskine, and others, whose descendants afterwards occupied the first rank among the Scottish nobility, and by the aid of whose arms his brother Edgar had been placed and sustained on the throne, were entirely favourable to this arrangement. He therefore prudently desisted from the attempt, and confined himself during the remainder of his reign to the northern portion of the kingdom. [Speech of Walter l'Espec at the battle of the Standard, in Ældred.] It has been inferred by modern writers who have recognised the foregoing as the territorial limits of Cumbria, that David held this government as a fief in sub-

ordination to Alexander, but this does not appear to have been the case. David seems to have regulated the affairs of his government as an independent prince. The motto of his seal during his brother's lifetime bears that he styled himself 'David, Comites Anglorum Regene Fratris, (contracted into Frīs); that is, David the count, brother of the Queen of the English. Annexed is a representation of David's seal:

Several of his public instruments, too, after he ascended the throne, when relating to matters affecting the southern districts, are addressed to the " Francis et Anglicis," Normans and English, [Anderson's Diplomata et Numismata, No. 17, 1 and 2]; and at a later period, or when referring to matters of more importance, to the " Francis et Anglicis, et Scottis et Galwensibus," that is, the Normans, English, Scotch, and Galwegians, which latter style was uniformly adopted by his successor and grandson Malcolm IV., [Idem, plates 19, 23, 25,] whilst the public instruments of Alexander are simply addressed to the Scots and English, " Scottis et Anglis " [Idem, page 9], showing that he only ruled over the northern portion of the kingdom in which these nations lived in the proportion of the order in which they are placed.

It was fortunate both for Alexander and David, and for the tranquillity of the government of the former, that during the entire period of his reign an unbroken peace was maintained with England. The marriage of their sister Matildis in 1100, during the life of their brother Edgar, with Henry king of England the brother of William Rufus, greatly facilitated this harmony, and it was further cemented by the union of Alexander with Sybilla, natural daughter of that monarch. Such an alliance, says Lord Hailes, was not held dishonourable in those days.

The people of the north were not reconciled to the sovereignty of the sons of Malcolm. According to their notions of the law of succession to the throne, both the family of Donald Bane, and that of Duncan the eldest son of Malcolm, had a prior right to it. Edgar had bestowed upon his cousin Madach, son of Donald Bane, the maormordom of Athol, erected by him into an earldom, and on his death, towards the end of the reign of David the First, it was obtained by Malcolm, the son of Duncan, the eldest son of Malcolm Canmore, "either," says Skene, "because the exclusion of that family from the throne could not deprive them of the original patrimony of the family, or as a compensation for the loss of the crown," [Skene's Highlanders, vol. ii. p. 139,] and thus this branch of the rival family were induced to remain in quiet, although various attempts were afterwards made to recover their rights, not only in the reign of Malcolm IV., but for nearly a hundred years after they were excluded from it.

The descendants of Donald Bane appear to have enjoyed another portion of the hereditary possessions of the family in the person of Ladman his son, and along with them some title which does not appear. Even the descendants of Macbeth seem, in the person of Angus the son of the daughter of Lulach, Macbeth's nephew, to have got the possessions and ancient maormordom of Moray erected into an earldom of that name. [Skene's Highlanders, vol. ii. p. 162.] According to the Annals of Ulster about 1116, a descendant of Malpedir, maormor of Moern or Garmoran, a district in northern Inverness-shire, one of the supporters of Donald Bane, and who had murdered Duncan, eldest son of Malcolm, in 1095, was in possession of his father's title and lands, and at the instigation of Ladman, in order probably to revenge his death, he combined with Angus earl of Moray, already referred to as of the family of Macbeth, to make an attempt to seize upon the person of Alexander. At his baptism Alexander had a donation

made to him of the lands of Blairgowrie and Liff by his godfather, Donald Bane, then probably maormor of Athol, and in the first year of his reign he began to build a palace or residence in the vicinity; but while engaged on this work the Highlanders of Moern (not Mearns, as commonly supposed) and Moray penetrated stealthily from their northern abodes to Invergowrie, where Alexander was, and surprised him by night. Alexander escaped to the shore, and crossing over the Tay to Fife, collected vassals, and followed them with surprising activity, through the 'Monthe' or Grampians, across the Spey and over the "Stockfurd into Ros." Of this passage Wintoun says,

> "He tuk and slew thame or he past
> Out of that land, that fewe he left
> To take on hand swylk purpose eft."

And again he adds,

> "Fra that day hys legys all
> Oysid hym Alysandyr the Fers to call."

So effectually, indeed, did he succeed in crushing the inhabitants of Moray that they were compelled to put to death Ladman, the son of Donald Bane, who had instigated them to the attempt on his life. [Skene's Highlanders, vol. i. p. 130.] The story that on this occasion the traitors obtained admission to the king's bed-chamber, and that he slew six of them with his own hand, is an invention of Boece, and like many other of his fables has obtained currency in Scottish history. Sir James Balfour, in his Annals [vol. i. pp. 6, 7.], has the following passage on this attempt against the king: "The rebells quho besett him in the night had doubtesley killed him, had not Alexander Carrone priuly carried the king save away, and by a small boate saived themselves to Fyffe, and the south pairts of the kingdome, quher he raissed ane armey, and marched against the forsaid rebells, quhome he totally ouerthrew and subdued; for wich grate mercey and preseruatione, in a thankfull retributione to God, he foundit the monastarey of Scone, and too it gaue hes first lands of Liffe and Innergourey, in A° 1114. About this tyme K. Alexander the I. reuardit for hes faithfull seruice Alexander Carrone, with the office of standart bearir of Scotland, to him and hes heirs for euer. He was called Scrimshour, becausse with a drauen suord, in a combat, he had strucke the hand from a courtier; wich surname of Scrinscoure, hes posterity to this day have kept." The name signifies a hardy fighter. See SCRIMGEOUR, surname of; also, DUNDEE, earl of.

During the remainder of the reign of Alexander, the Highlanders acquiesced in his occupation of the throne, he being now, even according to the Celtic laws, the legitimate heir of Malcolm Canmore.

The principal feature in Alexander's reign was his successful resistance to the efforts made by the English prelates to assert a supremacy over the church in Scotland. In 1109 when he first had occasion to nominate a bishop to the see of St. Andrews, to which place the primacy had been removed from Dunkeld, Alexander, with the approbation of his clergy and people, named Turgot, the monk of Durham already mentioned as the confessor and biographer of his mother the pious Queen Margaret. The consecration of Turgot was, however, long delayed. The archbishop of York pretended a right of consecrating the bishops of St. Andrews, but at this time Thomas, elected archbishop of York, had not himself received consecration. In consequence of a report that the bishop of Durham, concurring with the Scottish bishops and the bishop of the Orkneys, proposed to consecrate Turgot, in presence of the archbishop elect of York, Anselm, archbishop of Canterbury, in alarm, despatched a letter to the latter, informing him that consecration could not be performed by an archbishop elect or by any one acting under his authority, and requiring him to proceed to Canterbury to receive consecration himself. The Scottish clergy on their part contended that the archbishop of York had no right to interfere in the consecration of a bishop to the see of St. Andrews. While the two archbishops were engaged in mutual altercations concerning canonical order and the privileges of their respective sees, Alexander entered into a negotiation with the English king, and an immediate decision of the controversy was evaded by an ambiguous acknowledgment by all parties, which, confessing the independency of the Scottish church to be at least doubtful, seemed to prepare the way for its complete vindication at a future time. At the request of Alexander, Henry, the English king, enjoined the archbishop of York to consecrate Turgot, bishop of St. Andrews, "saving the authority of either church." In that form Turgot received consecration accordingly.

In the discharge of his episcopal functions Turgot met with obstacles, which induced him to form a resolution to repair to Rome to obtain the opinion of the pope for regulating his future conduct; a journey which his death soon after prevented him from carrying into effect. What the nature of these obstacles were, we are not informed, but as he perceived that he had lost that influence which he formerly enjoyed in the time of Queen Margaret, his spirit sunk, and in a desponding mood he asked and obtained permission to retire to his ancient cell at Durham, where he died, 31st August 1115.

A new bishop of St. Andrews was to be appointed, and to avoid any interference on the part of the archbishop of York, Alexander, soon after the death of Turgot, addressed a confidential letter to Ralph archbishop of Canterbury, who had succeeded Anselm, asking his advice and assistance for enabling him to provide a fit successor to Turgot. In this letter he observed, "That the bishops of St. Andrews were wont to be consecrated only by the Pope or by the archbishop of Canterbury." "The expression," says Lord Hailes "is flattering and artful. Alexander meant to relieve his kingdom from the pretensions of the one archbishop without acknowledging the authority of the other. He therefore left the right of consecrating doubtful between the Pope and the archbishop of Canterbury, while, at the same time, he seemed to place them both on a level." Eadmer, a monk of Canterbury, had been fixed upon by Alexander to fill the vacant see, but not receiving any answer to his proposal from the archbishop of Canterbury, the king allowed the see of St. Andrews, the chief bishopric in his kingdom, to remain vacant for many years. At length, in 1120, he despatched a special messenger to the archbishop of Canterbury, with a letter requesting the archbishop ' to set at liberty' Eadmer the monk, that he might be placed on the episcopal throne of St. Andrews. The archbishop consented that Eadmer should have liberty to accept the bishopric, and with that view he asked and obtained the approbation of the English king. In a letter to Alexander he said, "I send you the person whom you require *altogether free*," and concluded thus, "To prevent the inconveniencies which I foresee and dread, I would counsel you immediately to send him back to be consecrated by me." On his arrival in Scotland, Eadmer received the bishopric of St. Andrews on the 29th of June 1120. The election was made by the clergy and people, with the permission of the king; but on this occasion Eadmer neither received the pastoral staff nor the ring from the hands of Alexander, nor did he perform homage. Next day Alexander held a secret conference with him respecting the mode of his consecration, when the king expressed his aversion at his being consecrated by the archbishop of York. Eadmer, on his part, declared that the church of Canterbury had, by ancient right, a pre-eminence over all Britain, and he humbly proposed to receive consecration from that metropolitan see. He found, however, that Alexander was as much opposed to the pretensions of Canterbury as he was to those of York, and that he had determined to free the Scottish church from dependence on any foreign see but that of Rome. At Eadmer's proposal Alexander is described as having started from his seat with much emotion, and broken off the conference. He commanded the person, one William a monk of St. Edmundsbury, who had presided in the bishopric since the death of Turgot, to resume his functions. At the expiry of a month, the king, at the request of his nobility, sent for Eadmer, and with difficulty obtained his consent to a compromise, by which Eadmer was to receive the ring from Alexander, to take the pastoral staff from off the altar, as if receiving it of the Lord, and then to assume the charge of his diocese. While the king was absent with his army quelling some insurrection in the north, as the Highlanders of the district of Moray, particularly at this time, gave considerable opposition to his government, Eadmer was received into the see of St. Andrews by the queen, clergy, and people.

Finding, however, that his own sovereign Henry, who was then in Normandy, had, at the solicitation of the archbishop of York, written to the archbishop of Canterbury prohibiting him from con-

secrating Eadmer, and that Alexander had also received three letters from him requiring him not to permit the consecration, the new bishop of St. Andrews resolved to repair to Canterbury for advice. On hearing of his resolution Alexander sent for him, and said, "I received you altogether free from Canterbury; while I live, I will not permit the bishop of St. Andrews to be subjected to that see." "For your whole kingdom," answered Eadmer, "I would not renounce the dignity of a monk of Canterbury." "Then," replied the king passionately, "I have done nothing in seeking a bishop out of Canterbury." It seems to have been Alexander's design by soliciting a bishop from the province of Canterbury, to obtain one who would have no partiality for the see of York, and whom he hoped to win over to support the independency of the Scottish Church; but the zeal of Eadmer for Canterbury disappointed his views. Eadmer himself has given an ample account of the contest between him and Alexander; and Lord Hailes, in his Annals of Scotland, has generally followed his statements. The bishop complains that after the last interview with the king, the latter became rigorous and unjust, and would never afford him a patient hearing. He refused to allow Eadmer permission to visit Canterbury "for the counsel and blessing (meaning no doubt consecration) of the archbishop," contending that the church of Scotland owed no subjection to Canterbury, and that Eadmer himself had been freed from all subjection to it.

In the anomalous and uncomfortable position in which he found himself, Eadmer was induced to ask the advice of a friend in England, one Nicholas, whom Lord Hailes conjectures to have been an ecclesiastical agent, whose business it was to solicit causes at the court of Rome. This man advised him to obtain consecration from the Pope, under favour of the Scottish monarch, and in the meantime to be generous and hospitable to the Scots, as the best means of rendering them tractable and courteous. He concluded his letter thus: "I entreat you to let me have as many of the fairest pearls as you can procure. In particular, I desire four of the largest sort. If you cannot procure them otherwise, ask them in a present from the king, who, I know, has a most abundant store"—a remarkable evidence of the wealth and magnificence of the Scottish monarchs at this time.

Eadmer, in his perplexity, also asked the advice of John bishop of Glasgow, and of two monks of Canterbury, and the answer which they sent to him seems to have determined him upon resigning the see. It was in these terms: "If, as a son of peace, you desire peace, you must seek it elsewhere than in Scotland. As long as Alexander reigns, it will be vain for you to expect any friendly intercourse with him, or quiet under his government. We are thoroughly acquainted with his dispositions: it is his will to be everything himself in his own kingdom. He is incensed against you, although he knows no reason for his resentment; and he will never be perfectly reconciled to you, although he should see reason for a reconciliation. You must, therefore, either abandon this country, or, by accommodating yourself to its usages, dishonour your character and hazard your salvation. Should you choose to depart from among us, you will be constrained to restore the ring, which you received from the hands of the king, and the pastoral staff which you took from off the altar. Without complying with these conditions you will not be permitted to depart, unless you could make to yourself wings and fly away." Eadmer consented to restore the ring to Alexander, but with regard to the pastoral staff, he declared that he would replace it on the altar, whence he had taken it, 'and leave it to be bestowed by Christ,' and that since force had been used against him, he would relinquish the bishopric, and not reclaim it during the reign of Alexander, 'unless by the advice of the Pope, the convent of Canterbury, and the king of England.' Having thus, in effect, resigned his see, Eadmer was suffered quietly to leave the kingdom. He afterwards addressed a long epistle to Alexander, in which, after setting forth his pretensions to the bishopric, he added, in a tone of submission which would have better become him at an earlier period: "I mean not, in any particular, to derogate from the freedom and independency of the kingdom of Scotland. Should you continue in your former sentiments, I will desist from my opposition; for, with respect to the king of England, the arch-

bishop of Canterbury, and the sacerdotal benediction, I had notions, which, as I have since learned, were erroneous. They will not separate me from the service of God and your favour. In those things I will act according to your inclinations, if you only permit me to enjoy the other rights belonging to the see of St. Andrews." The archbishop of Canterbury, too, wrote Alexander, requiring him to recall Eadmer to Scotland; but Alexander would not listen either to the solicitations, though humbly enough expressed, of the one, or the requisition, however peremptory, of the other. He was resolved to uphold the independence of the Scottish church; and the undaunted spirit with which he maintained it throughout the whole contest, would have been equally displayed, as Lord Hailes justly remarks, in defence of the independence of his kingdom, had England ever attempted to call it in question during his reign.

In January 1123, about a year before Alexander's death, the pretensions of the archbishop of York were renewed, on the king procuring an English monk named Robert, who was prior of Scone, to be elected bishop of St. Andrews. The latter, however, was not consecrated till the fourth year of the reign of David I. about five years afterwards, when Thurstin, archbishop of York, performed the ceremony, under reservation of the rights of the Scots church.

While thus successful in his resistance to the claims of supremacy on the part of the metropolitan sees of York and Canterbury, Alexander, as was usual in those days, evinced his devotion to the church by the ample donations which he made to it. He bestowed upon the see of St. Andrews the famous tract of land called the Cursus Apri, or Boar's Chase, of which it is not possible now to assign the exact limits; but "so called," says Boece, "from a boar of uncommon size, which, after having made prodigious havoc of men and cattle, and having been frequently attacked by the huntsmen unsuccessfully, and to the imminent peril of their lives, was at last set upon by the whole country up in arms against him, and killed while endeavouring to make his escape across this tract of ground." The historian adds, that there were extant in his time manifest proofs of the existence of this huge beast; its two tusks, each sixteen inches long and four thick, being fixed with iron chains to the great altar of St. Andrews, having been placed there by the above named Bishop Robert, who obtained the grant of the boar chase from Alexander, although not consecrated bishop at the time it was bestowed. The legend that this extensive tract of land was conferred in 370 by Hungus or Hergustus, a Pictish king, who is unknown to history, is a monkish fiction utterly unworthy of attention.

In 1123, having narrowly escaped shipwreck near the island of Æmona, now called Inchcolm, in the Frith of Forth, Alexander built a monastery on that island, of the ruins of which a woodcut is given underneath.

The circumstances are thus related by Fordun: "About the year 1123, Alexander I. having some business of state which obliged him to cross over at the Queen's ferry, was overtaken by a terrible tempest blowing from the south-west, which obliged the sailors to make for this island, (Æmona,) which they reached with the greatest difficulty. Here they found a poor hermit, who lived a religious life according to the rules of St. Columba, and performed service in a small chapel, supporting himself by the milk of one cow, and the shellfish he could pick up on the shore; nevertheless, on these small means he entertained the king and his retinue for three days—the time which they were confined here by the wind. During the storm, and whilst at sea and in the greatest danger, the king made a vow that if St. Columba would bring him safe to that island, he would there found a monastery to his honour, which should be an asylum and relief to navigators. He was, moreover, farther moved to this foundation, by having, from his childhood, entertained a particular veneration and honour for that saint, derived from his parents, who were long married without issue, until imploring the aid of St. Columba, their request was most graciously granted." The monastery thus founded by Alexander was for canons regular of St. Augustine, and was richly endowed by the grateful and pious king its founder and patron. Being dedicated to St. Colm or Columba, the island obtained the name thereafter of Inchcolm, which it still retains. The king had previously brought a colony of canons regular of St. Augustine from the monastery of St. Oswald at Nastley, near Pontefract, in Yorkshire, and established them at Scone, the abbey of which he had founded in 1114, and dedicated to the Holy Trinity and St. Michael. This famous abbey, it is well known, enclosed the celebrated coronation stone which was removed to England by Edward I., and is still used at the coronation of the sovereigns of Great Britain at Westminster. The abbey of Scone, also, thus founded by Alexander, witnessed the crowning of the later Scoto-Saxon kings. By a royal charter he conferred upon the monks of this abbey the right of holding their own court, and of giving judgment either by combat, by iron, or by water; together with all privileges pertaining to their court; including the right in all persons resident within their territory, of refusing to answer except in their own proper court. [*Cartulary of Scone*, p. 16.] This right of exclusive jurisdiction was confirmed by four successive monarchs. In 1122, on the death of his queen, Sybilla, who died suddenly at the castle of Loch Tay, in Perthshire, on the 12th of June of that year, Alexander erected a priory on a small island on Loch Tay, for the repose of his soul and that of his consort. According to Spottiswood, this priory was a cell from the monastery of Scone, and was founded by Queen Sybilla herself, but this is evidently a mistake. Some very inconsiderable ruins of it still remain. Alexander also granted various lands to the monastery of Dunfermline which his father had founded, and is said to have finished the church. His queen Sybilla also conferred lands on it.

Notwithstanding the rude condition of the inhabitants of Scotland at that remote period, the personal state kept up by Alexander the First is described as having been scarcely, if at all, inferior to that of his brother-monarch of the richer country of England. It is well-known that in the reign of his father, Malcolm Canmore, an unusual splendour was introduced into the Scottish court by his Saxon consort, the good queen Margaret, who not only encouraged the importation and use of rich vestments from foreign countries, setting the example by being magnificent in her own attire, but increased the number of attendants on the person of the king, and caused him to be served at table on plate of gold and silver. [*Turgot's Memoir of Queen Margaret*.] Alexander I. seems to have given to his public appearances, as sovereign, a degree of splendour till then unknown in the northern end of the island. In his reign there appears to have been a considerable intercourse between Scotland and the East, as various oriental commodities and articles of Asiatic luxury were imported into this country. It is related of

this monarch, that, not content with endowing the church of St. Andrews—which had been founded in his reign by Turgot, its archbishop—with numerous lands, and conferring upon it various immunities, as an additional evidence of his devotion to the blessed apostle St. Andrew, after whom the see was called, he commanded his favourite Arabian horse to be led up to the high altar, his saddle and bridle being splendidly ornamented, while his housings were of a rich cloth of velvet. The king's body armour, of superb Turkish manufacture, and studded with jewels, with his spear and his shield of silver, were at the same time brought by a squire; and these, along with the horse and his furniture, the king, in the presence of his prelates and barons, solemnly devoted and presented to the church. The housings and arms were shown in the days of the historian who has recorded the event. [*Extract from the Register of the Priory of St. Andrews, in Pinkerton's Dissertation, Appendix*, vol. i. p. 464. *Winton*, vol. i. p. 286. See also *Tytler's History of Scotland*, vol. ii. p. 198.]

The rising commerce of the country in those early times was much aided and advanced by the settlement, in the districts contiguous to the Borders, of numbers of Flemish merchants, who, during the reign of Alexander, gradually spread into Scotland, and at a later period, namely, in the reign of David the First, were found in all the towns along the east coast, and even in the western parts of the kingdom, wherever traffic could be safely and profitably carried on. The money in circulation in Scotland at that period appears to have been of silver only. Indeed, down to the reign of Robert the Second, the gold coinage of England, then current in Scotland, seems to have been the only gold money in use. Of the early silver money of Scotland, the most ancient specimens yet found are the pennies of Alexander the First, which are now extremely rare. They are described as being of the same firmness, weight, and form as the contemporary English coins of the same denomination, and down to the time of Robert the First, the money of Scotland was precisely of the same value and standard as that of England. [See *Ruddiman's Introduction to Anderson's Diplomata*, pp. 54, 55.—*Tytler's History of Scotland*, vol. ii. p. 264.] The annexed engraving of the silver pennies of Alexander I. is from Anderson's *Numismata*.

Annexed is a seal of Alexander I., in which he is represented fully cased in the armour of that period:

Here we find the scaled mail-coat composed of mascles, or lozenged pieces of steel, sewed upon a tunic of leather, and reaching only to the mid thigh. The hood is of one piece with the tunic, and covers the head, which is protected with a conical steel cap, and a nasal; the sleeves are loose, so as to show the linen tunic worn next the skin, and again appearing in graceful folds above the knee; the lower leg and foot are protected by a short boot, armed with a spur. The king holds in his right hand a spear, to which a pennoncelle, or small flag, is attached, exactly similar to that worn by Henry the First; the saddle is peaked before and behind; and the horse on which he rides is ornamented by a rich fringe round the chest, but altogether unarmed. [*Seal in the Diplomata Scotiæ*, plate 7. *Tytler's History of Scotland* vol. ii. p. 360.]

Alexander the First died at Stirling on the 27th of April 1124, in the seventeenth year of his reign, and leaving no issue was succeeded by his youngest brother, David. He was interred before the high altar at Dunfermline, near to his father. During his reign, as during that of his brother and predecessor Edgar, the laws, institutions, and forms of government, except in the Gaelic portion of the kingdom, were purely Saxon; and to this particular epoch in our nation's history, may be traced the earliest existence in Scotland of some of the great officers of state, who after that period discharged some of the more important functions of the government, as the chancellor, the constable, &c. The former was the most intimate counsellor of the king, and generally the witness to his charters, letters, and proclamations, and the latter, an office of undoubted Norman origin, was the leader of the whole military power of the kingdom. The first appearance in Scotland of the now ancient office of sheriff is also referred to this reign, although the division of the country into regular sheriffdoms did not take place till a much later period. "During the reigns of Edgar and Alexander I.," says Skene, "the whole of Scotland, with the exception of what had formed the kingdom of Thorfinn (during the Norwegian conquest consisting of the Orkneys, the Hebrides, and a large portion of the Highlands), exhibited the exact counterpart of Saxon England, with its earls, thanes, and sheriffs, while the rest of the country remained in the possession of the Gaelic Maormors, who yielded so far to Saxon influence as to assume the Saxon title of earl." [*History of the Highlanders*, vol. i. p. 128.] The personal character of Alexander was bold and energetic, and his disposition fiery and impetuous. Strenuous in maintaining his authority, he had, early in his reign, applied himself to repressing the disorders and insurrections which were continually breaking out in the Celtic portion of his dominions, and his ardent temper and daring spirit contributed not a little to his success in overawing the turbulent inhabitants of the north, and reducing them to submission. The boldest chieftains are said to have trembled in his presence, and the epithet of 'Fierce' attached to his name seems to have arisen from the energy which he at all times displayed, and which was necessary for reclaiming the Scots from that savage barbarism into which they had relapsed under Donald Bane. Although terrible to the rest of his people, Alexander is described by Aldred, as being humble and courteous to the clergy, "not ignorant of letters," liberal even to profusion, and kind and benevolent to the poor.—*Hailes' Annals of Scotland*, vol. i., *and the authorities quoted in the preceding article.*

ALEXANDER II., king of Scotland, the fourth in succession from the subject of the foregoing memoir, to whom he stands in the relation of great grand-nephew, was born at Haddington 24 Aug., 1198. He was the only legitimate son of William surnamed the Lion, his predecessor on the throne. His mother, Ermangarde, was daughter of Richard Viscount de Beaumont, a descendant from Henry I. of England, through his mother, a natural daughter of that monarch. He succeeded his father December 4, 1214, being then only sixteen years of age, and was crowned at Scone on the 20th of the same month.

Some years before the death of William his father, that monarch had been engaged in warlike demonstrations against England, followed, (in 1209,) by a treaty of a singular character, of which the provisions have not yet been clearly ascertained. It appears that during the troubles in which John —the monarch who then sat upon the English throne—was involved, (in consequence of disputes with the head of the church and the dissatisfaction of his barons, which finally resulted in the concession by him of Magna Charta,) William—conceiving the opportunity to be favourable—took occasion to demand that the counties of Northumberland, Cumberland, and Westmoreland, (which until about the middle of the reign of Henry II. had constituted the county or province of Northumbria, and under that designation had been held

during the latter part of the reign of his grandfather David I., by the eldest son of that monarch, the father of William, as a fief of the English crown, but on the death of that monarch had been resumed by Henry II.,) should be restored to the Scottish nation. How far that claim—one of the *vexed* questions of Scottish history—was founded in right, does not properly fall to be considered in this biography, but will be treated of in that of Malcolm IV., the brother of William, on whose accession these counties were restored to Henry, and to which therefore we refer. We may, however, remark,—unwilling as we are to yield to any one in the assertion of the just rights of Scotland,— that there does not appear in the circumstances any warrant for assuming—as William then did, and as Scottish writers have hitherto done—that the intrusting of the government of these counties by Stephen in February 1139 to Prince Henry, son of David—as an individual lordship for which he rendered homage—can be construed into permanent cession of their possession from the English to the Scottish crown. It may more probably be inferred as done in guarantee of the fulfilment of the solemn engagement then entered into with David by Stephen, that the crown of England—usurped by him—should at his death descend to Henry, grand-nephew of David,—son of the empress Matilda his sister's daughter the rightful heiress,—on whose behalf alone it was that that wise and righteous prince had professed to take up arms. The retention in his own hands by the English king, during the entire period of their government by the heir to the Scottish throne, of the commanding strengths of Bamborough, Norham, and Newcastle on Tyne, (the two former situated near the Scottish border,) and the omission of all reference to the circumstance of the supposed cession on the part of English historians, gives additional probability to this aspect of the transaction. Its resumption, therefore, on the fulfilment of that stipulation towards the close of the reign of David, may in this view of the matter have involved no injustice on the part of the English monarch, and appears to have been peacefully acquiesced in by Malcolm, the then reigning king. In the history of the two kingdoms of that period, however, it will frequently be found that the occasion of distraction or civil contest on the part of the one was frequently availed of, to press to an issue assumed or disputed claims on the part of the other, and the fearful state of matters which then obtained in England—placed as it was under a papal interdict, the public services of religion suspended, the rites of interment withheld, the prelates banished, and the nobles insulted—presented an opportunity too tempting to be withstood by William, for making a demand which, if yielded to, would at once aggrandize his kingdom, and avenge his long captivity. Nor is there wanting, in the earlier history of that monarch himself, more than one incident to illustrate the truth of the foregoing remark.

In order to understand the position of the parties, however, on the occasion of the conclusion of this treaty, it is proper to observe that, according to the English historians, John,—notwithstanding the dangerous situation in which he stood, and the loss of reputation he had sustained by acquiescing in the conquest of the English provinces in France, —appears, on becoming aware of the military preparations of William, to have manifested a degree of energy unusual to him, and to have resolved to do some act that would give a lustre to his government. He is represented by them as having been successful in his military enterprises in Scotland, as also in others which he undertook against the Irish and Welsh. It was in these circumstances, therefore, that by the treaty in question, the king of Scotland bound himself to pay to John fifteen thousand merks (supposed to be equivalent to one hundred and fifty thousand pounds sterling of our present money) in two years, by four equal payments, "for procuring his good will (*benevolentia*), and for fulfilling certain conventions between them," contained in a charter which has not been preserved. For the performance of this treaty William gave John hostages. He likewise delivered his two daughters, Margaret and Isabella, to the king of England to be educated at his court, and "that they might be provided by him in suitable matches," but not to be considered as hostages. About thirty years thereafter it was stated in the English parliament that the conditions of the charter referred to were that the two Scottish princesses should be mar-

ried to king John's two sons, and that the money, together with a renunciation of his claim to the northern counties, was given by William as their marriage portion. Hubert de Burgh, the justiciary of England, who married the princess Margaret, positively denied, however, all knowledge of any such condition as the former; while some Scottish writers subsequently founded on its nonfulfilment a supposed claim for the restitution of the latter. [See *Life of William the Lion, post.*]

Shortly after Alexander came to the throne affairs in England became involved in a still greater degree of confusion than before. John, perfidious and perjured as tyrannical, had violated the provisions of Magna Charta, set his barons at defiance, and threatened alike to crush the liberties of the country and their power. In this emergency, they decided to renounce their allegiance to him, and sent a deputation to offer the crown of England to Louis, son of the king of France. At the same time such of them as held possessions in the northern counties applied to Alexander, and offered to put him in possession of these districts as the consideration for his aiding them against their oppressor. Although so young, Alexander was not unwilling to avail himself of the proposal, and an agreement was accordingly entered into to that effect. In accordance with this agreement, Alexander with an army marched into Northumberland, and on the 18th of October 1215, he received the homage of the barons of that county at Felton castle. The castle of Norham was besieged by him for forty days, during which time Eustace de Vesci,—one of the principal barons of the northern counties, who had made himself conspicuous by his opposition to John,—gave him investiture of the county of Northumberland by livery and sasine. The intelligence of these negotiations, however, again stirred up John to unwonted activity, and he resolved to crush the northern invasion before Louis should arrive in England. Accordingly, immediately after Christmas, whilst a deep fall of snow lay on the ground, at the head of a large force, consisting principally of foreign mercenaries, he advanced into Yorkshire and Northumberland, devastating the estates of the confederated barons, and burning and slaying wherever he came. All the castles and towns they could take were given to the flames, King John himself setting the example, as he fired with his own hands in the morning the house in which he had rested the preceding night.

On the approach northward of John, Alexander raised the siege of Norham, and retired within his own dominions. The English barons accompanied him, and those of the northern counties did homage to Alexander at the abbey of Melrose on the 15th January 1216. [*Chronicle of Melrose*, p. 190.] John with his mixed and savage host of foreign soldiery followed, burning, in their march, the towns of Werk, Morpeth, Alnwick, Mitford, and Roxburgh. After storming Berwick they entered Scotland, torturing, plundering, and massacring the inhabitants in their way. The towns of Dunbar and Haddington were likewise burnt to the ground. John was determined to have vengeance on Alexander for the assistance which he had given to the patriotic barons who had taken up arms against him. "We will smoke," he said, "the little red fox out of his covert." From this laconic description of him we may infer that Alexander the Second was both diminutive in stature and ruddy in complexion. John pursued his devastating course as far as Edinburgh, but was soon obliged to withdraw from a country which his troops had ravaged so completely that it no longer afforded them subsistence. In his retreat, his forces burnt the priory of Coldingham, which had been founded in the year 1098 by Edgar king of Scotland, and the town of Berwick; John himself, as was his usual practice, giving the example to his brutal soldiery by setting fire to the house in which he had lodged.

For the priory of Coldingham thus ruthlessly consumed by John's savage followers, Alexander, like all the rest of the Scottish kings since the time of Edgar its founder, had a great veneration. He had not only confirmed the charters which his predecessors had granted to it, but exempted the prior and his monks from a sum of twenty merks that they had been in the custom of paying yearly to his exchequer, under the name of *wattinga*,—a tax which appears to have been levied from the landholders in Scotland for the purpose of erecting and maintaining in repair the government fortresses. He also issued a writ to Robert de Bern-

ham, the mayor, and to the bailiffs of Berwick, enjoining them to allow free passage to foreign merchants, when on their way to the priory to purchase the wool and other commodities belonging to the monks, and prohibiting every one from seizing any property, moveable or unmoveable, belonging to the convent, within the barony or lordship of Coldingham, for debt on forfeiture. Besides these immunities, he released "the twelfth village of Coldinghamshire, or that in which the church is founded," from the aids and military service which had formerly been exacted. It was not likely therefore that he would allow John's destructive march to pass without taking dreadful reprisals.

Accordingly, in the month of February following this inroad, Alexander in his turn wasted the western marches with fire and sword and penetrated into Cumberland. Some of the undisciplined Scots, by which name the monkish historians distinguish the Highlanders in his army, plundered and burnt the abbey of Holmcultram, in revenge for the destruction of the priory of Coldingham by the English. These reverend chroniclers relate with apparent delight that two thousand of the Scots, on their way home with their booty, were drowned in the flooded current of the river Eden, as a judgment for their sacrilegious violation of a holy house. After a temporary retreat into his own territories, Alexander invaded Cumberland a second time, in the month of July, with all his army, except the Highlanders, whom he had chastised and dismissed [*Chron. Mel.*, p. 191], and on the 8th of August, he took possession of the city of Carlisle. The castle, however, held out against him. He then marched southwards quite through England to Dover, to join Louis, the son of the king of France, who by this time had arrived in England. In his progress Alexander assaulted Bernard castle, the seat of the Baliol family, then held by a garrison for John. Eustace de Vesci, who had given him investiture of Northumberland at Norham castle, was slain there. On arriving at Dover he found Louis besieging the castle, and as the English barons had done, he did homage to that prince for all his lands in England, and particularly for the counties of Northumberland, Cumberland,

and Westmoreland, which were then granted to him by charter. [*Rymer's Fœdera*, tom. ii. p. 217.] This he might very well do, for the French prince Louis had not only been offered and had accepted the crown of England, but actually had a claim to it in right of his wife. On this occasion Louis, on his part, swore that he would not conclude a separate peace, an oath which he was soon compelled to violate. On his return homeward Alexander met with some obstruction in passing the Trent, the bridge at Newark having been broken down by the army of King John, who expired at the castle of Newark, 19th Oct. 1216.

Some time before this (May 15, 1213) John had been reduced to the unworthy expedient of surrendering his dominions into the hands of the Pope, and of consenting to hold them henceforward only as his vassal, as a means of escaping from the consequences of the papal interdict, and threatened excommunication. When compelled by his barons and clergy (June 19, 1215) to sign the Great Charter, inwardly resolving to violate its provisions, he, as one means of effecting this, laid a statement of the matter, with a complaint of the violence imposed upon him, before his feudal lord, the supreme pontiff, who issued a bull, absolving him from his oath, annulling the charter, and prohibiting the barons from exacting the observance of it, on pain of excommunication. Strange to say, the English primate refused to obey the pope in publishing the sentence, and though suspended on account of this proceeding, and a new and particular sentence of excommunication was issued by name against the principal barons,—including not only the French prince Louis, but Alexander and his whole army, and the entire realm of Scotland,—the nobility and people, and even the clergy, of both kingdoms adhered to the combination against him, and so little zeal in the matter was manifested by the clergy of Scotland, that nearly a twelvemonth elapsed before it was published there. [*Chron. Melrose*, 192. *Fordun*, ix. 31.]

Although Alexander, as already stated, had taken the town of Carlisle, the castle held out, and was besieged by him unsuccessfully. While engaged in this siege, a portion of the army of Prince Louis was entirely defeated in the streets of Lincoln, 19th May 1217, the count de Perche, its commander-in-chief, being killed, and many of the chief commanders taken prisoners. On the news of this defeat, Prince Louis, who was still occupied with the siege of Dover, proceeded to London, where he learned the further defeat of a fleet bringing him reinforcements from France, and the general defection of the barons, as they had by this time become suspicious of his intention. In the general turn which men's dispositions had taken, the excommunication denounced by the legate failed not now to produce a mighty effect on them, and they were easily persuaded to consider a cause as impious, which had hitherto been unfortunate, and for which they had already entertained an unsurmountable aversion. Seeing his cause to be desperate, Louis now began to be anxious for the safety of his person, and entered into a negotiation with the earl of Pembroke, protector of the realm of England,—Henry the Third, the son and successor of King John, being then a minor,—and a peace was concluded, Louis stipulating for a full indemnity to the English of his party—with a restitution of their honours and fortunes, together with the free and equal enjoyment of those liberties which that wise noble had guaranteed in the name of the prince to the rest of the nation—and formally renouncing his pretensions to the crown of England. That Louis might be reconciled to the holy see, he did penance by walking barefooted to the legate's tent, in presence of both armies. He then departed with all his foreign forces to France.

On receiving intelligence of these events, Alexander, who was then on his march into England, made overtures of peace to the young king Henry III., and after some time spent in negotiation, a treaty was concluded between them. He then yielded up the town of Carlisle to the English, and in an interview which he had with King Henry at Northampton, he did homage to him, —but for his English possessions only, as Scottish writers allege,—and returned into Scotland. [*Chron. Mel.* 192, 194, 195. *Fordun* ix. 31.]

Alexander now sought to be reconciled to the Pope, and having procured a safe conduct from England, he proceeded to Tweedmouth, on the English side of the Border, and there met the archbishop of York and the bishop of Durham who had been delegated by the Pope's legate for the purpose, and received absolution from their hands, 1st December 1217, without being called upon to perform the ignominious penance which generally preceded absolution. Some days thereafter the delegates also removed the ban of excommunication from Alexander's mother, queen Ermengarde. The sentence was also removed from the whole body of the Scottish nation, except the prelates and the clergy, who had become obnoxious by reason of their reluctance to publish the bull.

In the spring of 1218, William, prior of Durham, and Walter de Wisbech, archdeacon of York, traversed Scotland, "from Berwick to Aberdeen," for the purpose of absolving the Scottish clergy from the sentence of excommunication. While upon this tour, on arriving at a town they summoned the clergy to attend them, and having required them to swear allegiance to the papal legate, and to make a candid confession of all matters concerning which they were asked, they absolved them, standing barefoot before the doors of their churches and abbeys. The commissioners were very sumptuously entertained, and their favour was courted by large bribes of money, and many presents. [*Ridpath's Border History*, p. 127.] On their return south they halted at the abbey of Lindores, where the prior of Durham was nearly suffocated with smoke, a fire having broken out in the chamber where he slept, through the carelessness and rioting of those who had the charge of the wine, "his chamberman," as Balfour pithily says, "being verey drunke." He died at Coldingham priory, which appears to have been partially restored after its burning by King John in 1216. The following is a woodcut of the ruins of this celebrated priory.

Against these proceedings the king appealed to Rome, while the clergy themselves sent a deputation of three bishops to the Pope. A judgment was obtained in their favour, which declared that the legate had exceeded his powers, and not only was absolution granted by Pope Honorius, but the liberties and privileges of the Scottish church were confirmed [*Fordun á Goodal*, vol. ii. pp. 40, 42.] For this favour one of the causes mentioned is the respect and obedience which Alexander had manifested to the papal see. This concession on his part in a few years thereafter (in 1225) led to one of still greater importance. The Scottish clergy having represented to the Pope, that from the want of a metropolitan they could not hold a provincial council, he authorized them to hold a general council of their own authority. Of this permission they were not slow to take advantage, and having assembled under its sanction, they drew up a distinct form of proceeding, by which the Scottish provincial councils were in future to be held; instituted the office of Conservator Statutorum, and continued to assemble frequent provincial councils, unfettered by the intervention of any foreign superior.

By one article of the treaty of peace concluded in 1217 between Alexander and Henry, it was stipulated that the king of Scotland should marry the princess Joan, the eldest sister of the king of England; and their nuptials, after some delays, occasioned by the detention of the princess in France, were celebrated on the 25th of June 1221. The princess Joan, on her marriage, was secured in a jointure of one thousand pounds of land rent. [*Fœdera*, tom. ii. p. 252.] Lord Hailes says, "The jointure lands were Jedworth, Lessudden, Kinghorn, and Crail. Any deficiencies were to be made good out of the castles and castellanys of Ayr, Rutherglen, Lanark, and the rents of Clydesdale. Kinghorn and Crail were, at that time, part of the jointure lands of the queen-dowager."

The peace with England and the marriage of Alexander to the English king's sister put a stop to all hostilities between the two nations for several years, and introduced a friendly intercourse between the two royal families, now so nearly related, which for a long time continued uninterrupted. The king and queen of Scotland made frequent visits to the court of England; where they were nobly entertained, and received many valuable proofs of friendship from King Henry. The alliance with England was still farther strengthened by the marriage of Alexander's two sisters, the princesses Margaret and Isabella, who had been sent to England in the preceding reign, to English barons of great power and influence, namely, Margaret, soon after her brother's marriage in 1221, to the celebrated Hubert de Burgh,

justiciary of England, and Isabella, in 1225, to Roger Bigot, eldest son of Hugh, Earl Bigot. [*Fordun*, ix. 32, 33. *Fœdera*, i. 227, 228, 374. *Matth. Paris*, 216.] For providing portions for his sisters, Alexander, in 1224, levied an aid of ten thousand pounds upon the nation. This grant is stated by some of our Scottish writers, in the loose manner in which they are accustomed to write of events which took place at that remote period, to have been authorized by Alexander's parliament; while, on the contrary, it was imposed by the simple order of the king himself, without the slightest appearance of a meeting of the three estates, or even of the council of the king. Such a thing as a parliament was then unknown in Scotland. The first meeting, indeed, of what may be termed one did not take place till 1289, fully sixty-five years later, when, after the death of Alexander III., the estates of the kingdom, that is, the five guardians or regents, ten bishops, twelve earls, twenty-three abbots, eleven priors, and forty-eight barons, calling themselves the community of Scotland, although no representatives of the burghs or of the people were among them, met at Brigham, now Birgham, an obscure village in Berwickshire, to take into consideration the proposal for a marriage between the prince of Wales, the son of Edward the First of England, and the young queen Margaret of Scotland, called "the Maiden of Norway." When Fordun (vol. ii. p. 34) asserts that Alexander the Second, immediately after his coronation, held his parliament in Edinburgh, in which he confirmed to the chancellor, constable, and chamberlain the same high offices which they had filled at his father's death, the word parliament so used may be held only to mean an assembly of the court, or the council of his nobles and great officers of the crown, and not a parliament, or even convention of estates, in the modern meaning of the word. [See *Tytler's History of Scotland*, vol. ii. sect. 3.]

Anciently the barons of the realm, with the crown vassals and higher clergy, constituted the *communitas regni*, which formed the parliament, as Mr. Skene terms it, of all Teutonic nations. To this body, composed of Celtic, Norman, and Saxon dignitaries and landholders, belonged the duty of counselling the monarch, and expressing the wants and wishes of the nation, without the great mass of the people having either a voice or a will in the matter, the principle of elective representation being altogether unknown to them. But there was another and even a higher body in the state, independent of the *communitas*, whose peculiar privileges were only exercised on great and rare occasions, namely, when there was a vacancy in the throne. This was the *Septem Comites Regni Scotiæ*, "the seven earls of Scotland." Until very recently, the existence of such a corporate body in the state seems to have been entirely unknown. To Sir Francis Palgrave belongs the merit of having made the discovery of a fact of so much importance to the right understanding of the history of Scotland. It is proved, he says in his 'Treasury Documents illustrative of Scottish History,' published in 1837, that "there existed in the ancient kingdom of Scotland, a known and established constitutional body denominated 'the seven earls of Scotland,' possessing privileges of singular importance as a distinct estate in the realm, severed equally from the other earls, and from the body of the baronage." These seven earls as a body derived their functions from the old Celtic constitution of the country, ancient Albania, or Scotland, north of the friths of Forth and Clyde, being divided into seven great provinces or governments. The Pictish names of these provinces were Fiv, Cait, Fotla, Fortrein, Circui, Ce, and Fidach, corresponding with, according to Geraldus Cambrensis, Fife, Caithness, Atholl and Garmorin, Stratherne and Menteth, Angus and Mearns, Moray and Ross, and Marr and Buchan. Three of these were provinces of the Southern Picts, namely, Fife, Stratherne and Menteth, and Angus and Mearns; the other four belonged to the northern Picts. These seven provinces formed the kingdom of the Picts or Scotland proper, previous to the ninth century. The Scottish conquest, in 843, having added to it Dalriada, which afterwards became Argyle, and Caithness having towards the end of the same century fallen into the hands of the Norwegians, the former was after that period substituted for the latter, and the earl of Argyle instead of the earl of Caithness was numbered among "the seven earls." The Pictish nation consisted of a confederacy of fourteen tribes

spread over the seven provinces named, in each of which one of the seven superior chiefs ruled under the Celtic name of maormor. In the reign of Edgar they assumed the Saxon title of earl, and their territories were exactly the same with the earldoms into which the north of Scotland was afterwards divided.

In the appendix to the first volume of Mr. Skene's valuable 'History of the Highlanders,' will be found a clear account of the 'seven ancient provinces of Scotland,' over which the seven earls presided. It was the privilege of these seven superior chiefs, by immemorial custom, as a peculiar estate in the realm, to appoint a king, whenever there was a vacancy, and to invest him with the royal authority, a right which they appear to have exercised after the Pictish kingdom had ceased to exist. Among the other documents preserved in the Treasury, illustrative of Scottish history, which the researches of Sir Francis Palgrave have brought to light, is a roll containing the appeal of the seven earls in 1290 to the authority and protection of Edward I. and the English crown, against William Fraser, Bishop of St. Andrews, and John Comyn, Lord of Badenoch, the Scottish regents, during the interregnum that succeeded the death of the Maid of Norway, on the ground that the regents were infringing or intending to infringe this their constitutional franchise; which appeal, it is now understood, led to the famous summons of the English monarch that the Scottish nobility and clergy should meet him at Norham in the English territories, on the 10th of May 1291, to decide upon the claims of the various competitors to the Scottish crown. Having given this explanation, which will form a key to much of what would be otherwise unintelligible or obscure in the early history of Scotland, we resume the regular narrative.

The external tranquillity which Scotland enjoyed after the peace with England and the marriage of Alexander to the sister of the English king, allowed Alexander leisure to suppress some dangerous insurrections that had broken out at home. In 1221, Somerled, a grandson of the celebrated lord of the Isles of that name, possessed the whole district of Argyle, which was then much more extensive than the modern Argyleshire, and having that year risen in rebellion, the king collected an army in Lothian and Galloway, and sailed for Argyle, intending to disembark his force, and penetrate into the interior of the country, but his ships were driven back by a tempest, and forced to take refuge in the Clyde. Alexander, however, was not discouraged, but resolved to proceed into Argyle by land. With a large army, which he had summoned from every quarter of his dominions, he made himself master of the whole of the insurgent district, and compelled Somerled to flee to the Isles, where, about eight years afterwards, he met a violent death. Winton says,

> " De king that yhere Argyle wan
>   Dat rebell wes till hym befor than
>   For wythe hys Ost thare in wes he
>   And Athe' tuk of thare Fewte,
>   Wythe thare serwys and their Homage
>   Dat of hym wald hald thare Herytage,
>   But of the Ethchetys of the lave
>   To the Lordies of that land he gave."

The estates of those who fled were bestowed on the principal men of the king's army as a reward for their having joined the expedition; but wherever the former vassals of Somerled submitted and were received into favour, they became crown vassals, and held their lands in chief of the crown. The district in which the forfeited estates were, was farther brought under the direct jurisdiction of the government, by being, according to the invariable policy of Alexander II., erected into a sheriffdom by the name of Argyle, the first sheriffdom bearing that name, while the ancestor of the Campbells was made hereditary sheriff of the new sheriffdom. [*Skene's History of the Highlanders*, vol. ii. p. 46.] The whole of the then northern Argyle, now part of Inverness-shire, was bestowed on the earl of Ross, as a reward for the assistance which he had rendered to the king on this and a former occasion.

Besides suppressing this insurrection in Argyle, Alexander was about the same time called upon to punish some disturbances of an alarming kind which had broken out in Caithness. In 1222, Adam bishop of Caithness was cruelly burnt to death in his own palace. He had proved himself extremely rigorous in enforcing the demand for tithes, leading the poor people's corn, as Balfour says, "too avariciously," and when the people of his diocese had assembled to consider what was to be done under the circumstances, one of them exclaimed, "short rede, good rede, slay we the bishop," meaning, "Few words are best, let us kill the bishop." The persons assembled unfortunately were too excited to pause or reflect—they followed the cruel advice, thus rashly given, but too literally. Rushing with eagerness to the bishop's house, they furiously assaulted it, set it on fire, and burnt the unhappy prelate in the flames of his own palace, with a monk who attended him, named Serlo. Some of the bishop's servants applied to the earl of Orkney and Caithness to protect their master from the fury of the mob; he answered that if the bishop came to him he would be sure of protection, but did not offer to go to his assistance. Alexander received intelligence of this cruel action when he was upon a journey towards England. He immediately turned back, marched into Caithness with an army, and put to death four hundred of those who had been concerned in the murder of the bishop. The earl of Orkney who might have prevented the catastrophe but did not, was believed to have favoured the conspiracy, but him the king pardoned, as he had no actual hand in the crime. He had to pay, however, a large sum of money, and give up the third part of his estate. Balfour says that in the following year, while Alexander was keeping his birth-day at Forfar, the earl of Orkney with a good sum of ready money redeemed the third part of his estate from the king, but on his return home he was murdered in his own castle, which was afterwards burnt, in imitation and revenge of the bishop's fate. This event, however, according to the chronicle of Melrose (p. 201) quoted by Lord Hailes, did not take place till 1231.

In the life of Alexander I. allusion has been made to the peculiar law of succession which prevailed amongst the Pictish or Gaelic tribes. [See p. 54, *ante*.] This law of Tanistry, as it was called, provided that on the death of a chief, the brother, or "he of the blood who was nearest," succeeded to the chiefship, to the exclusion of females and even sons, the brother being considered one degree nearer the original founder or patriarch of the race than the son, and if the person who ought to succeed was under fourteen years of age,—the ancient Highland period of majority,—his nearest male relation became chief, and continued so during his life, the proper heir inheriting the chiefship only at his death. [*Skene's History of the Highlanders*, vol. i. pp. 160, 161.] The establishment of such a law originated primarily, there cannot be a doubt, in the natural anxiety to avoid minorities in a tribe or clan, so that it might always have a competent leader in war, a principle which, however much opposed to the feudal notions of later times, flowed naturally from the patriarchal constitution of society in the Highlands, being peculiarly adapted to the circumstances of a people whose warlike habits and love of military enterprise, as well as addiction to armed predatory expeditions, demanded at all times a chief of full age and every way qualified to act as their leader and commander.

As, however, the Highlanders adhered strictly to succession in the male line and according to the lineal descent from the common ancestor, or founder of the tribe, any infraction of this rule was often productive of the most serious outbreaks and insurrections. This was remarkably the case in the old maormordom or province of Moray, which, at the period when Alexander the Second ascended the throne, included not only what now forms the counties of Elgin and Nairn, but a considerable part of Banffshire and nearly the half of Inverness-shire. This was always one of the most rebellious portions of the kingdom; and although the tribes of Moray, in common with the rest of the Highlanders, recognised in Alexander I. and his successor David I. the legitimate heirs of Malcolm Canmore, they were never without a pretext for disturbing the country. After the suppression of their attempt at insurrection early in the reign of the former, when Angus referred to (p. 54) as of the family of Macbeth,—whom Skene with reason supposes to be the same with Head or Heth, whose name with *Comes* attached to it appears as witness in numerous charters of David I., Head or Heth being the surname of the family,—was in in possession of the earldom, they remained quiet till 1130, Alexander's successor David I. being then on the throne. In that year, an Angus earl of Moray,—either the individual referred to above,

who escaped confiscation by causing his accomplice Ladman, younger son of Donald Bane, to be put to death, or a descendant of the same name,—taking advantage of David's absence at the English court, broke out into rebellion, and after having obtained possession of the northern districts of Scotland, advanced at the head of a numerous army, into Forfarshire; but Edward, son of Siward, earl of Northumberland, led an army into Scotland, with which he defeated and slew the earl at Strickathrow. Twelve years thereafter one Wimund, an English monk, who had risen to be bishop of Man, claiming to be the son of Angus, asserted his right to the earldom, and assumed the name of Malcolm Macheth. He was assisted by Somerled, thane of Argyle, whose daughter he married, and many of the northern chiefs. After having for several years sustained a struggle with David, he was at length betrayed by his own adherents, who put out his eyes and delivered him up to the Scottish king. He was sent a prisoner to the castle of Roxburgh, but after a tedious captivity, was pardoned, when he retired to the abbey of Biland in Yorkshire, where he died. [See Life of David I. *post.*]

On the death of David I. in 1153, the Tanistic law of succession would have conferred the right to the throne on Malcolm son of Duncan, the eldest son of Malcolm Canmore, but being then in possession of the earldom of Athol (p. 54), he does not appear to have brought it forward, preferring probably the certainty of possession under the feudal law to the risk of a hopeless conflict. On his death however, some years afterwards, it would appear that the law of Tanistry again came into conflict with the established system, not only as respects the succession to the crown, but in reference also to the family possessions of the earldom of Athol, and we find the celebrated Boy of Egremont, in the person of William, son of William Fitz-Duncan, a younger son of Duncan, appearing as a claimant of both, in opposition to Malcolm IV., the reigning monarch, and to his cousin Henry, son of Malcolm his father's brother, then earl of Athol. The people of the Highlands, ever prepared to avail themselves of an occasion to thrust out the race that governed them according to the Saxon laws, were the more encouraged to support the claim of this individual in the absence of Malcolm IV., then rendering military service to Henry II. in France, by the general dissatisfaction professed to be entertained on account of that servitude. Six of the seven great earls of Scotland, who governed the districts into which the ancient Pictish provinces of Scotland were divided —and in whose hands the nomination of the crown was vested [see p. 67]—sent a message to Malcolm, then at Toulouse, expressing their disapprobation of his proceedings, and indicating a withdrawal of their allegiance. On his return from France, he met the chiefs at Perth; and whilst by the intervention of his clergy he endeavoured to pacify them and regain their confidence, he was in 1160 attacked by a portion of the confederacy, but they were repulsed, and many of their followers slain. [See life of Malcolm IV. *post*.] Donald Bane, another son of William Fitz-Duncan, and grandson of Duncan, afterwards took up the claim, and supported by the northern chiefs, he for seven years held out the provinces of Moray and Ross against William the Lion, but in 1187, while his army lay at Inverness, a marauding party commanded by Roland of Galloway accidentally encountering him, when attended by few of his followers, attacked and slew him. In 1211 his son Guthred landed from Ireland and wasted the province of Ross. Notwithstanding that the king (William the Lion) went against him in person at the head of an army, he kept possession of the north of Scotland for some time, but was at last betrayed into the hands of William Comyn, by whom he was beheaded.

On the accession of Alexander II. to the throne, Donald Bane, or MacWilliam, the brother of Guthred, and the son of that Donald who was slain in 1187, prepared to assert his own pretensions to the crown, and in conjunction with Kenneth Macheth, who after an unsuccessful attempt to obtain the earldom of Moray in the reign of Malcolm IV. had taken refuge in Ireland, invaded Scotland at the head of a numerous body of Irish followers. They made an inroad into Moray, but were met by Ferchard, earl of Ross, an ally of the government, who defeated and slew them. Balfour in his annals says: "In the zeire 1215, Donald Bane, the sone of Mack-William, and Keneth Mack-Acht, with the son of a pittey king of Irland, and a good armey, invadit the heighe lands. Against quhom Machentagar leweys ane armey, and with them feights a werey bloodiey and creuell batell, quhom he totally ouerthrowes, the 17 day of Julay, and solemly presents the rebells heads to the king; for wich so gude seruice the king solemley knights Machentagar, and gives him a zeirly pensione during his lyffe." [Vol. i. p. 38.] Lord Hailes transcribed the same names, with a slight difference in the spelling, from the Chronicle of Melrose. "The author," he says, "being a Saxon, has corrupted the Gaelic names; Kenaukmacaht and M'Kentagar are unintelligible words." From the above retrospect, which was necessary to render the narrative clear, the reader will not be at a loss to understand that by Donald Bane is meant Donald M'William the grandson of William, and great-grandson of Duncan king of Scotland, and by Machentagar, Ferchard Macantagart, earl of Ross, who conquered and slew him and Kenneth Mack-Act, or Macheth, as already narrated.

The rebellion of Somerled in 1221, of which an account has been given in pages 66, 67, is the last of those persevering efforts made to replace the family of Duncan on the throne of his father Malcolm. By an intermarriage of their families at an earlier period Somerled had become closely related to the race of Duncan. The language of the old chronicler Winton, already quoted,

" Dat rebell wes till hym befor tham,"

would imply that he with the forces of Argyle had aided in the previous one of 1215. The death, therefore, of the last of the heirs of the direct line seems to have opened the way to a claim to the throne in his own right. In reading of these continuous struggles, and of the aid so frequently rendered by the Irish and Scottish branches of the Celtic family to the assertion of the old Pictish law, we see another proof of the tenacity with which under all discouragements they held to it. In the frequent interference also of the Irish in these internal struggles,—made too, it is worthy of being noted, generally on occasions when the occupant of the throne was embarrassed by other questions, —we seem to read over again the series of contests—brought to light by Skene and others—whereby the Irish Dalriadic tribe, not having then the Norman arms to encounter, at an earlier period of the national history more successfully submerged the existing government, and gave the name of Scotland, and race of monarchs—the true heirs according to their theory—to that country.

Although the family of Angus had become extinct by the death of Kenneth, yet by the Celtic law of succession, the claims of the family were transmitted to the next branch of the clan, and in 1228 the tranquillity of the same district was again disturbed by one Gillespic, claiming to be the chief of the province. This warrior, after burning some wooden castles, surprising and slaying a baron who had been sent against him, called Thomas of Thirlstane, to whom Malcolm IV. had given the district of Abertarff, set fire to the town of Inverness, and spoiled and wasted the crown lands in that neighbourhood. The king went against him in person, but for a while he eluded his pursuit. He was at last encountered and slain, by William Comyn earl of Buchan, the justiciary of the kingdom. As a reward for suppressing this insurrection Comyn got a grant from the king of the districts of Badenoch and Lochaber. In accordance with his usual policy, Alexander erected that portion of the extensive earldom of Moray, which was not then under the rule of the Bissets, the Comyns, and other Norman barons, into the separate sheriffdoms of Elgin and Nairn. "The authority of government," says Skene, "was thus so effectually established that the Moravians did not again attempt any resistance; and thus ended with the death of Gillespic, the last of that series of persevering efforts which the earls of Moray had made for upwards of one hundred years to preserve their native inheritance." [*Highlanders of Scotland*, vol. ii. p. 170.]

In 1233 the most serious insurrection which Alexander had yet to contend with occurred in Galloway, arising out of a similar principle to that which produced the disturbances in Moray; the adherence, namely, of the inhabitants to the ancient law of tanistry, as evidenced in their unwillingness to submit to female succession. The people of that extensive district, which forms the south-western angle of Scotland, were chiefly

of a Celtic race. Besides offshoots from the Scots of Kintyre, large bodies of colonists from Ireland formed, at various times, settlements there, during the ninth, tenth, and eleventh centuries, and from the frequent incursions of these and other settlers, the district obtained its name; either, as is most likely, from the word *Gall*, which originally signified stranger or wanderer, and in this sense was applied to the pirates who, in those days, infested the western coasts of Scotland,—hence the term used by the Irish annalists, in reference to them, namely the Gallgael, meaning Gaelic pirates or rovers,—or, as is generally supposed, from the Gaelic origin of the inhabitants. Although the name is now confined to the shire of Wigton and the stewartry of Kirkcudbright, it anciently had a more extensive application, as it comprehended the entire peninsula between the Solway and the Clyde, including Annandale in the south-east, and most of Ayrshire in the north-west, and was governed by its native chieftains, styled the lords of Galloway, who acknowledged a feudatory dependence on the Scottish crown. In the twelfth century, Fergus, one of the most potent of these, who was the son-in-law of Henry I. of England, endeavoured to throw off his allegiance to Malcolm IV., and raised a formidable insurrection in Galloway. Enraged at his daring, Malcolm marched into his territory, and though twice repulsed, he succeeded in a third effort, in the year 1160, in overcoming him. Fergus, after suing for peace, resigned his lordship and possessions to his two sons, Gilbert and Uchtred, and retired to the abbey of Holyrood, where he died in the following year. His two sons attended, as feudatories, William the Lion, in 1174, on his unfortunate expedition into England; but they no sooner saw him taken captive than, at the head of their savage followers, they returned to their native wilds, attacked and demolished the royal castles, and murdered many subjects of William who were settled in Galloway. To protect them against the vengeance of their own sovereign, they besought Henry, the English king, to receive their homage. In the meantime, before receiving an answer to their request, Uchtred was cruelly murdered by his brother Gilbert for his share of the inheritance. Gilbert renewed the negotiation with

Henry in his own name, and offered to pay him a yearly tribute of two thousand marks of silver, five hundred cows, and five hundred swine. To mark his detestation of the treacherous murder of Uchtred, Henry refused both the homage and the tribute. On regaining his liberty, King William invaded Galloway with an army, but instead of punishing Gilbert as he deserved, he accepted from him a pecuniary satisfaction. In the following year (1176) Gilbert accompanied William to York, where he was received into the favour of Henry, and did homage to him; the crown vassals as well as the kingdom of Scotland being then, in terms of the treaty which restored William to freedom, placed under feudal subordination to England. [See life of William the Lion, *post*.] From this Gilbert, who died in 1185, sprang, afterwards, in the third generation, Marjory countess of Carrick in her own right, the mother of Robert the Bruce. Meantime Roland, the son of the murdered Uchtred, seized the favourable moment of the death of his uncle Gilbert, to attack and disperse his faction, and to claim possession of all Galloway as his own inheritance, in which he was favoured by his own sovereign, William. Henry II., however, the English king, opposed his claims, and assembling a large army at Carlisle, prepared to invade Galloway. Roland resolved upon a desperate resistance, but the dispute was ultimately adjusted by Roland, after swearing fealty to Henry, being confirmed in the lordship of Galloway, on condition of surrendering the territory of Carrick to his cousin Duncan, the son of Gilbert. He is the Roland of Galloway who, in 1187, encountered and killed the pretender, Donald Bane, at Inverness, p. 69. On the restoration of the national independence, Roland obtained the office of constable of Scotland. He died in December 1200.

Alan, the eldest son of Roland, and the last male-heir of the line of the ancient 'lords of Galloway,' died in 1233. He succeeded as constable of Scotland, and was a personage of considerable importance in Scottish history. He had been twice married. By his first wife he had a daughter Helen, or Elena, married to Roger de Quincy, earl of Winchester. By his second wife, Margaret, the eldest of the three daughters, and eventual

heiresses of David, earl of Huntingdon, the brother of William the Lion, he had two daughters; his eldest daughter by his second marriage, Devorguil, becoming the wife of John de Balliol, lord of Bernard castle, transmitted to their son John Balliol, the competitor, afterwards king, the lineal right of succession to the throne. Devorguil's younger sister Christian, was the wife of William des Forts, son of the earl of Albemarle. Unwilling to have their country partitioned among the husbands of Alan's three daughters, the people of Galloway offered the lordship to Alexander, whose sense of justice prevented him from depriving the legitimate heirs of their right. They then requested that an illegitimate son of Alan, named Thomas, should be appointed their lord. To this application Alexander also refused to accede, on which the Galwegians broke out into open rebellion, having at their head the bastard Thomas, aided by an Irish chieftain named Gilrodh, who joined him with a large force from Ireland. To suppress this formidable outbreak, Alexander led an expedition against the rebellious Galwegians, who did not wait to be attacked by him, but rushed forth from their mountains and fastnesses with Celtic fury, and proceeded to ravage the adjacent country. They even contrived to surround Alexander, when he had got entangled among morasses, and he was in imminent danger till Ferchard, earl of Ross, came to his assistance, and assaulting the rebels in the rear, routed them with great slaughter. Galloway was restored to Alan's heiresses, and the inhabitants compelled to receive as their superior Roger de Quincey the husband of Elena. Thomas and his Irish ally escaped to Ireland, but in the following year they returned with a fresh force, and attempted to renew the rebellion. Gilrodh, on landing, burnt his vessels, as if resolved to conquer or die. The insurgents were, however, again defeated, and Gilrodh surrendered himself to the earl of March without resistance. He was sent bound to Edinburgh castle, but both he and Thomas were pardoned. Their Irish followers, crowding towards the Clyde, in the hope of being able to find a passage to their own country, fell into the hands of a band of the citizens of Glasgow, who are said to have beheaded them all except two, whom Balfour calls two of their chief commanders, and these they sent to Edinburgh, to be hanged and quartered there. The king's enforcing the rights of Alan's daughters, and at the head of an army breaking down the spirit of insurrection, was the introduction to the epoch of granting charters for the holding of lands, and of landholders giving leases to tenants, as well as of the security of property and the cultivation of the arts of husbandry in Galloway.

Notwithstanding the terms of amity in which Henry and Alexander lived, there were still several subjects of dispute between them, which now and then occasioned some disquiet, and afforded matter for discussion and negotiation; although their own pacific dispositions prevented an open rupture. Henry showed at times an inclination to extend the incidents of the homage of the king of Scotland to an unreasonable limit; and in 1234 he went so far as to solicit the Pope to exhort Alexander to acknowledge the superiority of England over Scotland, an exhortation which Alexander, when he received it, paid no attention to. Alexander, on his part, always insisted either on restitution being made to him of the three northern counties of England, or on the repayment of the fifteen thousand merks paid by his father to King John. The vacillating character of Henry III. exposed the peace between the two countries to the risk of constant interruption, but sometimes he would conciliate his brother-in-law's favour by gifts, concessions, and the warmest professions of friendship. An instance of this occurred in 1230, when Henry invited Alexander to York, where he celebrated Christmas, and entertained him with great state, and after loading him with presents, sent him home. In 1236, after an interview between the two monarchs at Newcastle, where they royally feasted each other, Henry bestowed the manor of Driffield on his sister, the queen of Scots, for life, and at a subsequent period he conferred on the same princess the manor of Staunton. [*Chron. Melr.* 203. *Fœdera*, i. 370, 379.] At length in September 1237, the matters in dispute between Henry and Alexander were heard at York, before Otho, or Eudes le Blanc l'Aleran, a cardinal deacon and the papal legate to England. The conference lasted for fifteen days, and twenty-four councillors of the two kings were present. The negociations terminated by a compromise. Henry, in full of all claims, consented to grant to Alexander lands in Northumberland and Cumberland, of the yearly value of two hundred pounds. Alexander agreed to accept of these as an equivalent, and did homage to Henry in general terms. Malcolm Macduff, earl of Fife, Walter Comyn, earl of Menteith, and others of the principal Scottish barons, bound themselves by oath to maintain this agreement on their monarch's part. [*Fœdera*, i. p. 374, 400. *Fordun*, i. 370. *Hailes' Annals of Scotland*, vol. i. p. 153.]

On this occasion the papal legate took an opportunity of intimating to Alexander his intention of soon visiting Scotland, in order, as he pretended, to inquire into the ecclesiastical affairs of his kingdom. Alexander, however, was fully aware of the true motive of this visit, namely, the exaction of money, and he had no desire to gratify the legate in the matter. The avarice of the court of Rome had, about this period, risen to such an exorbitant height as to be the subject of general complaint in all the nations of Christendom. The enormous amount of power which the Pope and his ministers universally possessed was used for purposes of extortion in every kingdom subject to their control. The venality of the popedom was so great that it guided all its dealings with princes and people everywhere abroad, and pervaded its tribunals at home. Simony was openly practised; neither favours, nor even justice could be obtained without a bribe, and he who paid the highest price was sure to obtain his suit. In 1226 Pope Honorius, under pretence that the poverty of the see of Rome was the source of all the grievances that existed, that they might be remedied, demanded from every cathedral in the Christian world two of the best prebends, and from every convent two monks' portions, to be set apart as a perpetual and fixed revenue of the papal see. This demand was felt to be so unreasonable that it was unanimously rejected, but about three years later he claimed and obtained the tenth of all ecclesiastical revenues, which he levied in the most oppressive manner, rapacious and insolent collectors of the tithes being sent into the different parishes, in many cases before the clergy had even drawn their own rents. Of all this Alexander was not ignorant, and he had not forgotten the conduct of the two deputies of the papal legate when, in 1218, they visited Scotland and grievously harassed the Scottish clergy. For a long period previous to his reign, Scotland had submitted, although reluctantly and impatiently, to the repeated visits of a papal legate who, under the pretext of watching over the interests, and reforming the abuses of the church, assembled councils, and levied large sums of money in the country, but now that the Scottish church had obtained from the Pope the right, however ambiguously and loosely worded the bull granting it might be, to hold provincial councils of herself, the presence of a papal legate in Scotland for any such purpose as that pretended by Otho was altogether unnecessary. Alexander, therefore, peremptorily declared that he would not allow any such visit. "I have never," he said, "seen a legate in my dominions, and as long as I live, I will not permit such an innovation. We require no such visitation now, nor have we ever required it in times past." He added a hint that should Otho venture to disregard his prohibition and enter Scotland, he could not answer for his life, owing to the ferocious habits of his subjects. The legate prudently abandoned all idea of the expedition then, but, as shall presently be seen, he carried his intention into effect a few years thereafter. [*Matth. Paris*, p. 377.]

Alexander's queen, Joan, had for some time been in declining health, and according to the superstition of the times, she sought relief at the shrine of Thomas à Becket at Canterbury, but in vain. She died on the 4th of March, 1238, in the presence of her two brothers, King Henry and Richard duke of Cornwall. She had no children.

About this time it would appear that despairing of heirs of his own body, Alexander publicly acknowledged, in presence and with consent of his barons, Robert Bruce, known in Scottish history as Bruce the Competitor, the grandfather of the hero of Bannockburn, as the nearest heir in blood to the crown. The birth of a son by Alexander's second wife, in 1241, put an end to his expectations of the throne at the time; and on the competition for the crown which took place after the death of the Maid of Norway, more than fifty years afterwards, he urged this as one of his strongest pleas. [See life of Robert the Bruce, *post.*]

In the following year (1239) Alexander married at Roxburgh Mary de Couci, daughter of Ingelram or Enguerrand de Couci, a lord of Picardy, Count de Dreux, in France. His family affected a rank and state scarcely inferior to that of a sovereign. The motto of the new queen's father is said to have been

> Je ne suis Roy, ni Prince aussi.
> Je suis le Seigneur de Couci.

The provision of Mary de Couci, on her marriage, was a third of the royal revenues, amounting to upwards of 4,000 merks. [*Matth. Paris*, p. 555.] Soon after this marriage, Alexander, being in England, met the papal legate Otho on his way to Scotland, and strenuously remonstrated with him on his intended visit. Through his earnest entreaty, however, but with extreme reluctance, and only at the joint request of the nobility of both kingdoms, the king at length consented to admit him within his dominions, and even permitted him to hold a provincial council at Edinburgh, but he insisted upon and obtained a written declaration from the legate, given under his seal, that this permission to enter the kingdom should not be drawn into a precedent. Not choosing, however, to countenance by his presence what he affirmed to be an unnecessary innovation, Alexander retired into the interior of his kingdom, nor would he suffer the legate to extend his pecuniary exactions beyond the Forth. [*Matth. Paris*, p. 422.] Under such circumstances the papal emissary tarried no longer than to collect those spoils which both clergy and laity, eager to get rid of him, poured into his rapacious hands. Secretly, and without leave asked, he then departed from Scotland. He had previously in this same year (1240), plundered the prelates and convents of England of large sums of money, partly by intrigues, and partly by menaces, and on his departure is said to have carried more money out of the kingdom than he left in it.

In 1241, the queen gave birth to a son at Roxburgh, whom the king called Alexander after himself. He succeeded him on the throne under the name of Alexander III.

Although the ties of relationship which had bound together Henry and Alexander, were now severed, yet so good a mutual understanding still subsisted between the two kings, that in 1242, when Henry prepared to visit his dominions on the continent, after he had declared war against Louis IX. of France, he committed to Alexander the care of the northern frontiers of his kingdom. He probably distrusted his own barons, who, discontented with his patronage of foreigners, were then preparing that confederacy against him which under Simon de Montfort, a few years later, virtually wrested all his regal authority from him. The king of Scotland, in the absence of the English sovereign, was the most likely person to have seized the opportunity of disturbing the borders; but the trust thus so honourably confided to him was as faithfully and honourably discharged. Alexander II. was not a prince to violate his faith, and he amply proved himself worthy of the confidence which the English monarch had reposed in him. [*Chr. Melr.* 203, 204. *Matth. Paris*, 395.]

In that age the great pastime of the nobles and knights was the tournament. At one of these feats of arms held in 1242, at Haddington, an incident occurred which led to important consequences. Between the noble house of Athole and the Bissets, an English family who held large possessions in the north of Scotland, a feud had long existed. At the tournament referred to, Walter de Bisset was foiled and overthrown by Patrick, earl of Athole, a young nobleman of great promise. It has been already stated (life of Alexander I. p. 54, *ante*), that the earldom of Athole was, towards the end of the reign of David I. obtained by Malcolm, the son of Duncan, the eldest son of Malcolm Canmore. Malcolm was succeeded as earl by his son of the same name. He left a son, Henry, who also enjoyed the earldom. The latter died in the beginning of the thirteenth century. By a son who predeceased him he had two granddaughters, Isabel and Fernelith. Isabel, the elder, married Thomas of Galloway, a younger son of Roland, and brother of Alan, lord of Galloway. Fernelith, the younger, married David de Hastings, an Anglo-Norman knight. This Patrick, earl of Athole, was the only child of the former, and the representative by the female line of the eldest branch of the

family of Duncan. In a short time after, the earl of Athole was murdered at Haddington, and the house in which he lodged set on fire by the assassins. Suspicion at once pointed to the defeated Bisset as the instigator, if not the actual perpetrator of the crime. The nobility, headed by the earl of March, immediately raised an armed force, and, excited to vengeance by David de Hastings, who had married Fernelith, the aunt and heiress of Patrick, and now earl of Athole, they demanded the life of both Walter and his uncle William Bisset, the chief of the family. The latter offered to maintain his innocence by single combat; and urged that, at the time of the murder, he was at Forfar, seventy miles distant. By the exertions of the king he was saved from death, but he was banished and his estates were forfeited. All his kindred were involved in his ruin. As his enemies secretly sought his life, the king took him under his protection and concealed him from their fury for three months. Escaping after that period first to Ireland and afterwards to England, Bisset found his way to the court of King Henry, to whom, as an English subject, he seems to have appealed against the judgment that had stripped him of all his possessions and exiled him from Scotland, on the plea "that Alexander, being the vassal of Henry, had no right to inflict such punishments on his nobles without the permission of his liege lord." So deep was his desire of vengeance for the injuries which he had sustained, that, forgetful of all feelings of gratitude to Alexander, to whose generous interposition on his behalf, he owed his life, he endeavoured, by the most insidious representations, to incite Henry to take up arms against him. He declared that the king of Scots was in league with France, and that he gave shelter and protection to traitors from England who had taken refuge in his dominions.

Henry, believing on good grounds that a strong anti-English feeling had begun to prevail in Scotland, and suspicious of the friendly correspondence which Alexander had, since his marriage to Mary de Couci, cultivated with France, gave but too ready an ear to these artful statements and insinuations. The personal intimacy of the two kings had now for some time ceased, and as national jealousies began to revive, the weak-minded English monarch was the more easily influenced against his former friend and brother-in-law. He complained to Alexander that he had violated the duty which he was bound to yield to him as his lord paramount, and Alexander is said to have replied that he owed no homage to England for any part of his dominions, and would perform none. Henry on this being reported to him, determined on an immediate invasion of Scotland. As one of his pretexts for preparing for hostilities, he alleged that "Walter Comyn, earl of Menteth, had given umbrage to England, by erecting two castles, the one in Galloway, the other in Lothian." [*Hailes*, vol. i. p. 159.] The Comyns were remarkable at this period for their championship of Scottish independence, and as the Walter Comyn mentioned was one of the principal noblemen in Scotland, Henry naturally enough looked upon him as representing the feeling against England prevalent amongst the Scottish nobility at the time. There was another pretext, "that Alexander had leagued himself with France, and had afforded an asylum to Geoffrey de Marais, and other English offenders." In 1242, as has been already stated, Henry declared war against Louis IX. of France, and made an expedition into Guienne, his stepfather, the count de la Marche, having promised to join him with all his forces. He was unsuccessful, however, in all his attempts against the French king. He was worsted at Taillebourg, was deserted by his allies, lost what remained to him of Poitou, and was obliged to return with loss of honour to England. This disgrace rankled in his breast, and Bisset's charge that Alexander was in league with France, touching him on the point where he was most sensitive, incensed him against Alexander. He secretly applied to the earl of Flanders for succours, and instigated no fewer than twenty-two Irish chiefs to make a descent on the Scottish coast. Having arranged all his plans, he proclaimed war against Alexander in 1244, and assembled a numerous and well-appointed army at Newcastle, prepared to cross the borders into Scotland. Some troops which had been sent to the assistance of Alexander by his brother-in-law, John de Couci, were intercepted by Henry. The

English monarch at this period was not on good terms with his nobles, most of whom were personally intimate with Alexander, and remembered their old association in arms with him against the tyrant, King John. From some one or other of them he doubtless obtained information of Henry's intentions, in time to send notice to his brother-in-law in Picardy for what aid he could furnish him with. He then determined upon a vigorous resistance, and was warmly seconded by his nobility. Measures were taken to strengthen the frontier fortresses of the kingdom; and at the head of a gallant army Alexander marched southward, resolved to be beforehand with Henry, and encounter his foes on English ground. From the description which the contemporary English historian, Matthew Paris, has given of the force under Alexander on this occasion it appears to have been a formidable one. "His army," he says, "was numerous and brave; he had a thousand horsemen tolerably mounted, though not indeed on Spanish or Italian horses. His infantry approached to a hundred thousand, all unanimous, all animated by the exhortations of their clergy, and by confession, courageously to fight and resolutely to die in the just defence of their native land." The horsemen were clothed in armour of iron network. Henry had a larger body of cavalry than the Scottish king, and his army included a force of five thousand men at arms, splendidly accoutred. [*Matth. Paris*, p. 645. *Chr. Melr.* p. 156.] The rival armies came in sight of each other at a place called Ponteland in Northumberland. No battle ensued, however. The English nobles held in high respect the character of the Scottish king, who, according to Matthew Paris, was justly beloved by all the English nation, no less than by his own subjects, and they did not fully approve of the rash enterprise of their own sovereign. While the Scottish army, undismayed by the superior array of their opponents, were prepared and eager for battle, the leaders of the English, on the other hand, were only anxious to avert hostilities. Henry soon saw that it would be dangerous to push matters to extremities. Through the mediation of Richard earl of Cornwall, the brother of the king of England, and the archbishop of York, a treaty of peace was concluded at Newcastle on the

13th of August, the terms of which were honourable to both sovereigns, and that without a sword being drawn, a bow bent, or a lance put in rest. Henry did not insist on an express act of homage from Alexander for the kingdom of Scotland, while Alexander, on his side, agreed always to bear good faith and affection to Henry as his liege lord, and not to enter into any alliance with the enemies of England, unless the English did him some wrong. [*Fœdera*, tom. i. p. 429.] The terms of the treaty have by Scottish writers been represented as favourable to Scotland, as in their opinion Henry by it undoubtedly conceded the point in dispute between them. Dr. Lingard, however, an acute and impartial investigator, describes it as " an arrangement by which, though Alexander eluded the express recognition of feudal dependence, he seems to have conceded to Henry the substance of his demand." This much is certain, that although the matter was not pressed to extremities, the claim of Henry was both revived and in part exercised early in the following reign. [*Life of Alexander III.*] It was also one of the stipulations of the treaty, that a proposal made in 1242, the year after a son was born to Alexander, of a marriage between Margaret the daughter of the king of England and the young prince of Scotland, should be carried into effect, as it subsequently was in 1251, when Alexander III. was only ten years old. Alan Durward, at that time considered the most accomplished knight and the best military leader in Scotland, Henry de Baliol, and David de Lindesay, with other knights and prelates, swore on the soul of their lord the king, that the treaty should be kept inviolate by him and his heirs.

In 1247 Alexander was again called to suppress an insurrection which had broken out in Galloway. Exasperated by the oppressions of their liege lord Roger de Quincy, earl of Winchester, the husband of Elena the eldest daughter of the deceased Alan, lord of Galloway, the people of that district suddenly rose against him, and besieged him in his own castle. In a sally which he made he was successful in cutting a passage through his rebellious vassals, and instantly sought redress from the king. Alexander chastised and subdued the insurgents, and reinstated de Quincy in his superiority.

The last expedition in which Alexander was engaged was undertaken in order to compel various of the chiefs in the western islands and in the north of Scotland who were at that time the vassals of Norway, to renounce their allegiance to that power, and to reduce the entire country under his own dominion. On setting out he declared " that he would not desist till he had set his standard upon the cliffs of Thurso, and subdued all that the king of Norway possessed to the westward of the German Ocean." [*Matth. Paris*, p. 550.] The principal of these chiefs was Ewen, great-grandson of the first Somerled, lord of the Isles, and grandson of his eldest son Dugall, who held certain of the western islands under the king of Norway. Ewen being the vassal of both sovereigns for different parts of his possessions, was placed in an awkward position between them, for if he consented to the demand of Alexander, he would only expose himself to the hostility of the Norwegian king, while if he refused it, he was sure to incur the vengeance of the king of Scots. Ewen seems to have considered it the better policy to remain true to the king of Norway. Alexander collected a great fleet and sailed for the western Islands, determined upon making every effort to obtain possession of them. It appears that so great was the attention which was paid to the building of ships in those days, that not only was Alexander possessed of a considerable naval force, but even the Hebridean chiefs, whose principal business was piracy, then esteemed an honourable profession, had formidable fleets. It is stated also that in 1231 Alan, lord of Galloway, who has been already mentioned, was able to fit out a fleet of a hundred and fifty ships, from his own territories, with which he drove Olave the Black, king of Man, from his dominions. This may help to furnish some idea of the extent of the naval strength of Alexander the Second, when he set forth to the western Isles to bring them under his sway.

Deeming it of the greatest consequence to gain over Ewen to his interest, he besought him to give up Kerneburgh, and other three castles, together with the lands which he held of Haco king of Norway, promising him that if he would come under his allegiance, he would reward him with many greater estates in Scotland, and take him into his confidence and favour. All Ewen's relations and friends advised him to yield to the king of Scotland and relinquish his fealty to the Norwegian monarch, but the Island chief remained steadfast to his allegiance, and declared that he would not break his oath to King Haco. [*Skene's History of the Highlanders*, vol. ii. p. 51.] Although, however, he is said to have refused all offers of compromise, he appears to have agreed to pay to Alexander an annual tribute of three hundred and twenty marks, [*Ayloff's Calendars of Ancient Charters*, p. 336], doubtless for such portion of his possessions as was under the actual government of the king of Scots. All our historians style this Ewen, Angus of Argyle, but this is evidently erroneous.

Alexander was not destined to see the end of his expedition. The subjection of the western Isles to the Scottish crown was reserved for his son and successor, Alexander III. When preparing to invade these islands, and so far on his progress as the Sound of Mull, this brave and prudent monarch was attacked with a fever, of which he died July 8, 1249, at Kerrara, a small island lying off the bay of Oban; being at the time of his death in the 51st year of his age, and 31st of his reign. A legend full of the superstitious feeling of the times, yet not without a certain degree of poetical interest, states that as Alexander lay in his bed there appeared to him three men; one of them dressed in royal garments, with a red face, squinting eyes, and a terrible aspect; the second was very young and beautiful with a costly dress, and the third was of larger stature than either, and of a still fiercer countenance than the first. The last personage demanded of him whether he meant to subdue the islands, and on his answering in the affirmative he advised him to return home; a warning to which he paid no attention. The three persons, says the tale, were supposed to be St. Olave, St. Magnus, and St. Columba. The latter certainly showed a most forgiving disposition in taking part with the two Norwegian saints, as the piratical invaders from Norway had always been bitter enemies of his monastery of Iona.

All historians agree in giving Alexander the Second the character of a wise, prudent, and magnanimous prince. Brave, and not unsuccessful in war, he was yet disposed to cultivate the blessings of peace. His rule was firm and strict, and under his sway Scotland advanced in prosperity and civilization; so that at his death he left it a more powerful nation than it had ever been in any previous period of its history. Though prompt and severe in the administration of justice, he was impartial and just, and his personal qualities were of that generous and popular nature which rendered him beloved equally by his nobility and people. Twenty-five statutes of Alexander II. were added to the code of Scottish laws; several of which, says Lord Hailes, require a commentary. His body was buried before the altar of the abbey of Melrose.

The burghs of Dumbarton and Dingwall are the only two which received charters from this monarch. The former town had been resigned by Maldwin, earl of Lennox, into his hands, and in 1222 he erected it into a free royal burgh, with extensive privileges. The latter was made a royal burgh by Alexander in 1227. To the church he was a generous benefactor, as he founded no fewer than eight monasteries for the mendicant friars of the order of St. Dominic, called the Black Friars, namely, at Aberdeen, Ayr, Berwick, Edinburgh, Elgin, Inverness, Stirling, and Perth. Boece, with his usual ingenuity, supposes that Alexander saw Dominic in France about the year 1217; but that was the year when he was deserted by the French prince Louis, and when Alexander was anxious to be reconciled to the Pope and to make peace with England. There is no evidence that Alexander ever was in France. Lord Hailes thus remarks on this conjecture of the inventive Boece: "The sight of a living saint may have made an impression on his young mind: but perhaps he considered the mendicant friars as the cheapest ecclesiastics. His revenues could not supply the costly institution of Cistercians and canons regular in which his great-grandfather, David I., took delight." Some idea may be formed of the value of land in Scotland in Alexander the Second's reign, from the circumstance that the monks of Melrose purchased from Richard Barnard, a meadow at Farningdun, consisting of eight acres, at thirty-five marks.

The following is the seal of Alexander II.,

taken from *Anderson's Diplomata et Numismata,* plate 31. Alexander is here represented clothed in a complete coat of mascled mail, protected by plates at the elbows. The surcoat also first worn in England by King John, is thrown over his armour, another proof, as Tytler remarks, of the

Seal of Alexander III.

progress of military fashions from England into Scotland at that period. His shield is hollowed, so as to fit the body, and completely defend it. The shield then in use in Scotland was the kite-shaped shield of the Normans, and previous to Alexander's time, it was plain and unornamented. The emblazonment of the lion rampant, which had been chosen as his armorial bearing by his father William, surnamed the Lion, and which ever after formed the arms of Scotland, appeared on Alexander's shield for the first time. In this he followed the example of Richard Cœur de Lion, who was the first to introduce into England heraldic emblazonments on the shield. In the above seal, Alexander's horse has no defensive armour, but is ornamented with a fringed and tasselled border across the chest, and an embroidered saddlecloth, on which the lion rampant again appears. The unicorns as supporters of the royal shield were added by the Stewarts to the arms of Scotland.

ALEXANDER III., king of Scotland, the only son of the preceding and of his queen Mary de Couci, was born at Roxburgh castle, on the 4th of September 1241. He succeeded to the throne on the death of his father, 8th July 1249, being then in the ninth year of his age, and was crowned at Scone on the 13th of the same month. This precipitancy was owing to the apprehension entertained by that portion of the Scottish nobles who were opposed to the English claim of supremacy over Scotland, that the English king Henry III., who esteemed himself the feudal superior of the Scottish sovereigns, would interfere in the arrangements preliminary to the young monarch's inauguration. In this proceeding they not only flattered the popular sentiment but were actuated by a regard to the interest of their order, as the privileges of the Scottish barons and clergy, and especially that of independent heritable jurisdiction within their lands, was not only not enjoyed in England, but proved a serious check upon the royal authority and power, and any assimilation of the two countries in this respect was calculated to place their continued enjoyment of them in danger. Of this party Walter Comyn, earl of Menteith, was the head. Indeed, all the power of the kingdom was, at this time, chiefly in the hands of the Comyns, a family descended from Robert Comyn, a Norman knight from Northumberland, who came into Scotland in the time of David the First. During the first years of Alexander's reign, (when, to use the words of Buchanan, " this family governed rather than obeyed him,") their influence in the administration of the country was characterized by a spirit of nationality and opposition to English interference in every shape that was or might be exhibited.

On the day of the coronation, the bishops of St. Andrews and Dunkeld, with the abbot of Scone, attended to officiate, when some of the counsellors, and among the rest, Alan Durward, the high justiciary, or lord chief justice, of Scotland, called also Ostiarius, and in the French *l'Huissier*, from his office as keeper of the palace gate or of the door of the king's chamber, objected to the young king being crowned so soon after his accession, on the grounds that " the day appointed for the ceremony was unlucky, and that the king, previous to his coronation, ought to receive the order of knighthood." Durward doubtless expected that, from his being at the head of the Scottish chivalry, as well as from having married a natural sister of the young king, the honour of knighting Alexander would devolve upon himself; but in this he was disappointed, as the earl of Menteith proposed that the bishop of St. Andrews should both knight the king and place the crown on his head, citing the instance of William Rufus as having been knighted by Lanfranc archbishop of Canterbury. [*Fordun*, b. x. c. i.] He also urged the danger of delay, as the English king, in a letter to the Pope, had solicited a mandate from his holiness to the young monarch of Scotland, that " being Henry's liegeman, he should not be anointed or crowned without his permission." He, therefore, strongly advised that the ceremony should be over before the Pope's answer could arrive. Henry, it would appear, had also requested a grant of the tenth of the ecclesiastical revenues of Scotland. Both requests were, however, rejected by the Pope, Innocent IV., the first as derogatory to the honour of a sovereign prince, and the second as without example. [*Fœdera*, vol. i. p. 163.] It is extremely likely that, chagrined and disappointed at not getting the full extent of his claim as feudal superior recognised by the treaty of Newcastle in 1244, Henry had made this application to Rome before the death of Alexander the Second, to be prepared to assert it effectually when his successor

came to the throne; as there could be no time to have done so in the short period, only five days, that elapsed between the accession and the coronation of Alexander the Third.

The advice of the earl of Menteith was followed. Without waiting for the result of Henry's application to the Pope, the Scottish nobles and prelates seated the young Alexander in the regal chair or sacred stone at Scone, which stood before the cross at the eastern end of the church, and invested him with the crown and sceptre and the other insignia of royalty. The barons, in token of their homage, cast their mantles at the feet of their young sovereign, who previous to the ceremony had been by David Bernham, bishop of St. Andrews, begirt with the belt of knighthood. The coronation oath was read in Latin, and then explained in French, that being then the language of the court, clergy, nobility, and barons of Scotland as well as of England, and the various countries more immediately connected with France. During the ceremonial an impressive incident occurred. While the king sat upon the inaugural stone, the crown on his head and the sceptre in his hand, a white-haired Highland sennachy or bard, of great age, and clothed in a scarlet mantle, advanced from the crowd, and bending before the king, repeated in the Gaelic tongue, the genealogy of the youthful monarch, deducing his descent from the fabulous Gathelus, who, according to legendary lore, married Scota, the daughter of Pharaoh, and was the contemporary of Moses! Alexander, though he did not comprehend a word of this singular recitation, is said to have liberally rewarded the venerable genealogist, who thus unexpectedly introduced this Celtic usage at the coronation of a Scoto-Saxon monarch.

The first act of the new reign, after the coronation of Alexander, was of a religious character, yet held at that period as of no less importance than the coronation itself. The virtues of the pious queen Margaret, the wife of Malcolm Canmore, having become the subject of universal belief as well as of monastic biography, according to the superstition of that age her remains were believed to have the faculty of working miracles, and an application was made to the Pope in 1246, by Alexander II., to admit her into the calendar of the saints. As the general reader is well aware, the evidence required to establish such a claim required to be full and distinct; and in the present instance, after a commission, consisting of the bishops of St. Andrews, Dunkeld, and Dunblane had made a favourable report, it was found invalid, because it had not incorporated the evidence of the witnesses, and a new commission was issued. If we can only get over the difficulty as to whether the class of miracles on which such claims are founded are to be admitted as proveable by any human testimony whatever, the most sceptical must admit that the evidence generally, such as it might be, was both abundant and strict. In consequence of these delays, it was not till 1249 that Queen Margaret became, as a canonized saint, the object of ecclesiastical dedication, and the abbey of Dunfermline, called after her name, had her bones "transferred" from the place were they were originally deposited "in the rude altar of the kirk of Dunfermline" to the choir of the abbey church. The young king Alexander III. with his mother, and a large assembly of nobles and clergy, were present at the ceremony. Robert de Keldelicht, the abbot, raised to the dignity of the mitre in 1244 in a bull, the terms of which are preserved in the registry, granted at the special request of Alexander II., saw the reward of his ambition and donations to the legate. The remains were placed in a silver sarcophagus, which the chroniclers state was adorned with precious stones. So interesting a scene could not take place without a miracle. The body of the wife refused to be translated until that of her husband had been first lifted to the intended spot, then

> " Syne in fayre manere
> Her corse thai tuk up and bare ben,
> And thame enterydd togyddyr, then
> Swa trowyed thai all that gadryd thare
> Qnhat honoure til hyr lord scho bare."
> *Wynton*, b. 7, c. 10.

The next proceeding of the new government was to change the stamp of the Scottish coin, the cross, which previously was confined to the inner circle being now extended to the circumference. This took place in 1250. The coins of this reign were pennies and half-pennies of silver, but though these only were issued, other denominations of money were named in accounting, as the shilling, the merk, and the pound, while foreign coins, which were from time to time imported by the merchants, were allowed to be current in the kingdom. To give some idea of the value of the Scottish silver penny, it may be stated that ten of them were equal to half a crown of our present money. Five pence was the yearly rent paid to the king by the burgesses of every royal burgh, for each rood of land possessed under burgh privileges. The vassal of a thane, or of any other subject, was fined in fifteen ewes, or six shillings, for disobeying the king's summons to join the royal army. Money was common only in the burghs, at markets and fairs, and through the more populous and cultivated parts of the kingdom. In secluded districts, cattle were more frequently referred to, as a common measure of value. [*Anderson's Diplomata Scotiæ, with Ruddiman's Introduction.*]

In 1251 some measures appear to have been employed by those at the head of affairs in Scotland for circumscribing, or at least for defining the limits of the power of the clergy, as the Pope directed a bull to the bishops of Lincoln, Worcester, and Litchfield in England, requiring them to examine into the abuses said to prevail in Scotland, and on these delegates he conferred ample powers of excommunication. [*Chartulary of Moray*, i. 30.] Lord Hailes, who has printed this bull in full in the appendix to the first volume of his Annals of Scotland, thinks it probable that it was never transmitted to the English bishops, no historian having made any mention of it.

The state of the kingdom at this time was unfavourable to the continuance of that peace and prosperity in which the firm and prudent administration of Alexander the Second had left it at his death. The king was a minor, and exposed to the continual demands of the sovereign of England for a recognition of his claim of feudal superiority, while the nobles, instead of joining together and acting in unison for the common welfare, were engaged against each other in a factious struggle for power. They were divided into two great parties. The one, composed of the potent family of the Comyns and their adherents, among whom was John de Baliol, lord of Galloway, were masters of the government. The chiefs of the other party

F

were Patrick Cospatrick, earl of March and Dunbar, Malise, earl of Stratherne, Niel or Nigel, earl of Carrick, Alexander, the steward of Scotland, Robert Bruce, lord of Annandale, and Alan Durward, the high justiciary. The latter party acted all along in alliance with Henry III. of England, who, by the marriage of his daughter to Alexander, soon obtained a fair pretext for interfering in the affairs of Scotland.

As stated in the life of Alexander the Second, (ante, p. 77,) the young prince his son had been betrothed when only a year old to Henry's eldest daughter, Margaret, who was about the same age, and their nuptials, although neither of them had reached their eleventh year, were solemnized at York, 26th December 1251, amidst circumstances of extraordinary splendour. Besides the bride's father and mother, King Henry and his queen, the mother of the young bridegroom, Mary de Couci, the queen-dowager of Scotland, with a train worthy of her high station, was present at the nuptials, [Rymer, vol. i. edition 1816, p. 278,] having come for the purpose from France, whither she appears to have retired soon after the death of Alexander the Second. There were also present the nobility and the dignified clergy of both countries, and in their suite a numerous assemblage of vassals. According to Matthew Paris, a thousand knights, in robes of silk, waited upon the princess at her bridal, and the primate of York contributed six hundred oxen, as part of the marriage feast, which, says the matter-of-fact chronicler, "were all spent upon the first course." With the hand of his daughter Henry gave the promise of a dowry of 5,000 merks, [Fœdera i. 467,] which, however, was not paid till several years afterwards.

In the midst of the marriage festivities, Alexander, according to custom, did homage to Henry for the lands which he held in England, but on his father-in-law requiring him to render fealty for his kingdom of Scotland, "according to the usage recorded in many chronicles," Alexander, by the advice of his council, returned this prudent answer: "I have been invited to York to marry the princess of England, not to treat of affairs of state, and I cannot take a step of so much importance without the knowledge and approbation of my parliament." [Matth. Paris, p. 829.] This famous reply, there cannot be a question, was dictated by the Comyns, whose policy at that period was strictly national, and against the claims of England. The word parliament as here used must be taken with the limitation of meaning pointed out in the life of Alexander the Second (ante, p. 66). It signifies no more than the states of the kingdom, that is a meeting of the regents and counsellors of the king, with the nobles, crown vassals, and superior clergy. Under the feudal system all vassals of the crown, holding their possessions and privileges by the tenure of fixed and certain services, were entitled to receive the royal summons to sit in parliament, as it would now be called, whenever the necessities of the kingdom compelled the king to demand their advice and assistance for his direction and support in providing for the common welfare of the realm.

While the young king remained at York, Alan Durward, the high justiciary of Scotland, who had accompanied him, and who by virtue of his office was one of his chief counsellors, was accused by Henry himself [Hailes' Annals, vol. i. p. 164] of a design against the Scottish crown, "for that he and his associates had sent messengers, accompanied with presents, to the Pope, soliciting the legitimation of his daughters by the king's sister; whereby, in the event of the king's death, they might succeed as lawful heirs of the kingdom of Scotland." Balfour in his Annals, [vol. i. p. 59,] says that "as conscious to this plot were accused likewise Walter Comyn, earl of Menteith, William Comyn, earl of Mar, and Robert, abbot of Dunfermline, chancellor of Scotland, who was accused that he had passed a legitimation under the great seal to the king's base sister, the wife of Alan, earl of Athole, great justiciary of Scotland." The story is taken from the Chronicle of Melrose. Whether there was any foundation for the accusation or not, it is certain that the chancellor hastily left the English court, where he had been with the young king, and returning to Scotland, resigned the seals, quitted his abbey, and assumed the habit of a monk at Newbottle, in Mid Lothian, [Chr. Melr. 219,] and that Henry, on the return of Alexander and his queen into Scotland, sent with them Geoffrey de Langley, keeper of the royal forests, to act in concert with the Scottish nobles, as guardian of the young king, but he proved so insolent and rapacious that he was soon dismissed. [*Matth. Paris*, 571.] Tytler says, but without giving any authority, that the accusers of Durward were the earls of Menteith and Mar, and that Henry placed these noblemen at the head of the new appointment of guardians to the young king, which he made at this time. [*Hist. of Scotland*, vol. i. p. 9.] It is not improbable that Henry's object in bringing this accusation against the popular and potent Alan Durward was as much to remove so dangerous a rival from about the person of the queen, as to obtain the services of so accomplished a soldier and so expert a leader, in his wars in Guienne, which he was conscious he had no means of securing otherwise than by driving him into a sort of banishment from his country, under a charge of meditated treason, not easily repelled. Two years after these transactions, the Pope, having induced Henry to embark in a project for the conquest of Naples, or as it was called, Sicily on this side the Fare, levied a tenth on all ecclesiastical benefices in England for three years, and in 1254 granted to Henry a twentieth of the ecclesiastical revenues of Scotland for the same term, which grant was renewed in 1255 for one year more, to be employed by the English king, as asserted by the chroniclers of the period, in the expenses of an expedition to the Holy Land. [*Chr. Melr.* i. 30. *Fœdera*, vol. i. 467.] We rather think, however, that while this was the pretext, the money thus received from Scotland for four years was by Henry intended to be applied, and was in fact expended, in a fruitless endeavour to secure the crown of Sicily for his second son Edmond, which had been promised him by the Pope. [*Fœdera*, vol. i. p. 502, 512, 530.]

At this time the Comyn party appear to have been in full possession of the government. Robert de Ros and John de Baliol, two of their friends, had the name of regents. In 1254 Simon de Montfort, the great earl of Leicester, the same powerful nobleman who, four years afterwards, attempted to wrest the sceptre from Henry's hand, was sent into Scotland, charged with a secret mission from Henry [*Fœdera*, vol. i. p. 523]; the precise nature or object of which can only be con-

jectured from subsequent events. In the following year complaints were sent from the young queen to the English court, that she was confined in the solitary castle of Edinburgh, "a place without verdure, and owing to its vicinity to the sea unwholesome," that she was not permitted to make excursions through the kingdom or to choose her female attendants, and that, although both she and Alexander had completed their fourteenth year, she was still secluded from the society of her husband. Henry had all along been in communication with the discontented nobles who were opposed to the Comyn party having possession of the government, and there can be no doubt that while he professed to interfere only for the good of his daughter, he fanned their mutual jealousies and animosities, and gave his countenance and support to their proceedings. He declared that he would protect them against the enemies of the king and the gainsayers of Queen Margaret, and promised to make no attempt to seize the person or impair the dignity of the king, and that he would never consent to the dissolution of his marriage with the queen. [*Fœdera*, vol. i. p. 559.] The particular causes of such a declaration are said by our historians to be unknown [*Hailes' Annals*, v. i. p. 165], and to be involved in much obscurity [*Tytler's History of Scotland*, vol. i. p. 11]; but there can be no doubt that when Henry engaged to support the interests of the party favourable to his claim as feudal superior over Scotland, and was preparing to interfere actively in the overthrow of those ministers who were opposed to it, he had found it necessary to make some declaration of the kind to satisfy them that his interference in Scottish affairs was meant to go no farther than a mere change in the party administering the government.

Alan Durward, who was serving with the English army in Guienne, had gained, by his military talents and address, the favour of the fickle monarch of England, and by his advice Henry sent Richard de Clare earl of Gloucester, and John Maunsell, his chief secretary, to Scotland, ostensibly to relieve the young queen from the real or pretended durance of which she complained, but in reality to assist the discontented nobles in their efforts to overturn the Comyns, and place the government in their own hands. While the regents and their protectors the earls of Menteith and Mar were engaged in preparations for holding a meeting of the estates at Stirling, Gloucester, in concert with the earls of Carrick, March, and Stratherne, surprised the castle of Edinburgh, restored the king and queen to liberty, and allowed them free conjugal intercourse. [*Chr. Melr.* p. 220. *Matth. Paris*, p. 908.] To aid this enterprise, Henry assembled a numerous army, and as he led it towards the borders, he issued from Newcastle, August 25, 1255, a proclamation declaring that in this progress to visit his dear son Alexander, he did not design anything prejudicial to the rights of the king, or the liberties of Scotland. [*Fœdera*, vol. i. pp. 560, 561.] The young king and queen were immediately conveyed to the north of England, and had an interview with Henry at Werk castle in Northumberland. Their safe conduct bore, "that they and their retinue should not tarry in England, unless with the general approbation of the Scottish nobility." [*Fœdera*, vol. i. p. 562]. Henry, soon after, visited Alexander at Roxburgh, within his own territories.

At the abbey of Kelso, whither the two kings had repaired with great pomp, a new regency was appointed, 20th September 1255. This proceeding was said to be by the advice of the English king, but there can be no doubt that these entire transactions were under his express direction or rather control and management throughout. The party of the Comyns were removed from the king's council and all their employments in the state. Those among them who were particularly named were Gamelin, chancellor of Scotland and bishop-elect of St. Andrews, William de Bondington, bishop of Glasgow, Clement, bishop of Dunblane, Walter Comyn, earl of Menteith, Alexander Comyn, earl of Buchan, William de Mar, earl of Mar, John de Balliol, Robert de Ros, John Comyn, and William Wishart, archdeacon of St. Andrews, of which see he was afterwards bishop. [*Fœdera*, vol. i. pp. 565, 567. *Chr. Melr.* p. 221.] The English faction, as the earl of March and his friends were accounted, to the number of fifteen, were appointed regents of the kingdom and guardians of the king and queen. [*Fœdera*, vol. i. p. 566.] The following are their names: Richard Inverkeithen, bishop of Dunkeld; Peter de Ram-

say, bishop of Aberdeen; Malcolm Macduff, earl of Fife; Patrick Cospatrick, earl of March and Dunbar; Malise, earl of Stratherne; Nigel, earl of Carrick; Alexander, the steward of Scotland; Robert de Brus; Alan Durward; Walter de Moray; David de Lindsay; William de Brechin; Robert de Meyners: Gilbert de Hay; Hugh Gifford de Yester. The government thus new modelled was to subsist for seven years, that is, till Alexander should have attained the age of twenty-one, and vacancies in the regency were to be supplied by the surviving regents. Alexander declared that he would not restore the Comyn party to favour until they had atoned for their offences against the king of England as well as against himself; except in the event of Scotland's being invaded by a foreign enemy, when they might be again taken into favour. To Henry he promised that he would treat his daughter with conjugal affection and all due honour; and to the regents that he would ratify all their public acts and reasonable grants. Patrick, earl of March and Dunbar, swore upon the king's soul, a customary form of oath in those days, that these engagements should be fulfilled, and Alexander subjected himself to the papal censures should he fail in performance. The instrument drawn up on the occasion was deposited in the hands of the English king [*Fœdera*, vol. i. p. 567.] It was considered by the Scottish party in general as derogatory to the dignity of the kingdom, and Bondington, bishop of Glasgow, Gamelin, bishop elect of St. Andrews, and the earl of Menteith, indignantly refused to affix their seals to a deed which, as they asserted, compromised the liberties of the country, and was prejudicial to the honour of the king. [*Chr. Melr.* p. 221.] Winton (book vii. chap. x.) says of it:

> "Thare wes made swylk ordynans,
> That wes gret grefe and displesans
> Till of Scotland ye thre statis,
> Burgens, Barownys, and Prelatis."

Before returning to England, Henry, with the view of raising money, proceeded to take cognizance of the offences of the late regents John de Baliol and Robert de Ros. As they both possessed estates in England, he held them to be amenable to his courts, even on a vague charge of disrespect and disloyalty to Alexander and his queen. John de Baliol obtained his pardon by the payment of a large fine, but Robert de Ros, to whom the castle of Werk belonged, not appearing to his summons, was deprived of his lands in England, which were confiscated by Henry. [*Matth. Paris*, p. 611.]

The tranquillity of the kingdom being thus, in the meantime, in some degree restored, the young king and queen, attended by a retinue of three hundred horse, visited the court of England in August 1256, and were royally entertained at London, Woodstock, and Oxford. On the second of September of that year Alexander was invested by his father-in-law in the earldom of Huntingdon as a fief held by his ancestors. [*Matth. Paris*, p. 626.] As a farther mark of his affection, Henry issued orders to all his military tenants in the five northern counties to assist the king of Scotland with all their forces. [*Fœdera*, vol. i. p. 605.] He farther declared that the grant which he himself had obtained from the Pope of a twentieth of the ecclesiastical revenues of Scotland should never be urged as a precedent to the hurt of the nation.

The late settlement of the government having been brought about by English influence, was generally unpopular in Scotland, and did not last longer than about two years. "The greater part," says Buchanan, [vol. vii. p. 60,] "of the nobility and the ecclesiastical order, their power being curtailed by the new ordinances, stigmatized them as an English thraldom and a commencement of slavery." The Comyns, taking advantage of this feeling, and working upon the sensitive national jealousy of England, now endeavoured to regain their former position in the government. That party was still powerful, there being at this time in the kingdom three earls and thirty-three barons of the name, [see COMYN, surname of]; and the number of their retainers, assisted by the forces of the other patriotic nobles, backed by the influence of Gamelin, late chancellor and bishop elect of St. Andrews, enabled the Comyns to present a formidable opposition to the regency. Gamelin had, towards the close of 1255, procured himself to be consecrated by William de Bondington, bishop of Glasgow, in direct opposi-

tion to an injunction of the regents. For this act of disobedience he was outlawed, and the revenues of his see were seized. [*Chron. Melr.* p. 221.] Gamelin immediately hastened to Rome and appealed to the Pope, who espoused his cause, declared him worthy of his bishopric, and excommunicated his accusers, ordering the sentence to be solemnly published in Scotland by Clement bishop of Dunblane and the abbots of Melrose and Jedburgh. [*Ibid.*] Enraged at the bold opposition of Gamelin, Henry, to whom the Pope had addressed an imperious letter, on his behalf, prohibited his return, and issued orders for his arrest, if he attempted to land in England. [*Fœdera*, vol. i. p. 652.]

In the meantime the Comyns received a powerful accession to their cause in the support given to them by Mary de Couci, the mother of the young king, who in 1257 returned to Scotland. That princess had, during her residence in France, taken for her second husband John de Brienne, the son of Guy of Lusignan, the titular king of Jerusalem. After the male line of Godfrey of Bouillon had become extinct, the sceptre of Jerusalem was held by Sybilla the daughter of Baldwin and granddaughter of Fulk, count of Anjou, grandfather of Henry the Second of England. Having such an adversary as Saladin the Great to contend with, Queen Sybilla, to strengthen her hands, found it necessary to marry one of the bravest of the knights then engaged in her service, and the husband she made choice of was Guy de Lusignan, the father of John de Brienne, a prince of a handsome person but of no very honourable renown. Although he lost his kingdom by the invasion of Saladin in 1187, he was still acknowledged by all the Christians as king of Jerusalem.

The queen-dowager was accompanied to Scotland by her second husband, and supported by their influence the Comyns and their party acquired strength enough to effect a counter-revolution in the government. It was now considered a favourable time to publish the sentence of excommunication which had been procured from the pope against the enemies of bishop Gamelin. The awful ceremony was performed by the bishop of Dunblane and the abbots of Jedburgh and Melrose, the delegates of the Pope, in the abbey church of Cambuskenneth, and repeated 'by bell and candle' in every chapel in the kingdom. [*Chr. Melr.* p. 182.] The Comyns hereupon declared that the king was now in the hands of persons accursed, and that the kingdom was in immediate danger of papal interdiction, and under the pretext of rescuing the king from such a state of things, and relieving him from the control of foreigners who, they said, filled all the highest offices of the state, they assembled in great strength, and headed by the earl of Menteith, they during the night attacked the court at Kinross, seized the person of the king while in bed, and carried him and the queen before morning to Stirling. They obtained at the same time possession of the great seal of the kingdom. The king and queen were kept separate till the party of the regents were dispersed. [*Matth. Paris*, p. 644.] The charge they brought against the young queen was that "she had incited her father, the king of England, to come against them with an army in a hostile manner, and make a miserable havoc" in the country. [*Ibid.* p. 821.] To strengthen their interest, the Comyns concluded an alliance with Lewellyn prince of Wales, who was then (1257) at war with England, whither Alan Durward had precipitately fled. Taking the young king with them, the forces of the Comyns marched southward to the borders, where it would appear the adherents of the late government had rallied and collected their strength. A negotiation was set on foot which led to a compromise between the rival factions at Roxburgh; the leaders of the defeated party agreeing to refer all disputes to a conference to be held at Forfar. This, however, was only an expedient to gain time, as the latter retired into England, and the earls of Albemarle and Hereford, with John de Baliol, were soon after sent by Henry to Melrose, where Alexander held his court for the time. Although their avowed object was to mediate between the two factions, their real intention was to seize, if possible, the person of the king, and carry him to England. Past experience, however, had led the Comyns to distrust their professions, and the person of Alexander was removed from the abbey of Melrose to the forest of Jedburgh, where the greater part of the Scottish forces had already assembled.

The king of England, obliged to suppress for the present his bitter opposition to bishop Gamelin, and to be silent regarding the obnoxious treaty of Roxburgh, was thus constrained to accede to the appointment of a new regency, consisting of ten persons, six of them being of the Comyn faction, with four of the former regents. This took place in 1258. At the head of the new regency, which may be said to have governed the country till the king came of age, were placed the queen-dowager and her husband. The regents were, Mary the queen-dowager; John of Brienne, her husband; Gamelin, bishop of St. Andrews; Walter Comyn, earl of Menteith; Alexander Comyn, earl of Buchan; and William, earl of Mar. Their colleagues were, Alexander, the steward of Scotland; Robert de Meyners; Gilbert de Hay; and Alan Durward. [*Matth. Paris*, p. 644. *Fœdera*, vol. i. p. 670.] Soon after, Walter earl of Menteith, one of the regents and the soul of the national party, died suddenly. In England it was reported that his death was occasioned by a fall from his horse. In Scotland it was believed that he had been poisoned by his wife, countess in her own right, that she might be free to indulge a guilty passion for one John Russel, an English knight, called by Boece an obscure Englishman, whom, disregarding the addresses of the Scottish nobles, she somewhat precipitately married. The suspicion of her guilt, perhaps groundlessly excited by the slighted suitors, was employed as a pretext for depriving her and her second husband of the earldom, driving them in disgrace from the kingdom, and at last dividing the inheritance between her heirs and those of her younger sister. The latter had married Walter Stewart, called Bailloch or "the freckled," a younger brother of the steward of Scotland, who laid claim to the earldom of Menteith in right of his wife, and by the favour of those in power obtained and kept it. [*Fordun*, x. 11. *Fœdera*, ii. p. 1082.]

It was the policy of the court of Rome in that age, when it asserted a right over all kingdoms and grasped at power wherever it could be claimed, to secure all ecclesiastical patronages to itself; and scarcely was the dispute relative to the regency settled than Alexander found himself likely to be involved in a difference with the Roman pontiff. The bishopric of Glasgow becoming vacant by the death of William de Bondington, Alexander in 1259 bestowed it upon Nicholas Moffat, archdeacon of Teviotdale, one of his own subjects. Disregarding the king's appointment, the Pope, Alexander IV., gave the vacant see to his chaplain, John de Cheyam, an Englishman, and archdeacon of Bath. Sensible, however, that this step would prove disagreeable to the young Scottish monarch, he requested the king of England to use his good offices with his son-in-law, to receive Cheyam, and put him in possession of his temporalities. "Although he is my subject," said Henry to the king of Scots, "I would not solicit you in his behalf, could any benefit arise to you from your opposition to a man on whom the Pope has already bestowed ecclesiastical jurisdiction." Alexander thought fit prudently to acquiesce in the Pope's nomination, but though Cheyam was kindly enough received at the Scottish court, the bishop himself knew that he was obnoxious to the government, and he took the first opportunity of leaving the kingdom, and enjoying the revenues of his see abroad. [*Fœdera*, vol. i. p. 683. *Chr. Melr.* p. 222.] Satisfied with Alexander's apparent submission to his wishes, the Pope recalled certain angry mandates which he had issued against him and his kingdom.

In 1260, Alexander, who had then attained his twentieth year, was invited by his father-in-law to visit him with his queen at London. Whatever may have been the motive of this invitation, the manner in which it was conveyed filled the regents and nobility of Scotland with suspicion as to the ulterior intentions of Henry. It appears that he sent to Alexander for the purpose a monk of St. Albans, who arrived at a time when the king and his nobles were assembled in council, to whom he declined to impart the special objects for which the meeting was desired by the English monarch, farther than that it was to treat of matters of great importance. Two of the regents, Alexander Comyn, earl of Buchan, and Alan Durward the justiciary, with William Wishart, chancellor of the kingdom, were despatched on a secret mission into England, to exact pledges from Henry as to his behaviour towards the young king while at his court. The conditions on which Alexander and his queen consented to visit England on this occasion were, that during his residence at the English court neither the king nor his attendants should be required to treat of state affairs, and that if the queen of Scotland became pregnant, or if she gave birth to a child during her stay with her father, neither she nor her infant were to be detained in England. To the latter stipulation particularly Henry gave his solemn oath. [*Fœdera*, vol. i. pp. 713, 714.]

Thus secured, Alexander, attended by a large concourse of the nobility, proceeded, in October 1260, to the court of England. The young queen followed him by slow stages, and on her approach to St. Albans, she was met by her younger brother Edmond, then a mere youth, who with a splendid retinue conducted her to London. Their reception was unusually magnificent, but Alexander, young as he was, did not allow the festivities which marked the occasion to divert his mind from two objects which had been strong inducements with him to comply with King Henry's invitation. He wished to exercise his rights over the earldom of Huntingdon, which he held of the English crown, as well as to obtain payment of his wife's marriage portion, which had been too long delayed. In this last matter, however, he was disappointed. The authority of the English monarch had been now for nearly two years usurped by the twenty-four barons, at the head of whom was Simon de Montfort, earl of Leicester, and Henry's exchequer was in too impoverished a state to allow him to discharge the debt at this time.

It was agreed that the queen should remain in England until she gave birth to the child of which she was then pregnant, and Henry entered into a solemn engagement that, in the event of the death of Alexander, he would deliver up the child to the following Scottish bishops and nobles to be conveyed to Scotland, namely, the bishops of St. Andrews, Aberdeen, Dunblane, and Galloway, and to Malcolm, earl of Fife, Alexander Comyn, earl of Buchan, Malise, earl of Stratherne, Patrick, earl of March and Dunbar, William, earl of Mar, John Comyn, Alexander, the steward of Scotland, Alan Durward, and Hugh de Abernethy, or to any three of them. This list would seem to indicate that the two rival factions into which the nation had been so long divided had at last united to resist English interference in the domestic affairs of Scotland. Alexander now returned to his own kingdom, and in the succeeding February (1261) the young queen was delivered at Windsor of a daughter named Margaret, afterwards married to Eric king of Norway. [*Fœdera*, vol. i. p. 713. *Chr. Melr.* p. 223.] With regard to the dowry promised with the queen it may be stated that in 1262 Alexander sent the steward of Scotland to England to demand payment of it from Henry. He paid an instalment of five hundred marks, which drained his treasury; and promised to make payment of the remainder at Michaelmas 1263 and Easter 1264. "I appoint such distant terms," he said, "because I mean to be punctual, and not to disappoint you any more." The marriage portion of the princess of England was in fact not all paid till some time after this, and only in small partial payments. [*Ibid.*]

Alexander having now (1262) arrived at full age, took the reins of government into his own hands, and in the administration of affairs he showed both prudence and courage. Combining the zeal, but tempered with discretion, for national independence which had characterized the Comyns, with something of the friendly disposition towards England which had been the most marked feature in the policy of their opponents, this strong-willed monarch was able at once to shake himself loose from the tutelage of either party, and to conduct the government in his own person, according to his own views and judgment. His first important undertaking after he came of age, was to accomplish the subjection to his sway of the chiefs of the western islands, an object which death had prevented his father, Alexander the Second, from effecting, although as related (*ante*, p. 78), he had prepared an expedition for the purpose. The king of Norway, at this time, held unquestioned possession of the Orkneys and the Shetland Isles, and claimed also to rule over the Hebrides. In 1255 the possessions of Angus Macdonald, lord of Islay, the descendant of Reginald, a son of Somerled, lord of the Isles, were ravaged by Alexander, because he would not consent to renounce his fealty to the king of Norway, and he was thus

compelled to become a vassal of Scotland. In 1262, Henry, the English king, interposed his good offices to prevent a rupture between Haco, king of Norway and Alexander, as to the possession of the Islands [*Fœdera*, vol. i. p. 753], which were remarkable at that period for their prosperous condition, their crowded population, and their advanced state of civilization. Haco returned an evasive answer, and after an unsuccessful embassy to the Norwegian court, Alexander determined upon at once endeavouring to bring the Islands under his sovereignty. For this purpose he instigated William, earl of Ross, at that time, says Skene, the most powerful nobleman in Scotland, and whose great possessions extended over the mainland opposite to the northern isles, to commence hostilities against them. This William was the son of Ferchard who acted such a prominent part in the reign of Alexander the Second (see pp. 70 and 72). Ferchard was surnamed Gilleanrias, "the priest's son,"—whence Anrias or Ross, the family name,—descended from a noble who figured amongst the earls that besieged Malcolm IV. in Perth in the year 1160. [See Ross, Earldom of.] Being joined by the Mathiesons, and other powerful dependents, the earl suddenly crossed over to the Isle of Skye, where he ravaged the country, burned villages and churches, and put great numbers, both of men and women, to the sword. [*Skene's Highlanders of Scotland*, vol. ii. p. 52.] The Norse Chronicles relate, that in their wanton fury his soldiers raised little children on the points of their spears, and shook them till they fell down to their hands. The complaints of the island chiefs of the atrocities committed by their savage invaders determined Haco to fit out an expedition to revenge the injuries offered to his vassals.

He accordingly repaired to Bergen to superintend in person the preparations of this armament. These were so vast and so threatening as to spread alarm, as to its destination and objects, even upon the coasts of England. When all was complete, he sailed from Herlover, on July 7, 1263. His own ship, described as having been entirely of oak, was of larger size than the rest, having twenty-seven banks of oars, that is, twenty-seven seats for the rowers. It is also said to have been ornamented with richly carved dragons, overlaid with gold. [*Norse Account of the Expedition, with Johnstone's Notes*, p. 25.] The Norwegian fleet reached the Shetland Isles within two days, whence steering for the Orkneys, Haco proposed to despatch a squadron of light vessels to ravage the south-eastern coasts of Scotland, but the principal nobles and knights on board his fleet declined to proceed unless he himself went with them, and he was constrained to bear up for Ronaldsvoe, now Ronaldshay, the most southern of the Orcadian group, situated about six miles from Duncansby head, on the coast of Caithness, and near to the mouth of the Pentland frith. Here he remained at anchor for some weeks, during which he levied contributions upon, and exacted tribute from, the inhabitants both of the neighbouring islands and of the opposite mainland of Caithness, a district which appears to have been reduced under the Scottish sway in the interval between the death of Alexander the Second and the arrival of Haco. It is recorded in the Norse Chronicle of the expedition that, while the fleet lay at Ronaldsvoe, "a great darkness drew over the sun, so that only a little ring was bright round his orb," which precisely fixes the date of this great invasion, as the remarkable phenomenon of an annular eclipse has been ascertained to have been seen at Ronaldsvoe on the 5th of August 1263.

Haco now sailed to the south. Crossing the Pentland frith, his galleys proceeded by the Lewes to Skye, where he was joined by the squadron of Magnus king of Man. Holding on his course to the Sound of Mull, Dugal of Lorn, the son of Ronald, the son of Reginald MacSomerled, and other Hebridean chiefs, united their forces to his, so that he soon found himself at the head of a fleet of above a hundred sail, most of them vessels of considerable size. Though far from being of the dimensions of the vessels of war of our day, these craft of Norway and the island chiefs were very formidable in piratical excursions. Dividing his force, he sent one powerful squadron, under Magnus and Dugal, to ravage the Mull of Kintyre, and lay waste the estates of those chiefs who had submitted to Alexander, while another was despatched to reduce the isles of Arran and Bute, in

the frith of Clyde. The comprehensive name of the Hebrides comprised in those days not only the numerous islands and islets extending along nearly all the west coast of Scotland, but also the peninsula of Kintyre, the islands of the Clyde, and even for some time the Isle of Man. With the remainder of his fleet Haco cast anchor at Gigha, a little island between the coast of Kintyre and Islay. While he lay here he was met by the island chief Ewen, mentioned in the life of Alexander the Second (page 77), as having refused to withdraw his allegiance from Norway, when that monarch in 1249 set out on his expedition against the western islands. Since then he seems to have reflected on the hazard of holding out against the king of Scotland, as he subsequently, although at what period does not appear, swore fealty to his successor, and on Haco's desiring him to follow his banner, he excused himself, on the ground that he had sworn an oath to the Scottish king, and that he had more lands of him than of the Norwegian monarch. He therefore entreated King Haco to dispose of all those estates which he had conferred upon him. Haco was satisfied with his reasoning, and after bestowing presents on him dismissed him honourably. The reguli or petty chiefs of the Hebrides were in those remote times called kings, and accordingly Ewen is called King John by Tytler, who evidently assumed that Ewen is the Celtic name of John, [*History of Scotland*, vol. i. p. 25], and King Ewen by Skene [*History of the Highlanders*, vol. ii. p. 52.]

The politic example of Ewen was not followed by the other island chiefs who had owned allegiance to Alexander, for Haco was soon after joined by Angus lord of Islay and South Kintyre, who had submitted to Alexander only eight years before (p. 88), giving his infant son as a hostage, and agreeing, by a formal instrument, that his whole territories should be forfeited, if he ever deserted; and even by Murchard, a vassal of the earl of Menteith in North Kintyre, who had obtained this district from the baron to whom it had been granted by Alexander the Second. [*Skene's Highlanders*, vol. ii. p. 53.] Roderic, the Norwegian leader, who had been despatched to reduce Bute, took the strong castle of Rothesay, its garrison having capitulated, part of whom he savagely murdered. He then laid waste the island, and carried fire and sword throughout the adjoining districts of Scotland. After sending a force under Sigurd, a Hebridean chief, to the assistance of the Ostmen, or descendants of the Danes settled on the eastern coasts of Ireland, who were anxious to throw off the English yoke, Haco, with his fleet, the greater part of which had now rejoined him, sailed round the point of Kintyre, and entering the frith of Clyde, anchored in the Sound of Kilbrannan, which lies between the island of Arran and the mainland.

By this time the Norwegian fleet had increased to a hundred and sixty sail, and the danger of a descent on the Scottish coasts became imminent. In this emergency Alexander despatched a deputation of Barefooted friars with overtures of peace to Haco; in consequence of which five Norwegian commissioners were sent to the Scottish court to arrange the preliminaries, when a truce was agreed upon. The defenceless state of the western and south-western portions of Scotland made the gaining of time a matter of the first importance to Alexander until an army could be collected sufficiently strong to repel the invaders. Alexander offered to resign to Haco the sovereignty of all the western or Hebridean isles, claiming as belonging to Scotland only those of Arran, Bute, and the two Cumbrays, in the frith of Clyde. [*Norse Account of the Expedition*, p. 71.] These moderate terms of the king of Scotland were refused by Haco, who carried his fleet across the frith to Millport Bay. Although the coast of Ayrshire was now open to a descent from his fleet, Haco, in consideration of the existing truce, restrained his followers from plunder, but provisions becoming scarce, the officers of the expedition earnestly entreated him for permission to land, that they might obtain by seizure supplies for the ships. Thus pressed, Haco despatched a last envoy to Alexander, of the name of Kolbein Rich, with the following chivalric proposal: "That the sovereigns should meet amicably at the head of their armies, and treat regarding a peace, which if, by the grace of God, it took place, it was well; but if the attempt at negotiation failed, the ambassador was to throw down the gauntlet from Norway, to challenge the Scottish monarch to

debate the matter with his army in the field, and let God, in his pleasure, determine the victory." Alexander was too wary to accept the challenge, although, says the Norse Chronicle, he "seemed in no respect unwilling to fight," and the truce was declared at an end. [*Norse Account of the Expedition*, p. 75.]

A fleet of sixty vessels, under the command of Magnus king of Man, and with him four Hebridean chiefs and two principal Norwegian officers, was now despatched by Haco, across the Clyde to Loch Long, where they took to their boats, and dragging them across the neck of land between Arrochar on the west and Tarbet on the east, which separates the salt and the fresh water lochs, they carried havoc and destruction through the numerous islands on Loch Lomond. Sturlas, a Norwegian poet, thus celebrates this exploit: "The persevering shielded warriors of the thrower of the whizzing spear drew their boats across the broad isthmus. Our fearless troops, the exactors of contribution, with flaming brands, wasted the populous islands in the lake and the mansions around its winding bays." A devastating expedition into Stirlingshire followed under another leader, who returned to the ships loaded with booty. Haco had now to contend with the storms and tempests of the end of autumn, which had been counted upon by the Scots as likely to bring wreck and disaster to the invaders. Ten of their best ships were lost by a storm in Loch Long, and on the first of October, while the main fleet of Haco lay at anchor in the capacious and usually well-sheltered bay between the island of Cumbray and the mainland of Ayrshire, it was overtaken by a tempest of so severe and protracted a character, the wind blowing right up the frith and sound upon his fleet, that the superstitious Norwegians ascribed its extreme violence to the powers of enchantment. [*Norse Account of the Expedition*, pp. 81, 87.] The galley of the king was in imminent peril, and several vessels were stranded. The storm increasing, Haco rowed to one of the Cumbray islands, and caused mass to be chaunted amid the roaring of the elements, in the hope that the dreaded powers of magic might be neutralized by the services of religion. Still the tempest continued, and his own ship, with five other galleys, was cast ashore, while those of the fleet that still rode out the gale, though mostly dismasted or otherwise disabled, were driven violently up the channel towards Largs. [*Ibid.* p. 85.]

The Scots collected on the surrounding heights watched with intense interest the dispersion of the invading armament, and crowding to the beach, immediately attacked with fury the crews of the Norwegian ships as they were successively driven ashore. The Norwegians defended themselves with great intrepidity, and Haco, taking advantage of a lull in the storm, succeeded in sending in boats with reinforcements to their relief, when the Scots deemed it expedient to retire, but only to return again at night to plunder the stranded vessels, among which were two transports. At daydawn next morning Haco landed with a large force, and ordered the transports to be lightened and towed to sea, with those vessels which had not been totally wrecked. The rays of the rising sun now shone upon the Scots army mustered on the heights above the village of Largs, and as it descended from the high grounds towards the beach it had truly a formidable appearance. It was led by the king in person, along with Alexander the steward of Scotland, the grandfather of the first sovereign of the name of Stuart who occupied the Scottish throne; and consisted of a numerous body of foot-soldiers, well accoutred and armed for the most part with bows and spears, with a force of fifteen hundred horsemen, chiefly knights and barons, many of them with their Spanish steeds sheathed in complete armour. All the horses had breastplates. The Norwegians on shore numbered little more than nine hundred men, commanded by three principal leaders. Two hundred of them, under Ogmund Krakidauts, occupied a rising ground in advance of the main body, which were posted on the beach. With the former was Haco, who, on the approach of the Scottish army, was anxiously entreated by his chiefs to row out to the fleet and send them reinforcements. The king insisted on remaining on shore, but they would not consent to his exposing his life unnecessarily, and he returned in his barge to his fleet at the Cumbrays. The Norwegians on the hill, being attacked with great fury by the Scots, who greatly outnumbered them, and pressed them on both flanks,

became apprehensive of being surrounded, and began to retire in scattered parties towards the sea. Their retreat soon changed into a flight, and the divisions drawn up on the beach supposing they had been routed, broke their ranks, and while many of the Norsemen threw themselves into their boats and attempted to regain their ships, the rest were driven along the shore amid showers of arrows, stones, and other missiles, to a place a little below Kelburne. In the meantime another violent storm had come on, which not only prevented Haco from sending ashore in time the expected reinforcements, but completed the ruin of the Norwegian fleet, already much shattered by the previous gales. The Norwegians on land, thus left to themselves, gallantly maintained the unequal contest, and repeatedly rallying, made an obstinate stand wherever the nature of the ground favoured their movements. Gathering round their stranded galleys they defended themselves with all their accustomed bravery, and kept their pursuers for some time in check. [*Ibid.* p. 97.] A young Scottish knight named Sir Piers de Curry was here slain. According to the Norse Chronicle, his helmet and coat of mail were plated with gold, and the former was set with precious stones. In the true spirit of chivalry he galloped frequently along the Norwegian line, endeavouring to provoke some one to single combat. Andrew Nicolson, one of Haco's chiefs who conducted the retreat, answered his defiance, and after a brief encounter, killed him with a blow which severed his thigh from his body, the sword cutting through his armour, and penetrating to the saddle. The Norwegians stripped him of his rich armour; but while doing so they were attacked furiously by the Scots, and many fell on both sides. [*Ibid.* p. 99.] The Norwegians would have been cut to pieces to a man, had not a reinforcement reached them towards evening from the fleet, the boats being pushed through a tremendous surf to the shore. These fresh troops instantly attacked the Scots upon two points, and their arrival gave new courage to the Norwegians, who began to form themselves anew. The contest was protracted till night, when, according to the Norse account, the Norwegians, uniting in a last grand effort, made a desperate charge against their assailants, who were posted on the heights over-hanging the shore, and succeeded in beating them back, after a short and furious resistance. The survivors then re-embarked in their boats, and though the storm continued to rage, got on board their shattered vessels in safety. [*Ibid.* p. 103]. Among the Norwegians of note who fell were Haco of Steine and Thorgisi Eloppa, both of King Haco's household, with many more of the principal Norwegian leaders. Sir Piers de Curry is the only name of mark mentioned as having fallen on the Scottish side.

Next morning the strand was seen covered with dead bodies and strewed with the wreck of the best appointed fleet which Norway had ever sent out. Alexander granted a truce to Haco, to enable him to bury his dead, and to raise above their bodies those rude memorials which to this day mark the site of the field of battle. The chief scene of the contest is supposed to have been a large plain southward of the village of Largs, still presenting a recumbent stone ten feet long, which once stood upright, and is believed to have been placed over the grave of a chieftain, and vestiges are found of cairns and tumuli formed, as is said, over pits into which the bodies of the slain were thrown.

Such was the battle of the Largs, famed in story, song, and tradition, and the most memorable event in the reign of Alexander the Third. The loss sustained by the Norwegians is thus feelingly alluded to in Lady Wardlaw's celebrated ballad of Hardyknute:—

> "In thraws of death, with wallert cheik,
>   All panting on the plain,
> The fainting corps of warriours lay,
>   Neir to aryse again:
> Neir to return to native land;
>   Nae mair, wi' blythsome sounds,
> To boist the glories of the day,
>   And shaw their shynand wounds.
>
> On Norway's coast, the widow'd dame
>   May wash the rock with teirs,
> May lang luik ower the shiples seis,
>   Before hir mate appeirs.
> Ceise, Emma, ceise to hope in vain;
>   Thy lord lyes in the clay;
> The valiant Scots nae reivers thole
>   To carry lyfe away."

After the stranded vessels had been burnt by his order, King Haco weighed anchor with the small remnant of his fleet that remained to him under the Cumbrays, and, being joined by the squadron which had been sent up Loch Long, he steered to the bay of Lamlash in the Island of Arran, and across the frith of Clyde, a few miles from the scene of his disasters and defeat. In Lamlash bay he met Sigurd, whom he had sent to inquire into the situation of the Ostmen of Ireland, and was assured by him that they would willingly receive his aid against the rule of England. The aged but heroic monarch, anxious to wipe out the disgrace of his repulse at Largs, was eager for the enterprise, but a council of his officers opposed the expedition, and it was accordingly abandoned. [*Norse Account,* p. 109.] He afterwards sailed past Sand, Gigha, the Calf of Mull, Rum, and Cape Wrath, to the Orkneys, where he arrived on the 29th October, abandoned by the island chiefs who had joined him, and even by many of his own followers, and with the loss of another vessel in the Pentland Frith. At Kirkwall a mortal illness, brought on by anxiety and disappointment as much as by overfatigue, seized upon Haco, under which he lingered for some weeks, and at last expired on the 15th December (1263). Thus ended the last great attempt of the Scandinavian monarchs to secure to themselves the possession of the Western Isles.

The tidings of the death of Haco and of the birth of an heir to the throne were received by Alexander on the same day, the queen having, on the 21st of January, been delivered at Jedburgh, of a son, who was named Alexander. [*Chr. Melr.* p. 225.]

To follow up the advantages which he had already gained, and complete the reduction of the isles, were now the chief objects of Alexander. With the intention of invading the Isle of Man, he raised an army, and compelled the island chiefs to furnish a fleet for the transport of his troops. Dreading his vengeance, and despairing of assistance from Norway, Magnus, king of Man, son of Olave the Black, who had been subdued by Alan lord of Galloway in 1231, sent envoys with offers of submission, and hastened himself to meet the Scottish king, which he did at Dumfries on his way to subdue the Isle of Man, where he swore fealty to the crown of Scotland, and became bound to furnish to his lord paramount, when required, ten war-galleys, five with twenty-four oars and five with twelve. [*Fordun*, b. 10. c. 18.] This Magnus, king of Man, died in 1265. A military force, under the earl of Mar, was next sent against those chiefs of the Western Isles who had joined or had favoured the invasion of Haco. Some of them were executed, and the rest reduced. After negotiations which lasted for nearly three years, a treaty of peace was at last, in 1266, concluded with Magnus, king of Norway, the successor of Haco, whereby the Hebrides and the Isle of Man, and all other islands in the western and southern seas, of which the Norwegians might have hitherto held, or claimed the dominion, were made over in full sovereignty to Scotland. The Shetland and Orkney islands remained in the possession of Norway. One of the articles of this important treaty provided that four thousand merks sterling of the Roman standard, in four yearly payments, and a perpetual quitrent of one hundred merks annually should be paid by Scotland to Norway, in consideration of the latter yielding up all claim to the isles. Another declared that such of the subjects of Norway as were inclined to quit the Hebrides should have full liberty to do so, with all their effects, whilst those who preferred remaining, were to become subjects of Scotland. To this latter class, the king of Norway, in fulfilment of his part of the treaty, addressed a mandate, enjoining them henceforth to serve and obey the king of Scotland as their liege lord; and it was further arranged that none of the islanders were to be punished for their former adherence to the Norwegians. [*Gregory's Highlands and Isles of Scotland*, p. 22.] To the treaty, which is dated the 20th of July, 1266, was added the penalty of a fine of ten thousand merks, to be exacted by the Pope from the party breaking it. The patronage of the bishopric of Sodor and Man was expressly ceded to Alexander, while the ecclesiastical jurisdiction was reserved in favour of the archbishop of Drontheim in Norway. [*Tytler's Hist. of Scotland.* vol. i. p. 41, *note*.]

After the treaty of cession, Alexander appears to have acted in a liberal spirit towards the island chiefs. Ewen of Lorn, (already referred to as a grandson of Dugall, eldest son of the first Somerled by his second wife, daughter of Olave the red, Norwegian king of the Isles,) was of course restored to the lands in that portion of the Hebrides termed by the Norwegians the Sudreys, which he had resigned into the hands of Haco (*ante*, p. 89), and which he had formerly held of Norway, and was further rewarded for his services and fidelity. By his death, however, without male issue, this branch of the descendants of Somerled, chief of the Macdonalds, became extinct. Angus Moir, of South Kintyre and Islay, grandson of Reginald the second son of the elder Somerled by the same marriage, the ancestor of the second race of the lords of the Isles, who had on its arrival joined the Norwegian expedition (*ante*, p. 89), having determined to remain in the isles, became, according to the treaty, a vassal of the king of Scotland, for his lands there, and was allowed to retain, under one king, all that he had formerly held under both. His son Alexander having subsequently married one of the daughters and co-heiresses of Ewen of Lorn, became the lineal representative of the elder branch of the race of Somerled. The isles of Skye and Lewis were conferred upon the earl of Ross, no part of these islands, or of Man, Arran, and Bute, being granted on this occasion by Alexander the Third to any of the descendants of Somerled, to whom they had formerly belonged. The former, however, viz. the isles of Skye and Lewis, afterwards reverted to that family, when on the utter ruin of the Albany family, accomplished by the revenge of James I., the Macdonalds, lords of the Isles, quietly succeeded to the earldom of Ross, through their descent from the last heiress of that line.

While thus fortunate in securing peace at home, Alexander had been able, in 1264, to allow a large body of Scottish auxiliaries under John Baliol, lord of Galloway, Robert de Brus, lord of Annandale, and John Comyn, to be sent to the assistance of his father-in-law, Henry III., who with his son Edward prince of England, afterwards Edward I., was in arms against his revolted barons, led by Simon de Montfort, earl of Leicester. Northampton was stormed by the royalists, but at the battle of Lewes, 14th May, Henry was defeated and made prisoner, as were also two of the Scottish leaders, John Comyn and Robert de Brus. In this battle great slaughter was made of the Scottish auxiliaries, who behaved with all their accustomed bravery. [*Matth. Paris*, p. 669. *Hemingford*, p. 581. *Knyghton*, p. 2447.] The battle of Evesham, 4th August, 1265, where Simon de Montfort was discomfited and slain, retrieved the fortunes of Henry, and the Scottish barons soon obtained their liberty. [*Chr. Melr.* p. 226.]

The long minority of Alexander, from the constant feuds and contentions among the nobles, and the anarchy which generally prevailed, had struck deep at the roots of the prosperity of his kingdom; but his wise, firm, and judicious rule after he came of age, was well calculated to heal the wounds that had been inflicted, and to restore confidence and tranquillity to his people, by whom he was universally beloved. After the Norse invasion and the reduction of the isles, the kingdom was not again, during Alexander's life, assailed by a foreign enemy, while its internal peace seems to have been no longer disturbed by the turbulence of its domestic factions. For three years after, Alexander was engaged in maintaining the independence of the national church against the exactions of the court of Rome, at the same time, with equal spirit and prudence, keeping in check the domineering spirit of his clergy. In the year 1266, Cardinal Ottobon de Fieschi, the legate of the Pope in England, demanded six merks from every cathedral in Scotland, and four merks from each parish church, for the expenses of his visitation. This demand the king firmly resisted, and appealed to the pontiff. To defray the expenses of the appeal, the clergy supplied him with two thousand merks. [*Fordun*, b. 10. ch. 21.] Soon after (in 1267) a dispute between the king and the bishop of St. Andrews arose from the excommunication of a certain knight named Sir John de Dunmore, for offences committed against the prior and convent of St. Andrews. The king required Gamelin, the bishop, to absolve him, without satisfaction. The latter refused, and not only ratified the sentence, but excommunicated all the adherents of Dunmore, the royal family only excepted. Irritated at his zeal, Alexander allowed the legate to levy part of the disputed contributions, and the

contention between the king and the bishop threatened to rise very high, when, to put an end to it, Dunmore, of his own accord, with creditable good sense, asked forgiveness of the church, made reparation, and was absolved; on which the king and the bishop were reconciled. The papal legate now demanded admittance into Scotland, but the king, having examined his commission, and consulted with his clergy, sent him a peremptory refusal. [*Ibid.* c. 23.] Foiled in this scheme, the legate, in 1268, summoned the Scottish prelates to attend him in England, at whatever place he should think fit to hold a council. He also required the Scottish clergy to send two representatives, who should be heads of monasteries. The Scottish bishops deputed two of their number, and the other clergy two; but though they acceded thus far, it was not to assist the council, but to watch its proceedings, as the cardinal-legate soon found; for when he had procured several canons to be enacted relative to Scotland, the Scottish clergy at once disclaimed obedience to them. Seeing them so resolute, the Pope, Clement IV., took up different ground, and in the course of the same year claimed from the clergy of Scotland a tenth of their revenues to be paid to Henry of England, as an aid for an intended crusade, an object which he thought they could have no excuse in declining to subscribe to. Here again, however, he was baffled, as both king and clergy united in a decided refusal to the requisition, Alexander declaring that Scotland was ready to equip a competent body of knights to proceed to the Holy Land. Accordingly David earl of Athole, Adam earl of Carrick, William Lord Douglas, John Steward, Alexander Comyn, Robert Keith, George Durward, John de Quincy, and William Gordon, all connected with the first families in Scotland, assumed the cross, and sailed for Palestine, whence few of them ever returned. The earl of Carrick here mentioned was Adam de Kilconath, the husband of the lady Marjory, only daughter of Nigel earl of Carrick, whose recent death in the Holy wars had left her heiress in her own right of the whole lands and earldom of Carrick. Her husband, Adam de Kilconath, who became earl of Carrick in her right, having also been slain in Palestine in 1270, she afterwards became the wife of Robert de Brus, the father of the restorer of the Scottish monarchy.

In the meantime, founding upon the papal grant, the king of England, in 1269, attempted to levy the tenth of the ecclesiastical revenues in Scotland, for the crusades. The attempt was spiritedly met by the Scottish clergy, who, not content with appealing to Rome, to show their independence both of the papal legate and the English king, assembled in a provincial council at Perth, under the authority of the bull of Pope Honorius IV., granted in the year 1225, during the reign of Alexander the Second. [See *ante*, p. 66.] At this council, over which one of their own bishops presided, they passed various canons for the regulation of the Scottish church, which remained in force till the Reformation, and with those of the council of 1242, are preserved in the Chartulary of Aberdeen. The first of them appointed a council of the national clergy of Scotland to be held annually, and the second decreed that each of the bishops should, in rotation, be " conservator statutorum," or protector of the statutes, and during the interval between each council he should enforce obedience to the canons, under pain of ecclesiastical censures. [*Fordun*, b. 10. c. 23, 24, 26. *Chr. Melr.* pp. 241, 242.]

In 1270, Alexander's queen gave birth to a second son, who was named David, but who died in his eleventh year. The country at this period enjoyed both peace and plenty, and few events of a domestic nature seem to have occurred of sufficient importance to deserve a place in history. The friendly relations which had been for some time maintained with England were not impaired by the death of Henry III., which took place November 16, 1272. At the coronation of Henry's son and successor, Edward I., at Westminster, 19 August, 1274, Alexander and his queen, Margaret, Edward's sister, were present, with a splendid train of his nobility. Before proceeding to London, Alexander took care to obtain from his royal brother-in-law a letter declaring that his friendly visit to him, on this occasion, should not be construed into anything prejudicial to the independence of Scotland. In those feudal times such a precaution was customary, and we find Edward himself, when twenty years afterwards he sent

some ships to the assistance of the king of France, his feudal superior for the duchy of Normandy, requiring from that monarch a similar declaration. About six months after she had attended her brother's coronation, Alexander lost his queen, who died 26th February 1275, in the prime of her age.

In 1275, a tenth of the church revenues of Scotland was again required by the Pope, for the relief of the Holy Land. Benemund de Vicci, corrupted into Bagimont, was sent to collect this contribution, which was paid by all the clergy, except the regulars of the Cistertian order; that order having compounded with the Pope, by granting a general aid of fifty thousand merks; and thus the amount of their annual revenues throughout Europe remained unknown. Bagimont was prevailed upon by the Scottish clergy to apply to Rome on their behalf for an abatement of the tax; but the Pope, remembering no doubt their former resistance to his demands, refused to grant any commutation, and it was rigidly exacted. The rent-roll by which this tax was levied is known in history by the name of " Bagimont's roll," the estimate being made not according to " the ancient extent, but the true value." [*Fordun*, b. 10. c. 35.] Two years thereafter, Alexander was involved in a dispute with the bishop of Durham, who accused him of encroachments on the English marches. The king of Scots sent five ambassadors to the court of Edward, with the declaration that he had only maintained the marches according to ancient usage, that is, " to the floodmark towards the south," [*Fœdera*, vol. ii. p. 84,] and bearing a proposal that commissioners should be appointed by both crowns to adjust the matter. This dispute, which Lord Hailes thinks, and with good reason, related only to a salmon fishing at the mouth of the Tweed, was, soon after, amicably settled.

In 1278 Alexander attended the English parliament at Westminster on Michaelmas day, when he took the general and traditional oath of fealty to Edward in the following terms : " I, Alexander, king of Scotland, do acknowledge myself the liegeman of my lord Edward king of England, against all deadly." This Edward accepted, " saving the claim of homage for the kingdom of Scotland, whenever he or his heirs should think proper to make it." [*Fœdera*, vol. ii. p. 126.] On this occasion Robert de Brus, eldest son of the lord of Annandale, and who was, by marriage, earl of Carrick, — having seven years before espoused Martha or Marjory, countess of Carrick in her own right, the widow of his old companion in arms, and fellow-crusader, Adam de Kilconath, — by the command of Alexander and with the approbation of Edward, performed the accompanying ceremony of homage, in these words: " I, Robert earl of Carrick, according to the authority given to me by my lord the king of Scotland, in presence of the king of England, and other prelates and barons, by which the power of swearing upon the soul of the king of Scotland was conferred upon me, have, in presence of the king of Scotland, and commissioned thereto by his special precept, sworn fealty to Lord Edward king of England in these words: ' I, Alexander king of Scotland, shall bear faith to my lord Edward king of England and his heirs, with my life and members, and worldly substance; and I shall faithfully perform the services, used and wont, for the lands and tenements which I hold of the said king.' " This having been sworn by the earl of Carrick, was confirmed and ratified by the king of Scotland. [*Ibid.*] Both kings were then and always amicably disposed towards each other, and the time had not yet come for Edward to advance those claims of supremacy over the kingdom of Scotland which, whether well or ill founded, had so often created disquiet between the two kingdoms, and were only finally got rid of on the field of Bannockburn. It is remarkable that the ceremony of homage, under the reservation on Edward's part of the claim of fealty for the kingdom of Scotland, should have been on this occasion performed by the father of that Bruce who, after the long struggle for independence, should have at last succeeded in rescuing the kingdom from the claim for ever. The following portrait of Alexander III. is from a print of the parliament of Edward I. in which the above ceremony was performed, published in Pinkerton's portraits of illustrious persons of Scotland, taken from a copy, in the collection of the earl of Buchan, from an ancient limning formerly in the College of Arms, London.

In 1281 the treaty which, in 1266, had been concluded with Norway, was farther cemented by the marriage of Margaret, the only daughter of Alexander, who was then twenty-one years old, to Eric king of Norway, then in his fourteenth year. A dowry of fourteen thousand merks was given with the princess, who was accompanied to the Norwegian court by Walter Bailloch earl of Menteith and his countess, the abbot of Balmerino, Sir Bernard Montalto, and other knights and barons. The alliance thus happily formed between the two countries was calculated to put an end to those troubles which the restless chieftains of the western islands so frequently occasioned by their turbulence and ambition, and the wavering fealty of whom even the late treaty of peace had failed to secure for any length of time to Scotland. It appears that notwithstanding the submission of King Magnus, Alexander had been compelled in 1275 to lead an armed force against the Isle of Man, and in 1282, the very year following the marriage of the princess Margaret, Alexander Comyn earl of Buchan and constable of Scotland, proceeded with an army to suppress some disturbances in the lately ceded islands. [*Fœdera,* vol. ii. p. 205.]

Soon after the marriage of his sister, Alexander the prince of Scotland, then in his nineteenth year, was united, in 1282, to Margaret, the daughter of Guy earl of Flanders. The ceremony took place at Roxburgh, and the rejoicings lasted for fifteen days. The king himself was, at this time, only in his forty-first year, and might reasonably have expected a lengthened reign, while the marriages of his son and daughter, thus so auspiciously formed, gave an almost certain hope that his sceptre would be transmitted to descendants of his own line. But a singular train of calamities following each other in rapid succession, soon destroyed all such hopes and expectations. The queen of Norway died about the end of 1283, leaving an only child, known in Scottish history as "the Maiden of Norway;" and very soon after, on the 28th of January 1284, the prince of Scotland, who had always been of a weak constitution, also died, at the abbey of Lindores in Fife, leaving no issue. Prince David, the youngest son of Alexander, had, as already stated (p. 95), died in 1281, the year of his sister's marriage. Both princes were interred at Dunfermline.

Being thus bereaved of his children, the first care of Alexander was to take the necessary measures for the settlement of the succession. On the 5th of February, 1284, the estates of the kingdom assembled at Scone, when the prelates and barons became bound to acknowledge Margaret, princess of Norway, as their sovereign, "failing any children whom Alexander might have, and failing the issue of the prince of Scotland, deceased;" it not being then known whether his widow was pregnant. [*Fœdera*, vol. ii. p. 266.]

In the following year, being earnestly entreated by the lords of his council and the estates of the realm, Alexander deemed it prudent to contract a second marriage, and accordingly sent Thomas Tartar, the lord chancellor, with Sir Patrick Grahame, Sir William St. Clair, and Sir John de Soulis, knights, as ambassadors to France, to choose for his bride Joletta, the beautiful and accomplished daughter of the count de Dreux. This lady accompanied them to Scotland, and their nuptials took place at Jedburgh, April 15, 1285. In the midst of the marriage rejoicings, an incident occurred which, in that superstitious age, dismayed and distressed the guests who had thronged to the royal festivities. Amidst the masques and pastimes usually produced on such occasions, and when the enjoyment of the scene was at its height, a spectral image of death glided with fearful gestures among the revellers, and after striking terror into all present, vanished suddenly. The thing was nothing more than a well-acted piece of mummery, or clever pantomimic representation by a person expert in such performances, which were not unusual in the "Moralities" and "Mysteries" as enacted in those days by the monks, but it was held as if foreshadowing those misfortunes which so soon after befell Scotland, beginning with the sudden and violent death of the king himself. [*Fordun*, b. 10. c. 11.] To the north of the burgh of Kinghorn, on the sea-coast of Fife, and northern shore of the Frith of Forth, there stood in Alexander's time a castle, bearing the name of the burgh, which was often the residence of the Scottish kings, but of which no vestige now remains. This castle and the domains attached to it, were frequently pledged, along with others, in security for the jointure of their queens. The young queen Joletta appears to have been residing here on the 16th March 1286, when Alexander the Third, who had been enjoying the chase towards Burntisland and Inverkeithing, turned his horse's head, in the dusk of the evening, towards Kinghorn. The road then wound along the top of the rocks which overhang the sea, and as it was dangerous to proceed in the dark, his attendants strongly urged him to remain at Inverkeithing till the morning. Disregarding their remonstrances the king galloped forward, and when little more than a mile west from Kinghorn, his horse stumbled, and he was thrown over a lofty and rugged precipice, and killed on the spot. The place is still familiarly known in the traditions of the district as the King's Wood-End. The accompanying cut represents the scene of this unhappy catastrophe. This event, the greatest national calamity that Scotland ever sustained, took place when Alexander was in the 45th year of his age, and 37th of his reign. His corpse, after being embalmed, was solemnly interred at Dunfermline, among the kings of Scotland.

The loss of a sovereign so deservedly beloved

—although at the time they could not have foreseen the premature death of his granddaughter the princess of Norway, much less the contest for the succession to the crown, the overweening claims of the king of England, or the subsequent intestine war and the struggle for independence which embittered it, in which the best blood of Scotland was shed and many noble families ruined and cast into exile—yet the many amiable qualities of the deceased monarch, the series of domestic disappointments by which his government had been preceded, and those presentiments of coming calamities which so often cast their shadows before them, tended to

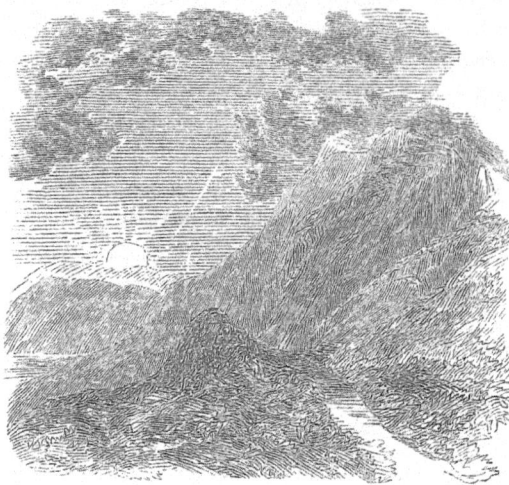

Scene of the death of Alexander III.

overwhelm the people of Scotland with grief and dismay, and the misfortunes and miseries which followed, caused it to be long and deeply deplored. "Neuer," says honest Balfour, "was ther more lamentatione and sorrow for a king in Scotland than for him; for the nobility, clergie, and above all, the gentrey and comons, bedoued hes coffin for 17 dayes space with riuoletts of teares." [*Annals of Scotland*, vol. i. p. 77.] The oldest specimen of the Scottish language known to be in existence is a sort of monody, written on the death of Alexander, which has been preserved by Winton:

" Quhen Alysandyr, oure kyng, wes dede,
　　That Scotland led in luwe and le,
　　Away wes sons of ale and brede,
　　Of wyne and wax, of gamyn and gle.
　　Oure gold wes changyd into lede.—
　　Christ, born in-to virgynyte,
　　Succour Scotland, and remede,
　　That stad is in perplexyte."

Winton, vol. i. p. 401.

The death of Alexander, so disastrous to Scotland, is said to have been foretold, the day previous, to the earl of March, who was one of the chiefs of the English faction during Alexander's minority, at his castle of Dunbar, by Thomas of Ercildon, commonly called Thomas the Rhymer. On the night preceding the king's death, Thomas having arrived at the castle, was jocularly asked by the earl if the next day would produce any remarkable event; to which the bard replied, "Alas! for to-morrow, a day of calamity and misery! Before the twelfth hour shall be heard a blast so vehement that it shall exceed those of every former period, a blast which shall strike the nations with amazement, shall humble what is proud, and what is fierce shall level with the ground! The sorest wind and tempest that ever was heard of in Scotland!" Next morning, discovering no unusual appearance in the weather which indicated a storm, the day on the contrary being remarkably clear and mild, the earl and those who were with him began to doubt the powers of the prophet, as Thomas was esteemed, and having ordered him into their presence, they upbraided him as an impostor, and hastened to enjoy their wonted repast. But his lordship had scarcely seated himself at table, and the shadow of the dial fallen on the hour of noon, when an express, his horse covered with foam, appeared at the castle-gate, and demanded an audience. On being asked what news he brought, he exclaimed: "I do indeed bring news, but of a lamentable kind, to be deplored by the whole realm of Scotland! Alas, our renowned king has ended his fair life at Kinghorn!" "This," cried Thomas, gathering himself up in the consciousness that his prediction had been fulfilled, "This is the scaithful wind and dreadful tempest which shall blow such a calamity and trouble to the whole realm of Scotland!" Whether "the sun-set of life had given mystical lore" to this singular personage, or he had uttered his prediction in the usual mystical language of soothsayers, leaving its fulfilment to accident or the weather, as chance might determine, it is certain that the story has been generally credited from that time till the present, and it would be very difficult now to shake the universal belief in it. As indicating at least the impression which seems to have prevailed, that the death of Alexander foreboded greater disaster and woe to Scotland, than any former event in our annals, it is not without a certain degree of histo-rical interest, and could not well be omitted in any narrative of Alexander's life.

The appearance and manners of Alexander the Third were in the highest degree noble and digni-fied, and such as befitted a king. Though tall and large-boned, his limbs were well-formed and strongly knit. His figure was majestic, and his countenance handsome and expressive. His sin-cerity of character and excellent understanding were such as to command the respect while they won the attachment of his people. He is described as having been affable in demeanour, easy of ac-cess, firm of purpose, and of a just yet generous disposition. His kingdom he governed with wis-dom and energy. With England he maintained constant peace and amity, yet, as Lord Hailes justly remarks, never submitted to any concessions which might injure the independence or impair the liberties of the realm or the church of Scotland. In the administration of the laws he was diligent and impartial, and his inflexible love of justice, and patience in hearing disputes, were amongst the qualities which endeared him to his subjects. For the punishment of offenders and the redress of wrongs, he divided Scotland into four great dis-tricts, and made an annual progress through each, attended by his justiciary and his principal nobles. In passing from one county to another he required the attendance of the sheriff with the whole force of the shire; and the train of retainers of the nobles who accompanied him being, while travel-ling, limited by law, the people were thus relieved of the charge of supporting the royal retinue. He greatly contributed to diminish the burdens of the feudal system, and to restrain the license and op-pressions of the nobility; keeping them in quiet subjection to his authority, and obliging each to act peaceably in his own allotted sphere. In his private life, Alexander was upright, temperate and pious, and in all his domestic relations kind and affectionate. During his reign, according to For-dun, "the church flourished, its ministers were treated with reverence, vice was openly discour-aged, cunning and treachery were repressed, injury ceased, and the reign of truth and justice main-tained throughout the land." [*Fordun*, b. 10, ch. xli.]

In Alexander's reign the little trade that was in the country became so flourishing that foreign merchants were attracted to Scotland in numbers, from the maritime and commercial cities of Italy, France, Germany, and the Low countries, who were allowed to traffic with the burgesses, and had free and safe access to markets in every burgh town. The imports were chiefly wine, cloth and rich stuffs, armour and other commodities, while the staple exports of the kingdom consisted almost solely of fish, wool, and hides. The exportation of Scottish merchandise was, however, prohibited by Alexander under severe laws, owing to the fre-quent losses of valuable cargoes, by pirates, wrecks, and unforeseen arrestments. Notwithstanding this restriction, which showed very narrow ideas on the subject of trade, Scotland, we are told, speedily became rich in every kind of wealth, and in the production of the arts and manufactures. Agriculture, too, had made great progress in Alex-ander's peaceful reign, and, besides the produce of the ground, flocks and herds abounded everywhere. According to Winton:

> "Yowmen, pewere karl, or knawe
>   That wes of mycht an ox til hawe,
>   He gert that man hawe part in pluche;
>   Swa wes corn in his land enwche;
>   Swa than begouth, and efter lang
>   Of land wes mesure, ane ox-gang.
>   Mychty men that had má
>   Oxyn, he gert in pluchys ga.
>   Be that vertu all his land
>   Of corn he gert be abowndand."
>   Vol. i. p. 400.

Indeed, Scotland at that period presented such a field for commercial enterprise that a number of

Lombard merchants, who were in that age the most active traders in Europe, and then filled every mart in England, arrived in the kingdom, and offered to establish manufacturing and mercantile settlements in various parts, specifying particularly an island near Cramond, and the mount above Queensferry. All they asked in return was to be allowed certain spiritual immunities. Their proposal was, however, opposed by some of the most powerful of the nobility, though Alexander himself is said to have been desirous of encouraging them; and their negotiations on the subject were defeated only by his sudden and premature death. [*Fordun*, b. 10. ch. xli. xlii.]

In the period of two hundred and thirty years, which elapsed from the accession of Malcolm Canmore to the death of Alexander the Third, that is, from the middle of the eleventh to near the close of the thirteenth century, a great change had taken place on Scotland as a nation. The vast moral revolution which the Saxon connexion and influence of Malcolm's queen, Margaret, at first remotely worked upon the country had, during that time, extended its effects more and more throughout all its relations, to the great improvement of the people, and their steady advance in civilization. But a sad reverse was now to take place in their destinies. The line of Scotland's ancient kings terminated with Alexander the Third, and the continuous train of miseries and wasting calamities in which the kingdom was involved for more than a generation after his unhappy death, from the long and fierce struggle that ensued for the succession to the throne, in which the national liberty and independence were frequently at stake, marks a peculiar era in the history of Scotland, and caused the memory of so good a king to be long held in affectionate remembrance by the Scottish people.

During the interval from what is usually called in Scottish annals "the Saxon Conquest,"—when by the aid of a Northumbrian Saxon army, Malcolm Canmore was enabled, first to drive Macbeth beyond the Forth, and four years afterwards to defeat and slay him at the battle of Lumphanan in Aberdeenshire,—to the death of Alexander the Third, the last of Malcolm's dynasty, the advance made in civilization, in the useful arts,

and in the habits of social life among the people of Scotland was most remarkable. This was chiefly owing in the first instance, to the settlement of the Anglo-Saxon nobles and leaders in the Lothians and lowlands, and, in the second place, to the introduction of the feudal system by the Norman adventurers who followed them. The revolution that in the course of these changes took place in the laws and customs and forms of government was strikingly favourable to the progressive improvement of the country. The Saxon and Norman colonization of the southern and midland districts exercised a far more direct and beneficial influence on the national character than ever was, or could be, derived from the Celtic race; much of what is peculiar and distinctive in its formation being mainly ascribable to this important accession to the population; and from this period the Saxon domination may be said to have been firmly and securely established in Scotland. In the reign of Edgar one of its principal effects was to confine the Celtic portion of the community to the mountainous districts, while the more enlarged and comprehensive policy of Alexander led him to extend the Saxon institutions to those portions of the country which he may be said to have conquered, and, as we have seen, by the erection of separate sheriffdoms, to bring them more immediately under the operation and subjection of the laws and government.

The changes which took place on the Scottish church and clergy were among the most important of the effects produced by the Saxon conquest, and in this respect it may be truly said, as Mr. Daniel Wilson has remarked, to have been " even more an ecclesiastical than a civil revolution." [*Archæology and Prehistoric Annals of Scotland*, p. 604.] By the marriage of Malcolm Canmore with the Saxon princess Margaret, the sister of Edgar Atheling, much of elegance and refinement were introduced into the Scottish court. By her influence, joined to that of the Saxon refugees, not only were several of the more gross and barbarous customs of the Scots abolished, and various wise and beneficial laws adopted from the system of the Anglo-Saxon jurisprudence, but the whole form and fabric of religion was reformed, and the Scottish church assimilated as much as possible to the English, and to that of Rome; so that, as Mr. Wilson says, "in the period which intervened between the landing of the fugitive Saxon princess at St. Margaret's Hope and the death of her younger son David, nearly all the Scottish sees were founded or restored, many of the principal monasteries were instituted, their chapels and other dependencies erected, and the elder order of Culdee fraternities with their missionary bishops for the first time superseded by a complete parochial system." [*Ibid.*] The change to the better on the ecclesiastical architecture of Scotland that followed was proportionately great. The Scottish clergy, although not so wealthy as their English brethren, appear to have been equally anxious to improve the splendour of their churches, and the commodiousness of their dwellings. Even before the reign of Malcolm Canmore there were at Dunkeld, Brechin, Abernethy, and St. Andrews, religious edifices, as grand and suitable in their way as the state of the arts and manners of those times would admit; but the attention paid to religious matters by his pious queen Margaret, and the encouragement given by her to foreign clergymen to resort to this kingdom, to whom new establishments required to be assigned, fixed a new era in the style and character of the ecclesiastical buildings in Scotland. The Anglo-Saxon and Norman nobles who were driven into this country by the oppressions of William of Normandy, historically styled the Conqueror, also gave an impetus, by their advice and benefactions, to the changes and improvements which took place in the ecclesiastical architecture of the people amongst whom they had found a home. Previous to this period, the churches had been in form, square or oblong, generally built of timber or baked clay, and covered with lead, thatching, or tiles. In imitation of the only parts of the military architecture of the period that could be, in any degree, accommodated to religious purposes, beside some of these square churches, round towers had been erected, either as ornamental, or as secure repositories for valuable things in times of danger. In many instances these round towers may have served as belfries, and in others as places for conveying signals; while in some, it is not unlikely, they were used as prisons. In the ecclesiastical architecture in-

troduced at this period, the nave and the aisles, the chancel and the choir, were distinct parts of the same structure. The relative positions of the nave and the aisles were arranged by the practice of building these sacred edifices in the form of a cross. The native style of ecclesiastical architecture which had been in use was, in the progress of the reformation in the church, entirely superseded by the mode prevalent in England, as its ecclesiastical system had also been. What immediately succeeded appears to have been what is called the early or older Norman, to which Mr. Wilson gives the name of the Romanesque style. Of this the oldest and one of the most interesting specimens now remaining in Scotland is the nave of the church founded and endowed by Queen Margaret at Dunfermline, where her nuptials with Malcolm took place in 1070, which she dedicated to the Holy Trinity, and which was the origin of, and partly incorporated into, the Benedictine abbey of Dunfermline. The erection of the little chapel of St. Margaret in the castle of Edinburgh is assigned to the same period. This has been supposed, on good grounds, to have been erected over the place used for her devotions by Queen Margaret during her residence in the castle till her death in 1093. "It is in the same style," says Mr. Wilson, "though of a plainer character, as the earliest portions of Holyrood abbey, begun in the year 1128; and it is worthy of remark, that the era of Norman architecture is one in which many of the most interesting ecclesiastical edifices in the neighbourhood of Edinburgh were founded, including Holyrood abbey, St. Giles' church, and the parish churches of Duddingston, Ratho, Kirkliston, and Dalmeny." [*Memorials of Edinburgh*, vol. i. p. 129.] As specimens of the early Norman the following may also be mentioned, namely, the parish churches of Leuchars, in Fifeshire; Borthwick, in Mid Lothian; Gulane, in East Lothian; Uphall, and Abercorn, in West Lothian; St. Helen's, Cockburnspath, in Berwickshire; Mortlack and Monymusk, in Aberdeenshire; St. Columba's, Southend, Kilchonchan, Campbeltown; and "the beautiful little ruined church of St. Blane, on the island of Bute, with its Norman chancel arch and graceful First-pointed chancel; besides various others more or less perfect still remaining in Argyleshire—all presenting interesting features illustrative of the development of the Romanesque style in Scotland, and furnishing evidence of the great impetus given to church building at the period." [*Wilson's Archæology*, p. 614.] We learn from the work just quoted that the portions which remain of the original Norman structure of Alexander the First's foundation on Inchcolm, (of which the cut given in p. 58 will illustrate our remarks,) erected about 1123, are characterized by the same unornate simplicity that marks the little chapel of St. Margaret in the castle of Edinburgh, which has already been referred to, and that it was not till the reign of David the First that any certain examples were furnished of the highly decorated late Norman work. The architecture of Kelso abbey, founded in 1128 by David the First, (in the same year with Holyrood abbey,) and the singularly rich details of which have made it one of the most celebrated remains of the middle ages in Scotland, is Saxon or early Norman, with the exception of four magnificent central arches, which are decidedly Gothic; and is a beautiful specimen of this particular style, being regular and uniform in its structure. Though built under the same auspices, and nearly about the same period as the abbeys of Melrose and Jedburgh, it totally differs from them in form and character, being in the shape of a Greek cross. Melrose abbey, founded in 1136, was partially consumed by fire in 1322, and what now remains of the re-edified structure exhibits a style of architecture of the richest Gothic, which has been ascertained to belong to a later age than that of David. The well-known masterly description of it by Sir Walter Scott in the ' Lay of the Last Minstrel,' may, however, not unfitly be applied to the richer portions of the early Scottish Gothic style, which were constructed at the close of this period.

" The darkened roof rose high aloof
   On pillars lofty and light and small;
The keystone that locked each ribbed aisle
Was a fleur-de-lys or a quatre-feuille;
The corbells were carved grotesque and grim;
And the pillars, with cluster'd shafts so trim,
With base and with capital flourish'd around,
Seem'd bundles of lances which garlands had bound."

The chief object of architectural interest in Jedburgh abbey is the Norman door, which, for the elegance of its workmanship, and the symmetry of its proportions is unrivalled in Scotland.

Although not strictly pertaining till a later period to Scotland, perhaps the most interesting specimen of later Norman work is the cathedral of St. Magnus at Kirkwall in Orkney, the most perfectly preserved cathedral of that epoch, the foundation of which was laid in the year 1138, by Rognwald or Ronald, Norwegian earl or count of Orkney, the nephew of the sainted Magnus. Like St. Mungo's in Glasgow, it boasts of being a complete cross church, with all its essential parts entire, and these are the only two cathedral edifices now existing in Scotland, to which this description applies. A remarkably curious and indeed unique example of the architecture of the period is the little church and tower of St. Rule, at St. Andrews. The Norman prevailed about a hundred years, during which period the ecclesiastical architecture of England and Scotland was much the same in character as well as details. The next style that was introduced was the First-pointed or early English, which was adopted about 1170, and was used till about 1242—a period of seventy years. Of this, which is considered an improvement on the later Norman, the crypt and choir of Glasgow cathedral, built between 1188 and 1197, the nave of Dunblane cathedral, Kilwinning abbey, the ruined abbey of Dryburgh, and the chancel of St. Blane's, Bute, already mentioned, are fine examples. Subsequently the ecclesiastical architecture of Scotland assumed a somewhat different style from that of England, and became more distinctive and peculiar in its character. The magnificent abbey of Aberbrothwick, which was founded by William the Lion in 1178, and which furnishes a most interesting specimen of the early Scottish Gothic, is thought to mark the historic epoch in which the native styles had their rise. [*Wilson's Archæology*, p. 618.] As an illustration of the progressive character of Scottish architecture, and the slow rate at which ecclesiastical structures in that age were erected, the reader is presented with the following view of " The North Aisle of the Nave of Dunfermline Abbey, looking west."

The architectural distinctions which are here observable indicate a difference of ages in the styles adopted as well as in the periods of erection. The nave is the only portion of the original abbey church which remains. At the time of the removal of the relics of the sainted queen Margaret, in the beginning of the reign of Alexander the Third, as already related (see p. 81) the choir was remodelled according to the prevailing first pointed style of the thirteenth century, and on this occasion the nave also must have undergone some modifications. The interior of the nave is thus referred to in 'Billings' Baronial and Ecclesiastical Antiquities of Scotland,' article *Dunfermline*: "Towards the western extremity the clustered pillar supports the deeply moulded pointed arch,"—this later style probably indicating the period when the new church was rebuilt,—"while further on," viz. towards the front of the engraving, "the supporting pillars are circular with the stunted hard Norman capital, and the arches are semicircular. The cylindrical shafts of the easternmost arch on either side are adorned by large zigzags," indicat-

ing the varieties of the early Norman. In the middle ages the most skilful *architects* were generally monks or secular clergymen, who were at once the patrons and chief practitioners of the highest branches of the art; hence the peculiarly rich and splendid style of their architectural work, and as a guild of lay *masons* was generally organized wherever any great ecclesiastical erection was going on, hence, too, that singular progressive unity of purpose traceable throughout the various styles of the ecclesiastical architecture of that period.

During the reigns of Alexander the Second and Alexander the Third, Scotland began for the first time to assume that position among the nations of Europe which it continued to sustain while it remained an independent kingdom. Its geographical and political isolation, and smallness of extent and power in proportion to the neighbouring realm of England, as well as its intestine wars, and as has been remarked, "very partial share in the great movements of mediæval Europe, including the crusades," had hitherto prevented its importance from being acknowledged; but its growing influence and gradual development of strength under the monarchs of the period included within what is called " the Saxon Conquest," could not fail to be, in course of time, duly recognised by the other powers; and the marriages of the second Alexander, first to Joan, the sister of John king of England, the daughter of a French lady and educated in France, and afterwards to Mary de Couci; of Alexander, prince of Scotland, the son of Alexander the Third; and latterly of Alexander himself, to other illustrious ladies connected with that kingdom, could not fail to mark the consideration in which Scotland was at this period beginning to be held. It may here be stated that Enguerrand de Couci, the father of Mary de Couci, the mother of Alexander the Third, was one of the most accomplished knights of the age in which he lived, and conspicuous above his contemporaries for his virtues and abilities. He stood so high in the estimation of his brother knights and nobles that they at one period seem to have entertained a project of placing him on the throne of France. Winton (vol. ii. p. 482), says that on account of his brave actions, his possessions, and three marriages with ladies of royal and illustrious families, he was surnamed Le Grand. He was also one of those famous romantic poets of chivalry, who in the middle ages were known by the name of Troubadours, as were also many of his family. His grandfather, Raoul I., lord of Couci, accompanied Philip Augustus in the earlier crusades, to Palestine. His nephew Renaud, Castellan de Couci, with whom Raoul is sometimes confounded, is the hero of the old French ballad of ' The Knight of Curtesy and the Lady of Faguel.' Having gone to the Holy Land with Richard Cœur de Lion, he was mortally wounded in defending a castle in 1191, and desired his squire, after his death to carry his heart to his mistress Gabrielle de Vergy, wife of the lord of Fayel. The squire was intercepted by the husband, and the heart of the unfortunate Castellan was by his orders dressed for supper and eaten by his wife, who, on being informed of the horrible fact, refused all sustenance, and died of voluntary starvation. The fame of the father of his future consort as a votary " of the gay science," and one of the most esteemed Provençal

poets, as well as one of the most gallant knights of the age, must have been well known to the Scottish king, and no doubt had its effect, with the attractions of the daughter, in directing the affections of Alexander II. towards her, on the death of Queen Joan.

The de Coucis were long an illustrious family in France, and in the reign of Charles the Sixth, the then lord de Couci, one of the greatest warriors of his age, married the daughter of the duke de Lorraine. Our historians have universally contented themselves with mentioning the name of the mother of Alexander the Third, without giving any account of her lineage or her father's illustrious qualities both as a poet and a knight. The propensity to verse, song, and the dance, was one of the characteristics of the Norman chivalry, and through the means of the Norman settlers in Scotland, a similar taste must have been gradually encouraged at the Scottish court. Of this fondness for mirth and the gay poetry of the troubadours, which appears to have prevailed to some extent at the Scottish court during the reigns of Alexander the Second and Third, a valuable proof seems to be furnished by the celebrated chesspiece, of which a woodcut is given. This chesspiece is

preserved in the collection formed by Sir John Clerk at Penicuick house, and was found by John

Adair, geographer for Scotland, in 1682, somewhere in the north, while engaged in making a survey of the kingdom. The piece consists in all of seven figures, and is supposed, although not we think on very sufficient grounds, to be of Scottish manufacture.

In this curious and ingenious piece of art, a representation and description of which is given in 'Wilson's Archæology and Prehistoric Annals of Scotland,' page 579, (where it is supposed to belong to the fourteenth century), the queen, probably intended for Queen Mary de Couci, is represented crowned and seated on her throne, with a lapdog on her knee, and what is apparently a book, perhaps of troubadour poetry, in her right hand. On her left stands a knight in full armour, with drawn sword and shield, who appears to be reciting verses, while a trouvere or minstrel on her left seems to be accompanying him on the crowde, a musical instrument then in use which somewhat resembled the violin. The four female figures behind have hold of each other by the hand, while the one next the minstrel bears a palm-branch. The whole seems intended to embody some display before the queen of the joyous science, in which the troubadours took so much delight.

ALEXANDER, a surname in Scotland, probably derived originally from the first king of that name, but chiefly borne by the earls of Stirling and their descendants. The family of Alexander, earls of Stirling, is traced from a remote period by genealogists, who derive it from a branch of the Macdonalds. Somerled, king of the Isles, who lived in the reign of Malcolm the Fourth, and was slain in battle about 1164, had by his second wife Effrica, daughter of Olave the Red, king of Man, three sons, Dugall, Reginald, and Angus. After Somerled's death, the Isles, with the exception of Arran and Bute, which had come to him with his wife, descended to Dugall, his eldest son by his second marriage. Dugall also possessed the district of Lorn. On his death the Isles did not immediately pass into the possession of his children, but appear, according to the Highland law of succession, to have been acquired by his brother Reginald, who, in consequence, assumed the title of king of the Isles. [*Skene's History of the Highlanders*, vol. ii. p. 49.] The portion of property which fell to Reginald's share on his father's death consisted of Islay among the Isles, with Kintyre and part of Lorn. The genealogists of the noble family of Stirling have confounded this Reginald with his cousin Reginald the Norwegian, king of Man and the Isles, who was contemporary with him, and who was the son of Godred the Black, king of Man, the brother of Effrica, Somerled's second wife. Reginald, lord of Islay and South Kintyre and king of the Isles, was the father of Donald, the progenitor of the clan Donald, who had three sons, Roderick, Angus, and Alexander, Roderick's male descendants became extinct in the third generation. The second son, Angus, lord of Islay, the Angus Mohr

of the Sennachies, and the first of his race who acknowledged himself a subject of the King of Scotland, was ancestor of the earls of Ross, lords of the Isles, of the lords Macdonald, and of the earls of Antrim in Ireland. His grandson, John, lord of the Isles, took for his second wife, the princess Margaret, daughter of Robert II., and his third son by her, Alexander, Lord of Lochaber, forfeited in 1431, had two sons, Angus, ancestor of the Macalisters of Loup, Argyleshire, and Alexander Macalister, who obtained the lands of Menstrie, Clackmannanshire, in feu from the family of Argyle, and was ancestor of the earls of Stirling. His posterity took the surname of Alexander from his Christian name. He had a son, Thomas, 2d baron of Menstrie, who is mentioned as an arbiter in a dispute between the abbot of Cambuskenneth and Sir David Bruce of Clackmannan, 6th March 1505. Thomas' son, Andrew, 3d baron, was father of Alexander, Alexander, 4th baron, who had a son, Andrew, 5th baron. This gentleman was father of another Alexander Alexander, 6th baron of Menstrie, who died in 1594, leaving an only son, Sir William Alexander, 7th baron of Menstrie and first earl of Stirling, a Memoir of whom is subjoined in larger type.

Sir William Alexander, the first earl of Stirling, married Janet, daughter and heiress of Sir William Erskine, titular archbishop of Glasgow, parson of Campsie, chancellor of the cathedral of Glasgow, and commendator of Paisley, a younger son of Erskine of Balgony, and cousin of the regent earl of Mar. By her he had seven sons and three daughters.

The earl's eldest son, William, Viscount Canada and Lord Alexander, was appointed an extraordinary lord of session in Scotland, in room of his father, 27th January 1635. He spent a winter in Nova Scotia as deputy-lieutenant, but the hardships he endured while there injured his constitution. He died at London in 1638, during the lifetime of his father. By his wife, Lady Mary Douglas, daughter of William, first marquis of Douglas, he had a son William, the second earl of Stirling, who died within six months after succeeding to the title, under eight years of age.

Earl William was succeeded by his uncle Henry, who was the third son of the first earl,—the second son, Anthony, who had been knighted, and was master of works in Scotland, having, like his eldest brother Alexander, died before his father.

The third earl died in 1644, leaving an only son, also named Henry, who became the fourth earl. He died in 1691, leaving issue four sons, whereof Henry the eldest succeeded as fifth earl, but died without issue 4th December 1739. His three younger brothers having also died without issue in his lifetime, the title became dormant.

The first earl of Stirling's third son, John, married the daughter and heiress of John Graham of Gartmore, of which estate the earl obtained a charter 23d January 1636. By this lady the Hon. John Alexander had a daughter but no sons; and in 1644, he sold Gartmore to Graham of Donnans, progenitor of the baronets of Gartmore, and the Grahams of Gallangad.

Charles, the first earl's fifth son, had an only son Charles, who died without issue. Ludovick the sixth son died in infancy, and James the youngest died without issue male.

In 1830, a gentleman of the name of Mr. Alexander Humphrys, or Alexander, came forward, and claimed the titles and honours as descended from a younger branch of the family by the female side, his mother Hannah, the wife of William Humphrys, Esq. of the Larches, Warwickshire, assuming to be countess of Stirling in her own right. She died in September 1814, and in April 1825 he began to style himself earl of Stirling and Dovan, but was in 1839, tried before the High Court of Justiciary, Edinburgh, on a charge of forging certain documents on which he founded his claim. The jury declared the documents forgeries; but found the charge against Humphrys of having forged them not proven. The result of the trial was to put an end to his pretensions to the earldom. Another supposed descendant, Major-general Alexander, of the United States service, generally styled Lord Stirling, distinguished himself during the revolutionary war in North America, and died in 1783. See STIRLING, earl of.

The noble family of Alexander, earls of Caledon in Ireland, is descended from a junior branch of the house of Stirling.

ALEXANDER, SIR WILLIAM, first earl of Stirling, an eminent poet and statesman, styled by Drummond of Hawthornden, "that most excellent spirit and earliest gem of our north," was the son of Alexander Alexander of Menstrie, in Stirlingshire, and was born, about 1580, in Menstrie House, which is celebrated also as the birthplace of Sir Ralph Abercromby, and of which a wood-cut is given at page 5. All his patrimony was the small estate of Menstrie, of which he was the seventh proprietor, but he acquired both fortune and rank for himself. After completing his education, he accompanied the seventh earl of Argyle to the continent as his travelling tutor and companion. On his return to Scotland, he lived for some time in retirement, employing himself in composing amatory verses. His first poetical effusions were inspired by a passion which he entertained for a lady, whom he fancifully calls "Aurora." His suit was unsuccessful. The lady of his love married a much older person, and like another Petrarch he continued to address her in lachrymatory sonnets. These, a hundred in number, were published in London in 1604, under the title of 'Aurora, containing the First Fancies of the Author's Youth.' He subsequently married Janet, daughter and heiress of Sir William Erskine, cousin of the regent earl of Mar, as stated above. He next turned his attention to grave and moral subjects, with a view to the direction of princes and rulers, in a series of tragedies, formed upon the Greek and Roman models, at least in their chorusses between the acts. One of these, founded upon the story of Darius, was published in Edinburgh in 1603. He had been early introduced to the royal notice, as his residence was near the castle of Stirling, where James the Sixth often held his court, and shortly after that monarch, with whom he had ingratiated himself by his poetry, had removed to England,

in the year stated (1603), Alexander followed him to London. At court he distinguished himself by his genius and accomplishments, and soon obtained the place of gentleman of the privy chamber to Prince Henry, the eldest son of King James. To this youthful and amiable prince he addressed his 'Paraenesis, or Exhortation to Government,' a poem containing important and useful lessons to an heir of royalty. After Prince Henry's death he published it, re-addressed to the new heir-apparent, Prince Charles. From this poem we may quote one short specimen :

"O heavenly knowledge! which the best sort loves,
  Life of the soul! reformer of the will!
  Clear light! which from the mind each cloud removes,
  Pure spring of vertue, physick for each ill!
  Which, in prosperity, a bridle proves,
  And, in adversity, a pillar still.
    Of thee the more men get, the more they crave,
    And think, the more they get, the lesse they have."

In 1607 the tragedy of Darius, above referred to, was republished with three others, namely, Croesus, The Alexandraean, and Julius Caesar, under the title of 'Monarchic Tragedies.' They had another title, 'Elegiac Dialogues for the Instruction of the Great,' and were dedicated to the king. None of them were adapted to the stage. The point of these moral 'Monarchic Tragedies' was to illustrate the superiority of merit to dignity. Thus, in Croesus, we have the following lines :

"More than a crown true worth should be esteemed.
  One Fortune gives, the other is our own ;
  By which the mind from anguish is redeemed,
  When Fortune's goods are by herself o'erthrown."

And in Darius there is the following sentiment ·

"Who would the title of true worth were his,
  Must vanquish vice, and no base thoughts conceive.
  The bravest trophy ever man obtained
  Is that which o'er himself himself hath gained."

We are afraid, however, that the tragedies were monarchic in more senses than one. Instead of such moral truisms, had he checked the intemperate spirit of kingcraft and selfish policy of James, or pointed out, as soon as they began to display themselves in his son Charles, the folly and danger of that love of the prerogative and fatal duplicity which afterwards led him to the block, he would have rendered a benefit to these monarchs, and done good service to humanity. One of these plays, called 'The Alexandræan,' gave rise to the following Latin epigram by Arthur Johnston, editor of his 'Whole Works.'

" Confer Alexandros; Macedo victricibus armis
   Magnus erat, Scotus carmine Major uter ?"

Prince Henry died in 1612, and in 1613 Alexander was appointed one of the gentlemen ushers of the presence to Prince Charles, afterwards Charles I. In the same year he published a 'Supplement,' to complete the third part of Sir Philip Sydney's romance of 'Arcadia,' which had been written some years before. In 1614 he received the honour of knighthood from king James, who used to call him his " philosophic poet," and was made Master of Requests. The same year he published at Edinburgh his largest work, a sacred poem entitled 'Doomsday, or the Great Day of Judgement,' of which there have been several editions. It is supposed that Milton has copied from this in some parts of his Paradise Lost, or at least derived some of his suggestions from it. At this period he commenced his political career. The object which first attracted his attention was the settlement of a colony in North America, in a part of the Council of New England's patent from King James, which they were desirous of surrendering. Of this great tract of country he had a royal grant, dated at Windsor the 10th September 1621, by which the said extensive territory was then given to him to hold hereditarily, with the office of hereditary lieutenant, and was thenceforth to be called Nova Scotia. The following sketch of this proposed settlement is abridged from Bancroft's History of the Colonization of America. Sir Frederick Gorges, governor of Plymouth in New England, a man of energy of character, and zeal for discovery, having a few months previous, November 3, 1620, obtained from James a patent for the famous association, which has but one parallel in the history of the world, whereby forty English subjects, incorporated as " The Council established at Plymouth for the planting, ruling, and governing New England in America," obtained an exclusive right to possess and rule over territory extending from the fortieth to the forty-eighth

degree of north latitude, and from the Atlantic to the Pacific, that company, under a grant from whom the Pilgrim fathers about the same time obtained the privilege of a settlement, being unwilling to witness the Roman Catholic religion and the French monarch in possession of the eastern coast of North America, sought to secure the safety of the northern frontier of the region assigned to them (now the present state of Maine), by inviting the Scottish nation to become the guardians of its frontier, and Sir William Alexander, as a man of influence with King James, and already animated with the ambition, so common to the courtiers of that age, of engaging in colonial adventure, was persuaded to second a design which promised to establish his personal dignity and advance his interest. Accordingly, without difficulty a patent was obtained by him, as already stated, on the 10th September 1621, for all the territory lying east of the St. Croix, and south of the St. Lawrence. Immediate attempts were made to effect a Scottish settlement. A ship was sent out in 1622, but it only came in sight of the shore ; and those on board, declining the perils of colonization, returned to the permanent fishing station at Newfoundland. In the following spring a second ship arrived, but the two vessels in company hardly possessed courage to do more than survey the coast. After making a partial survey of the harbours, and the adjacent lands, they postponed the formation of a colony, and returned with a brilliant account of the soil, climate, and productions of Nova Scotia, which is still to be read in Purchas and other authors.

The territory thus ceded, however, and designated Nova Scotia, had already been included in the French province of Acadia and New France, which, with a better title on the ground of discovery, had been granted by Henry the Fourth of France, in 1603, and had been immediately occupied by his subjects, and it was not to be supposed that the reigning French monarch would esteem his rights to his rising colonies invalidated by a parchment under the Scottish seal, or prove himself so forgetful of his kingly duty and honour as to withdraw his protection from the emigrants who had settled in America on the faith of the crown. [*Bancroft's History of the United States,* edition 1843, p. 134.] The accession of Charles the First in 1625, and his marriage with Henrietta Maria, the daughter of the French king, might have been expected to lead to some adjustment between the rival claimants of the wilds of Acadia, but England would not recognise the rights of France; and King Charles, by a charter dated at Oatlands, July 12, 1625, confirmed Sir William Alexander, and his heirs, in the office of lieutenant of Nova Scotia, with all the prerogatives with which he had been so lavishly invested by King James, and the right of creating an order of baronets of Nova Scotia. All who paid a hundred and fifty pounds for six thousand acres were to receive the honour of a knight baronetcy, and his majesty, by letter to his privy council of Scotland, dated 19th July 1625, fixed the quantity of land that Sir William might grant to the baronets created by him as the qualification and to sustain the title, to be "thrie myles in breadth, and six in lenth, of landis within New Scotland, for their several proportions." The difficulty of infefting the new-made baronets in their remote possessions was overcome by a royal mandate, converting the soil of the Castle Hill of Edinburgh, for the time being, into that of Nova Scotia, and they were accordingly invested with their honours on this spot. Sir William Alexander was to have the precedence of all the baronets. He had the same year (1625) published a pamphlet entitled 'An Encouragement to Colonies,' the object of which was to show the advantages which were likely to accrue to the nation from the prosecution of the scheme. The grants of such title of baronet, though following, in the first instance, in consequence of the voluntary surrender of Sir William, before or after he became earl of Stirling, were afterwards held of the crown, by charter of *Novodamus* to the respective parties. No baronet, however, obtained such grant from the king, without having previously obtained the portion of lands for its qualification, from Sir William Alexander, the lord proprietor of the country. Sir William was also invested with the privilege of coining small copper money. The sale of lands proved to the poet a lucrative traffic, and he forthwith planted and began to settle a colony at Port Royal, where he built a fort.

The version of the Psalms of David into Scottish verse, prepared by King James, had been committed to Sir William Alexander by his majesty for revisal; but from the following extract of a letter to his friend Drummond of Hawthornden, of date 28th April 1620, it would appear that the pedantic monarch, with characteristic vanity, thought his own translation of one of the psalms better than those of the two first poets of his time. "Brother," says Alexander, "I received your last letter, with the Psalm you sent, which I think very well done. I had done the same long before it came; but he (meaning King James) prefers his own to all else; though, perchance, when you see it, you will think it the worst of the three. No man must meddle with that subject, and therefore I advise you to take no more pains therein." On the 28th of December 1627 he received a license from Charles I. to print the late king's version of the Psalms, with the exclusive copyright for thirty-one years. The first edition was accordingly published at Oxford in 1631, but the earl derived little benefit from the privilege thus conferred upon him, as King James' translations of the Psalms, although the use of them was attempted to be enforced by King Charles throughout his dominions, were rejected by the Scottish church and people, and not encouraged by the English, and in the civil war that followed they were lost sight of altogether.

In 1626 Sir William Alexander was appointed principal secretary of state for Scotland. On the 2d of February, 1628, he had another charter, under the great seal of Scotland, in which he was described as the king's hereditary lieutenant of Nova Scotia, and had a grant of certain islands and territories, the bounds of which were most extensive; and the whole were erected into an entire and free lordship, then, and at all times thereafter, to be called and designated the "Lordship of Canada," from the great river then bearing that name, on both sides of which lay the territories granted. This colony, as well as that of Nova Scotia, was founded and established at the sole private expense of Sir William Alexander, the grantee; and both grants were confirmed to him by the parliament of Scotland in 1633.

On the 4th of September, 1630, he was created

Lord Alexander of Tullibody, and Viscount Stirling in the Scottish peerage. Charles the First had, in 1627, entered into a war with France, in support of the Huguenots of that kingdom, which continued until April 1629, when it was terminated by articles of peace, concluded at Susa in Piedmont. During this war, Sir David Kertk of Dieppe, a Calvinist, called Kirk by the English and American historians, and his two brothers, Louis and Thomas, having received the command of three English ships, sailed in 1628 on an expedition against Quebec, then in the hands of the French, which they summoned to surrender. The garrison, though destitute alike of provisions and military stores, returned a proud defiance; but after the Kertks had defeated a squadron sent to its relief, and reduced the garrison to extreme suffering and the verge of famine, Quebec capitulated 19th July, 1629. "Thus," says Bancroft, "did England, one hundred and thirty years before the enterprise of Wolfe, make the conquest of the capital of New France." Before, however, this conquest had been achieved, peace had been proclaimed betwixt England and France, and an article in the treaty already mentioned promised the restitution of all acquisitions made in America subsequent to its date, April 14, 1629.

In consequence of a letter from his majesty, Charles the First, to the lords of the privy council in Scotland, on the subject of the dispute betwixt the English and French concerning the title of lands in America and particularly New Scotland, their lordships, with the other estates of the realm, being assembled in convention, 31st July 1630, unanimously agreed that his majesty should "be petitioned to maintain his right of New Scotland, and to protect his subjects, undertakers of the said plantation, in the peaceable possession of the same, as being a purpose highlie concerning his majestie's honour, and the good and credit of this his ancient kingdom." The removal of the colony planted at Port Royal was nevertheless commanded by his majesty, together with the destruction of the fort built for its protection, and the evacuation of Port Royal itself, by a letter to Sir William Alexander, then Viscount Stirling, dated Greenwich, 10th July 1631. This fort it seems was one which had been erected by Lord Stirling's son, Sir William

Alexander, "on the site of the French cornfields, previous to the treaty of St. Germains (afterwards referred to). The remains of this fort may be traced with great ease; the old parade, the embankment and ditch have not been disturbed, and preserve their original form." [*Haliburton's History of Nova Scotia.* Halifax, 1829, vol. ii. page 156.] The removal of the colony from Port Royal, although it was declared to have been only for a time, occasioned a great private loss to Lord Stirling, and operated as a discouragement to the planting and settling of Nova Scotia. At the same time King Charles wrote to the lords of the council, 12th July, 1631, "We will be verie careful to maintain all our good subjects who do plant themselves there;" and granted letters patent, 28th of the same month, wherein he declared, that he agreed to give up the fort and place of Port Royal, without prejudice nevertheless to his right or title, or that of his subjects, for ever; and even held out the prospect of its garrison, colonies, and inhabitants being allowed to return in consequence of approbation to that effect being obtained from the French king. To their lordships he also wrote, under date 19th February, 1632, with a warrant in Lord Stirling's favour for £10,000 sterling, "in no ways for quitting the title, right, or possession of New Scotland, or of any part thereof, but only for satisfaction of the losses that the said viscount hath, by giving order for removing of his colonie at our express command, for performing of an article of the treatie betwixt the French and us." This is doubtless what Sir Thomas Urquhart, in his 'Discovery of a most Exquisite Jewel,' &c., (8vo, 1652,) refers to, when he charges Lord Stirling with having sold the colony to the French "for a matter of five or six thousand pounds English money;" but it so happens that this sum of ten thousand pounds was never paid either to Lord Stirling or any of his heirs.

That fanciful knight speaks very slightingly of Lord Stirling's plans of colonization, and especially of his project of raising money by the creation and sale of baronetcies in what he calls "that kingdom of Nova Scotia," and says that "the ancient gentry of Scotland esteemed such a whimsical dignity to be a disparagement, rather than any addition to their former honour." Their descendants, however, are of a different opinion. The order of baronets of Scotland and Nova Scotia is considered highly honourable. From the beginning of the reign of Charles the First, when it was first instituted, to the end of the reign of Queen Anne, when the last member was created, upwards of two hundred and eighty baronets of this order were made in all; and of these creations about one hundred and seventy exist at present. The badge of the order is a medal bearing the arms of Nova Scotia, encircled by the motto, "*Fax mentis honestæ gloria,*" suspended from the neck by an orange tawny riband.

Owing to the capture of Quebec by Sir David Kertk, the king of France detained four hundred thousand crowns, part of his sister the queen of England's portion. This brought about a treaty with King Charles, who empowered his ambassador, Sir Isaac Wake, to conclude the dispute 29th June 1631, but it was not till 29th March 1632 that the treaty was signed, by which King Charles agreed to make his subjects withdraw from all the places occupied by them; and for that effect gave orders to those who commanded in Port Royal, the fort of Quebec, and Cape Breton, to render up these places and fort into the hands of such persons as the French king should please to appoint; which put an end to all differences, and the remaining half of the queen's portion was paid by the French king. [*Prince's Annals of New England.*] This treaty is known in history as the treaty of St. Germains. Although by this treaty Nova Scotia was not ceded at all, but only Port Royal commanded to be given up, the French from Quebec and the surrounding district thereafter suddenly broke into the country of Nova Scotia, on the unsupported pretence of a right to the possession of it, by the treaty just referred to. The troubles in England, in which King Charles was involved, prevented his breaking with the French court, and the French availed themselves of the opportunity of the convulsed state of Britain to take possession of Nova Scotia, and keep it for a long time, without being molested, or any effectual remonstrances being made against their aggression.

In June 1633 the patents or grants to Sir William Alexander, viscount of Stirling, were solemnly ratified by the Scottish parliament, and at the coronation of King Charles at Holyrood on the 14th of the same month, with a view to perpetuate the name of the lordship of Canada in his family, the king, by other letters patent, created him viscount of Canada, and earl of Stirling. His salary as secretary of state for Scotland was only one hundred pounds sterling, but the privilege which, as already stated, he had received from the king, of issuing small coins, as well as his sale of baronetcies, added much to his fortune. As, however, the intrinsic value of these coins was inferior to their nominal, this monopoly was unpopular. They were called "turners," from the French town *Tournois*, where this money was first coined, and which, being a mixture of copper and brass termed billon, was known by the name of "turners" from this circumstance, as also "billons" from the mixture of which they were composed. Thus the poet Beattie, in the only known composition of his in the Scottish language, referring to the disposition which prevailed on the part of the Scots to look to English to the neglect of native literature, after the death of Allan Ramsay, thus uses the word:

> " Since Allan's death, nae body car'd
> For anes to speer how Scotia far'd;
> Nor plack nor thristled turner war'd
>   To quench her drouth;
> For, frae the cottar to the laird
>   We a' run south."

It was called the thristled, that is, thistled turner, to distinguish it from the French coin, which, owing to the friendship subsisting between the Scots and the French, circulated in Scotland even so late as the reign of Louis the Fourteenth. The Scottish turner, or *tournois*, bore the national emblem of the thistle. It was sometimes called a bodle, or black farthing, value two pennies Scotch; being half a plack, value fourpence Scotch, or one-third of a penny English. The motto of the earl of Stirling was "*Per Mare, per Terras,*" which, with his armorial bearings, he caused to be placed in front of a spacious mansion he had erected at Stirling. His motto, in allusion to his poetry and his coinage, was thus parodied by the sarcastic Scott of Scotstarvet, "*per metres, per turners,*" which became current among the people. The house remains, but has been long known by the name of Argyle's lodging; the arms of the Alexanders having after his death in 1640, when it passed into that family, been removed to make way for those of Argyle. "This baronial edifice is a very excellent specimen," says Billings, in his 'Baronial Architecture of Scotland,' "of that French style which predominated in the north in the early part of the seventeenth century. Its characteristic features are, round towers or turrets, whether at the exterior or interior angles, with conical summits, rows of richly ornamented dormer windows, and a profuse distribution of semi-classic mouldings and other decorations." The accompanying cut represents it as originally constructed, and before the cone-topped tower

was substituted by the polygonal one erected in 1674. It is taken from the highly interesting work above referred to. The original portion bears the date of 1632. After the additions made to it in 1674, James VII., when duke of York, became its inmate as guest of Argyle, "an incident," says Billings, "noticed in connection with the circumstance, that the guest was subsequently instrumental in putting his host to death." It was here the great Duke John held his council of war, when suppressing the rebellion of 1715. The

building subsequently came into possession of the Crown, and is now used as a military hospital for the garrison. [*Nimmo's Stirlingshire*, p. 342.] Besides being secretary of state, an office which he is said to have held with no small degree of reputation till his death, his lordship was by Charles the First appointed a member of the privy council, keeper of the signet in Scotland, commissioner of exchequer, and an extraordinary lord of session; a plurality of offices doubtless sufficient for one man.

In 1637, by a privy seal precept dated 30th July, the earl was created earl of Dovan in Scotland, with precedency from June 1633. He continued to procure the creation of baronets of those persons respectively who concurred with him in the great enterprise of fully planting Nova Scotia, and he made up their territorial qualifications for receiving the dignity, by surrender of portions of the lands in their favour. This, we are told, he did down to 31st July 1637, at which time he ceased to make them, intelligence having reached him that the French had overrun the country and held it in possession. Thus, twelve years after the commencement of this great undertaking,— when one hundred and eleven baronets having fulfilled the stipulated conditions of the institution, had each received grants of sixteen thousand acres, which were erected into free baronies of regality, and two parliaments of Scotland, in 1630 and 1633, had ratified and confirmed all the privileges of the order,—it fell to the ground.

In 1638 Lord Stirling's eldest son and heir, William, lord Alexander, died, when his lordship made a surrender of all his honours and estates into the hands of King Charles, who, by a charter of *Novodamus*, under the great seal of Scotland, dated the 7th of December 1639, regranted them to the earl, to hold to himself and the heirs male of his body, whom failing to the eldest heirs female. Shortly after this, Lord Stirling died at London, on the 12th of September 1640, and was interred at Stirling on the 12th of April thereafter. His corpse was deposited in a leaden coffin in the family aisle in the church of Stirling, aboveground, and remained entire for a hundred years. He never relinquished any of the rights vested in him under his patents, and an assignment of them in trust was executed by him only two weeks before his death. The accompanying portrait of his lordship is taken from one given in Walpole's Royal and Noble authors :

The province of Nova Scotia finally came under the undisputed possession of Great Britain in 1763. By the fourth article of the treaty of Paris, of 10th February of that year, the French king renounced all pretensions to Nova Scotia in all its parts, and thus, with Canada, its sovereignty was re-acquired by Great Britain, in whose possession it now remains. The baronets of Scotland and Nova Scotia in the year 1836, held a meeting at Edinburgh for the purpose of reviving the objects for which their order was created, and a " Case, showing their rights and privileges, dignitorial and territorial," was shortly thereafter published by Richard Broun, Esq., the secretary of the order, afterwards Sir Richard Broun, baronet, of Colstoun, Dumfries-shire ; but there is very little likelihood now of their ever regaining the lands in Nova Scotia which were originally granted with their titles. Since Queen Anne's time no new Nova Scotia baronets have been made. Those created are styled baronets of Great Britain, and no payment of money can now purchase the title, although of course expenses attend the passage of a patent, on the title being conferred. —By his countess, as already stated in the preliminary notice, the earl of Stirling had seven sons and three daughters, but only three sons and two daughters survived him.

A complete edition of Lord Stirling's works, revised by himself, was published in 1637, in one volume folio, under the title of ' Recreations with the Muses.' This work contained his four ' Monarchick Tragedies,' his ' Doomsday,' the ' Paraenesis to Prince Henry,' and the first book of an intended heroic poem, entitled ' Jonathan.' His poems are generally of a grave and moralizing character, and possess considerable merit. Mr. George Chalmers has remarked, that he must be allowed to have sentiments that sparkle, though not " words that burn," [*Apology for the Believers,* &c., p. 420] ; and Mr. Alexander Chalmers adds to this remark that " his versification is, in general, much superior to that of his contemporaries, and approaches nearer to the elegance of modern times than could have been expected from one who wrote so much." His works were highly praised by writers of his own day. The opinion of Drummond of Hawthornden has been already quoted. Michael Drayton, who commended Lord Stirling's poems highly, expresses a wish to be known as the friend of a writer " whose muse was like his mind ;" and John Davies of Hereford, in a book of epigrams, published about the year 1611, praises the tragedies of his lordship, and says that " Alexander the Great had not gained more glory with his sword than this Alexander had gained by his pen." Higher approbation even than this, as coming from a higher authority in matters of literature, is afforded in the verdict of Addison, who said of Lord Stirling's " whole works," that " he had read them over with the greatest satisfaction." Dr. Currie, in his Life of Burns, says, " Lord Stirling and Drummond of Hawthornden studied the language of England, and composed in it with precision and elegance. They were, however, the last of their countrymen who deserved to be considered as poets in that century." Dean Swift, in one of his poems, has brought their names together as

" Scottish bards of highest fame,
Wise Hawthornden and Stirling's lord."

His plays appear to be mere dramatic poems, more fitted for perusal in the closet than representation on the stage, and accordingly none of them seem ever to have been acted. Three poems by his lordship and a few of his letters, with 'Anacrisis, or a Censure of Poets,' occur in the folio edition of Drummond's works. The latter of these productions is considered very creditable to his lordship's talents as a critic. As a proof of the unpopularity of Lord Stirling in his native country on account of his small copper money, it is stated by Burnet, in his Memoirs of the Dukes of Hamilton, that he durst not come to Scotland to attend to the king's affairs as secretary of state. His productions are as follows:

Darius: a Tragedy. Edin. 1603, 4to. Reprinted with the Tragedy of Crœsus and a Parænesis to the Prince, 1604, and still further augmented with the Alexandrian Tragedy and Julius Cæsar. Lond. 1607, 4to.

Aurora; containing the first Fancies of the Author's youth. Inscribed to the Lady Agnes (Anne) Douglas, (afterwards Countess of Argyle). Lond. 1604, 4to.

The Monarchicke Tragedies. Lond. 1604, 1607, 4to. 3d edition. Lond. 1616, small 8vo.

An Elegie on the Death of Prince Henrie. Edin. 1612, 4to. Including an Address 'To his Majestie,' and 'A Short Viewe of the State of Man.'

Doomesday, or the Great Day of the Lord's Judgement. Edin. 1614, 4to.

A Supplement of a Defect in the third part of Sidney's Arcadia. Dublin, 1621, fol.

An Encouragement to Colonies. Lond. 1625, 4to.

A Map and Description of New England, with a Discourse of Plantation and the Colonies, &c. Lond. 1630, 4to.

Recreations with the Muses, being his whole works, with the exception of Aurora, and including Jonathan, an Unfinished Poem. Lond. 1637, fol.

ALEXANDER, JOHN, a painter of some eminence during the earlier half of the eighteenth century. Neither the place of his birth nor the date is recorded, but he was a descendant of the more celebrated George Jamesone, through his lawful daughter, Mary Jamesone. He studied his art chiefly at Florence. On his return in 1720, to Scotland, he resided at Gordon castle, having found a liberal patroness in the duchess of Gordon, a daughter of the earl of Peterborough. He painted poetical, allegorical, and ornamental pieces; also portraits and historical landscapes. Many of the portraits of Queen Mary are by Alexander. He had begun, it is stated, a picture of Mary's escape from Lochleven castle, which he did not live to finish.

ALISON, the name of a family possessing a baronetcy of the United Kingdom, conferred 25th June, 1852, on Sir Archibald Alison, LL.D., D.C.L., and F.R.S., born at Kinley, Salop, 29th December, 1792. His father, the Rev. Archibald Alison, author of 'Essays on Taste,' of whom a memoir follows, was a scion of the family of Alison of Newhall, parish of Kettins, Forfarshire. By the mother's side he is descended lineally from Edward I. and Robert the Bruce. Sir Archibald was educated at the university of Edinburgh, and admitted advocate in 1814; advocate depute from 1828 to 1830; sheriff of Lanarkshire, 1835, author of 'Principles of the Criminal Law of Scotland,' Edinburgh, 1832; 'Practice of the Criminal Law;' 'History of Europe,' 20 vols. 8vo, the first published in 1833; 'Essays,' contributed to Blackwood's Magazine; 'Principles of Population,' 1845; 'England in 1815 and 1845, or a Sufficient and Contracted Currency;' 'Life of the Duke of Marlborough,' 1847; married, 21st March 1825, Elizabeth Glencairn, youngest daughter of Lieutenant-colonel Patrick Tytler, second son of William Tytler, Esq. of Woodhouselee; issue, Archibald, born 21st January 1826, lieutenant-colonel in the army, military secretary to Lord Clyde when commander-in-chief in India, lost an arm at Lucknow, and has a medal and clasps for his services in the Crimea; Frederick Montagu, born 11th May 1835, a captain in the army, aid-de-camp to the same commander; and one daughter, Ellen Frances Catherine, Mrs. Cutlar Fergusson of Craigdarroch. Sir Archibald's brother, William Pulteney Alison, M.D., LL.D., F.R.S., professor of practice of physic, university of Edinburgh, and first physician to the Queen in Scotland, retired from his chair in 1855, and died in 1859.

ALISON, ARCHIBALD, The Rev., author of 'Essays on the Nature and Principles of Taste,' was the second son of a magistrate of Edinburgh, and some time lord provost of that city, where he was born in 1757. In 1772 he went to the university of Glasgow, and afterwards became an exhibitioner at Baliol college, Oxford, where he took the degrees of A.M. and LL.B. Entering into holy orders he obtained the curacy of Brancepeth, county of Durham, and was subsequently made prebendary of Sarum. Having acquired the friendship of the late Sir William Pulteney, he was indebted to him for preferment in the church. In 1784 he married at Edinburgh the eldest daughter of the celebrated Dr. John Gregory, by whom he had six children. In 1800, on the invitation of Sir William Forbes, baronet, and the vestry of the Episcopal chapel, Cowgate, Edinburgh, he became senior minister of that place of worship. The congregation having removed to St. Paul's church, York Place, in the same city, he continued to officiate there until a severe illness, in 1831, compelled him to relinquish all public duties. He was one of the early fellows of the Royal Society of Edinburgh, and the intimate friend of many of its most distinguished members. He was also a fellow of the Royal Society of London. His principal work, the 'Essays on the Nature and Principles of Taste,' published in 1790, has passed through several editions, and was translated into French. He died 17th May, 1839. His works are :

Essay on the Nature and principles of Taste. Edin. 1790, 4to. 3d. edit. 1815, 2 vols. 8vo. 4th edit. 1816, 2 vols. 8vo.
A Discourse on the Fast Day, 1809, 8vo.
A Thanksgiving Sermon, 1814, 8vo.
Sermons, chiefly on particular occasions. Edin. 1814, 8vo. Vol. ii. 1815, 8vo. 5th edit. 1815, 2 vols.
Life and Writings of the Hon. Alexander Fraser Tytler, Lord Woodhouselee. Trans. Ed. R. Soc. viii. 515. 1818.

ALLAN, a name meaning, in the British, *Alan*, swift like a greyhound ; in the Saxon, *Alwin*, winning all ; and in the Celtic, *Aluinn*, when applied to mental qualities or conduct, illustrious. The primary meaning of the word, however, is sparkling or beautiful, and it is on that account the name of several rivers, particularly one in Perthshire, which waters the fertile district of Strathallan. It is the opinion of Chalmers that the Alauna of Ptolemy and of Richard of Westminster, (in his *Itinera Romana*, a work referable to the second century,) was situated on the Allan, about a mile above its confluence with the Forth, so that the name has an ancient as well as a classical origin. The popular song of 'On the banks of Allan Water,' is supposed to refer to a smaller stream of the same name, a tributary of the Teviot. Allan is also not unfrequently a Christian name in Scotland, as Allan Ramsay.

ALLAN, DAVID, an eminent historical painter, the son of David Allan, shoremaster at Alloa, was born there on 13th February 1744. His mother, Janet Gullan, a native of Dunfermline, died a few days after his birth, and it is related of him that, when a baby, his mouth was so small that no nurse in his native place could give him suck, and a countrywoman being found, after some inquiry, a few miles from the town, whose breast he could take, he was, one very cold day, after being wrapped up in a basket, amidst cotton, to keep him warm, sent off to her under the charge of a man on horseback. On the road the horse stumbled, the man fell off, and the little Allan being thrown out of the basket among the snow which then covered the ground, received a severe cut on his head. While yet a mere child of little more than eighteen months old, he experienced another narrow escape from a premature death. The servant girl who had the care of him, while out with him in her arms one day in the autumn of 1745, thoughtlessly ran in front of some loaded cannons, at the very moment that they were fired by way of experiment, but she and the child were providentially not touched.

Like that of many other great painters, his genius for designing was discovered by accident. Being when a boy kept at home from school, on account of a burnt foot, his father seeing him one day doing nothing, reproved him for his idleness, and giving him a bit of chalk, told him to draw something with it on the floor. He accordingly attempted to delineate figures of houses, animals, &c., and was so well pleased with his own success, and so fond of the amusement, that the chalk was seldom afterwards out of his hand. His sense of the ludicrous was great, and he could not always resist the propensity to satire. Having when about ten years of age drawn a caricature on his slate of his schoolmaster, a conceited old *dominie*, who used to strut about the school attired in a tartan nightcap and long tartan gown, and circulated it among the boys, it fell into the hands of the object of it, who straightway complained to Allan's father, and he was in consequence withdrawn from his school. On being questioned by his father as to how he had the impudence to insult his master in such a way, he answered, "I only made it like him, and it was all for fun." In one account of his life it is stated that the first rude efforts of his genius were formed merely by a knife, and displayed a degree of taste and skill far above his years; and these having attracted the notice of Mr. Stewart, then collector of the customs at Alloa, that gentleman, when at Glasgow, mentioned the merits of young Allan to Mr. Foulis, the celebrated printer, and he was sent, on the 25th of February 1755, when eleven years of age, to the Messrs. Foulis' academy of painting and engraving at Glasgow, where he remained seven years. In the year 1764 some of his performances attracted the notice of Lord Cathcart of Shaw Park, near Alloa. At the expense of his lordship, Mr. Abercromby of Tullibody, and other persons of fortune in Clackmannanshire, to whom his talents had recommended him, among whom were Lady Frances Erskine of Mar, and Lady Charlotte Erskine, he afterwards proceeded to Italy, and studied for sixteen years at Rome. In 1775, he received the gold medal given by the academy of St. Luke, in that city, for the best specimen of historical composition ; the subject being ' The Origin of Painting, or the Corinthian Maid drawing the Shadow of her Lover ;' an admirable engraving of which was executed at Rome by Dom. Cunego in 1776, and of which copies were published by him in February 1777, after his return to London. Mr. Allan presented the medal received by him for this painting to the Society of Antiquaries of Scotland, on the 7th January 1783, and an account of it was published in their transactions, vol. ii. pp. 75, 76. The only other Scotsman who had ever received the gold medal of St. Luke's academy was Mr. Gavin Hamilton. After a residence of two years in London, he returned to Edinburgh, in 1779, and, on the death of Alexander Runciman in 1786, was appointed director and master of the academy established by the board of trustees for manufactures and improvements in Scotland. In 1788 he published an edition of the Gentle Shepherd, with characteristic etchings. In ' Observations on the Plot and Scenery of the Gentle Shepherd,' from Abernethy and Walker's edition (Edinburgh : 1808), reprinted in edition of A. Fullarton & Co., 1848 (vol. ii. p. 25.), the following passage occurs : " In 1786, an unexpected visit was paid at New Hall house, (the romantic seat of Mr. John Forbes, advocate, situated in the parish of Penicuick, Edinburghshire, the scenery round which is supposed to have been that of the Gentle Shepherd,) by Mr. David Allan, painter in Edinburgh, accompanied by a friend, both of whom were unknown to the family. His object was to collect scenes and figures, where Ramsay had copied his, for a new edition of the pastoral. Mr. Allan was an intelligent Scottish antiquarian, and well acquainted with everything connected with the poetry and literature of his country. His excellent quarto edition was published in 1788, with aquatinta plates, in the true spirit and humour of Ramsay. Four of the scenes at New Hall are made use of with some figures collected there ; and in his dedication to Hamilton of Murdiston in Lanarkshire, the celebrated historical painter, he writes, ' I have studied the same characters' (as those of Ramsay), ' from the same spot, and I find that he has drawn faithfully, and with taste, from nature. This likewise has been

my model of imitation, and while I attempted, in these sketches, to express the ideas of the poet, I have endeavoured to preserve the costume as nearly as possible, by an exact delineation of such scenes and persons as he actually had in his eye.'" Mr. Allan published also, some time after, a collection of the most humorous old Scottish songs, with similar drawings ; these publications, with his illustrations of the Cottar's Saturday Night, the Stool of Repentance, the Scottish Wedding, the Highland Dance, and other sketches of rustic character, all etched by himself in aquatinta, procured for him the title of the Scottish Hogarth. One of his subjects, representing a poor man receiving charity from the hand of a young woman, is here copied.

As an instance of simple character and feeling without caricature, it gives a tolerably good idea of his natural manner, and illustrates the particular locality of Edinburgh of that epoch, where its scene is laid. It, as well as the view of the General Assembly, which appears in another part of this volume, was also etched by himself. He likewise etched and published various subjects drawn when in Italy, exhibiting the peculiarities of the people, and especially the devotional extravagances of the church of Rome of that time, which appear to have excited his sense of the ludicrous. Besides these he published four engravings, done in aquatinta by Paul Sandby, from drawings made by himself when at Rome, where, in a vein of quiet drollery, he holds up to ridicule the festivities of that city in connection with the sports of the carnival. Several of the figures were portraits of persons well known to the English who visited Rome during his stay there, and their truthfulness gave much satisfaction at the time.

His personal appearance was not in his favour. "His figure," says the author of his life in Brown's Scenery edition of the Gentle Shepherd, 1808, "was a bad resemblance of his humorous precursor of the English metropolis. He was under the middle size; of a slender, feeble make; with a long, sharp, lean, white, coarse face, much pitted by the small pox, and fair hair. His large prominent eyes, of a light colour, looked weak, near-sighted, and not very animated. His nose was long and high, his mouth wide, and both ill-shaped. His whole exterior to strangers appeared unengaging, trifling and mean. His deportment was timid and obsequious. The prejudices naturally excited by these external disadvantages at introduction, were soon, however, dispelled on acquaintance; and, as he became easy and pleased, gradually yielded to agreeable sensations; till they insensibly vanished, and were not only overlooked, but, from the effect of contrast, even heightened the attractions by which they were so unexpectedly followed. When in company he esteemed, and which suited his taste, as restraint wore off, his eye imperceptibly became active, bright and penetrating; his manner and address quick, lively, and interesting — always kind, polite, and respectful; his conversation open and gay, humorous without satire, and playfully replete with benevolence, observation, and anecdote." He resided in Dickson's close, High street, Edinburgh, where he received private pupils in his art. One of the most celebrated of his pupils was the late Mr. H. W. Williams, commonly called Grecian Williams. "The satiric humour and drollery," says Mr. Wilson, in his Memorials of Edinburgh, (vol. ii. page 40), "of his well-known 'rebuke scene' in a country church, and the lively expression and spirit of the 'General Assembly,' and

others of his own etchings, amply justify the character he enjoyed among his contemporaries as a truthful and humorous delineator of nature." "As a painter," says the author of his life already quoted, "at least in his own country, he neither excelled in drawing, composition, colouring, nor effect. Like Hogarth, too, beauty, grace, and grandeur, either of individual outline and form, or of style, constitute no part of his merit. He was no Corregio, Raphael, or Michael Angelo. He painted portraits, as well as Hogarth, below the size of life; but they are recommended by nothing save a strong homely resemblance. As an artist and a man of genius, his characteristic talent lay in *expression*, in the imitation of nature with truth and humour, especially in the representation of ludicrous scenes in low life. His vigilant eye was ever on the watch for every eccentric figure, every motley group, or ridiculous incident, out of which his pencil or his needle could draw innocent entertainment and mirth." He died at Edinburgh on the 6th of August 1796, in the 53d year of his age, and was interred in the High Calton burying-ground. He had married in 1788 Shirley Welsh, the youngest daughter of Thomas Welsh, a carver and gilder in Edinburgh. He had five children, three of whom died in infancy. His surviving son, David, went out as a cadet to India in 1806. He also left a daughter named Barbara.—*Brown's Scenery edition of the Gentle Shepherd, appendix.*

ALLAN, ROBERT, a minor poet, some of whose lyrics and songs have long been popular in Scotland, was born at Kilbarchan, in Renfrewshire, 4th November, 1774. He was a handloom weaver, and all his life in humble circumstances. To relieve the tedium of his occupation he occasionally had recourse to poetry. In 1836, a volume of his poems was published by subscription, but made no great impression. The principal poem in the volume, entitled 'An Address to the Robin,' is written in the Scottish dialect. His most popular pieces are 'The bonny built wherry;' 'The Covenanter's Lament;' 'Woman's wark will ne'er be dune;' 'Haud awa' frae me, Donald;' and the ballad 'O speed, Lord Nithsdale.' He had a numerous family, all of whom were married except his youngest son, a portrait painter of great promise, who emigrated to the United States. Desirous of joining his son, Allan sailed for New York, where he arrived 1st June 1841, but died there on the 7th, six days after his arrival, from the effects of a cold caught on the banks of Newfoundland. He is represented as having been a most single-hearted and unaffected being, and much of the simplicity of his character is reflected in his poems.

ALLAN, SIR WILLIAM, an eminent historical painter, was born at Edinburgh, in 1782, of humble parentage, his father being one of the doorkeepers of the Court of Exchequer. He was educated partly at the High School of his native city, under William Nicol, the friend of Burns, and served his apprenticeship to a coach-painter, George Sanders the celebrated miniature-painter being in the same employment. All his spare hours were devoted to drawing. He studied for several years at the Trustees' Academy, having Wilkie as a fellow-student. These two great painters began drawing from the same example, and thus continued for months, using the same copy, and sitting on the same form. The friendship thus commenced in their youth increased with their years, and ceased but with the life of Wilkie, who died nine years before him. One of his first pieces engraved was 'Flora parting with Ascanius,' in Home's 'Adventures of the young Ascanius,' 1804. After the close of his studies in Edinburgh, Allan removed to London, and was admitted to the school of the Royal Academy, where he remained some time. Not ultimately finding professional employment in London, he determined upon proceeding to Russia, to try whether encouragement could not be obtained in that country, and that he might study the rude and picturesque aspects there presented, and find suitable and striking materials for his pencil. Hastily communicating his intention to his friends in Scotland, with one or two letters of introduction to some of his countrymen at St. Petersburg, he embarked in 1805 in a vessel bound for Riga. Owing to adverse winds the ship, almost a wreck, was driven into Memel in Prussia, where, though ignorant of the German language, he took up his abode at an inn, and at once commenced portrait-painting. He began with the portrait of the Danish consul, to whom he had been introduced by the captain of the vessel. Having, in this way, recruited his nearly empty purse, he pro-

ceeded overland to St. Petersburg, encountering on the road various romantic incidents, and passing through a great portion of the Russian army on their way to the battle of Austerlitz. On his arrival at the Russian capital, he was introduced to many valuable friends, through the kindness of Sir Alexander Crichton, then physician to the Imperial family; and was soon enabled to pursue his art diligently and successfully. Having attained a knowledge of the Russian language, he travelled into the interior, and remained for several years in the Ukraine, making excursions at various times to Turkey, Tartary, the shores of the Black Sea, the Sea of Azoph, and the banks of the Kuban, amongst Cossacks, Circassians, Turks, and Tartars; visiting their huts and tents, studying their history, character, and costume, and forming a collection of their arms and armour, for his future labours in art, as he had resolved to devote his great powers to historical painting.

In 1812, Mr. Allan began to think of returning to Scotland, but was prevented by the French invasion of Russia of that year. The whole country was thrown into confusion and alarm by the Emperor Napoleon's advance to Moscow, and thus was Allan forced to remain, when he witnessed not a few heart-rending miseries incident to that eventful period. In 1814, however, he was enabled to set out on his return home, and, after a lapse of ten years, he once more trod the streets of Edinburgh. His improvement had been so rapid and so remarkable, that the most eminent of his countrymen in literature and art visited, and were in daily intercourse with, the young and enterprising artist, and he numbered among his friends Scott, Wilson, Lockhart, and other distinguished literati of the day in Edinburgh, which city he resolved to make his future residence. His first efforts, after his return, were directed to embodying on the canvass, some of those romantic and striking scenes which had been suggested by his travels and adventures in the strange countries he had visited. His 'Circassian Captives,' a work full of novel and original matter, character, and expression, and remarkable for the completeness of its design, and the masterly arrangement of its parts, was exhibited at Somerset House, London, in 1815, and immediately made his name generally known. To this great picture succeeded 'Tartar Banditti;' 'Haslan Gheray crossing the Kuban;' 'A Jewish Wedding in Poland;' and 'Prisoners Conveyed to Siberia by Cossacks,' which, with many others, he brought together, and exhibited in Edinburgh, along with the armour and costumes he had collected in his travels. The exhibition proved highly attractive, and the artist rose higher in the estimation of his countrymen. His picture of 'The Circassians' was purchased by Sir Walter Scott, John Wilson, the poet, his brother, James, the naturalist, Lockhart, and a number of the artist's other friends, and it was resolved to raffle it in Edinburgh. In a letter to the Duke of Buccleuch, dated 15th April, 1819, Sir Walter Scott, who took a great interest in Allan, thus gives an account of the circumstance, and of the artist himself;—"A hundred persons subscribed ten guineas apiece to raffle for his fine picture of the Circassian chief selling slaves to the Turkish pacha—a beautiful and highly poetical picture. There was another small picture added by way of second prize, and, what is curious enough, the only two peers on the list, Lord Wemyss and Lord Fife, both got prizes. Allan has made a sketch, which I shall take to town with me when I can go, in hopes Lord Stafford, or some other picture-buyer, may fancy it, and order a picture. The subject is the murder of Archbishop Sharpe on Magus Moor, prodigiously well treated. The savage ferocity of the assassins, crowding on one another to strike at the old prelate on his knees, contrasted with the old man's figure, and that of his daughter endeavouring to interpose for his protection, and withheld by a ruffian of milder mood than his fellows—the dogged, fanatical severity of Rathillet's countenance, who remained on horseback, witnessing, with stern fanaticism, the murder he did not choose to be active in, lest it should be said that he struck out of private revenge—are all amazingly well combined." The picture which Allan executed from the sketch here described by Sir Walter Scott, was worthy of his genius. It was afterwards engraved, and is well known. The painting itself is in the possession of Mr. Lockhart, of Milton-Lockhart. Sir Walter added:—"Constable (the eminent publisher) has offered Allan three hundred pounds to make sketches for an edition of the 'Tales of my Landlord,' and other novels of that cycle, and says he will give him the same sum next year, so, from being pinched enough, this very deserving artist suddenly finds himself at his ease. He was long at Odessa with the Duke of Richelieu, and is a very entertaining person."

During the visit of the Grand Duke Nicholas, afterwards Czar of Russia, to Edinburgh, about this time, he purchased several of Allan's pictures; one, the 'Siberian Exiles,' and another, 'Haslan Cheray,' both already mentioned. Allan's works were now readily bought. His most affecting picture, 'The Press-Gang,' was purchased by Mr. Horrocks of Tillyheeran; his 'Knox admonishing Mary, Queen of Scots,' a work full of character, by Mr. Trotter of Ballendean; and his 'Death of the Regent Moray,' by the then duke of Bedford. A serious malady in his eyes, which was a source of suffering for several years, caused a cessation from all professional labours. A change of climate being advised by his physician, he went to Italy, and after spending a winter at Rome, he proceeded to Naples, and thence made a journey to Constantinople. He afterwards, with restored health, visited Morocco, Greece, Spain, and the wild range of country from Gibraltar to Persia, and from Persia to the Baltic, for the purpose of studying the scenery and manners of the various nations through which he passed. These he faithfully embodied on his canvass, and among his greatest pictures in this style may be noticed, 'The Discovery of the Cup in the Sack of Benjamin;' 'The Polish Captives;' 'The Slave Market at Constantinople,' which was purchased by Alexander Hill, Esq., print-publisher; 'Tartar Banditti Dividing their Spoil;' 'The Moorish Love-Letter;' 'Byron in the Fisherman's Hut, after Swimming the Hellespont,' which was bought by his friend Robert Nasmyth, Esq., who was also the purchaser of his whole-length cabinet portraits of 'Scott and Burns.' The eastern pieces named were executed after his return to Edinburgh, with numerous others, descriptive of oriental scenery, persons, and manners. The history of his own land also furnished him with subjects for his powerful and graphic pencil. Besides 'The Murder of Archbishop Sharpe,' and 'The Death of the Regent Moray,' he devoted his genius to many other scenes illustrative of our Scottish annals, so fruitful in remarkable and striking events. His painting of Mary and Rizzio is one of the best of these historic pictures.

In his famous picture of 'The Ettrick Shepherd's House-heating,' executed in 1819, he introduced a portrait of his friend Sir Walter Scott, who had always a great regard for him. His figure of 'The Author of Waverley in his Study,' done shortly before Sir Walter's death, is considered one of his most successful efforts in this department of art. He also finished an admirable painting of Sir Walter's eldest son, when cornet of dragoons, holding his horse, which hangs over the mantelpiece of the great library at Abbotsford. He was there during the last melancholy scenes of Scott's life. Mr. Lockhart says, " Perceiving, towards the close of August 1832, that the end was near, and thinking it very likely that Abbotsford might soon undergo many changes, and myself, at all events, never see it again, I felt a desire to have some image preserved of the interior apartments as occupied by their founder, and invited from Edinburgh, for that purpose, Sir Walter's dear friend, William Allan, whose presence, I well knew, would, even under the circumstances of that time, be nowise troublesome to any of the family, but the contrary in all respects. Mr. Allan willingly complied, and executed a series of beautiful drawings. He also shared our watchings, and witnessed all but the last moments."

In 1834 he visited Spain, with the object of collecting fresh materials for the subjects of his art. He sailed for Cadiz and Gibraltar, proceeded into West Barbary, and crossing again into Spain, travelled over the greater part of Andalusia, intending to go on to Madrid, but was recalled to Scotland, by news from home.

In 1835 Mr. Allan was elected a member of the Royal Academy, and in 1838 he was chosen president of the Royal Scottish Academy of Painting, Sculpture, and Architecture, on the death and in the room of Mr. Watson, the original president. In 1841, on the death of Sir David Wilkie, he was appointed her Majesty's limner for Scotland, and in the following year he was knighted. He was an honorary member of the Academies of New York and Philadelphia.

Having long intended to paint a picture of the Battle of Waterloo, he several times visited France and Belgium to make sketches of the memorable field, and to collect the requisite materials for his purpose. The view he chose was from the French side, Napoleon and his staff being the foreground figures. This picture was, in 1843, exhibited at the Royal Academy, London, and purchased by the Duke of Wellington, who expressed his high satisfaction at the truthfulness of the arrangement and detail in his work. He was subsequently induced, by the success of the first, to paint another great picture of Waterloo, from the British side, with the view of entering the lists of the Westminster Hall competition of 1846. This piece also gained the approbation of the Duke of Wellington, and was much praised by the public, but though voted for by W. Etty, R.A., one of the best judges in the committee, as worthy of public reward, it was not judged deserving of a prize.

In 1844 Allan revisited Russia, and had an opportunity of again seeing his early patron, the Emperor Nicholas. While there he painted a picture of 'Peter the Great teaching his subjects the art of shipbuilding,' which is now in the winter palace of St. Petersburgh.

After his return to his native city, he continued his professional labours, with the enthusiasm that ever marked his character. His last energies were expended on a national piece, and one commemorative of the most remarkable event in the history of Scotland's independence, namely, 'The Battle of Bannockburn,' on the same extensive scale as his latter picture of Waterloo. On this picture he worked with as much diligence as his weakened condition would admit, for already his last illness was upon him. So eager was he to complete the work in time for the ensuing exhibition of the Royal Academy, that, it is stated, he had his bed carried into his painting room that he might sleep near his work. When the pencil at length fell from his hand he was too far gone in illness to be removed, and he died in his painting room, in front of his latest picture. He was never married, his niece having kept house for him.

Sir William died at his residence, 72 Great King Street, Edinburgh, on the 23d February, 1850, in the 69th year of his age. He had for many years been afflicted with chronic disease of the windwipe, and had latterly become much enfeebled. His genius as an artist was of the highest order, and he possessed singularly unassuming manners and an amiable disposition. As an instance of his kindly feeling, it may be stated that on a few of the scholars of Mr. John Robertson, the first teacher in Gillespie's hospital, Edinburgh, who had been educated in that institution under his charge, wishing to have the portrait taken of their old master, two of them waited on Sir William Allan to ascertain if his engagements would permit him to do it, and on what terms, when, appreciating their motives, he at once generously agreed to paint Mr. Robertson's portrait without remuneration, and it is now in the hall of the hospital. Sir William was much esteemed, not only by his brother artists, but by an extensive circle of friends. A picture of his commemorative of the Ettrick Shepherd's birthday, at Hogg's house at Altrive, after a day's sport in trouting and rambling on the mountains, contains nineteen portraits of the Shepherd's intimate friends and his own, in rural costumes, among whom, besides Hogg and himself, are Sir Walter Scott; his son-in-law John Gibson Lockhart; the two Ballantynes, James and John; Professor Wilson and his brother James; Captain Thomas Hamilton, author of 'Cyril Thornton;' Alexander Nasmyth, the celebrated landscape painter; David Brydges; Constable the publisher; James Russell, the comedian; and James Bruce, piper to Sir Walter Scott; a list of names calculated to make the painting interesting, although not among the most finished of the artist's performances. It is now the property of Mrs. Gott of Armsly House.

Sir William Allan was for a long period the only resident historical painter of his country, and for seventeen years master of the Trustees' academy, at Edinburgh, where he and Wilkie first began their career. His excellence as a painter consisted in his dramatic power of portraying a story, and his general skill in composition, rather than in character or in colour. He will be remembered in the history of Scottish art by the impulse which he gave to historical composition; while his name will always be endeared to the admirers of Sir Walter Scott by the strong partiality which the latter evinced on all occasions for his friend "Willie Allan." With the office of limner to the queen for Scotland, which Allan received in 1842, the honour of knighthood is always conveyed to its holder. A small salary also accompanies it. The office was revived by George the Fourth, and given to Sir Henry Raeburn, and at Raeburn's death it was conferred on Sir David Wilkie, who was succeeded by Sir William Allan. At the death of the latter, Sir James Watson Gordon, R.A., president and trustee of the Royal Scottish Academy, was appointed in his place. A portrait of Sir William Allan is given separately. Besides Wilkie, John Burnet the engraver, Alexander Fraser the painter, and others eminent in art, were his fellow students at the Trustees' Academy, Edinburgh. When he first went to London, Opie, the Cornish painter, was then at the height of his reputation, and in the first picture which Allan sent to the Royal Academy, he imitated Opie's style, so far as colour went, with something like servility. This picture, called 'A Gipsy and Ass,' was exhibited in 1805. His 'Russian Peasants Keeping Holiday,' was exhibited in 1809. Besides the pictures above mentioned, he also painted the following:—'Circassian Prince on Horseback selling two boys of his own nation to a Cossack chief of the Black Sea;' 'Circassian Chief selling to a Turkish Pasha Captives of a neighbouring tribe taken in war;' 'The parting between Prince Charles Stuart and Flora Macdonald at Portree;' and 'Jeanie Deans' first interview with her father after her return from London.'

ALLARDICE, surname of, see BARCLAY-ALLARDICE.

ALPIN, king of the Dalriadic Scots, reigned contemporary with his cousin, Drust IX., king of the Picts. He is usually said to have been the son of Achaius, or Eoganan, that is, in the Celtic, Eochy-annuine (the poisonous), but Pinkerton thinks that the name of his father is lost beyond all recovery, and, indeed, the history of the country at a period so remote is so enveloped in darkness as to be considered in many respects fabulous. He succeeded his brother, Dungal the Brown, in 834. His kingdom comprehended the mountainous country of Argyleshire, as far as the mouth of the Clyde, but, anxious to extend his territories, he sailed from Kintyre, and landed in the bay of Ayr, with a powerful force. After laying waste the district between the rivers Ayr and Doon, following the course of these rivers, he penetrated to the ridge which separates Kyle from Galloway, destruction for a time marking his progress. He soon, however, received a check. The chiefs, recovered from their first alarm, and thirsting for revenge, collected their followers, and coming up with the invading army, in the parish of Dalmellington, in Ayrshire, a furious conflict ensued, when Alpin was numbered among the slain. This event happened about 837. The battle was fought near the site of Laicht castle, which derived its name from the stone of Alpin, a gravestone known and recognised nearly four centuries after this last of the Dalriad kings had been slain on the spot. The word *laicht* signifies a grave or stone, and there are still the remains of an old castle in the parish of Dalmellington, at a place called Laicht, which was demolished by the proprietor in 1771, to enclose some ground. Two farms in the parish are still called Over and Nether Laicht, and several cairns are found which indicate the scene of the battle. It is also remarkable that the foundation charter of the town of Ayr, granted by William the Lion in 1197, when describing the limits of its exclusive trade, names Laicht Alpin, the stone or grave of Alpin, as one of its distinguishing boundaries. Alpin left two sons, Kenneth MacAlpin, under whom the Scots and Southern Picts were united, and Donald II., who succeeded Kenneth. Alpin's attempt to extend his territories appears, says Skene, from the register of St. Andrews, to have been confined to Galloway, the province of which in those days comprehended Ayrshire, and belonged to the Southern Picts, and it is said by that chronicle, that it was his conquest of that territory which transferred the kingdom of the Picts to the Scots. The latter event is called the Scottish Conquest. Kenneth his son apparently fought but one battle, and that, according to the same chronicle, at Forteviot, in the very heart of the territory of the Southern Picts. [*Skene's History of the Highlanders*, vol. i. p. 65.] This Alpin is not to be confounded with another Alpin or Elpin, who was

king of the Picts, and who reigned from 775 to 779 —*Chalmers' Caledonia.*—*Ritson's Annals*, vol. ii.

ALSTON, CHARLES, an eminent physician and lecturer on botany, was born in Lanarkshire in 1683, and first studied at the university of Glasgow. While a student there, he had the good fortune to be taken under the patronage of the duchess of Hamilton, and spent his early years at Hamilton palace. By the assistance of her grace he was enabled to accomplish the design of devoting himself to the medical profession, and in the year 1716 he went, with the celebrated Dr. Alexander Monro, to Leyden; where, after studying for three years under the celebrated Boerhaave, he took his degree of M.D. On his return he commenced practice in Edinburgh, and, by the interest of the duke of Hamilton, heritable keeper of Holyrood house, he obtained the sinecure office of king's botanist. He began his lectures on botany in 1720, in the king's garden at Holyrood house, which he enriched by large collections he had made in Holland. In 1738 he was chosen to succeed Professor Preston, in the chair of Botany and Materia Medica united, in the university of Edinburgh; and in conjunction with Dr. Monro, Dr. Rutherford, Dr. Sinclair, and Dr. Plummer, laid the foundation of the high character since enjoyed by Edinburgh as a school of medical science. In 1740, for the assistance of his pupils, he published an Index of the plants demonstrated to them in the Edinburgh medical garden. He continued to lecture till his death on the 22d of November 1760. In the fifth volume of the Edinburgh Medical Essays he published a short paper on the efficacy of the powder of tin in destroying or expelling worms from the bowels. He was the author of several botanical works, the principal of which is entitled 'Tirocinium Botanicum Edinburgense,' 1753. In the same year one of his papers, in which he endeavoured to overturn the Linnæan doctrine of the sexual system of plants, was published in the first volume of the 'Edinburgh Physical and Literary Essays.' He also engaged in a controversy with Dr. Whytt about quicklime; but the most valuable of all his works are his 'Lectures on the Materia Medica,' which appeared in two volumes 4to in 1770, edited by his friend and successor in the professor's chair, Dr. John Hope.

H 2

In botany a genus of the *Polyandria monogynia* class and order is called Alstonia after Dr. Alston.

The following is a list of Dr. Alston's works :

Index Plantarum in Horto Medico Edinburgensi. Edin. 1740, 8vo.

Index Medicamentorum simplicium triplex. Edin. 1752, 12mo.

Dissertations on Quick Lime and Lime Water. Edin. 1752, 12mo. The 2d edition, with additions. 1754, 8vo.

Tyrocinium Botanicum Edinburgense. Edin. 1753, 8vo. 1765, 8vo.

Dissertation on Botany, translated from the Latin by a Physician. Edin. 1754, 8vo, perhaps a translation of the Tyrocinium.

A second Dissertation on Quick Lime and Lime Water. Edin. 1755, 12mo.

A third Dissertation on Quick Lime and Lime Water. Edin. 1757, 8vo.

Lectures on the Materia Medica, containing the Natural History of Drugs, their Virtues and Doses; also Directions for the Study of the Materia Medica, and an Appendix on the Method of Prescribing. Lond. 1770, 2 vols. 4to, edited by Dr. Hope.

Powder of Tin, an Anthelmentic Medicine. Med. Ess. v. p. 89, 1736.

Dissertation on Opium. Ib. p. 110, 1736.

Case of Extravasated Blood in the Pericardium. Ib. v. p. 609.

A Dissertation on the Sexes of Plants. Ess. Phys. and Lit. p. 205, 1754.

Two Letters on Lime and Lime Water. Phil. Trans. 1751, Abr. x. p. 204.

ALTRIE, in the peerage of Scotland, an extinct barony originally conferred on Robert Keith, the second son of William fourth earl Marischal, who was commendator of the Cistertian Abbey of Deer in Aberdeenshire, and had the whole lands belonging to that monastery erected into a temporal lordship, with the title of Lord Altrie, 29th July 1587. His lordship was selected by King James VI., to go to Denmark to negotiate his marriage with the princess Anne in 1589, but excused himself on account of his age and infirmities, when his nephew George, fifth earl Marischal, was appointed in his stead. The first Lord Altrie is supposed to have been dead before 1606. He was succeeded by his said nephew, the fifth earl Marischal, the founder of Marischal College, Aberdeen, when the title of Lord Altrie merged in the superior title, and became extinct on the death of George the tenth earl Marischal. See MARISCHAL, earl, and KEITH, surname of.

ALVES, a surname derived from a parish in Elginshire of that name.

ALVES, ROBERT, a minor poet, was born at Elgin in 1745, and studied at Aberdeen, where he took his degrees of philosophy in 1766. His poetical talents gained him the friendship of Dr. Beattie and other gentlemen of literary tastes. He afterwards became parish schoolmaster at Deskford, and in 1773 removed to Banff. In 1779 he went to Edinburgh, where he maintained himself by teaching the classics. He is said to have left Banff on account of a disappointment in love. In 1782 he published a volume of poems, which attracted little notice. In 1789 appeared another of his works, entitled 'Edinburgh, a poem, in two parts, and the Weeping Bard, in sixteen cantos,' which were not without merit. He died on the 1st of January 1794, leaving a laborious work in the press, entitled 'Sketches of a History of Literature,' which was afterwards published. [*Campbell's History of Scottish Poetry.*] The works of Alves are :

Poems. Edin. 1782, 8vo.

Edinburgh, a Poem; also the Weeping Bard. Edin. 1789, 8vo.

Sketches of the History of Literature, containing Lives and Characters of the most eminent writers in different Languages, ancient and modern, with Critical Remarks on their works, together with several Literary Essays; to which is prefixed, a short biographical account of the Author. Edin. 1794, 8vo. Edin. 1795, 8vo.

Banks of Esk, and other Poems. Edin. 1801, 12mo.

ANCRUM, earl of, one of the titles of the marquis of Lothian, conferred in 1633, on Sir Robert Kerr, of Ancrum, an accomplished poet and courtier, the descendant of Sir Andrew Kerr of Fernihirst, a border chief who acted a prominent part in the reigns of James IV. and James V., particularly in resisting the inroads of the English. The title devolved on Robert fourth earl and first marquis of Lothian, on the death of Charles, second earl of Ancrum, and is now by courtesy borne by the eldest son of the marquis of Lothian. [See LOTHIAN, marquis of, and KERR, surname of.] The name of Ancrum is derived from Alncromb or Alncrumb, signifying the crook of the Ale or Aln, and is exactly descriptive of the situation of the village of Ancrum, which stands on a rising ground on the south side of the Ale, where that stream fetches a curve before falling into the Teviot. A ridge in the sequestered parish of Ancrum in Roxburghshire is called Lilliard's edge, from a battle fought there in 1544, on an invasion of the English under Sir Ralph Evers and Sir Brian Latoun, in which a young Scottish woman named Lilliard who had followed her lover, on seeing him fall, rushed forward, and fighting bravely, by her gallantry aided to turn the fight in favour of her countrymen. The heroine was slain in the engagement, and an old broken and defaced stone is still pointed out to mark the spot where she fell. It is said to have once borne the following inscription, recast from the well-known lines on Sir Thomas Widdrington in the ballad of Chevy Chase:

"Fair maiden Lyliard lies under this stane;
Little was her stature, but great was her fame;
Upon the English loons she laid many thumps,
And when her legs were cutted off she fought upon her
stumps."

The leaders of the Scotch were the regent earl of Arran and the earl of Angus. (See vol. ii. p. 46.)

ANCRUM, earl of, see KERR, SIR ROBERT.

ANDERSON, a surname meaning literally the son of Andrew, but as held by families of Lowland origin, denoting more properly a son of St. Andrew, that is, a native Scotsman, as indicated by the Cross of St. Andrew, the patron saint of Scotland, in their shield. The Mid Lothian Andersons, to one branch of which belongs the family of the author of this work, have for crest a crosslet above the crescent; motto, "Gradatim." The crest evidently has reference to the crusades.

The Gaelic sept of Anderson are said to be an offshoot of the old potent stem of Clan Anrias, from which spring the Mac Andrews, the Mac Gilanders, and the Gillanderses (*Skene*, vol. ii. p. 228). The chief of the sept is Anderson of Candacraig, Aberdeenshire.

ANDERSON, ADAM, author of the largest British compilation upon commercial history, was born about the year 1692. He left Scotland early in life, and obtained the situation of clerk in the South Sea House, London, in which he remained for forty years, and rose to be chief clerk of the Stock and New Annuities in that establishment. He retained that post till his death, which happened on the 10th January 1765. He was one of the trustees for the Settlement of Georgia, and also a member of the court of assistants of the Scots Corporation in London. In 1764, a year before his death, was published his elaborate work, entitled 'An Historical and Chronological Deduction of the Origin of Commerce, from the Earliest Accounts to the Present Time ; containing a History of the large Commercial Interests of the British Empire,' &c. London, two volumes folio. An improved edition of this work was subsequently published by David M'Pherson, in four volumes. Mr. Anderson was twice married. By his first wife he had a daughter. His second wife survived him till 1781. He was her third husband.—*Chalmers' Biog. Dict.*

ANDERSON, ALEXANDER, an eminent mathematician, was born at Aberdeen, near the close of the sixteenth century. Having at an early period of his life proceeded to Paris, he settled there as a private teacher or professor of mathematics. Between the years 1612 and 1619 he published various treatises on geometrical and algebraic science. His pure taste and skill in mathematical investigation pointed him out to the executors of the celebrated geometrician Vieta, Master of Requests at Paris, who died in 1603, as the fittest person to revise and publish his valuable MSS., which he did with learned comments, and neat demonstrations of propositions left imperfect. He subsequently produced a specimen of the application of geometrical analysis, distinguished for its clearness and classic elegance. His works are now scarce. They consist of six thin quarto volumes, including the edition of the works of Vieta. The date of his death, as of his birth, has not been ascertained. [*Hutton's Mathematical Dictionary.*] The following is a list of his works :

Supplementum Apollonii Redivivi ; sive Analysis Problematis ad Apollonii Doctrinam desiderati, a Marino Ghetaldo relicti. Huic subnexa est, variorum problematum practice. Paris, 1612, 4to.

Αἰτιολογία, pro Zetetico Apolloniani Problematis a se jam pridem edito in Supplemento Apollonii Redivivi, &c. Paris, 1615, 4to.

Francisci Vietæ de Æquationum Recognitione et Emendatione Tractatus duo. Paris, 1615, 4to.

Vindiciæ Archimedis, sive Elenchus Cyclometriæ Lausbergii. Paris, 1616.

Diacrisis Animadversionis in Franc. Vietam a Clem. Cyriaco. Paris, 1617.

Exercitationum Mathematicarum Decas prima. Paris, 1619.

ANDERSON, DAVID, of Finshaugh, a citizen and merchant of Aberdeen, the brother, or, as another account says, the cousin of the preceding, and uncle of George Jamesone the Scottish Vandyke, had likewise a strong turn for mathematics and mechanics, and from his being able to apply his knowledge to so many practical and useful purposes, he was popularly known at Aberdeen by the familiar name of Davie Do-a'-things. He removed a large rock which obstructed the entrance to Aberdeen harbour. He left three daughters, yet "his widow," we are informed by Mr. David Laing, in the information supplied to Allan Cunningham for his Memoir of Jamesone the painter, "was rich enough and generous enough to found and endow an hospital in Aberdeen for the maintenance and education of ten poor orphans." One of his daughters was married to the Rev. John Gregory, minister of Drumoak, and their son was the celebrated James Gregory, inventor of the reflecting telescope. From her is supposed to have been derived that taste for mathematical science which afterwards distinguished the Gregorys. A portrait of him by his nephew, the celebrated painter above referred to, is still extant in Aberdeen.

ANDERSON, ANDREW, a printer at Edinburgh, who, in the reign of Charles II., obtained a patent for printing everything in Scotland for 41 years, thus monopolizing the whole trade to himself—a thing that would not be tolerated in our more enlightened days. He was the son of George Anderson, who, in 1638, introduced the art of letter-press printing into Glasgow, having been invited from Edinburgh by the magistrates for that purpose, and it appears from the council records of the former city that he was to be allowed £100 for the liquidation of his expenses, " in transporting of his gear to that burgh," and in full of his bygone salaries from Whitsunday 1638 till Martinmas 1639. His son Andrew succeeded him in Glasgow, but afterwards removed to Edinburgh, and was made king's printer for Scotland, in 1671. For many years after this period the art of printing remained in the very lowest state in Scotland, owing mainly to the exclusive nature of the royal grant to Anderson. This privilege was afterwards restricted to Bibles and Acts of parliament, which continued exclusively in the hands of the king's printers for Scotland, till 1839, when the license was thrown open, under certain conditions and restrictions, to the printing trade generally.

ANDERSON, ANDREW, lieutenant-general in the East India Company's service, founder of an institution at Elgin for the support of old age and the education of youth, was the son of a private soldier and a poor half-witted woman of the name of Marjory Gilzean, belonging to the town of Elgin, to whom he was privately married. Andrew, who was born about the year 1746, was brought up by his mother in a state of great misery, in what had been the sacristy of Elgin cathedral, where she led a wretched and lonely life, supported by charity; her infant's bed being a hollow sculptured stone, which had formerly been used as a font. He was educated at the grammar school of that town as a pauper, doing all the drudgery of the school in return for his education. Afterwards he was bound apprentice to his father's brother, a staymaker in the adjoining parish of St. Andrews Lhanbryd, whose harsh treatment induced him, while yet very young, to run away from home. Having contrived to reach London, he was taken in by a tailor, who afterwards employed him as his clerk. Being sent with a suit of clothes to an officer in the East India Company's

service, a countryman of his own, then about to proceed to India, that gentleman, pleased with his appearance, and satisfying himself that he had obtained a good education, advised him to enlist in his regiment, and offered to take him as his servant. Anderson accordingly went out as a drummer, and from his steadiness and good conduct, and singular facility in the acquirement of languages, soon obtained promotion. He had early made himself master of the Hindostance, and was frequently employed as interpreter. His conduct at the taking of Seringapatam, in 1799, was honourably noticed at the time in the public papers. Having amassed a large fortune, he ultimately retired with the rank of lieutenant-general in the Bombay army. In 1811 he returned to Elgin, and resided for several summers there, or in the neighbourhood, passing the winter in London, where, on the 23d November 1815, he executed a trust-disposition and deed of settlement, assigning his whole property, after the payment of a few minor legacies, for the purposes of founding and endowing an Hospital, a School of Industry, and a Free School at Elgin, to be called the Elgin Institution for the support of old age and education of youth. He died in London on the 16th of December 1824.

The funds left by General Anderson amounted to £70,000, and the Elgin Institution, which stands at the east end of Elgin, was founded in 1832, for the maintenance of aged men and women, and the maintenance and education of poor or orphan boys and girls. The philanthropic and splendid monument which he may be said to have thus raised to his own memory is a beautiful and appropriate piece of architecture. Built of native sandstone, it is a quadrangular structure of two stories, surmounted by a circular tower and dome. The institution for the children contains a school of industry. The children are apprenticed also to some trade or useful occupation. The house governor and teacher of the school of industry has a salary of £55 per annum, with board and lodging in the institution. A public school, on the Lancasterian system, is attached to the institution as a free school, for the education of male and female children whose parents, though in narrow circumstances, are still able to maintain and clothe them

ANDERSON, JAMES, the author of the 'Diplomata Scotiæ,' was the son of the Rev. Patrick Anderson, one of the persecuted presbyterian ministers, who at the Restoration was ejected from his living and afterwards suffered imprisonment in the Bass, and was born at Edinburgh, August 5, 1662, and graduated at the university there. It appears from the registers of the university of Edinburgh that he was a student under Mr. William Paterson, the professor of philosophy in 1667, and took his degree in the class of Mr. James Wishart, on the 27th of May 1680. Having chosen the law for his profession, he served an apprenticeship with Sir Hugh Paterson of Bannockburn, writer to the signet, and on the 6th of June 1691 he was admitted a member of that society. In 1704, an English lawyer, of the name of Atwood, having published a pamphlet claiming for England a direct superiority over Scotland, Mr. Anderson was led to publish an 'Historical Essay, showing that the Crown and Kingdom of Scotland is imperial and independent,' which appeared in 1705. This work procured for him not only a reward, but the thanks of the Scottish parliament, which ordered Atwood's pamphlet as well as the Historia Anglo-Scotica of Drake, to be burnt by the common hangman. Having projected a series of engravings of fac-similes of the charters and seals, medals and coins, of the Scottish monarchs from the earliest times, in November 1706, he obtained from the Scottish parliament a vote of three hundred pounds sterling towards this object. By this aid he was enabled to make great progress in his arduous work; but before March 1707 he had not only expended this sum, but five hundred and ninety pounds sterling of his own on the undertaking, and was forced again to apply to parliament, now about to expire. A committee reported the facts, and the parliament, while they approved of his conduct, voted him an additional grant of one thousand and fifty pounds sterling; and recommended him to the queen 'as a person meriting her gracious favour.' One of the last acts of the union parliament was 'a recommendation in favour of Mr. James Anderson.' This induced him to remove to London, to superintend the progress of the work, though the money is said never to have been paid. In June 1715 he was appointed postmaster-general for Scotland, a situation which he held only for two years, having been superseded on the 29th of November 1717, for some cause which does not appear, by Sir John Inglis of Cramond. When he lost this appointment he issued proposals for publishing his 'Diplomata.' The following advertisement appeared in Watson's Scots Courant of the 25th of February 1718: "Proposals being printed for publishing a book, which will consist of above one hundred copperplates, containing the ancient charters and seals of the kings of Scotland, and the alphabets and abbreviations made use of in ancient writings, collected pursuant to an order of the parliament of Scotland, by Mr. Anderson, writer to the signet: any who encourage that book may have copies of the proposals at Mr. Anderson's house above the general post office, Edinburgh, and may also see specimens of the work at any time between the hours of two and five in the afternoon." In 1727 appeared the first and second volumes of his 'Collections relating to the History of Mary Queen of Scotland;' to which he soon after added two more volumes, 4to. This work was intended as a counter publication to Jebb's *Vita et Rebus Gestis Mariæ Scotorum Reginæ*, published at London, in 1725, in two folio volumes, which represented Mary and her cause in a favourable light. In preparing his work on Queen Mary, Mr. Anderson, through the influence of the Duke of Devonshire, obtained admission to the state paper office, "whence," says Chalmers, "he drew some documents that lost their efficacy from suspicions of his candour." Mr. Chalmers, in his life of Ruddiman, makes the following very just remark: "That such an antiquary as Anderson is represented to have been should entitle Mary, queen of *Scotland*, is astonishing, when the charters and seals of his own *Diplomata* would have shown him that she was *Scotorum Regina*, as her predecessors had been *Scotorum Reges*. Ruddiman, with his usual acuteness, remarks, 'That it is a sure indication of forgery when an old charter speaks of the king as *Scotiæ Rex*.'" [*Chalmers' Ruddiman*, p. 156, *note*, ed. 1794.] Anderson was one of a society of the critics of Edinburgh, which was formed for publishing a correct edition of Buchanan's works, with the declared aim of vindicating "that incomparably learned and pious author from the calumnies of Mr. Thomas Ruddiman." It does not appear that they ever carried their design into execution, farther than preparing a series of "Notts" upon the annotations of Ruddiman, which are still in manuscript. He died at London of an apoplectic stroke, on the 2d of April 1728, at the age of sixty-six, leaving unfinished his great work, on which he had been engaged for so many years. He had married in his youth a daughter of John Ellis of Elliston, an advocate in Edinburgh, by whom he had several sons, who survived him, and a daughter Margaret who married George Crawford, the author of the Peerage. One of his sons, Patrick Anderson, was comptroller of the stamps at Edinburgh. In his latter years, Anderson found himself in embarrassed circumstances, from the poverty which had gradually fallen upon him from his ill-directed projects, arising from his want of prudence and over sanguine temperament. In his distress he pledged his ancient charters and his copperplates to Thomas Paterson of Conduit Street, London, a friend who had patronized his labours and relieved his necessities. In 1729 the plates were sold by auction, and brought £530. It was at the request of Mr. Paterson that Ruddiman was induced to finish what Anderson with less erudition and diligence had begun. At last in 1739, eleven years after his death, the work was published in one volume folio, under the title of 'Selectus Diplomatum et Numismatum Scotiæ Thesaurus,' with an elaborate preface by Thomas Ruddiman. It was printed, in one large folio volume, by Thomas and Walter Ruddiman, for Thomas Paterson in Conduit Street, Andrew Millar in the Strand, London, and Gawin Hamilton at Edinburgh.

The following is a list of Anderson's works:

An Historical Essay, showing that the Crown of Scotland is Imperial and Independent, in answer to Mr. Atwood. Edin. 1705, 8vo.

Collections relating to the History of Mary Queen of Scotland. Edin. 1727–28, 4 vols. 4to.

Selectus Diplomatum et Numismatum Scotiæ Thesaurus: de Mandato Parliamenti in subjiciuntur ad faciliorum Rei Antiquariæ cognitionem Characteres et Abbreviaturæ, in duas partes distributus: 1. Syllogen complectuntur veterum diplomatum, sive Chartarum regum et procerum Scotiæ, una cum eorum Sigillis, a Duncano II. ad Jacobum I. i. e. ab anno 1094 ad 1412. 2. Continet Numismata tum aurea quam argentea singulorum Scotiæ regum ab Alexandro I. ad supra dictam regnorum coalitionem perpetua serie deducta Quæ operi consummando deerant, supplevit, et prefatione, Tabu-

larum explicatione, aliisque Appendicibus; rem Scotiæ diplomaticam nummariam, et genealogicam haud parum illustrantionibus, auxit et locupletavit Thomas Ruddimanus. Edin. 1739, fol. This splendid work is enriched with fac-similes of charters, &c. beautifully engraved by Sturt. The original price was 4 guineas common paper, and 6 fine. Mr. Ruddiman's Introduction was afterwards translated, and published by itself. Edin. 1773, 12mo. It is a work of extreme rarity, and great value. In the fifth division it exhibits the characters and abbreviations used in ancient MSS.

ANDERSON, JAMES, D.D., the brother of Adam Anderson, author of the Commercial History, whose life has been previously given, was for many years minister of the Scotch church, in Swallow street, Piccadilly, London. He wrote a treatise on 'The Constitutions of the Free Masons,' being the chaplain of that body in London; and an elaborate folio volume, entitled 'Royal Genealogies, or the Genealogical Tables of Emperors, Kings, and Princes, from Adam to these Times,' London, 1732. Neither the date of his birth nor of his death is known.

ANDERSON, JAMES, LL.D., an eminent writer, the son of a farmer, was born at Hermiston, near Edinburgh, in 1739. His ancestors were farmers, and for many generations had occupied the same land. His parents died when he was very young, and at the age of fifteen he entered upon the management of the farm which they had possessed. Early perceiving the great advantage of a scientific acquaintance with agriculture, he attended the chemistry class of Dr. Cullen, in the university of Edinburgh, studying at the same time several collateral branches of science. He adopted a number of improvements on his farm, and was among the first to use the small two horse plough on its introduction into Scotland. In the midst of his agricultural labours, so great was his desire for knowledge and so unwearied his application, that he contrived to acquire a considerable stock of general information. In 1771, under the signature of Agricola, he contributed to Ruddiman's Edinburgh Weekly Magazine a series of 'Essays on Planting,' which in 1777 were collected into a volume. In 1773 he furnished the article Monsoon to the first edition of the Encyclopædia Britannica, in which he predicted the failure of Captain Cook's first expedition in search of a southern polar continent. In 1776 appeared his Essay on Chimneys.

Previous to the year 1777, Mr. Anderson had removed to a large uncultivated farm of 1,300 acres, named Monkhill, which he rented in Aberdeenshire, and which, by his skill and care, he brought into excellent condition. In that year appeared 'Observations on the Means of Exciting a Spirit of National Industry,' with regard to agriculture, commerce, manufactures, and fisheries; and, besides his Essays on Planting, various pamphlets on agricultural subjects, which raised his reputation very high as a practical agriculturist. In 1780, the university of Aberdeen conferred on him the degree of LL.D. He had married in 1768, Miss Seton of Mounie; by whom he had thirteen children; and with the twofold object of educating his family, and enjoying literary society, in 1783 he went to reside in the neighbourhood of Edinburgh. His place of residence was situated within the parish of Leith, and when the magistrates and heritors attempted to levy an assessment upon householders for the maintenance of the poor, he brought the measure before the court of session, and succeeded in persuading the judges that the laws of Scotland did not authorise the establishment of a poor's rate. He considered himself as having rendered an essential service to his country, by his resistance in this case, and several editions of his papers during the process, though never published, were printed for the use of his friends. Having, in a tract privately circulated, projected the establishment of the North British Fisheries, he was requested by the Lords of the Treasury in 1784 to survey the western coast of Scotland, and in 1785 he published the result of his inquiries, under the title of 'An Account of the present state of the Hebrides and Western Coast of Scotland, being the Substance of a Report to the Lords of the Treasury.' In the Report of a committee appointed May 11, 1785, to inquire into the state of the British fisheries, very honourable mention is made of his labours. On the 22d December 1790 he commenced a weekly publication of a literary and scientific nature, called 'The Bee,' which continued till the 1st January 1794. He wrote a great part of the work himself, and besides many of the principal papers without signature, all those which were signed Senex, Alcibiades, and Timothy Hairbrain, were from his pen.

When the Board of agriculture applied to parliament for a reward to Mr. Elkington, on account of his mode of draining by boring, Dr. Anderson addressed several letters to the president of that Board. These letters were published, and though the language he used in them was considered as rather intemperate, yet it afterwards appeared that his assertions were well founded, and that Elkington's plan contained nothing but what had been fully explained by Dr. Anderson more than twenty years before in his Agricultural Essays. About this time, also, he read an Essay on Moss before the Royal Society of Edinburgh, which was soon after published. In it he first advanced the very singular idea that moss, contrary to the mode of all other plants, vegetates below, while its upper stratum is undergoing putrefaction by exposure to the air.

About the year 1797 he removed with his family to London, and for several years wrote the agricultural articles in the Monthly Review. From 1799 to 1802 he conducted another journal called 'Recreations in Agriculture, Natural History, Arts, and Miscellaneous Literature,' which ended with the sixth volume. Although the work contains a number of communications from others, the greater part of it was written by himself. It met with the greatest encouragement from the public, but the irregularity of his printers and booksellers caused him to discontinue it. The thirty-seventh number of his 'Recreations' was his last publication in March 1802. After this period he published nothing more, except his correspondence with General Washington and a pamphlet on scarcity, but devoted himself almost entirely to the relaxation of a quiet life, and particularly to the cultivation of his garden at Isleworth; in which he had constructed a model of his patent hothouse, to act by the rays of the sun, without the application of artificial heat. With this he amused himself by making experiments, in order to ascertain what degree of heat and moisture was most salutary to different plants. As an instance of his unwearied attention to every department of rural economy, may be mentioned a discovery which he made about this time, respecting the most effectual mode of exterminating wasps. Having observed that in the district where he resided these insects were very destructive to every species of fruit, he resolved to study their natural history. He soon ascertained, by his inquiries and observations, that the whole hive, like that of bees, was propagated from one female or queen, and that the whole race, except a few queens, perished during winter, and he naturally concluded that to destroy the queens, in the months of May and June, before they began to drop their eggs, was the surest way of diminishing their number. With this view he even procured an association to be formed, which circulated handbills with directions, and offered a reward for every queen wasp that should be brought in, within a specified period.

Dr. Anderson died at Westham, near London, on 15th October 1808, of a gradual decline. Having been some time a widower, in 1801 he had married a second wife, a lady belonging to Isleworth, who survived him; as did also five sons and a daughter. In his younger days, and while engaged in the active pursuits of agriculture, Dr. Anderson was remarkably handsome in his person, of middle stature, and of robust constitution. Extremely moderate in his living, the country exercise animated his countenance with the glow of health; but the overstrained exertion of his mental powers afterwards impaired his strength, ultimately wasted his faculties, and brought on premature old age. He possessed a very independent mind, and his manners were agreeable and unconstrained. In the relative duties of a husband and a father, he displayed the greatest prudence and affection; and in the social circle he was distinguished by his humorous pleasantry, and abounded in anecdote. In conversation he entered with zeal and spirit into any favourite subject, and his remarks were generally full of interest. He was among the first of that long list of practical writers of which the present century has produced so many who directed the public attention to the improvement of agriculture, and there was no agricultural subject of which he treated without throwing upon it new light. Besides the works mentioned, he wrote also many papers in the periodicals, and an Account of Ancient Fortifications in the Highlands, which was read to the Society of Scottish Antiquaries. — *Scots Mag.* 1809. — *Edin. Ency.*

The following is a list of his works :

A Practical Treatise on Chimneys; containing full directions for constructing them in all cases, so as to draw well, and for removing Smoke in houses. Lond. 1776, 12mo.

Free Thoughts on the American Contest. Edin. 1776, 8vo.

Essays relating to Agriculture and Rural Affairs. Edin. 1775, 8vo. 1777, 8vo. Lond. 1796, 3 vols. 8vo. Fifth edit. with additions and corrections. Lond. 1800, 3 vols. 8vo.

Miscellaneous Thoughts on Planting and Training Timber Trees, by Agricola. Edin. 1777, 8vo.

Observations on the Means of exciting a Spirit of National Industry, chiefly intended to promote the Agriculture, Commerce, Fisheries, and Manufactures of Scotland. Edin. 1777, 4to.

An Inquiry into the Nature of the Corn Laws, with a view to the new Corn Bill proposed for Scotland. Edin. 1777, 8vo.

An Enquiry into the Causes that have hitherto retarded the advancement of Agriculture in Europe, with Hints for removing the circumstances that have chiefly obstructed its progress. Edin. 1779, 4to.

The Interest of Great Britain with regard to her American Colonies considered. 1782, 8vo.

The True Interest of Great Britain considered, or a Proposal for establishing the Northern British Fisheries. 1783, 12mo.

An Account of the present State of the Hebrides, and Western Coasts of Scotland, with Hints for encouraging the Fisheries, and promoting other Improvements in these countries; being the Substance of a Report to the Lords of the Treasury. Edin. 1785, 8vo, illustrated with a geographical map.

Observations on Slavery, particularly with a view to its effects on the British Colonies in the West Indies. Manchester, 1789, 4to.

Papers drawn up by him and Sir John Sinclair, in reference to a Report by a Committee of the Highland Society on Shetland Wool. 1790, 8vo.

The Bee, consisting of Essays Philosophical and Miscellaneous. Edin. 1791–94, 6 vols. 8vo.

Observations on the Effects of Coal Duty upon the remote and thinly peopled coasts of Britain. Edin. 1792, 8vo.

Thoughts on the Privileges and Power of Juries, with Observations on the present State of the Country with regard to Credit. Edin. 1793, 8vo.

Remarks on the Poor Law in Scotland. Edin. 1793, 4to.

A Practical Treatise on Peat Moss, considered as in its natural state fitted for affording fuel, or as susceptible of being converted into mould, capable of yielding abundant crops of useful produce, with full directions for converting and cultivating it as a soil. Edin. 1794, 8vo.

A General View of the Agriculture and Rural Economy of the County of Aberdeen, with Observations on the means of its improvement. Chiefly drawn up for the Board of Agriculture, in two parts. Edin. 1794, 8vo.

An Account of the different kinds of Sheep found in the Russian dominions, and among the Tartar Hordes of Asia, by Dr. Pallas, illustrated with six plates, to which are added five appendixes, tending to illustrate the natural and œconomical history of sheep, and other domestic animals. Edin. 1794, 8vo.

On an Universal Character, in two letters to Edward Home, Esq. Edin. 1795, 8vo.

A Practical Treatise on Draining Bogs and Swampy Grounds, with cursory remarks on the originality of Elkington's mode of draining. Also disquisitions concerning the different breeds of sheep and other domestic animals, being the principal additions made in the fourth edition of his Essays on Agriculture. Lond. 1794, 1798, 8vo.

Recreations in Agriculture, Natural History, Arts, and Miscellaneous Literature. Lond. 1799–1802, 6 vols. 8vo.

Selections from his Correspondence with General Washington, in which the causes of the present scarcity are fully investigated. Lond. 1800, 8vo.

A Calm Investigation of the Circumstances that have led to the present scarcity of Grain in Britain; suggesting the means of alleviating that evil, and of preventing the recurrence of such a calamity in future. Lond. 1801, 8vo.

A Description of a patent Hot-house, which operates chiefly by the heat of the Sun, and other subjects; without the aid of Flues, or Tan-bark, or Steam, for the purpose of heating it, &c. Lond. 1804, 12mo.

The Antiquity of Woollen Manufactures in England.— Gents. Mag. August 1778, and other papers in that work.

A Disquisition on Wool-bearing Animals. American Trans. iv. 149. 1799.

On Cast Iron. Trans. Ed. R. Soc. i. 26. 1788.

A further Description of ancient Fortifications in the North of Scotland. Archæol. vi. 87. 1782.

ANDERSON, JOHN, M.A., author of the celebrated Defence of Presbyterianism, was born in the reign of Charles the Second, but the precise year has not been ascertained. All that is known of his early life is, that, after receiving a university education, he was for some time the preceptor of the celebrated John duke of Argyle and Greenwich; and that he subsequently resided for twenty-five years in Edinburgh, where he kept a school. Having been educated for the church, he was, about the beginning of the eighteenth century, minister of the parish of Dumbarton, and afterwards was transported to Glasgow. The general use of the English liturgy in the Episcopalian congregations, as we learn from Wodrow's correspondence, was exciting, about this period, the utmost alarm in the minds of the Presbyterian clergy and people, and a violent controversy on the subject was carried on for some time between the ministers of the rival churches. Into this controversy Mr. Anderson entered with much zeal. The first of his publications known is styled 'A Dialogue between a Curat and a Countreyman concerning the English Service, or Common Prayer Book of England,' 4to, printed at Glasgow about 1710. In this work, in opposition to the statements in Sage's 'Fundamental Charter of Presbytery Examined,' he proved that the liturgy which had been used by the first Scottish reformers for at least seven years after the overthrow of popery, was not the

English liturgy, but that used by the English church at Geneva, since known by the name of John Knox's liturgy, or the old Scottish liturgy. In 1711 appeared a 'Second Dialogue,' in which he set himself to oppose the sentiments of South, Hammond, Beveridge, and Burnet. These works were followed by 'A Letter from a Countreyman to a Curat,' which called forth several answers, particularly one by Robert Calder, an Episcopalian clergyman, the friend of Dr. Archibald Pitcairn, to which he speedily replied in a pamphlet entitled 'Curat Calder Whipt.' Soon after he published 'A Sermon preached at Ayr, at the opening of the Synod, on April 1, 1712.' In 1714 appeared his famous work, under the title of 'A Defence of the Church Government, Faith, Worship, and Spirit of the Presbyterians, in Answer to a Book entitled "An Apology for Mr. Thomas Rhind,"' &c., 4to. In 1717 he received a call from the congregation of the North-West church, Glasgow, but was not settled there till 1720, after his case had been before both the synod and the Assembly, some of the members of his presbytery having objected to his removal. His colleagues, it seems, had taken offence at a letter addressed by him to Walter Stewart of Pardonan, published by him in 1717, in which he says, "I confess I was under a great temptation of being eager for a settlement in Glasgow, for what minister would not be fond of a larger stipend and a double charge?" In the latter year (1720) he published, in 12mo, six 'Letters upon the Overtures concerning Kirk Sessions and Presbyteries,' which, like all his controversial writings, abound in curious historical information, interspersed with severe satirical remark. He wrote several other political and theological tracts besides those mentioned, now gone into oblivion. The precise year of his death is not known, but as his successor was appointed in 1723, his decease must have taken place before that year. His grandson, Professor Anderson, the founder of the Andersonian Institution, Glasgow, caused the following memorial to his memory to be inscribed upon the family tombstone erected over his grave, on the front of the North-West church, Glasgow: "Near this place ly the remains of the Rev. John Anderson, who was preceptor to the famous John

Duke of Argyle and Greenwich, and minister of the gospel in Dumbarton in the beginning of the eighteenth century, and in this church in 1720. He was the author of 'The Defence of the Church Government, Faith, Worship, and Spirit of the Presbyterians,' and of several other ecclesiastical and political tracts. As a pious minister and an eloquent preacher, a defender of civil and religious liberty, and a man of wit and learning, he was much esteemed; he lived in the reign of Charles II., James II., William III., Anne, and George I. Such times, and such a man, forget not, reader, while thy country, liberty, and religion are dear to thee."—*Wodrow's History.*

ANDERSON, JOHN, F.R.S., founder of the Andersonian Institution, Glasgow, and grandson of the subject of the preceding article, was the eldest son of the Rev. James Anderson, minister of Roseneath, Dumbartonshire, in the manse of which parish he was born in the year 1726. His father died when he was yet young, and he went to live at Stirling with his aunt, Mrs. Turner, widow of one of the ministers of the High church of that town, where he received the first part of his education. At the age of twenty he was one of the officers of the Burgher corps of Stirling, raised for the defence of the town against the forces of the Pretender, and the carabine he carried on that occasion is preserved in the Museum of the university founded by him. He afterwards studied at the college of Glasgow. In 1756 he was appointed professor of oriental languages in that university. In 1760 he was removed to the chair of natural philosophy. Embued with an ardent zeal for the diffusion of useful knowledge, he instituted a class, in addition to his usual one, for the instruction of the working classes and others, who were unable to attend the regular course of academical study, which he continued to teach twice a-week, during session, till his death. In 1786 he published 'Institutes of Physics,' which in ten years went through five editions. Having, like many other good men, hailed the first burst of the French Revolution in 1789, as calculated to promote the cause of liberty, he went to Paris in 1791 with the model of a gun he had invented, the peculiar advantage of which consisted in the recoil being stopped by the condensation of common air within the body of the carriage. To this ingenious invention he had unsuccessfully endeavoured to obtain the attention of our own government. This model he presented to the national convention, who hung it up in their hall, with the superscription, "The Gift of Science to Liberty!" A six-pounder being made from his model, he tried numerous experiments with it, in presence, among others, of the celebrated Paul Jones, then in Paris, who expressed his approbation of the new species of gun. While Professor Anderson remained in the capital of France, he witnessed many of those stirring and momentous scenes, which at that period attracted the notice of all Europe, and he was one of those who, on the 14th July, from the top of the altar of liberty, sung *Te Deum* with the bishop of Paris, when the ill-fated Louis XVI. took the oath to the Constitution! An expedient of his for furnishing the people of Germany with French newspapers and manifestoes, after the emperor Leopold had drawn a cordon of troops round the frontiers, to prevent their introduction, was tried, and found very useful. It consisted of small balloons of paper, varnished with boiled oil, and filled with inflammable air, and the newspapers being tied to them, they were sent off when the wind was favourable, and picked up by the people. A small flag which these paper balloons carried, bore an inscription in German to the following purport:

"O'er hills and dales and lines of hostile troops, I float majestic,
Bearing the laws of God and Nature to oppressed men,
And bidding them with arms their rights maintain."

On his return to Glasgow, Professor Anderson resumed his college duties with his usual fervour. He died on the 13th January 1796, in the 70th year of his age, and 41st of his professorship. By his will, dated 7th May 1795, he bequeathed all his money and effects for the establishment at Glasgow of an institution, to be called Anderson's University, for the education of the unacademical classes.

The institution was endowed by the founder with a valuable philosophical apparatus, museum, and library, valued at three thousand pounds sterling; and it was incorporated by charter from the magistrates and council of Glasgow, on the 9th June following the testator's death. The plan of Professor Anderson contemplated four colleges, for arts, medicine, law, and theology, each college to consist of nine professors, the senior professor being president or dean, but the funds not allowing of this at the outset, the managers wisely began on a small scale, and the institution has gradually grown in influence and importance, and is now in a state more corresponding with the original design of the founder. The first teacher was Dr. Thomas Garnet, professor of natural philosophy, and author of a 'Tour through the Highlands,' as well as various scientific works, who commenced on 21st September 1796, by reading in the Trades' Hall, Glasgow, popular and scientific lectures on natural philosophy and chemistry, addressed to persons of both sexes, and illustrated by experiments. With the view that the institution should be permanently established the trustees purchased, in 1798, extensive buildings in John Street, and in the same year a professor of mathematics and geography was appointed. After a successful period of tuition of four years, Dr. Garnet, on the foundation of the Royal Institution of Great Britain in 1800, was chosen its first professor of chemistry, and accordingly removed to London in October of that year, but was obliged to resign the situation on account of ill health, and died in 1802, aged 36. He was succeeded in Anderson's Institution, Glasgow, by the celebrated Dr. George Birkbeck, the founder of Mechanic's Institutes, who, at the age of twenty-one, was appointed professor of natural history, and in addition to what had formerly been taught, introduced a familiar system of instruction, which he conducted gratis, chiefly for the benefit of operatives. One of the great benefits of this institution from the commencement, indeed, has been that instruction is communicated to students of all classes, divested of those technicalities by which it is frequently overlaid and obscured by educational institutions of greater name. Dr. Birkbeck resigned in August 1804, and was succeeded in the following month by Dr. Andrew Ure, the well-known chemist. Dr. Ure continued to discharge the duties of his office with great success for the long period of twenty-five years, when he

removed to London. In the meantime the institution had grown in public estimation, and several professors had been appointed. The original buildings too had become insufficient, and the trustees finally purchased from the city the Grammar school buildings, situated in George Street, which, with extensive additions and alterations, were rendered fit for a complete college establishment, containing halls for the professors, the museum, library, &c. The new buildings were opened in November 1828, and continue to be used with marked success. There are now thirteen professors, and the subjects taught are natural philosophy, chemistry, natural history, logic and ethics, mathematics and geography, oriental languages, drawing and painting, anatomy, theory and practice of medicine, surgery, materia medica, medical jurisprudence, veterinary medicine, and German and modern literature. The Institution, or as it is called, the Andersonian University, is placed under the inspection of the Lord Provost and other officials as ordinary visitors, but it is more immediately superintended by eighty-one trustees, who are elected by ballot, and remain in office for life, unless disqualified by non-attendance. They are chosen from nine classes of citizens, namely, tradesmen, agriculturists, artists, manufacturers, physicians and surgeons, lawyers, divines, philosophers, and kinsmen or namesakes. Nine of their number are annually elected by the trustees as managers of the establishment for the year, and they in turn elect from their number, by ballot, the president, secretary, and treasurer.

A posthumous work of Professor Anderson, entitled 'Observations on Roman Antiquities discovered between the Forth and the Clyde,' was published at Edinburgh in 1800. — *Glasgow Mechanic's Magazine*, 1825. — *Cleland's Annals of Glasgow*.

ANDERSON, JOHN, historian of the Hamiltons, was born June 6, 1789, at Gilmerton House, in the county of Mid-Lothian. He was the eldest son of James Anderson, supervisor of excise, Oban, whose father, William Anderson, was a farmer at Upper Liberton, and a burgess and guild-brother of the city of Edinburgh. His mother was Elizabeth, daughter of John Williams, the well-known author of the 'Mineral Kingdom,' who then resided at Gilmerton. After receiving the proper education, and attending the university of Edinburgh, he was in 1813 admitted a licentiate of the Edinburgh Royal College of Surgeons, and had scarcely passed his college examinations, when he was appointed, by the Marquis of Douglas, afterwards, on the death of his father in 1819, Duke of Hamilton, first Surgeon of the Royal Lanarkshire Militia, and he retained that situation, and the patronage and confidence of his grace, until his death. He settled at Hamilton, and obtained an extensive practice. In 1825, he published, in quarto, a large and elaborate work, entitled ' Historical and Genealogical Memoirs of the House of Hamilton,' to which, in 1827, he added a supplement. For more than two years previous to his death, he had been engaged collecting materials for a Statistical Account of Lanarkshire; and he also contemplated writing a Genealogical History of the Robertsons of Struan. In the peculiar line of literature which he selected for himself, he was distinguished by sound and pertinent information, deep research, untiring perseverance, and a ready and perspicuous style. He died 24th December 1832, his last illness being caused by extraordinary fatigue in attending patients under the cholera morbus. He was (says a writer in the *New Monthly Magazine*) universally known in the neighbourhood of his residence; and from his unassuming manners, his social disposition, and extensive benevolence, was as generally respected. His maternal grandfather, John Williams, F.S.A., Scotland, was, though a native of Wales, long connected with Scotland, and in his lifetime eminent both as an antiquarian and a geologist. He was a mineral surveyor by profession, and on his first coming to Scotland he took the coal-mines of Brora, in the parish of Golspie, from the Earl of Sutherland, and a farm near them named Waterford. His daughter, Elizabeth, the mother of Dr. Anderson, (and of the author of the ' Scottish Nation,') was born at Brora, 13th April 1765, just a fortnight before the late Duchess-Countess of Sutherland. The farm proved a bad speculation, as Mr. Williams lost a large sum of money in improving it to no purpose. After he had put up an engine at the coal-mine, the latter took fire, by which he lost a considerable sum, indeed nearly all that he

possessed. At that time the earl and countess were at Bath, on account of the health of the earl, who died there. The young countess, their daughter, on succeeding to the Sutherland title and estates, was an infant scarcely a year old. The factor, a Mr. Campbell Combie, was a very harsh and arbitrary person, and would not do anything for Mr. Williams. He refused even to entertain his claim either for the loss he had sustained by the coal-mines, or for the money he had expended in improvements on the farm. Fortunately, at this juncture Mr. Williams was appointed by government one of the persons to survey the forfeited estates in Scotland, and in this employment he was engaged for eighteen months. He afterwards took a coal-mine at West Calder, and subsequently went to Gilmerton about 1775. In 1777 he published ' An Account of some remarkable ancient Ruins lately discovered in the Highlands and Northern parts of Scotland,' being the vitrified forts found in various parts of the country. He was one of the first to direct attention to these remains, and his theory regarding them has generally been adopted by subsequent writers on the subject. In 1789 appeared, in 2 vols. 8vo., his most celebrated work, ' The Natural History of the Mineral Kingdom.' Of this last work he sent a copy to George the Third, one to the unfortunate Louis the Sixteenth of France, and one to the Empress Catherine of Russia. The two former never acknowledged receipt. The Empress was the only one of these potentates who took any notice of the gift. Whatever was her character otherwise, it is worthy of note that she patronized literary and scientific men, and invited them to her court. Mr. Williams received a communication from St. Petersburg, requesting him to proceed to Russia, to survey for minerals in that empire, and he accordingly left Scotland for that purpose about the end of 1792, or early in 1793. On his way home, after fulfilling his mission, he was seized with a fever and died at Verona in Italy, May 29, 1795. He was one of the twelve original members of the Scotch Antiquarian Society, and his portrait is in that Institution in Edinburgh. In the Transactions of that society there appeared from his pen, a paper entitled ' A Plan for a Royal Forest of Oak in the Highlands of Scotland.' An edition of 'the Mineral Kingdom,' edited by a Dr. Millar of Edinburgh was published in 1810, containing a Life of Mr. Williams, which was incorrect in many respects, and not sanctioned by his family.

ANDERSON, JOHN, an enterprising character, founder of the town of Fermoy, in Ireland, son of David Anderson of Portland, was born in lowly circumstances in the West of Scotland. While very young he learned to read and write, and having made a few pounds in some humble employment, he settled in Glasgow about 1784. By a speculation in herrings he acquired five hundred pounds, and with this sum he went to Cork, and became an export merchant, dealing in provisions, the staple trade of the place. In a few years he realized twenty-five thousand pounds. This sum he laid out in the purchase of four-sixths of the Fermoy estate, in the province of Munster. With characteristic energy he resolved to make a town at Fermoy, which at that period was no more than a dirty hamlet, consisting of a few hovels, and a carman's public house, at the end of a narrow old bridge. He began by building a good hotel, and next erected a few houses, and a square. At his own expense he rebuilt the ruinous bridge over the Blackwater, on which the town is situated. Having learned that government intended to erect large barracks in Munster, he offered, in 1797, a most eligible site for them, rent free. The offer was accepted, and two very large and handsome barracks were built. He next erected a theatre, and a handsome residence for himself. He invited various families, having more or less capital, to settle at Fermoy, and placed himself at the head of the little community. As his manners were pleasing, his society was courted by the nobility and gentry of the neighbourhood. He was never ashamed of his origin, and often spoke of his success in the world with laudable pride. On one occasion, in the very height of his prosperity, he was entertaining a large company at his residence in Fermoy. Amongst the party were the late Earls of Kingston and Shannon, and Lord Riversdale. The conversation turned on their host's great success in life, and Lord Kingston asked him to what he chiefly attributed it. "To education, my lord," he replied, " every child in Scotland can easily get the means of learning to read and write.

When I was a little boy my parents sent me to school every day, and I had to walk three miles to the village school. Many a cold walk I had in the bitter winter mornings; and I assure you, my lords," he added, smiling, "that shoes and stockings were extremely scarce in those days." Still continuing his attention to business, he established a bank, an agricultural society, and a mail coach company. The first coach which ran between Cork and Dublin was set a-going by him. He also built a large schoolhouse and a military college; the latter afterwards became a public school. For the erection of a Protestant church he gave three thousand pounds, and five hundred pounds and a site rent free for a Catholic chapel. The government offered him a baronetcy, which he declined. It was, however, conferred, in 1813, by George IV., when Prince Regent, upon his son, Sir James Caleb Anderson, the well-known experimentalist in steam-coaching, as a mark of his Royal Highness's gracious approbation of the services rendered to Ireland by his father. Having embarked in some dangerous speculations, Mr. Anderson, in his latter years, sustained great reverses. In Welsh mining alone he lost £30,000. On the sale of the Barrymore estates, he was a heavy purchaser, by which, owing to the fall in the price of land in Ireland, after the close of the war, he became a considerable loser; while his banking operations were affected by the changes in the currency. He left behind him, however, a noble monument in the handsome town of Fermoy, which has now 7,000 inhabitants. Mr. Madden, in his ' Revelations of Ireland,' has devoted a chapter to the enterprise of this "Scotchman in Munster," to which we are mainly indebted for the materials of this sketch. Mr. Anderson married a Miss Semple, by whom he had two sons and two daughters.

ANDERSON, ROBERT, M.D., editor and biographer of the British Poets, born at Carnwath in Lanarkshire on 7th January 1750, was the fourth son of William Anderson, feuar there, and Margaret Melrose, his wife. After receiving the rudiments of his education at his native village, he was sent to the grammar school at Lanark, the master of which was Robert Thomson, who had married a sister of the poet Thomson. Two of his schoolfellows at this school were Pinkerton the historian, and James Græme, who died young, and whose poems were afterwards included in his edition of the British poets. When only ten years old his father died in his fortieth year, leaving his widow with four sons very slenderly provided for. Robert, the youngest, showed very early a taste for reading and study, and being destined for the church, he was sent, in the year 1767, to the university of Edinburgh, where he became a student of divinity. Subsequently changing his views, he entered upon the study of medicine; and after finishing his medical studies he went to England, and was for a short time employed as surgeon to the Dispensary at Bamborough castle, Northumberland. On the 25th September 1777 he married Anne, daughter of John Grey, Esq. of Alnwick, a relative of the noble family of that name. He took his degree of doctor of medicine at Edinburgh, in May 1778. He afterwards practised as a physician at Alnwick, but his wife's health failing, and having by his marriage secured a moderate independence, he finally returned to Edinburgh in 1784, where, in December 1785, his wife died of consumption, leaving him with three daughters, the youngest of whom soon followed her mother to the grave. In 1793 he married Margaret, daughter of Mr. David Dale, master of Yester school, Haddingtonshire. He now devoted himself to literary pursuits, and produced various works, chiefly in the department of criticism and biography. The principal of these is 'The Works of the British Poets, with prefaces Biographical and Critical,' in fourteen large octavo volumes, the earliest of which was published in 1792-3; the thirteenth in 1795, and the fourteenth in 1807. His correspondence with literary men of eminence was extensive. He was the friend and patron of all who evinced any literary talent. In particular he was the friend of Thomas Campbell the poet, who through his influence procured literary employment on his first coming to Edinburgh; and to Dr. Anderson Mr. Campbell dedicated his 'Pleasures of Hope,' as it was chiefly owing to him that that most beautiful poem was first brought before the world. It was in the year 1797, when Campbell was only nineteen years of age, that his acquaintance with Dr. Anderson commenced,

which forms such an important epoch in the history of both. The following account of it by Dr. Irving is extracted from Beattie's Life of Campbell: "Campbell's introduction to Dr. Anderson, which had no small influence on his brilliant career, was in a great measure accidental. He had come to Edinburgh in search of employment, when he met Mr. Hugh Park, then a teacher in Glasgow, and afterwards second master of Stirling school. Park, who was a frank and warmhearted man, was deeply interested in the fortunes of the youthful poet, which were then at their lowest ebb. His own character was held in much esteem by the doctor; and he was one day coming to pay him a visit, when the young ladies (Dr. Anderson's daughters) observed from the window that he was accompanied by a handsome lad, with whom he was engaged in earnest conversation, and who seemed reluctant to take leave. Their curiosity was naturally excited, and Campbell's story was soon told—being merely the short and simple annals of a poor scholar, not unconscious of his own powers, but placed in the most unfavourable circumstances for the development of poetical genius. Park knew that he had obtained distinction in the university of Glasgow; and he fortunately had in his pocket a poem [an Elegy written in Mull the previous year] which his young friend had written in one of the Hebrides. Dr. Anderson was struck with the turn and spirit of the verses; nor did he hesitate to declare his opinion that they exhibited a fair promise of poetical excellence. The talents, the character, and the prospects of so interesting a youth formed the chief subject of conversation during the afternoon. He expressed a cordial wish to see the author without delay, and Park's kindness was too active to neglect a commission so agreeable to himself. Campbell was accordingly introduced, and his first appearance produced a most favourable impression." [*Beattie's Life of Campbell*, vol. i. p. 194.] As Campbell was anxious to obtain some literary employment, Dr. Anderson, with his characteristic zeal and sympathy in the cause of friendless merit, did not rest until the object had been attained. He warmly recommended the young poet to Mr. Mundell, the publisher, who made Campbell an offer of twenty pounds for an abridged edition of

Bryan Edwards's 'West Indies,' which Campbell accepted, and which was his first undertaking for the public press. He afterwards consulted Dr. Anderson as to the publication of his 'Pleasures of Hope,' as his experience as an author gave peculiar weight to his opinions on this point. The manuscript, we are told, was then shown to Mr. Mundell, and after some discussion between Dr. Anderson and the publisher, the copyright was sold to him on the terms mentioned in the life of Campbell. "In the literary society," says Dr. Beattie, "which Dr. Anderson drew around him, the poem was a familiar topic in conversation, and he had soon the pleasure of finding that the opinion of other judicious critics, respecting its merits, was in harmony with his own." At that period, says Dr. Irving, "the editor of the British Poets had a very extensive acquaintance; and it was through him that Campbell formed his earliest connexions with men of letters. His house at Heriot's Green was frequented by individuals who had then risen, or who afterwards rose to great eminence. As he had relinquished all professional pursuits, his time was very much at the disposal of his friends, whatever might be their denomination. He was visited by men of learning and men of genius, and perhaps in the course of the same day by some rustic rhymer, who was anxious to consult him about publishing his works by *superscription*. I remember finding him in consultation with a little deformed student of physic, from the north of Ireland; who, in detailing his literary history, took occasion to mention that at some particular crisis he had no intention of *persecuting* the study of poetry." [*Ibid.* vol. i. p. 241.] Before committing it to press, the manuscript of the 'Pleasures of Hope,' by the advice of Dr. Anderson, underwent a careful revisal, and at his suggestion the opening of the poem was entirely rewritten.

In 1796 Dr. Anderson published 'The miscellaneous works of Tobias Smollett, M.D., with memoirs of his life and writings,' six volumes octavo; which passed through six editions. His life of Smollett was also published separately, the eighth edition of which appeared in 1818, under the title of 'The Life of Tobias Smollett, M.D., with critical observations on his

Works.' He also published an elaborate 'Life of Samuel Johnson, LL.D., with critical observations on his Works,' the third edition of which appeared in 1815. In 1820 he published an edition of Dr. Moore's Works, with memoirs of his life and writings. Among his other publications may be mentioned 'The Poetical Works of Robert Blair,' with a Life, 1794. His latest production was a new edition of Blair's Grave and other poems, with his life and critical observations, Edinburgh, 1826. He was for several years editor of the Edinburgh Magazine, afterwards incorporated with the Scots Magazine, and a contributor to various periodicals. Dr. Anderson died of dropsy in the chest on the 20th February 1830, in the 81st year of his age, and was buried, by his own desire, in Carnwath churchyard. In the year 1810 his eldest daughter was married to David Irving, LL.D., author of the Life of George Buchanan, the Lives of Scottish Writers, and other works. Mrs. Irving died suddenly in 1812, leaving a son. Dr. Anderson's habits were so regular, and his disposition so cheerful and animated, that old age stole on him imperceptibly. As an instance of the strong interest which he ever took in the cause of civil and religious liberty, it may be mentioned, that, on the evening before his death, he asked for a map of Greece, that he might, to use his own words, form some notion of the general elements of this new state, which had then worked out its independence. As a literary critic he was distinguished by a warm sensibility to the beauties of poetry and by extreme candour. His personal character was marked by the most urbane manners, the most honourable probity, and by unshaken constancy in friendship.—*New Monthly Magazine for July* 1830. —*Annual Obituary.—Encyclopedia Britannica, 7th edition.*

ANDERSON, WALTER, D.D., a respectable clergyman of mediocre talents, who was afflicted with an incurable *furor scribendi*, which exposed him to the ridicule of his acquaintances, was upwards of fifty years minister of Chirnside. The date and place of his birth are unknown. His first work was a 'Life of Crœsus, King of Lydia,' in four parts, 12mo, 1755, which owed its origin, it is said, to a joke of David Hume. One day, being at the house of Ninewells, which stood within his parish, and was the property of Hume's brother, and conversing with the great historian on his success as an author, he is said to have thus addressed him: " Mr. David, I daresay other people might write books too ; but you clever folks have taken up all the good subjects. When I look about me, I cannot find one unoccupied." Hume waggishly replied, " What would you think, Mr. Anderson, of a history of Crœsus, king of Lydia ? That has never yet been written." He caught at the idea, and hence the life of the Lydian king. This singular work was honoured with a serio-burlesque notice in the second number of the first Edinburgh Review, started by Hume, Smith, Carlyle, and others ; and received rather a severe critique in the second number of the Critical Review, then first established in London by Smollett. In 1769, undeterred by the ill success of his first attempt, he published a History of the Reigns of Francis IV. and Charles IX. of France, two volumes quarto. In 1775 appeared a continuation, being 'The History of France, from the beginning of the reign of Henry III. down to the period of the edict of Nantes,' one volume quarto. In 1783 he published two additional volumes, bringing the history down to the peace of Munster. Not one of these works ever sold, and as he published at his own risk, it is related that the cost of print and paper was defrayed by the sale, one by one, as each successive heavy quarto appeared, of some houses which he possessed in the town of Dunse, until they had all ceased to be his property. He also produced an essay, in quarto, on the philosophy of ancient Greece, which displayed considerable erudition, though sadly deficient in style, and may be said to have been the only production of his which merited or received any praise. He subsequently published a pamphlet against the principles of the first French Revolution, which fell still-born from the press. With the view of drawing attention to the work, and thereby promoting its sale, he wrote an addition or appendix to the pamphlet, of much greater extent than the pamphlet itself, with which he went to Edinburgh to get it printed. Having called upon Principal Robertson he informed him of his plan, which caused him to exclaim in surprise :

" Really, this is the maddest of all your schemes —what! a small pamphlet is found heavy, and you propose to lighten it by making it ten times heavier ! Never was such madness heard of !" " Why, why," answered Dr. Anderson, " did you never see a kite raised by boys ?" " I have," answered the principal. " Then you must have remarked that, when you try to raise the kite by itself, there is no getting it up : but only add a long string of papers to its tail, and up it goes like a laverock !" The venerable historian was highly amused by this ingenious argument, but succeeded in dissuading the infatuated author from his design. Dr. Anderson died at an advanced age in July 1800, at the manse of Chirnside.

His works may be enumerated as follows :

The History of Crœsus, king of Lydia, in four parts ; containing Observations on the Ancient Notion of Destiny or Dreams, on the Origin and Credit of the Oracles, and the principles upon which their Oracles were defended against any attack. Edin. 1755, 4to.

The History of France, during the reigns of Francis II. and Charles IX. To which is prefixed, a Review of the General History of the Monarchy, from its origin to that period ; comprehending an Account of the various Revolutions, Political Government, Laws, and Customs of the Nation. Lond. 1769, 2 vols. 4to.

The History of France, from the commencement of the reign of Henry III. and the rise of the Catholic League, to the peace of Vervins, and the establishment of the famous Edict of Nantz, in the reign of Henry IV., and from the commencement of the reign of Lewis XIII. to the general peace of Munster. Lond. 1775-1788, 8 vols. 4to.

The Philosophy of Ancient Greece investigated, in its origin and progress to the æras of its greatest celebrity in the Ionian, Italic, and Athenian schools ; with Remarks on the Delineated Systems of their Founders, and some Account of their Lives and Characters, and those of their most eminent Disciples. Edin. 1791, 4to.

ANGUS, a very ancient name in Scotland ; the first on record who bore it being the brother of Loarn and Fergus, the earliest kings of the Dalriadic Scots. Pinkerton says : " The Irish accounts bear that Loarn, Angus, and Fergus, three sons of Erc, led the Scots back to Britain in 503, [after having been compelled to retreat to Ireland about fifty years before—that is, about the middle of the fifth century, or about two hundred years after their first arrival in Argyleshire,] and that Loarn was the first king and was succeeded by Fergus. What became of Angus we are not told. It would seem that, either from incapacity or preference of private life, he aspired not to any share of the power of his brothers. But though Loarn be left out of the regal list in the Scottish accounts, yet neither he nor Angus is unknown to them. Fordun, lib. iii. cap. i., says that Fergus, son of Erc, came to Scotland *cum duobus fratribus Loarn et Tenegus,* 'with his brothers Loarn and Tenegus,' which last word is a not uncommon corruption of Angus with Fordun. The register of the priory of St. Andrews, written about 1250, also says of Kenneth, son of Alpin, *sepultus in Yona insula, ubi tres filii Erc, scilicet Fergus, Loarn, et Enegus, sepulti fuerant;* 'he was buried in Iona, where the three sons of Erc, namely Fergus, Loarn, and Enegus were buried.'" [*Enquiry into the History of Scotland*, vol. ii. p. 92.] It would appear that Cantyre, (from the Gaelic word *Ceantir*, Headland), was the portion of Fergus, Loarn possessed the district called after him Lorn, and Angus is supposed to have colonized Islay, as it was enjoyed by Muredach his son, after his decease. See LORN, marquis of, and ARGYLE, duke of; also DALRIADA.

ANGUS, styled by the annalists Angus MacFergus, was also the name of the most powerful king the Picts ever had. He reigned between 731 and 761, in which latter year he died. Belonging originally to the southern Picts, he had, in 729, raised himself to the command of that portion of the Pictish tribes, and in the year 731, by the conquest of Talorgan MacCongusa, his last opponent, he obtained the throne of the whole Pictish nation. In consequence of his success a league was entered into between the principal tribes of the northern Picts and the Dalriads or Scots of Argyle, who were ever ready for war with their Pictish enemies. Angus, however, crushed this formidable union, and almost annihilated the Scots of Dalriada; "and yet," says Skene, "it was his power and his victories which laid the germ of that revolution that resulted in the overthrow of the Pictish influence in Scotland." [*History of Highlanders*, vol. i. p. 55.]

ANGUS, was also the name of a king of the Dalriads, who began to reign in 804 and died in 811. At a very early period the district of country lying between the North Esk on the north, and the Tay and Isla on the south, was called Angus, which it still retains, though also called Forfarshire from the county town. Its more ancient name is commonly supposed to have been so named from Angus, a brother of Kenneth the Second, to whom this territory was granted by Kenneth, after the union of the Picts and Scots. Gaelic scholars, however, think that the name denotes a hill of a particular description, or which was applied to a special use; and it is supposed to have been derived from the Hill of Angus, a little to the eastward of the church of Aberlemno, in ancient times the usual place of rendezvous for the inhabitants of the surrounding country, during the predatory incursions of the Danes and Norwegians. It seems more probable that the hill itself took its name from the district.

ANGUS, earldom of, one of the most ancient titles in Scotland. According to Chalmers, Dubican, the son of Indechtraig, and maormor or earl of Angus, died in 939. Maolbride his son died during the reign of Culen, who was murdered by Rohard, thane of Fife, in 970. His successor Cunechat, Cruchne, or Conquhare, maormor of Angus, had a daughter Finella, styled the lady of Fettercairn, to whose name an historical interest is attached as being the murderess of Kenneth the Third, king of Scots, in consequence of having caused her son Crathilinthus to be put to death as related in the life of that monarch. See KENNETH III. This event happened in the year 994, and the Lady Finella was afterwards put to death for her crime, in the romantic ravine called Den Finella. Her memory is still preserved in the names of various other places in the county of Kincardine.

In the reign of Malcolm Canmore flourished Gilchrist, earl of Angus, who was living after the year 1120. He married Finella or Fynbella, the sister of the thane of Mearns, by whom he had a son Gilibrede, the second earl of Angus, properly so called instead of maormor, who succeeded him, and was engaged in the battle of the Standard, under King David

the First, in 1138. Earl Gilibrede was one of the twenty barons who were given up to Henry as hostages for the performance of the disgraceful conditions entered into by King William the Lion, in 1174, when imprisoned at Falaise in Normandy, in order to obtain his release. He died about 1180. He married a daughter of Cospatrick, the third earl of March, by whom he had six sons, namely, Gilchrist, third earl of Angus; Magnus, earl of Caithness, [see CAITHNESS, earldom of]; Gilbert, ancestor of the Ogilvys, earls of Airlie, [see OGILVY, surname of, and AIRLIE, earl of]; Adam, William, and Anegus.

Gilchrist, third earl of Angus, married a sister of William the Lion. He was the father of Duncan the fourth earl, whose son, Malcolm the fifth earl, married Mary, daughter and heiress of Sir Humphrey Berkeley, knight, by whom he had a daughter, Matildis, countess of Angus in her own right. She married first John Cumin who, in her right, became earl. He died in France in 1242. She married, secondly, in 1243, Gilbert de Umfraville, lord of Redesdale, Prudhow, and Herbottle in Northumberland, who in consequence also became earl of Angus. He died in 1245. He was one of the most famous barons of that age and guardian of the northern parts of England. [*Dugdale's Baronage*, vol. i. p. 504.]

His only son by the countess, also bore the name of Gilbert de Umfraville. He succeeded as the eighth earl. He was governor of the castles of Dundee and Forfar, and of the whole territory of Angus, in 1291, when the regents of Scotland, during the competition for the crown, agreed to deliver up the kingdom and its fortresses to Edward I. of England. On this occasion the earl declared that he had received his castles in charge from the Scottish nation, and that he would not surrender them to England, unless Edward and all the competitors joined in an obligation to indemnify him. The English monarch and the competitors submitted to these conditions of Angus, who was the only person in Scotland who acted with integrity and spirit at this national crisis. [*Fœdera*, vol. ii. p. 531.] He married the third daughter of Alexander Cumin, earl of Buchan, and died in 1307. He had three sons. The eldest, Gilbert, having died before his father, he was succeeded by Robert his second son, who was the ninth earl of Angus. By Edward the Second, Earl Robert was appointed joint-guardian of Scotland, 21st July 1308, and had a commission to be sole guardian 20th August 1309, but did not act upon it, as Robert de Clifford was constituted to that office. Robert de Umfraville, earl of Angus, was forfeited by King Robert the First, for his adherence to the English interest. In 1319, he was one of the commissioners of England to treat with those of Scotland for peace between the two nations. He appears to have died about 1326. By his first wife Lucia, daughter of Philip de Kyme, he had a son Gilbert, who succeeded him, and a daughter, Elizabeth, married to Gilbert de Burdon. His second wife, Alianore, who was afterwards the wife of Roger Mauduit, brought him two sons, Sir Robert, and Thomas.

Gilbert de Umfraville, the tenth earl of Angus, was among the disinherited barons who invaded Scotland in 1332. He claimed the earldom of Angus, of which his father had been deprived by forfeiture in the reign of Robert the First. He had a like right to the superiority of the barony of Dunipace in Stirlingshire, which Bruce had granted to William de Lindesay. He had a share in the decisive victory obtained by Edward Baliol over the forces of King David I. at Dupplin Moor, 12th August 1332. He was much engaged in the wars of Scotland, and in the fourteenth year of Edward the Third he was joined in commission with Lord Percy and Lord Neville, to conclude a truce with the Scots. At the battle of Durham, 20th August 1346, when David the Second was defeated and made prisoner, he was one of the chief commanders of the English army, and ten years afterwards he was one of the commissioners for treating of the liberation of that monarch. He was also frequently a commissioner for guarding the marches. He died 7th January 1381, possessed of great estates in the counties of Northumberland, Cumberland, York, Lincoln, and Suffolk, leaving his niece his next heir, his son, Sir Robert de Umfraville, having predeceased him. This lady was Alianore, the daughter of his sister, Elizabeth, and Gilbert de Burdon, and the wife of Henry Talboys.

The title of earl of Angus after the forfeiture, came into the possession of the Stewart family, having been bestowed before 1329 upon Sir John Stewart of Bonkil, great-grandson of Sir John Stewart of Bonkil, second son of Alexander, high steward of Scotland. He died in December 1331. He had married Margaret, eldest daughter of Sir Alexander de Abernethy, and had an only son Thomas, the second earl of Angus of the Stewart family. The latter took to wife Margaret, daughter of Sir William St. Clair of Roslin, by whom he had one son Thomas, the third earl, and two daughters, Lady Margaret, married first to Thomas the thirteenth earl of Marr, who died without issue in 1377, and secondly to William, first earl of Douglas, by whom she was the mother of George de Douglas, the first earl of Angus of the Douglas family. The second daughter, Lady Elizabeth, married Sir Alexander Hamilton of Innerwick, and had issue.

Thomas, the third earl of Angus, of the Stewart family, succeeded his father in 1361, being then an infant. He died without issue in 1377, when the title devolved on his sister Lady Margaret. On her resignation of it in parliament in 1389, King Robert the Second granted the earldom of Angus, with the lordships of Abernethy in Perthshire, and of Bonkil in the county of Berwick, in favour of George de Douglas her son and the heirs of his body, whom failing to Sir Alexander de Hamilton and his wife Elizabeth, the sister of the said countess, and their heirs. The earldom being afterwards restricted to heirs male, is now vested in the Duke of Hamilton, the representative in the male line of the above named George earl of Angus. See DOUGLAS, earl of, (page 45, vol. ii.); and HAMILTON, duke of, (page 422, vol. iii.)

ANGUS, styled *Angus Mohr*, the great, lord of Islay, was son and successor of Donald, (from whom the Macdonalds take their name) second son of Reginald, son of Somerled, king of the Isles, whose youngest son was also named Angus. During the life of Angus Mohr the expedition of Haco, king of Norway, to the Isles took place, as related in the life of Alexander the Third, [see *ante*, page 88.] Angus joined Haco with his fleet, but in consequence of the treaty which was afterwards entered into between the kings of Norway and Scotland he was allowed to retain his possessions undisturbed, [see page 93.] His son, Angus Oig, or the younger, was faithful to Robert the Bruce, and when the latter, with the few followers who adhered to him, after taking refuge in the Lennox, proceeded to Kintyre, he was hospitably received by Angus, and entertained for three days in his castle of Dunaverty, the ruins of which still remain; and this at a time when he had been denied an asylum everywhere else. At the head of two thousand men, whom he had raised, Angus Oig engaged on Bruce's side at the battle of Bannockburn, where he displayed great valour. On the forfeiture of Alexander, lord of Lorn, and his son and heir, John, who were opposed to the claims of Bruce, a portion of their territories was bestowed on Angus Oig, and in this way the Isles of

Mull, (the possession of which had, for some time, been disputed betwixt the lords of Islay and Lorn,) Jura, Coll, and Tiree, with the districts of Duror and Glencoe, fell to the share of Angus Oig. He also received a portion of Lochaber, and the lands of Morvern and Ardnamurchan. As a measure of precaution, however, Bruce procured from Angus Oig the resignation of his lands in Kintyre, and bestowed them upon Robert, the son and heir of Walter, the high steward and the princess Marjory Bruce, to whom he also gave the keeping of Tarbert castle, then the most important position on the Argyle coast. Before King Robert's death, Angus Oig was the most powerful chieftain in Argyle or the Isles. He and the Bruce died about the same time, that is about 1329. Under David the Second the lands of Kintyre reverted to the descendants of Angus Oig. [*Gregory's Western Highlands and Isles*, pages 22—27.]

ANGUS, earl of, see DOUGLAS, George, William, and Archibald.

ANNAND, WILLIAM, dean of Edinburgh, was born at Ayr in 1633. His father, who bore the same name, was rector of that town under the episcopacy, and rendered himself very unpopular by his strong attachment to the episcopal form of worship. Having in August 1637 been appointed to preach at the opening of the synod of Glasgow, he chose for his text 1 Tim. ii. 1, 2, and, says Baillie, "in the last half of his sermon, from the making of prayers, ran out upon the liturgy, and spake for defence of it in whole, and sundry most plausible parts of it, as well, in my poor judgment, as any in the isle of Britain could have done, considering all circumstances; howsoever, he did maintain to the dislike of all in an unfit time, that which was hanging in suspense betwixt the king and the country. Of his sermon among us in the synod, not a word; but in the town, among the women, a great din." On the following day Mr. Lindsay, minister of Lanark, preached, and as he was entering the pulpit, "some of the women in his ear assured him that if he should twitch (touch) the service-book in his sermon, he should be rent out of his pulpit: he took the advice, and let the matter alone." During the day the women contented themselves with railing and invectives, and "about thirty or forty of our honestest women, in one voice, before the bishop and magistrates, did fall, in railing, cursing, scolding, with clamours on Mr. Annand: some two of the meanest were taken to the tolbooth." Late in the evening Mr. Annand went out with three or four of the clergy, when he was immediately assaulted by some hundreds of enraged women, "of all qualities," who with fists and staves "beat him sore; his cloake, ruff, hatt were rent. However, upon his cries, and candles set out from many windows (it was a dark night), he escaped all bloody wounds; yet he was in great danger even of killing." The following day the magistrates accompanied him to the outskirts of the town, to prevent farther molestation. [*Baillie's Letters and Journals*, ed. 1841, vol. i. pp. 20, 21.] In 1638, five years after his son's birth, he was obliged to remove to England, on account of his adherence to the king and his zeal in the cause of episcopacy. In 1651 the younger Annand was admitted a student of University college, Oxford. In 1656, being then Bachelor of Arts, he received holy orders from Dr. Thomas Fulwar, bishop of Ardfert, or Kerry, in Ireland, and was appointed preacher at Weston on the Green, near Bicester, in Oxfordshire. He was afterwards presented to the vicarage of Leighton-Buzzard, in Bedfordshire. In 1662 he returned to Scotland, in the capacity of chaplain to John, earl of Middleton, high commissioner from the king to the Estates. In the end of 1663 he was inducted to the Tolbooth church at Edinburgh, and some years after transferred to the Tron church. In April 1676 he was appointed by the king dean of Edinburgh. In 1685 he acted as professor of divinity in the university of St. Andrews, and on the 30th of June of that year he attended, by order of government, the earl of Argyle at his execution. He was the author of seven theological treatises, principally in favour of the episcopal worship and government, all published in London but the last, which came out at Edinburgh in 1674. He died on 13th June 1689, and was interred in the Greyfriars' churchyard, Edinburgh.—*Biographia Britannica.*

The titles of Dean Annand's works, which, notwithstanding their Latin names, were all written in English, are as follows:

Fides Catholica; or the doctrine of the Catholic Church, in eighteen great ordinances, &c. Lond. 1661–2, 4to.

A Sermon in Defence of the Liturgy, on Hosea xiv. 2. 1661, 4to.

Panum Quotidianum; or Daily Bread, in defence of set forms of prayer. Lond. 1662, 4to.

Pater Noster; or Our Father, an explanation of the Lord's Prayer. Lond. 1670, 8vo.

Mysterium Pietatis; or the Mystery of Godliness. Lond. 1672, 8vo.

Doxologia, Lond. 1672, 8vo.

Dualitas; including Lex Loquens; or the Honour of Magistracy; and Duorum Unitas; or The Agreement of Magistracy and Ministry, &c. Edin. 1664.

ANNANDALE, lord of, a title possessed by the de Bruses, the ancestors of ROBERT the BRUCE; the lordship of Annandale in Dumfries-shire, having been bestowed by David the First, soon after his accession to the throne, in 1124, on Robert de Brus, the son of a Norman knight who came into England with William the Conqueror. Besides his large estates in Yorkshire, he thus became possessed of an extensive property in Scotland, which he held by the tenure of military service. [See BRUCE, surname of.] After the battle of Bannockburn, the lordship of Annandale was bestowed by Robert the Bruce on his nephew, Sir Thomas Randolph, earl of Moray. With the hand of his daughter Agnes, who married Patrick, ninth earl of Dunbar and March, it went, after the death of her brother John, third earl of Moray, to the Dunbars, earls of March. On their attainder, it came into possession, in 1409, of Archibald, fourth earl of Douglas, and on the forfeiture, in 1455, of James, ninth and last earl of Douglas, it was lost to that family. Annandale now belongs chiefly to the earl of Hopetoun.

ANNANDALE, earldom of, an extinct title, formerly in the possession of a family of the name of Murray. Sir William Murray, the first of this noble family, is said to have been descended from the house of Duffus [see DUFFUS]. He married Isabel, the sister of Thomas Randolph, earl of Moray, and daughter of Sir Thomas Randolph, great chamberlain of Scotland, by Isabel, sister of King Robert Bruce, and by her had two sons, William and Patrick. His great grandson, Sir Adam Murray of Cockpool, made a considerable figure in Scotland in the reigns of King Robert the Second and Robert the Third. A descendant of his, Mungo Murray of Broughton, the second son of Cuthbert Murray of Cockpool, was the ancestor of the Murrays of Broughton in the stewartry of Kirkcudbright. Sir James Murray of Cockpool, the twelfth designed of Cockpool, who died in 1620, married Janet, second daughter of Sir William Douglas of Drumlanrig, ancestor of the dukes of Queensberry, by whom he had three daughters, the eldest of whom, Margaret, was married to Sir Robert Grierson, younger of Lag, by whom she had an only son, Sir John Grierson of Lag, who had no sons. His eldest daughter, Nicholas, married David Scot of Scotstarvet, and had one daughter, Marjory, by whose marriage with David fifth viscount Stormont, the Murrays of Cockpool, earls of Annandale, are lineally represented by the present earl of Mansfield [see STORMONT, viscount of].

Sir James Murray's brother, John, who succeeded to the estates of the family on the death, in 1636, of an intermediate brother, Richard, was raised to the peerage by James the Sixth, with whom he was a great favourite, and whom, on his majesty's accession to the throne of England, he accompanied to London, as one of the gentlemen of the privy chamber, by the titles of Viscount of Annand, and Lord Murray of Lochmaben. The date of his creation does not appear; but he had a charter "to John Viscount of Annand," of the palace in Dumfries, and the lands of Haikheuch and Caerlaverock, 20th February 1623. He was created earl of Annandale by patent dated at Whitehall, 13th March 1624. His lordship married Elizabeth, daughter of Sir John Shaw, knight, and died at London in September 1640. He was succeeded by his son James, second earl of Annandale, who in March 1642 succeeded as third viscount of Stormont. He died at London 28th December 1658, leaving no issue. The titles of earl of Annandale, viscount of Annand, and Lord Murray of Lochmaben, in consequence became extinct, and those of Viscount Stormont and Lord Scoon devolved on David, second Lord Balvaird [see MURRAY, surname of].

The title of Marquis of ANNANDALE (now dormant) was formerly possessed by a brave and powerful Border family of the name of Johnstone, which, as far back as can be traced, were in possession of most extensive estates in the upper district of Annandale; and of the numerous families bearing that name the Johnstones of Lochwood were acknowledged the chiefs. This distinguished family maintained their ground, not only against the English borderers, but also against the lords of Sanquhar, whose descendants became earls of Dumfries, and against the powerful and ancient family of the Maxwells, lords of Nithsdale.

In the reign of King Robert the Second, Sir John de Johnstone, the ancestor of the Annandale family of that name, made a conspicuous figure. In 1371, he was one of the guardians of the west marches, and frequently had an opportunity of exerting himself against the English borderers, particularly in 1378,

> "When at the wattyr of Sulway,
> Schyr Ihon of Ihonystown on a day
> Of Inglis men wencust a grete dele.
> He bare hym at that tyme sa welle
> That he and the Lord of Gordowne,
> Had a sowerane gud renown
> Of ony that was of thar degre
> For full thai war of gret bownte."
>
> *Wyntoun*, b. ii. p 311.

He died about 1383, leaving a son Sir John Johnstone of Johnstone. A lineal descendant of his in the eleventh degree, James Johnstone of that ilk, was by Charles the First created Lord Johnstone of Lochwood, by patent dated at Holyroodhouse, 20th June 1633. In March 1643 he was created earl of Hartfell. In 1644 he was imprisoned by order of the committee of estates, as a favourer of the marquis of Montrose. After the battle of Kilsyth, August 1645, he joined Montrose, and being taken at Philiphaugh, 13th September of the same year, he was carried to St. Andrews, where, with several others, he was sentenced to death, 26th November 1645, and ordered to be executed first of all, with Lord Ogilvy. But the night before the time fixed for the execution, Lord Ogilvy escaped out of the castle of St. Andrews, and the marquis of Argyle, suspecting it to have been done by means of the Hamiltons, obtained a pardon for the earl of Hartfell, who was as obnoxious to the Hamiltons as Lord Ogilvy was to Argyle. He died in March 1653.

His only son, James the second earl of Hartfell, was, on the restoration of Charles the Second, sworn a privy councillor. The title of earl of Annandale having become extinct by the death of James Murray, the second earl, in 1658, the earl of Hartfell made a resignation of his peerage into the hands of his majesty, who, 13th February 1661, granted a new patent to him as earl of Annandale and Hartfell, viscount of Annand, Lord Johnstone of Lochwood, Lochmaben, Moffatdale, and Evandale. He died 17th July 1672. His son William, who succeeded as second earl of Annandale and third of Hartfell, was appointed an extraordinary lord of session, 23d November 1693. He was also constituted one of the lords of the Treasury, and president of the parliament of Scotland, which assembled at Edinburgh 9th May 1695, and sat till 17th July following. On the 24th of June 1701 he was created marquis of Annandale, and on the accession of Queen Anne was appointed lord privy seal. In 1703 he was ap-

pointed president of the privy council. In 1704 he was invested with the order of the Thistle. In 1705 he represented her majesty as high commissioner to the General Assembly of the church of Scotland, as he had already done King William in 1701. He was also constituted in 1705 one of the principal secretaries of state, but not approving of the Union, he was dismissed from that office in the following year, and strenuously opposed the Union treaty in parliament. He was afterwards on several occasions elected a representative peer. In 1711 he was again lord high commissioner to the General Assembly. On the accession of George the First he was, 24th September 1714, appointed keeper of the privy seal, and a few days after sworn a privy councillor. He died at Bath on the 14th January 1721. His lordship married, first, Sophia, only daughter and heiress of John Fairholm of Craigiehall, in the county of Linlithgow, by whom he had James, second marquis of Annandale, two other sons, who both died unmarried, and two daughters, of whom the eldest, Lady Henrietta, married, in 1699, Charles Hope of Hopetoun, created earl of Hopetoun in 1703, and had issue. His first wife having died in 1716, the marquis married secondly, in 1718, Charlotte Van Lore, only child of John Vanden Bempde of Pall Mall, London; by whom he had George, third marquis of Annandale, and another son named John, who died young.

James, the second marquis of Annandale, resided much abroad, and dying unmarried at Naples, 21st February 1730, was buried in Westminster Abbey. The estate of Craigiehall went to his nephew, the Hon. Charles Hope, and his titles and the other estates to his half brother George, third marquis of Annandale, who was born 29th May 1720. The loss of his brother, Lord John, in 1742, occasioned a depression of spirits, which finally deranged his mind. In 1745 David Hume, the historian, went to live with him, the friends and family of the marquis being desirous of putting his lordship under his care and direction. He resided with him a year. On 5th March 1748 an inquest from the court of Chancery found the marquis a lunatic since 12th December 1744. He died 24th April 1792, when the title of Marquis of Annandale became dormant; claimed by Sir Frederic John William Johnstone of Westerhall, baronet; and by Mr. Goodinge Johnstone. It is understood that the titles of earl of Annandale and Hartfell devolved upon James, third earl of Hopetoun, who, however, did not assume them, but took the name of Johnstone in addition to that of Hope.

In the parish of Johnstone, Dumfries-shire, are the ruins of the castle or tower of Lochwood, said to have been built during the fourteenth century, and which, from the thickness of its walls and its insulated situation amidst bogs and marshes, must have been a place of great strength. It was in allusion to this circumstance that James the Sixth is said to have remarked, "that the man who built Lochwood, though he might have the outward appearance of an honest man, must have been a knave at heart." In 1593, it was burnt by Robert, the natural brother of Lord Maxwell, who, with savage glee, exclaimed while it was in flames, "I'll give Dame Johnstone light enough to show her to set her silken hood." In revenge for the destruction of Lochwood's "lofty towers, where dwelt the lords of Annandale," the Johnstones, aided by the bold Buccleuch, the Elliots, the Armstrongs, and the Grahams, attacked and cut to pieces a party of the Maxwells near Lochmaben, and among the slain fell Robert the incendiary. The surviving few then took refuge in the church of Lochmaben, but the church with all that was in it was burnt to ashes by the Johnstones, and it was this sacrilegious act which in its turn occasioned the memorable battle of Dryfe

Sands, 7th December 1593, in which the Johnstones finally prevailed. Lord Maxwell, while engaged in single combat with the laird of Johnstone, was slain behind his back by the cowardly hands of Will of Kirkhill. The Maxwells lost, on the field and in the retreat, about 700 men. Many of those who perished or were wounded in the retreat, were cut down in the streets of Lockerby; and hence the phrase currently used in Annandale to denote a severe wound,—" A Lockerby lick." Sir James Johnstone of Johnstone, warden of the west marches, was murdered, 6th April 1608, by John, seventh Lord Maxwell, the son of the Lord Maxwell slain on Dryfe Sands, at a meeting betwixt them, in presence of Sir Robert Maxwell of Orchardton, brother-in-law of Sir James, to which meeting each of them came with one attendant. Their attendants quarrelling, Sir James Johnstone turned about to separate them, when he was treacherously shot in the back with two bullets by Lord Maxwell, who, being taken at Caithness some years afterwards, was beheaded for the same, at the cross of Edinburgh, 21st May 1613.

ANSTRUTHER, a surname derived from the lands of Anstruther, in the county of Fife, on a portion of which the burgh of Anstruther-easter, of which the laird of Anstruther is superior, is built. The family of Anstruther of Anstruther is very ancient, having been settled in Fife in the very early periods of Scottish history. During the reign of David the First, William de Candela, obviously of Norman origin, possessed the lands of Anstruther, as appears from a charter granted in favour of the monks of Balmerinoch, by his son William, wherein he is designated " Filius Willielmi de Candela, domini de Anstruther." Henry his son first assumed the name of his lands, and in a charter of confirmation of his father's grant, dated in 1221, he is styled " Henricus de Aynistrother, dominus ejusdem, Filius Willielmi," &c. From these early proprietors the family of Anstruther are lineally descended.

About the year 1515 Robert Anstruther and David his brother, younger sons of Robert de Anstruther, the sixth in descent from the original William de Candela, having gone to France, were promoted to be officers of the Scots guards in the service of the French king. David married a lady of distinction in France, and his descendant, Francis Cæsar Anstruther, contracted into Anstrude, was by Louis the Fifteenth, in 1737, raised to the dignity of a French baron, by the title of Baron de Anstrude of the seigniory of Barry.

Sir James Anstruther, the twelfth in direct descent from William de Candela, was, in 1585, appointed heritable carver to James the Sixth. In 1592, he had the honour of knighthood conferred upon him, and was appointed one of the masters of the household to his majesty. He died in 1606.

His son, Sir William, succeeded to his father's offices, and was, besides, appointed one of the gentlemen of the bedchamber. On James' accession to the English throne, he accompanied his majesty to London, and at his coronation was created a knight of the Bath. He was also in great favour with Charles the First, by whom he was appointed gentleman usher of his majesty's privy chamber. He died in 1649; and was succeeded by his younger brother, Sir Robert, who was, by Charles the First, appointed one of the members of the privy council, and one of the gentlemen of his majesty's bed-chamber. He was an able diplomatist, and frequently employed in negociations of state, both by James the Sixth and Charles the First. In 1620, he was sent ambassador extraordinary to the court of Denmark, to borrow money from King Christian, with power to grant security for it in the king's name. At this time he got from the Danish king,

in a compliment, a ship's load of timber for building his house in Scotland. In April 1627, he was commissioned as minister plenipotentiary, to treat with the emperor and the states of Germany, at Nuremberg, about the concerns of the elector palatine, and other affairs of Europe. He was also appointed by Charles the First, and Frederick, king of Bohemia, elector palatine, their plenipotentiary to the diet at Ratisbon, for settling all differences between the Roman emperor Ferdinand and the elector palatine. His commission for this purpose is dated at Westminster 2d June 1630, and is signed by King Charles and Frederick, and has both their seals appended. He went also as ambassador to the meeting of the princes of Germany at Hailburn.

His second son, Sir Philip, succeeded to the Anstruther estates. He was a zealous and gallant cavalier, and had a command in the royal army at the battle of Worcester, where he was taken prisoner. He was fined in a thousand merks by Cromwell, and his estates were sequestrated till the Restoration in 1660. He married Christian, daughter of Majorgeneral Lumsden of Innergelly, and had five sons, two of whom were created baronets, and the other three knights. He died in 1702.

Sir William Anstruther, the eldest son, represented the county of Fife in the Scottish parliament, in 1681, when James duke of York was his majesty's high commissioner in Scotland, and strongly opposed the measures of the court. He sat in parliament for the county of Fife till 1709, and took an active part in the proceedings, those more particularly for securing and establishing the Protestant religion, and the government, laws, and liberties of the kingdom. In 1689 he was appointed by William the Third one of the ordinary lords of Session, and soon after was made one of his majesty's privy council and of Exchequer. In 1694 he was created a baronet of Nova Scotia. From Queen Anne, he received a charter dated at Kensington, 20th April 1704, of the baronies of Anstruther and Ardross, and many other lands, and of the heritable bailiary of the lordship and regality of Pittenweem; and of the office of searcher, and giver of coquets for the ports of Anstruther and Elie. The same charter constitutes him heritably, one of the *cibi cidæ*, or carvers, and one of the masters of the household to her majesty and her successors within the kingdom of Scotland; offices which belonged to his predecessors, and which his descendant, the present baronet, continues to hold. On the 9th November of the same year he was nominated one of the lords of Justiciary, in the room of Lord Aberuchil. He married Lady Helen Hamilton, daughter of John, fourth earl of Haddington, and died at Edinburgh in January 1711. He was the author of a volume, entitled ' Essays, Moral and Divine,' interspersed with poetry, published at Edinburgh in 1701, in 4to. Its contents are, 1st, Against Atheism. 2d, Of Providence. 3d, Of Learning and Religion. 4th, Of trifling studies, stage plays, and romances; and 5th, Upon the incarnation of Jesus Christ, and redemption of mankind. The work does not seem to have done much credit to his literary powers, as his friends did all they could to dissuade him from publishing it; and after his death, his son bought up every copy that could be found, for the purpose of suppressing it. [*Campbell's History of Scottish Poetry*, page 141.] He was succeeded by his son Sir John, after mentioned.

Sir James Anstruther of Airdrie, the second son of Sir Philip, was an advocate, and principal clerk of the Bills. His son, Philip, adopted a military life, and rose to the rank of lieutenant-general in the army, but dying unmarried, his estates went to his cousin, Sir John Anstruther of Anstruther.

Sir Robert Anstruther of Balcaskie, the third son of Sir Philip, acquired the estate of Balcaskie, and was created a baronet of Nova Scotia in 1694, the same year as his elder brother, Sir William.

Sir Philip Anstruther, the fourth brother, was made a knight. He was designed of Anstruther-field, from lands he so named near Inverkeithing.

Sir Alexander Anstruther, knight, the fifth brother, married in 1694, Jean Leslie, Baroness Newark, daughter and heiress of David second lord Newark, and was father of William, third lord Newark, and Alexander, fourth lord. The title of Lord Newark, which became dormant on the death of the latter in 1791, was claimed in 1793, by his eldest son, but unsuccessfully. [See NEWARK, Lord.]

Sir John Anstruther of Anstruther, the son of Sir William, married, in 1717, the lady Margaret Carmichael, eldest daughter of James second earl of Hyndford, and on the failure in the male line of that noble house, and the title becoming extinct in 1817, their descendant, Sir John Anstruther of Anstruther, succeeded to the entailed estates of the earldom, and assumed the name of Carmichael. [See HYNDFORD, Earl of, and CARMICHAEL, surname of.] Sir John died in 1746, and was succeeded by his son, also named John.

Sir John, the third baronet of this branch of the family, was the author of a work on drill husbandry, published in 1796, which is understood to have been useful at the time of its publication, but is chiefly remembered from a *bon mot* connected with it. On its appearance one of Sir John's friends jocularly remarked that no one could be better qualified to write on the subject, as there was not a better drilled husband in the county of Fife. Sir John married, in 1750, Janet, daughter of James Fall, Esq. of Dunbar. She was a very superior woman, and seems to have had a considerable influence with her lord. Sir John died in July 1799.

His eldest son, Sir Philip, succeeded. He married in 1778, Anne, only child of Sir John Paterson, of Eccles, baronet, and assumed in consequence the additional surname of Paterson. He died without issue in 1808.

He was succeeded by his brother, the Right Hon. Sir John Anstruther, of Cassis in Staffordshire, a distinguished lawyer, who had been created a baronet of Great Britain, 18th May 1798, when appointed chief justice of the supreme court of Judicature in Bengal. He married Maria, daughter of Edward Brice, Esq. of Berner's Street, London, and had issue two sons and a daughter. He retired from the Bench in 1806, and died in 1811.

Sir John, his eldest son, died in 1817. His only son, a posthumous child, born 6th February 1818, and named John after his father, inherited the titles and estates at his birth. He was accidentally killed while on a shooting excursion in November 1831, and the baronetcies and possessions of the family reverted to his uncle, Sir Windham Carmichael Anstruther of Elie and Anstruther, the eighth baronet of Nova Scotia, and fourth of Great Britain.

Sir Robert Anstruther, above mentioned, the founder of the Balcaskie branch, was thrice married. His first wife, whose name was Kinnear, an heiress, died without issue. His second wife, Jean Monteith Wrea, also an heiress, brought him six sons and two daughters; and by his third wife, Marion, daughter of Sir William Preston of Valleyfield, he had one son and two daughters. He was succeeded by his eldest son, Sir Philip, whose eldest son, Sir Robert, born 21st April 1733, married Lady Janet Erskine, youngest daughter of Alexander, fifth earl of Kellie, and had three sons and three daughters. Robert, the eldest, was the celebrated General Anstruther. He was born 3d March 1768, and entered at a very early period of life into the army. His first commission was in the Guards, and in 1793 he accompanied his regiment to Holland. In 1796 he joined the Austrian army in the Brigau, under the Archduke Charles then at war with France; and in one of the victories gained by the Austrians, he received a wound in the left side. In 1797 he returned home, purchased a company in the 3d Guards, and was appointed deputy quarter-master-general. In 1798 he went upon a diplomatic mission to Germany, whence he returned in the spring of the ensuing year, and in the autumn of 1799 he embarked with the expedition to the Helder. In 1800 Captain Anstruther went to Egypt as quarter-master-general to the army, under the command of Sir Ralph Abercromby, at which time the order of the Crescent was conferred upon him by the Turkish monarch. In 1802 he was appointed adjutant-general in Ireland. In 1808 he went to Portugal as brigadier-general, and distinguished himself at the battle of Vimiera. In the subsequently disastrous campaign in Spain, under the gallant Sir John Moore, General Anstruther commanded the rear-guard of the army, which he brought safely into Corunna on the night of 12th January 1809; but survived only one day the extraordinary exertions he had made, and the fatigue he had endured during the retreat. He died 14th January 1809, and lies interred in the north-east bastion of the citadel of Corunna. Sir John Moore by his own desire was buried by the side of General Anstruther. He married 16th March, 1799, Charlotte Lucy, only daughter of Col. James Hamilton, grandson of James, fourth duke of Hamilton, and had issue Sir Ralph Abercromby Anstruther, Bart., who succeeded his grandfather in August 1818, one other son and three daughters.

ARBUCKLE, JAMES, A.M., a minor poet, was born in Glasgow, in 1700. He studied at the university of that city, where he took his degrees. He afterwards kept an academy in the north of Ireland, hence he is called an Irishman by Campbell, in his Introduction to the History of Poetry in Scotland. He was the friend of Allan Ramsay. He published a volume of poems, and had begun a translation of Horace, but died before it was finished, in 1734. Some of his translations and imitations of Horace are among his best pieces. He wrote 'Snuff, a Poem,' which, according to the advertisement, was "printed at Edinburgh by Mr. James M'Ewen and Company for the author, and sold by Mr. James M'Ewen, bookseller in Edinburgh, and by the booksellers in Glasgow," 1719. This poem was dedicated to "His Grace, John, Duke of Roxburgh," and contained some pleasing enough conceits, very prettily turned. As an instance the following may be quoted:

"Though in some solitary pathless wild
Where mortal never trod, nor nature smiled,
My cruel fate should doom my endless stay,
To saunter all my ling'ring life away,

Yet still I'll have society enough,
While blest with virtue, and a Pinch of Snuff;
Enough for me the conscious joys to find,
And silent raptures of an honest mind."

ARBUTHNOTT, viscount of, a title possessed by a family of ancient descent, bearing that surname, in Kincardineshire; the first of whom, Hugo de Aberbothenoth, flourished in the reign of King William the Lion, and derived his name, in 1105, from lands which came to him by marriage with a daughter of Osbertus Oliphard, sheriff of Mearns. Those lands now form the greater part of the parish of Arbuthnott, and have passed to the present viscount through no less than twenty-two generations. Previous to the twelfth century the name was Aberbothenothe; about 1335, it had become Aberbuthnot, and about 1443, Arbuthnott.

The name of Aberbothenothe is understood to mean "the confluence of the water below the baron's house," being derived from *Aber*, the influx of a river into the sea, or of a smaller stream into a larger; *Both*, or *Bothena*, a dwelling, a baronial residence; and *Neth* or *Neoth-ea*, the stream that descends or is lower than something else in the neighbourhood; a derivation which is perfectly applicable to the site of the ancient castle, and to the present residence of the noble family of Arbuthnott. [See *Statistical Account*, vol. xi.]

In the reign of Alexander the Second, Duncan de Aberbothenothe was witness to a donation of that sovereign in 1242. His son, Hugh, is witness, along with his father, designed Duncanus Dominus de Aberbothenoth, to a charter of Robert, the son of Warnebald, to the monastery of Aberbrothwick. His son and successor, Hugh, called from the flaxen colour of his hair, Hugo Blundus or le Blond, to distinguish him from two predecessors of the same name, was laird of Arbuthnott in 1282, in which year he bestowed the patronage of the church of Garvock, in pure alms, on the monastery of Arbroath, "for the safety of his soul," which patronage, with many others, at the Reformation, fell into the hands of the king. Along with the patronage he gave one ox-gang of land, lying adjacent to the church of Garvock, with pasturage for 100 sheep, 4 horses, 10 oxen, and 20 cows. Hugo le Blond died about the end of the thirteenth century, and was buried at Arbuthnott, where there is an ancient full-length stone statue of him, in a reclining posture, with the face looking upwards, and the feet resting on the figure of a dog. His own and his wife's arms, the latter being the same with those of the once powerful family of the Morevilles, constables of Scotland, are cut on the stone on which the statue lies.

In 1355 Philip de Arbuthnott, fourth direct descendant from Hugh le Blond, was a benefactor to the church of the Carmelite friars, Aberdeen. His son and heir, Hugh Arbuthnott, was accessary with several other gentlemen of the Mearns, upon great provocation, to the slaughter of John Melville, of Glenbervie, sheriff of that county, about 1420. According to tradition, Melville had, by a strict exercise of his authority as sheriff, rendered himself obnoxious to the surrounding barons, who teased the regent, Murdoch, duke of Albany, by repeated complaints against him. At last, in a fit of impatience, the regent incautiously exclaimed to Barclay, laird of Mathers (ancestor of Captain Barclay Allardice of Urie), who had come to him with another complaint against Melville, "Sorrow gin that sheriff were sodden, and supped in broo." Most of those who have related this story state, that it was the king, James the First, who made this exclamation, but his majesty was then a prisoner in England. Barclay, immediately returning home, assembled his neighbours, the lairds of

Lauriston, Arbuthnott, Pitarrow and Halkerton, who appointed a great hunting party in the forest of Garvock, to which they invited the devoted Melville; and having prepared a large fire and cauldron of boiling water in a retired place, they decoyed the unsuspecting Melville to the fatal spot, knocked him down, stripped him, and then threw him into the cauldron. After he was *boiled* or *sodden* for some time, they each took a spoonful of the soup. To screen himself from justice, Barclay built a fortress in the parish of St. Cyrus, called the Kaim of Mathers, on a perpendicular and peninsular rock, sixty feet above the sea, where, in those days, he lived quite secure. The laird of Arbuthnott claimed and obtained the benefit of the law of clan Macduff, which, in case of homicide, allowed a pardon to any one within the ninth degree of kindred to Macduff, Thane of Fife, who should flee to his cross, which then stood near Lindores, on the march between Fife and Strathern, and pay a fine. The pardon is still extant in Arbuthnott House. The rest were outlawed. He died in 1446.

His descendant, Sir Robert Arbuthnott of Arbuthnott, was knighted by King Charles the First, and for his enduring loyalty ennobled in 1641, by being created Viscount Arbuthnott and Lord Inverbervie. Robert the second viscount of Arbuthnott succeeded his father in 1655, and died in June 1682. By his first wife, Lady Elizabeth Keith, second daughter of William seventh earl Marischal, he had a son Robert, third viscount, and a daughter, and by his second wife, Catherine, daughter of Robert Gordon of Pitlurg and Straloch, he had three sons and three daughters. The Hon. Alexander Arbuthnott, the second son by the second marriage, who was appointed one of the barons of the Court of Exchequer in Scotland at the union of 1707, married Jean, eldest daughter of Sir Charles Maitland of Pitrichie in Aberdeenshire, heir to her brother, Sir Charles, who died in 1704, and he in consequence assumed the name and arms of Maitland.

John, the seventh viscount of Arbuthnott, married in December 1775, Isabella, second daughter of William Graham, Esq. of Morphie, county of Kincardine, and by her, who died in 1818, he had John, the eighth viscount, General Hugh Arbuthnott, long M.P. for Kincardineshire, five other sons, and two daughters.

The eighth viscount succeeded on his father's death 27th February 1800, and in June 1805 he married Margaret, daughter of the Hon. Walter Ogilvy of Clova, sister of the ninth earl of Airlie, with issue, six sons and two daughters.

To the noble family of Arbuthnott belonged the subjects of the two following notices:—

ARBUTHNOT, ALEXANDER, an eminent divine, and zealous promoter of the Reformation in Scotland, was the second son of Andrew Arbuthnot of Pitcarles, the fourth son of Sir Robert Arbuthnott of Arbuthnott, and the brother of the baron or proprietor of Arbuthnott, in Kincardineshire, and not the baron himself, as generally stated by his biographers. His mother was Elizabeth, daughter of James Strachan of Monboddo, and sister of Alexander Strachan of Thornton. He was born in 1538. According to Archbishop Spottiswood, he studied at the university of St. Andrews, but Dr. Mackenzie says that he received his education at King's college, Aberdeen. [*Mac-*

henzie's *Lives of Scots Writers*, vol. iii. p. 186.] The former is likely to be correct, as in the year 1560 his name appears the ninth in a list of young men at St. Andrews best qualified for the ministry and teaching, given in to the first General Assembly. [*Calderwood's History of the Church of Scotland*, vol. ii. p. 45.] In 1561 he went to France, and for the space of five years prosecuted the study of the civil law at Bourges, under the famous Cujacius. This has led his biographers to state that it was with the view of following the profession of an advocate in his native country; but it was then usual for students of divinity to make civil law a branch of their studies. He returned to Scotland in 1566, and was soon after licensed as a minister of the Reformed church. On the 15th July 1568 he received a presentation to the church of Logie Buchan, one of the common kirks of the cathedral of Aberdeen. He was a member of the General Assembly which met at Edinburgh on the first of July of that year, and was intrusted with the charge of revising a book entitled 'The Fall of the Roman Church,' published by one Thomas Bassenden, a printer of that city, which had given great offence and incurred the censure of the Assembly, chiefly on account of an assertion contained in it, that the king was the supreme head of the church. For this, and for having printed at the end of the Psalm-Book, an indecent song called 'Welcome Fortune,' the Assembly ordained Bassenden to call in all the copies of these books which he had sold, and to sell no more of them, and to abstain for the future from printing anything without the license of the magistrates, and the revisal by a committee of the church of such books as pertain to religion. [*Booke of the Universall Kirk of Scotland*, p. 100.]

In the year 1569, Mr. Alexander Anderson, the principal of King's college, Aberdeen, with the sub-principal and three of the regents of that university, having been ejected from their offices, on account of their adherence to popery, and refusal to sign the Confession of Faith, Mr. Arbuthnot was promoted to the vacant principalship on the 3d July of that year, and three weeks afterwards he was presented to the church of Arbuthnott in Kincardineshire, "provyding he administrat the sacraments of Jesus Christ, or ellis travell [that

is, labour] in some others als necessar vocation to the utility of the kirk, and approvit by the samen." The emoluments of his two parochial charges were probably his only support as principal, the funds of the college having been greatly dilapidated by his predecessor, Principal Anderson, when he found that he was likely to be deprived for his adherence to popery. To the university Principal Arbuthnot rendered the most important services, both in the augmentation of its funds, and by his assiduity and success in teaching. "By his diligent teaching and dexterous government," says Archbishop Spottiswood, "he not only revived the study of good letters, but gained many from the superstitions whereunto they were given." In 1572 he was a member of the General Assembly held at St. Andrews, which strenuously opposed a scheme of church government called 'The Book of policy,' proposed by the regent Morton and his party, for the purpose of restoring the old titles in the church, and retaining among themselves all the temporalities annexed to them. The same year he established his character as a man of learning, by the publication at Edinburgh, in quarto, of his 'Orationes de Origine et Dignitate Juris,' a production which was honoured with an encomiastic poem by Thomas Maitland, who represents Arbuthnot as one of the brightest ornaments of his native country. [*Delitiæ Poetarum Scotorum*, tom. ii. p. 153.] "To enhance the value of this eulogium," says Dr. Irving, "it must be recollected that Maitland was a zealous Catholic."

From this time Arbuthnot began to take a lead in the General Assembly, and during the minority of James the Sixth, he appears to have been much employed on the part of the church, in its tedious contest with the regency, concerning the plan of ecclesiastical government to be adopted. Of the General Assembly which met at Edinburgh 6th August, 1573, he was chosen moderator. In that of Edinburgh March 6th, 1574, he was appointed, with three others, to summon before them the chapter of Murray, accused of giving their letters testimonial in favour of George Douglas, bishop of that see, "without just trial and due examination of his life, and qualification in literature." [*Calderwood's Hist. of the Church of Scotland*, vol. iii. p. 304.] This assembly also authorized him, with Mr. John Row and others, to draw up a plan of ecclesiastical polity for the approval of the members. He was at the Assembly which met at Edinburgh in August, 1575. "Efter the Assemblie," (says James Melville,) "we passed to Anguss in companie with Mr. Alexander Arbuthnot, a man of singular gifts of lerning, wesdome, godliness, and sweitness of nature, then principall of the collage of Aberdein; whom withe Mr. Andro [Melville] communicat anent the haill ordour of his collage in doctrine and discipline, and aggreit as therefter was sett down in the new reformation of the said collages of Glasgow and Aberdein." [*Melville's Diary*, p. 41.] He was again chosen moderator of the General Assembly which met at Edinburgh 1st April 1577. In the Assembly which met in that city in October of the same year he was appointed, with Andrew Melville and George Hay, to attend a council which was expected to meet at Magdeburg for the purpose of establishing the Augsburg Confession. [*Booke of the Universall Kirk of Scotland*, page 169.] The council, however, was not convened. A copy of the heads of the policy and jurisdiction of the church having been, by order of that General Assembly, presented to the earl of Morton as regent of the kingdom; for the solution of doubts and the removal of difficulties, he was referred to Principal Arbuthnot, Patrick Adamson, and Andrew Melville, and nine other commissioners of inferior eminence. [*Ibid.* p. 171.] In the General Assembly which met at Edinburgh 24th April 1578, it was resolved that a copy of the same should be presented to the king, and another to his council; and that if a conference should be demanded, they, on their part, would nominate Arbuthnot, Andrew Melville, and ten others, to attend at any appointed time. [*Ibid.* p. 175.] In the Assembly which convened at Stirling, 11th June of the same year, Arbuthnot, with some others, was empowered to confer with several of the nobility, prelates, and gentry, relative to the polity of the church. In the General Assembly which met at Edinburgh on the 24th April 1583, Arbuthnot, with David Ferguson and John Durie, was directed to wait upon the king and council, to request, in name of the Assembly,

the dismissal of M. Manningville, the French ambassador, whose popish practices had excited much alarm, as well as to complain of sundry other grievances. He was also named in a commission, with Mr. Robert Pont and five others, or any four of them, to visit the university of St. Andrews, for the purpose of inquiring how the rents thereof were bestowed, what order and diligence were used by the regents or professors in teaching, and how order was kept among the students. With Messrs. Andrew and George Hay he was also empowered to present to the king and council such heads, articles, and complaints as the Assembly might determine, and to confer, treat, and reason thereupon, and to receive his majesty's answer to the same. [*Calderwood*, vol. iii. pp. 707, 708.] The leading part which he took in ecclesiastical matters seems to have rendered him an object of suspicion and displeasure to James the Sixth; for when, in the same year (1583), he was appointed by the Assembly minister of St. Andrews, the king commanded him to remain in his college, under pain of horning. The Assembly saw in this arbitrary exertion of the royal prerogative, an infringement of their rights. They therefore remonstrated against it, but his majesty answered generally that he and his council had good grounds and reasons for what had been done. Arbuthnot is said to have had some bias towards the episcopal form of ecclesiastical polity, but whatever might be his private sentiments, he adhered with steadiness to the presbyterian party. It is thought, and indeed Dr. Mackenzie confidently asserts, that he had given offence to the king by printing Buchanan's History of Scotland, in the year 1582, [*Lives of Scots Writers*, vol. iii. p. 192,] and other authors have also supposed that he was the identical Alexander Arbuthnot who at that period held the office of king's printer. On this point Dr. Irving particularly quotes James Man, who, in his 'Censure of Ruddiman's Philological Notes on Buchanan,' (p. 99. Aberdeen, 1753, 12mo,) maintained, "with ridiculous pertinacity," as Chalmers in his Life of Ruddiman says, that Principal Arbuthnot was indeed the printer of Buchanan's History. The mistake has been corrected by Chalmers, who, on referring to the writ of privy seal, found that the Alexander Arbuthnot therein mentioned as king's printer was denominated a burgess of Edinburgh, and therefore was a different person from the principal of King's college, Aberdeen. [*Life of Ruddiman*, p. 72.]

The restriction placed on him by King James is supposed to have seriously affected his health and spirits. He fell into a decline, and died unmarried, at Aberdeen, on the 10th of October 1583, before he had completed the age of forty-five. On the 20th of the same month his remains were interred in the chapel of King's college.

Principal Arbuthnot appears to have possessed a degree of good sense and moderation which eminently qualified him for the conduct of public business, and his death was regarded as a severe calamity to the national church and to the national literature. Andrew Melville honoured his memory by an elegant epitaph in Latin, which will be found in Irving's Life of Arbuthnot (*Lives of Scots Poets*, vol. ii. p. 177), quoted from the *Delitiæ Poetarum Scotorum*, (tom. ii. p. 120). James Melville, in his Diary, has pronounced Arbuthnot one of the most learned men of whom Europe could at that time boast. His character has been thus delineated by Archbishop Spottiswood: "He was greatly loved of all men, hated of none, and in such account for his moderation with the chief men of these parts, that without his advice they could almost do nothing; which put him in a great fashrie, whereof he did oft complain; pleasant and jocund in conversation, and in all sciences expert; a good poet, mathematician, philosopher, theologue, lawyer, and in medicine skilful; so as in every subject he could promptly discourse, and to good purpose." Notwithstanding the violence of the times in which he lived, the name of Principal Arbuthnot has never been found subjected to censure. Even the papists themselves appear to have revered his virtues. Nicol Burne, in his 'Admonition to the Antichristian Ministers of the Deformit Kirk of Scotland,' written in 1581, while he has treated the rest of the Protestant clergy with the utmost contempt, thus respectfully speaks of Arbuthnot:

" Bot yit, gude Lord, quha anis thy name hes kend,
    May, or thay de, find for thair saulis remeid:
With thy elect Arbuthnot I commend,
    Althocht the lave to Geneve haist with speed."

Three Scottish poems, published in Pinkerton's 'Ancient Scottish Poems,' have been attributed to Principal Arbuthnot. Dr. Irving in his Life of Arbuthnot gives extracts from two of these, 'The Miseries of a Pure [poor] Scholar,' and 'The Praises of Wemen,' which show the author to have been an ingenious and pleasing poet. The Maitland MSS. preserve several of his pieces not hitherto published. [See *Irving's Lives of Scottish Poets*, vol. ii. p. 169.] Principal Arbuthnot left in manuscript an account of the Arbuthnott family, entitled 'Originis et incrementi Arbuthnoticæ familiæ descriptio historica,' which is still preserved. It was afterwards translated by George Morrison, minister of Benholme, and continued to the period of the Restoration by Alexander Arbuthnott, episcopalian minister of Arbuthnott, the father of the celebrated wit, the subject of the succeeding notice.

ARBUTHNOT, JOHN, M.D., one of the most conspicuous, and certainly the most learned, of the wits of Queen Anne's reign, was the son of Alexander Arbuthnott, episcopalian clergyman at Arbuthnott in Kincardineshire, and a near relative of the noble family of that name, and his wife, Margaret Lamy, from the parish of Maryton, near Montrose. He was born in the parish of Arbuthnott in April 1667, and received the elementary part of his education at the parish school. About the year 1680 he and his elder brother Robert, afterwards a banker in Paris, went to Marischal college, Aberdeen, where he applied himself diligently to all the academical branches of instruction, and after finishing his medical studies, he took his doctor's degree. At the revolution his father, not complying with the new order of things, was deprived of his living, and in consequence retired to the castle of Hallgreen near Bervie, in the neighbourhood of which he possessed, by inheritance, a small property called Kingorney; and his two sons were compelled to trust to their own exertions for getting forward in the world. The subject of this memoir accordingly resolved to push his fortune in London, and on his arrival there, he was hospitably received into the house of a Mr. William Pate, a woollen-draper. For some time he supported himself by teaching the mathematics, and soon distinguished himself by his writings. His first work appeared in 1697, entitled an 'Examination of Dr. Woodward's Account of the Deluge,' being an answer to a work of that gentleman bearing the title of an 'Essay towards a Natural History of the Earth,' which had appeared two years before. This laid the foundation of Arbuthnot's fame, which was much extended by an able treatise published by him in 1700, 'On the usefulness of the Mathematics to young students in the universities.' In 1704, in consequence of a curious and instructive dissertation 'On the Regularity of the Births of both sexes,' communicated to the Royal Society, and published in the Philosophical Transactions of that year, No. 328, he was elected a member of that learned body. It would appear from the signature to his letters, that on first going to London he himself continued to spell his name with the two t's at the end of it, as is the correct way, but in process of time one of the t's was dropped as unnecessary.

In 1705 Prince George of Denmark, the consort of Queen Anne, was suddenly taken ill at Epsom. Dr. Arbuthnot, happening to be on the spot, was called to his assistance, and, under his care, his royal highness soon recovered. Arbuthnot was, in consequence, appointed physician extraordinary to the queen, and in the month of November, 1709, he was promoted to be fourth physician in ordinary to her majesty; that is, one of her domestic physicians. His skill having been the means of recovering her majesty from a dangerous illness, drew from his friend Gay the following elegant pastoral compliment:

" While thus we stood, as in a stound,
    And wet with tears, like dew, the ground,
    Full soon, by bonfire and by bell,
    We learnt our liege was passing well:
    A skilful leech, so God him speed,
    They say had wrought this blessed deed ;
    This leech ARBUTHNOTT was yclept;
    Who many a night not once had slept,
    But watch'd our gracious sovereign still,
    For who could rest when she was ill?
    Oh! may'st thou henceforth sweetly sleep !
    Sheer, swains! oh, sheer your softest sheep,
    To swell his couch, for well I ween
    He saved the realm who saved the queen."

In the month of April, 1710, he was admitted a Fellow of the Royal college of physicians. The confidence reposed in him by his royal mistress appears by the terms in which he is spoken of by Dean Swift, who calls him " the queen's favourite physician," and again, " the queen's favourite." Being thus distinguished by his professional abilities, his influence at court, and his literary attainments, Arbuthnot acquired the friendship not only of the leading men of the Tory party, to which he belonged, such as Harley and Bolingbroke, but that of all the wits and scholars of his time. On Swift's visit to London in 1710, a strict intimacy was formed between them, and soon after Pope was added to the number of his friends, as were also Prior and Gay.

In the year 1712, appeared the first part of 'The History of John Bull,' of which it has been justly said, that " never was a political allegory managed with more exquisite humour, or a more skilful adaptation of characters and circumstances." The doubt entertained respecting the author of this satire has been dispelled by Swift and Pope, who both distinctly attribute it to Dr. Arbuthnot. Pope declared that Arbuthnot was the " sole author." The object of this highly humorous production was to throw ridicule upon the splendid achievements of Marlborough, and to render the country discontented with the war then raging with France. Arbuthnot, who was one of the literary phalanx attached to the fortunes of Harley and the Tories, was aware how entirely that minister's power depended on a peace with France, and, therefore, he applied all the vigour of his wit to the accomplishment of that end. The ingenuity of the story contained in the ' History of John Bull,' united to its intelligible, straightforward, comic humour, procured for it a favourable reception everywhere ; but to politicians, the exquisite skill of its satire gave it a peculiar relish. After the accession of the house of Hanover, a supplement to the ' History ' appeared ; but it has been doubted whether this is a genuine production of Arbuthnot's pen. Some are of opinion that the first two parts as printed in Swift's works, are all that proceeded from Arbuthnot.

Early in the year 1714 he entered into an engagement with Pope and Swift, jointly to write a satire on the abuses of human learning, in the style of Cervantes. The name by which the intended hero was to be called was assigned to that assemblage of wits and learned men of which these three formed the nucleus, and it was called the 'Scriblerus' Club.' Harley, Atterbury, Congreve, and Gay, were members; and of them all no one was better qualified than Arbuthnot, both in point of wit and erudition, to promote the object of the society, which was to ridicule the absurdities of false taste in learning, under the character of a man of capacity enough, but no judgment, who had industriously dipped into every art and science. But the prosecution of this noble design was prevented by the queen's death, which deeply affected Pope, Swift, and Arbuthnot, who were all warmly attached to Lord Oxford's ministry; and a final period was afterwards put to the project, by the separation and growing infirmities of Dean Swift, by the bad health of Dr. Arbuthnot, and other concurring causes. The work in consequence was never completed, the first book of 'the Memoirs of Martinus Scriblerus' being only a part of it. "Polite letters," says Warburton, the editor of Pope's works, "never lost more than in the defeat of this scheme; in the execution of which work each of this illustrious triumvirate would have found exercise for his own peculiar talents, besides constant employment for those they had all in common. Dr. Arbuthnot was skilled in every thing which related to science; Mr. Pope was a master in the fine arts; and Dr. Swift excelled in the knowledge of the world. Wit they had all in equal measure; and this so large that no age perhaps ever produced three men to whom nature had more bountifully bestowed it, or in whom art had brought it to higher perfection." The first book of 'Martinus Scriblerus' was published after the death of Dr. Arbuthnot in 1741, in the quarto edition of Pope's prose works, and there seems to be every reason to believe that Arbuthnot was the sole author. It has, it is true, been printed in the collected editions of the works both of Swift and Pope; yet the internal evidence is sufficient to prove it the entire production of Arbuthnot, to whom Warton has attributed the fifth, sixth, seventh, eighth, tenth, and twelfth chapters, whatever may be determined of the other parts of the memoirs. The medical and antiquarian knowledge displayed in the other chapters,

and the ridicule on Dr. Woodward in the third, afford strong presumption of their having had the same authorship as the rest. The humorous essay concerning the origin of the sciences, usually appended to the 'Memoirs of Martinus Scriblerus,' appears from Spence to have been a joint production of Arbuthnot, Pope, and Parnell.

The death of Queen Anne in July 1714 put an end to Arbuthnot's connexion with the court, and completely destroyed the hopes of the Tory party. He felt severely the change in his circumstances, but his satirical humour and spirit of wit enabled him to derive some relief even from his altered prospects. In a letter to Swift, dated 12th August, he thus writes: "I have an opportunity calmly and philosophically to consider that treasure of vileness and baseness that I always believed to be in the heart of man, and to behold them exert their insolence and baseness; every new instance, instead of surprising and grieving me, as it does some of my friends, really diverts me,—and in a manner proves my theory." In a subsequent letter, alluding to the dispersion of the queen's courtiers on her death, he says, "The queen's poor servants are like so many poor orphans exposed in the very streets." To divert his chagrin he paid a visit to his brother Robert at Paris, under whose care he left two of his daughters. On his return, in the beginning of September, having been deprived of his apartments in St. James' palace, he took a house in Dover Street, where he assiduously devoted himself to the practice of his profession and to literary occupation. His spirits appear to have suffered considerably at this time, for, in a letter to Pope, dated September 7th, 1714, he says, "I am extremely obliged to you for taking notice of a poor, old, distressed courtier, commonly the most despisable thing in the world. This blow has so roused Scriblerus that he has recovered his senses, and thinks and talks like other men. From being frolicsome and gay, he is turned grave and morose." This depression of spirits, however, had not given him a distaste for the society of his friends: "Martin's office," he adds, in allusion to his 'Martinus Scriblerus,' "is now the second door on the left hand in Dover Street, where he will be glad to see Dr. Parnell, Mr. Pope, and his old friends, to whom he can still afford a half pint of claret." He is said, with Pope, to have assisted Gay in the farce of 'Three Hours after Marriage,' which was brought out in 1716, but met with no success.

In the autumn of 1722, Arbuthnot visited Bath, for the benefit of his health. He was accompanied by his brother, who had shortly before arrived in England. Mr. Robert Arbuthnot was a person of a singularly benevolent character, and is thus commemorated in a letter from Pope to the Hon. Robert Digby, "Dr. Arbuthnot is going to Bath,—his brother, who is lately come to England, goes also to the Bath, and is a more extraordinary man than he, and worth your going thither on purpose to know him. The spirit of philanthropy, so long dead to our world, is revived in him. He is a philosopher all of fire; so warmly, nay so wildly in the right, that he forces all others about him to be so too, and draws them into his own vortex. He is a star that looks as if it were all fire, but is all benignity, all gentle and beneficial influence. If there be other men in the world that would serve a friend, yet he is the only one, I believe, that could make even an enemy serve a friend."

On the 30th September 1723, Arbuthnot was chosen second censor of the College of Physicians. In the autumn of 1725 he had a dangerous illness. On this occasion he was visited by Pope, who thus communicated the intelligence of his illness to Dean Swift: "Dr. Arbuthnot is, at this time, ill of a very dangerous distemper, an imposthume in the bowels, which is broke; but the event is very uncertain. Whatever that be (he bids me tell you, and I write this by him) he lives and dies your faithful friend, and one reason he has to desire a little longer life is, the wish to see you once more." In 1727 he was chosen an elect of the Royal college of Physicians, when he pronounced the Harveian oration for that year. In the same year he published his great work, entitled 'Tables of Ancient Coins, Weights, and Measures, explained and exemplified in several dissertations,' 4to. This volume, which does great honour to the antiquarian knowledge and industry of the writer, though not wholly free from inaccuracies, has ever since been considered a standard work. In 1732 he published a professional treatise 'On the nature and choice of Aliments;' and in the following year an essay 'On the effect of Air on Human Bodies;' both founded on the doctrine of Boerhaave, the prevailing system of the time. He is supposed to have been led to write these works from the consideration of his own malady, an asthmatic affection, which gradually increasing with his years, became at last incurable. A little before the appearance of the latter publication he sustained a severe loss in the death of his son Charles, a clergyman of the Church of England, "whose life," he says, "if it had so pleased God, he would willingly have redeemed with his own." Another son had died previously in the year 1730.

In his latter years Dr. Arbuthnot was grievously afflicted with asthma, and in 1732 he retired to Hampstead, a village situated on the declivity of a high hill in the neighbourhood of London, for the benefit of the pure air of that elevated spot. "I came out to this place," he says, in an affecting letter to his friend Swift, dated October 4, "so reduced by dropsy and an asthma, that I could neither sleep, breathe, eat, nor move. I most earnestly desired and begged of God that he would take me." His attachment to Swift is strongly and tenderly manifested at the conclusion of this letter. "I am afraid, my dear friend, we shall never see one another more in this world. I shall to the last moment preserve my love and esteem for you, being well assured you will never leave the paths of virtue and honour; for all that is in this world is not worth the least deviation from that way." In the same strain of earnest friendship he had a little while previously addressed a letter to Pope. "As for you, my good friend, I think, since our first acquaintance, there have not been any of those little suspicions or jealousies that often affect the sincerest friendships; I am sure not on my side. I must be so sincere as to own, that though I could not help valuing you for those talents which the world prizes, yet they were not the foundation of my friendship; they were quite of another sort; nor shall I at present offend you by enumerating them; and I make it my last request that you will continue that noble disdain and abhorrence of vice which you seem naturally endued with; but still with a regard to your own safety; and study more to reform than chastise, though the one cannot be effected without the other. A recovery in my case, and at my age, is impossible; the kindest wish of my friends is *euthanasia* [meaning a happy and easy death]. Living or dying I shall always be yours."

Finding no relief from the change of air, Arbuthnot left Hampstead, and returned to his house in London, situated in Cork Street, Burlington-gardens, where he died, on the 27th February, 1735. His only surviving son, George, filled the lucrative post of secondary in the Exchequer-office, under Lord Masham, and was one of the executors of Pope. He died 8th September 1779, aged 76. He also left two daughters, one named Anne, who both died unmarried. The subjoined portrait of Dr. Arbuthnot is taken from an engraving from a scarce print formerly in the collection of Sir William Musgrave, Bart.

Among Arbuthnot's more humorous pieces, besides the 'History of John Bull' already mentioned, 'A Treatise concerning the Altercations or Scoldings of the Ancients,' and 'The Art of Political Lying,' are the most celebrated. He did not excel in poetry, and seldom attempted it. In Dodsley's Collection there is a didactic poem written by him, remarkable for its philosophical sentiment, with the title of 'Know Thyself!' His well known epitaph on Colonel Chartres, a noted usurer of the time, beginning "Here continues to rot," &c. is a masterly specimen of his powers of satire. He was also skilled in music; and Sir John Hawkins mentions an anthem and a burlesque song of his composition. [*Hist. of Music*, vol. v. p. 126.] In 1751 two 12mo volumes were published, entitled 'The Miscellaneous Works of the late Dr. Arbuthnot,' containing some of his genuine productions, but the greater portion of the contents were declared by his son to be spurious.

By his brother wits Dr. Arbuthnot was held in high estimation. Pope dedicated to him his 'Prologue to the Satires,' and Swift has more than once mentioned him with praise in his poems, for instance when he feelingly laments that he was

> " Far from his kind Arbuthnot's aid,
>   Who knows his art, but not his trade."

"His good morals," Pope used to say, "were equal to any man's; but his wit and humour superior to all mankind." "He has more wit than we all have," said Swift to a lady, who desired his opinion of him, "and his humanity is equal to his wit." His character is thus given by Dr. Johnson: "Arbuthnot was a man of great comprehension, skilful in his profession, versed in the sciences, acquainted with ancient literature, and able to animate his mass of knowledge by a bright and active imagination; a scholar, with great brilliance of wit; a wit, who, in the crowd of life, retained and discovered a noble ardour of religious zeal; a man estimable for his learning, amiable for his life, and venerable for his piety." He was distinguished in an eminent degree for genuine benevolence and goodness, while his warmth of heart and cheerfulness of temper rendered him much beloved by his family and friends, towards whom he displayed the most constant affection and attachment. Notwithstanding his powers of satire, all his contemporaries seem to have united in his praise. "His very sarcasms," says Lord Orrery, "are the satirical sarcasms of good nature; they are like slaps on the face given in jest, the effects of which will raise a blush, but no blackness will appear after the blows. He laughs as jovially as an attendant upon Bacchus, but continues as sober and considerate as a disciple of Socrates. He is seldom serious, except in his attacks upon vice, and there his spirit rises with a manly strength, and a noble indignation. No man exceeded him in the moral duties of life, a merit still more to his honour, as the united powers of wit and genius are seldom submissive enough to confine themselves within the limitations of morality." In the Biographia Britannica Arbuthnot is said, but at what particular period we are not informed, to have been for some time steward to the corporation of the Sons of the Clergy. He was in the habit of writing essays on the current events of the day in a great folio paper book, which used to lie in his parlour, and such was his good nature and indulgence to his children, that he suffered them to tear out his manuscript at one end for their kites, while he was writing them at the other.

No correct list of his productions has ever been given. The following is as near as can be ascertained:

Examination of Dr. Woodward's Account of the Deluge, &c., with a Comparison between Steno's Philosophy and the Doctor's, in the case of Marine Bodies dug up out of the Earth. By J. A., M.D. With a Letter to the Author, concerning an Abstract of Agostino Scilla's Book on the same subject, by W. W. Lond. 1695, 1697, 8vo.

Essay on the Usefulness of Mathematical Knowledge. Lond. 1700.

Sermon preached to the People at the Mercat-cross of Edinburgh, on the subject of the Union. Lond. 1707, 8vo. A Satire supposed to have been written by Arbuthnot.

Law is a Bottomless Pit, or the History of John Bull, exemplified in the case of the Lord Strutt, John Bull, Nicholas Frog, and Louis Baboon, who spent all they had in a lawsuit, in 4 parts; with an appendix. Lond. 1712, 8vo.

Tables of the Grecian, Roman, and Jewish Measures, Weights, and Coins, reduced to the English Standard, and Explained and Exemplified in several Dissertations. Lond. 1705, 8vo. The same, by his son, with a Poem to the King. Lond. 1727, 4to.

Miscellaneous Pieces by him, Swift, Pope, and Gay. Lond. 1727, 3 vols. 8vo.

Essay, concerning the Nature of Aliments, the Choice of them, &c. Lond. 1731. Another edition, with Practical Rules of Diet in the various Constitutions and Diseases of Human Bodies. Lond. 1732, 8vo. 1751, 1756, 8vo. In German. Hamb. 1744, 4to.

An Essay on the Effects of Air on Human Bodies. Lond. 1733, 1751, 1756, 8vo. In French. Paris, 1742, 12mo.

Miscellaneous Works of the late Dr. Arbuthnot. Glasg. 1750, 2 vols. 8vo. These volumes, now very scarce, were disclaimed in an advertisement by the author's son, dated, London, Sept. 25, 1750.

Oratio Anniversaria Harvejana, Anni 1727, in his miscellaneous works. 1751, 8vo.

Argument for Divine Providence, drawn from the equal number of births of both sexes. Phil. Trans. 1700, Abr. v. p. 606.

———

ARGYLE, duke of, a title belonging to the ancient family of Campbell of Lochawe. [See CAMPBELL, surname of.] The name of Argyle is derived from two Gaelic words, *Earra Ghaidheal*, "the country of the western Gael;" or, according to Skene, from *Oirirgael*, as the ancient district of Argyle (which comprehended also Lochaber and Wester Ross) was called by the Highlanders. By the historians the whole of this extensive district is included under the term of Ergadia. [*History of the Highlanders*, vol ii. p. 33.] In the middle ages the Macdougalls of Lorn held sway over Argyle and Mull; while the Macdonalds, lords of the Isles, were supreme in Islay, Kintyre, and the Southern Islands. The power of the Macdonalds was broken by Robert the Bruce, and their estates bestowed on the Campbells, who originally belonged to the ancient earldom of Garmoran, which comprehended Moydert, Arasaig, Morar, and Knoydert. Argyle was erected into an earldom in 1457, and into a dukedom in 1701.

ARGYLE, earl, marquis, and duke of, see CAMPBELL, Archibald, and John.

ARMSTRONG, the name of a famous border family, which, with its various branches, chiefly inhabited Liddesdale. According to tradition, the original surname was Fairbairn, and belonged to the armour-bearer of an ancient king of Scotland, who, having his horse killed under him in battle, was straightway remounted by Fairbairn on his own horse. For this timely assistance, the king amply rewarded him with lands on the borders, and in allusion to the manner in which so important a service was performed, Fairbairn having taken the king by the thigh, and set him at once on the saddle, his royal master gave him the name of ARMSTRONG, and assigned him for crest, "an armed hand and arm, in the hand a leg and foot in armour, couped at the thigh, all proper." Amongst the clans on the Scottish side of the border, the Armstrongs were formerly one of the most numerous. They possessed the greater part of Liddesdale, which forms the southern district of Roxburghshire and of the debateable land. All along the banks of the Liddel, the ruins of their ancient fortresses may still be traced. The habitual depredations of this border-race had rendered them so active and daring, and at the same time so cautious and circumspect, that they seldom failed either in their attacks or in securing their prey. Even when assailed by superior numbers, they baffled every assault by abandoning their dwellings, and retiring with their families into thick woods and deep morasses, accessible by paths only known to themselves. One of their most noted places of refuge was the Tarras-moss, a frightful and desolate marsh, so deep that two spears tied together could not reach the bottom. Although several of the Scottish monarchs had attempted to break the chain which united these powerful and turbulent chieftains, none ever had greater occasion to lower their power, and lessen their influence, than James the Fifth. The hostile and turbulent spirit of the Armstrongs, however, was never entirely broken or suppressed, until the reign of James the Sixth, when their leaders were brought to the scaffold, their strongholds razed to the ground, and their estates forfeited and transferred to strangers; so that throughout the extensive districts formerly possessed by this once powerful and ancient clan, there is scarcely left, at this day, a single landholder of the name. Their descendants have been long scattered, some of them having settled in England, and others in Ireland. The most celebrated of these border chiefs was 'Johnie Armstrang' of Gilnockie, who lived in the early part of the sixteenth century, and is the hero of one of our best historical ballads. A notice of him follows. 'Jock o' the Syde,' the hero of another ballad, was also an Armstrong, and a noted moss-trooper in the reign of Mary, queen of Scots. The site of his residence, the Syde, is pointed out on a heathy upland, about two miles to the west of New Castletown, in Liddesdale, while the ruins of Mangerton Tower, the seat of his maternal uncle, are still visible, on the haugh below. Sir Richard Maitland of Lethington, in a poetical complaint which he wrote " agains the Thievis of Liddisdaill," thus speaks of this famous border reaver:

> " He is weel kenned, Johne of the Syde;
> A greater thief did never ryde;
> He never tyres,
> For to break byres;
> Ower muirs and myres
> Ower gude ane guyde."

A lineal descendant of Johnie Armstrong, in the reign of Charles the First, kidnapped the person of Lord Durie, the president of the Court of Session, and kept him upwards of three months in secret confinement in an old castle in Annandale, called Graham's tower. The motive for this extraordinary and daring stratagem was to promote the interests of Lord Traquair, who had a lawsuit of importance before the court, in which there was reason to believe that the judgment would be unfavourable and decided by the casting vote of the president. [See GIBSON, Sir Alexander, Lord Durie.] Near Penton Linns, a romantic spot on the Liddel, was another border stronghold, called Harelaw tower, once the residence of Hector Armstrong, who betrayed his guest, the earl of Northumberland, to the regent Murray.

ARMSTRONG, JOHN, a celebrated border chief of the early part of the sixteenth century, was a native of the parish of Canonbie, in the county of Dumfries, and the brother of Christopher Armstrong, laird of Mangerton, chief of the clan or sept of the Armstrongs. His stronghold was Gilnockie Tower, now a roofless ruin, situated a few miles from Langholm, at a place called the Hollows, on the banks of the river Esk. The terror of his name was spread far and wide, and at the head of a band of brave and faithful followers, he levied *black mail*, or protection money, for many miles within the English border. All who refused were sure of being plundered and harassed to the utmost. The marauding system on the borders had, during the long minority of King James V., been carried to a formidable extent, especially under the connivance of the earl of Angus, the warden of the marches, who had bound the border chiefs to his interests by those feudal confederacies, named 'bands of manrent,' which compelled the parties to defend each other against the authority of the law. Having resolved to suppress the foraying chieftains, the king raised a powerful army, chiefly composed of horsemen, "to danton the thieves" of Teviotdale, Annandale, Liddesdale, and other parts of the country, and about the beginning of June 1529, he set out, at the head of eight thousand men, on an expedition through the border districts. To prevent the mosstroopers and their chiefs from taking alarm, he ordered all the gentlemen of the borders to bring with them their best dogs, as if his only purpose was to hunt the deer. The leaders thus thrown off their guard, were not apprehensive of any danger, and to insure their destruction the more readily, the principal border nobles who were known to be their protectors and secret encouragers, namely the earl of Bothwell, lord of Teviotdale, Lords Home and Maxwell, Scott of Buccleuch, Ker of Fairniehurst, with the lairds of Johnstone, Polwarth, Dolphington, and other powerful chiefs, were seized and imprisoned in separate fortresses in different parts of the kingdom. This being done, the king, accompanied by some of the borderers who had secured their pardon, marched rapidly through Ettrick Forest and Ewesdale, and seized Piers Cockburn of Henderland and Adam Scott of Tushielaw, commonly called the king of the border, and ordered both to be hanged before the gates of their own castles. So little did they expect the fate that awaited them that, it is recorded, when James approached the castle of Cockburn of Henderland, the latter was in the act of providing a great entertainment to welcome him. Armstrong, on his part, came to meet the king at a place about ten miles from Hawick called Carlinrigg chapel, at the head of thirty-six attendants, his usual retinue, he and his followers arrayed in all the pomp of border chivalry. As the ballad says,

> The Elliots and Armstrongs did convene;
>   They were a gallant companie :—
> " We'll ride and meet our lawful king,
>   And bring him safe to Gilnockie.
>
> Make kinnen and capon ready then,
>   And venison in great plentie;
> We'll welcome here our noble king;
>   I hope he'll dine at Gilnockie ! "

> They ran their horse on the Langholm holm,
>   And brak their spears wi' mickle main ;
> The ladies lookit frae their loft windows :—
>   " God bring our men weel hame again !"

We are told by Pitscottie that Armstrong was the most redoubted chieftain that had been for a long time on the borders of Scotland or England. He always rode with twenty-four able gentlemen, well horsed, and from the borders to Newcastle every Englishman, of whatever state, paid him tribute. Armstrong is said to have incautiously made this display, by the crafty advice of some of the courtiers, who knew that it would only the more exasperate the king against him; and the effect was precisely so, for James, seeing this bold border chief so gallantly equipped, on his approach, fiercely ordered the tyrant, as he styled Armstrong, to be removed out of his sight and instantly executed, exclaiming, " What wants that knave that a king should have ? "

> There hang nine targats at Johnie's hat,
>   And ilk ane worth three hundred pound,—
> " What wants that knave that a king should have,
>   But the sword of honour and the croun ? "

Armstrong saw at once the snare into which he had fallen, and made every effort to preserve his life. He offered, if James would pardon him, to maintain at his own expense, forty men, ready at a moment's notice, to serve the king, and engaged never to injure any Scottish subject.

> " Grant me my life, my liege, my king,
>   And a bonnie gift I'll gie to thee,—
> Full four-and-twenty milk white steeds,
>   Were a' foaled in ae year to me.
>
> I'll gie thee a' thae milk white steeds,
>   That prance and nicher at a speir,
> And as muckle gude English gold
>   As four o' their braid backs can bear."

He further undertook to produce to his majesty, within a certain day, any man in England, of whatever degree, duke, earl, or baron, either alive or dead. But James was inexorable.

> " Away, away, thou traitor strang !
>   Out o' my sight sune may'st thou be !
> I grantit never a traitor's life,
>   And now I'll not begin wi' thee !"

Seeing his death resolved upon, Armstrong haugh-tily exclaimed, " It is folly to ask grace at a graceless face, but had I guessed you would have used me thus, I would have kept the Border-side, in despite of the king of England and you both; for I well know that King Henry would give the weight of my best horse in gold to know that I am sentenced to die this day."

> " To seik het water aneath cauld ice,
>   Surely it is a great follie !—
> I have asked grace at a graceless face,
>   But there is nane for my men and me.
>
> But had I kenn'd ere I cam frae hame
>   How thou unkind wadst been to me !
> I wad hae keepid the border syde
>   In spite of all thy force and thee.
>
> Wist England's king that I was ta'en,
>   O then a blythe man he wad be !
> For anes I slew his sister's son,
>   And on his breast bane brak a tree."

He and all his followers, some accounts make them forty-eight, were hanged on the trees of a little grove at Carlinrigg chapel, two miles north of Moss Paul, on the road between Hawick and Langholm, and tradition still points out their graves in the solitary churchyard of the place. He left a son Christopher who succeeded as laird of Gilnockie. On the borders Armstrong was long missed and mourned as a brave warrior, and a stout defender of his country against England. It is said by Buchanan that James executed Armstrong and his retinue, in direct violation of his solemn promise of safety. We are told that this bold chief never molested any of his own countrymen, and it appears from his own statement that his plunderings were chiefly committed on the English ; yet the Armstrongs are accused of having, in the course of a few years, destroyed not less than fifty-two parish churches in Scotland, and they openly boasted that their chieftain, Johnny Armstrong, would be subject neither to James nor to Henry, but would continue his excesses in defiance of both. The fate of this renowned border leader has been commemorated in many of the rude ballads of the border districts. The celebrated ballad of ' Johnie Armstrang,' some of the verses of which have been quoted, was first published by Allan Ramsay, in his ' Evergreen,' in

1724, having been copied, as he tells us, by himself from the mouth of a gentleman of the name of Armstrong, who was the sixth generation from the renowned borderer. The tower of the Hollows, or Holehouse, once the residence of this famous border chieftain, was a place of considerable strength in its day; its ruins are now used as a cowhouse to a neighbouring farmer. The younger son of Christopher Armstrong of Mangerton, the brother of this Armstrong of Gilnockie, went to Ireland, some years after the death of Queen Elizabeth, and settling in county Fermanagh, became the founder of a numerous family, whose descendants now possess extensive estates in Fermanagh, King's county and Wicklow; and one of whom was created a baronet of Great Britain in 1841.

ARMSTRONG, JOHN, M.D., poet and miscellaneous writer, was born about 1709 at Castleton, a parish forming the southern extremity of Roxburghshire, of which his father and afterwards his brother were ministers. In history and poetry, and very frequently still in conversation, its name is Liddesdale, from the river Liddel which runs through it from east to west. Dr. Armstrong has sung the beauties of his native vale, in his highly-finished poem on 'The Art of Preserving Health,' Book III. :

> ———————"Such the stream,
> On whose Arcadian banks I first drew air.
> Liddal, till now—except in Doric lays,
> Tuned to her murmurs by her love-sick swains—
> Unknown in song; though not a purer stream
> Through meads more flowery,—more romantic groves,
> Rolls toward the westward main.   Hail, sacred flood!
> May still thy hospitable swains be blest
> In rural innocence; thy mountains still
> Teem with the fleecy race; thy tuneful woods
> For ever flourish, and thy vales look gay,
> With painted meadows, and the golden grain!"

After receiving the rudiments of his education at home, he was sent to the university of Edinburgh, where he distinguished himself before his twentieth year, by gaining a prize medal for a prose composition, prescribed by a literary society in that city, and by other promising marks of genius during his studies. Having chosen the medical profession, he took his degree as physician February 4, 1732.

His inaugural dissertation, *De Tabe Purulenta*, gained him some reputation, as being superior to the general run of such essays. Soon after he went to London, where he commenced practice as a physician. In 1735 he published anonymously 'An Essay for abridging the study of Physic,' being a humorous attack on quacks and quackery, in the style of Lucian. This work gained him credit as a wit, but did not advance his practice as a physician. In 1737 he published a work on the venereal disease. This was followed by 'The Economy of Love;' for which poem he received fifty pounds from Andrew Millar, the bookseller, but which greatly injured his reputation. In a subsequent edition, published in 1768, he carefully expunged many of the youthful luxuriances with which the first abounded. In 1744 appeared his principal work, entitled 'The Art of Preserving Health,' in blank verse, one of the best didactic poems in the language. This valuable work established at once his reputation both as a physician and a poet. In 1746 he was appointed one of the physicians to the hospital for sick and lame soldiers. In 1751 he published his poem on Benevolence, and in 1753 his Epistle on Taste, addressed to a Young Critic. In 1758 he produced his prose 'Sketches or Essays on various subjects, by Lancelot Temple, Esq.,' in two parts, which evinced considerable humour and knowledge of the world, and in which he is said to have been assisted by Mr. Wilkes, whose acquaintance he had made soon after his first arrival in London. In 1760 he received the appointment of physician to the army, then in Germany, where, in 1761, he wrote 'Day, a Poem, an Epistle to John Wilkes, Esq. ;' his friendship with whom was not of long continuance, the subject of politics having divided them; Wilkes's continued attacks upon Scotland being the cause of their quarrel. Having in that epistle hazarded a reflection on Churchill, the satirist retorted severely in his poem of 'The Journey.'

At the peace of Paris in 1763 Armstrong returned to London, and resigning his connection with the army, resumed his practice, but not with his former success. In 1770 he published a Collection of his Miscellanies, containing amongst others, the Universal Almanack, a new prose piece, and the Forced Marriage, a tragedy, which had been refused by Garrick. In 1771 he made the tour of France and Italy, in company with the celebrated artist Fuseli, who survived him for half a century. In his journey he met his friend Dr. Smollett, to whom he was much attached. On his return he published an account of it under the name of ' A short Ramble, by Lancelot Temple.'

Wilkes, his former friend, joined Churchill in assailing Dr. Armstrong, having published a scurrilous attack upon him in the Public Advertiser, contained in a series of three letters, commencing with one signed *Dies*, in which, to cloak his purpose, Wilkes reflected on himself. That letter appeared March 23, 1773, and was followed by one signed *Truth*, March 24, and by another signed *Nox*, April 1. In the Gentleman's Magazine for January 1792, the following substance of a conversation which took place between Armstrong and Wilkes on the appearance of these letters, is inserted. It was taken down at the time by Mr. Wilkes, and is quite characteristic of both parties.

On Wednesday, April 7, 1773, Dr. Armstrong called on Mr. Wilkes in Prince's Court, about two in the afternoon, and without the least ceremony or compliment, began—

Dr. Armstrong. Did you, Sir, write the letters in the Public Advertiser?

Mr. Wilkes. What letters do you mean, Doctor? There are many letters almost every day in the Public Advertiser.

Dr. A. Sir, I mean the three letters about me, and *Day, Day*, Sir.

Mr. W. You may ask the printer, Mr. Woodfall. He has my orders to name me, whenever he thinks it proper, as the author of every thing I write in his paper.

Dr. A. I believe you wrote all those letters.

Mr. W. What all three, Doctor? I am very roughly treated in one of them, in the first signed *Dies*.

Dr. A. I believe you wrote that on purpose to begin the controversy. I am almost sure of it.

Mr. W. I hope you are more truly informed in other things. I know better than to abuse myself in that manner, and I pity the author of such wretched stuff.

Dr. A. Did you write the other letters, Sir?

Mr. W. The proper person to inquire of, is Mr. Woodfall. I will not *answer interrogatories*. My time would pass in a strange manner, if I was to answer every question which any gentleman chose to put to me about anonymous letters.

Dr. A. Whoever has abused me, Sir, is a villain; and your endeavours, Sir, to set Scotland and England together are very bad.

Mr. W. The Scots have done that thoroughly, Doctor, by their conduct here, particularly by their own nationality, and the outrages of Lord Bute to so many English families. Whenever you think proper to call upon me in particular as a gentleman, you will find me most ready to answer the call.

Dr. A. D——n Lord Bute! It had been better for Scotland he had never been born. He has done *us* infinite mischief.

Mr. W. And us, too; but I suppose we are not met for a dish of politics?

Dr. A. No; but I wish there had been no *Union*. I am sure England is the gainer by it.

Mr. W. I will not make an essay on the advantages and disadvantages of the Union.

Dr. A. I hate politics; but I have been ill used by you, Mr. Wilkes, on the occasion.

Mr. W. On the contrary, Doctor, I was the injured friend.

Dr. A. I thought you for many years the most amiable friend in the world, and loved your company the most; but you distinguished yourself by grossly abusing *my* countrymen in the North Briton—although I never read much of that paper.

Mr. W. You passed your time, I am satisfied, much better. Who told you, Doctor, what particular numbers I wrote? It is droll, but the bitterest of those papers, which was attributed to me, was a description of Scotland, first printed in the last century, on Charles I.'s return from thence in 1633. Were you ever, Doctor, personally attacked by me? Were you not, although a Scotsman, at the very time of the North Britons, complimented by me, in conjunction with Churchill, in the best thing I wrote, the mock 'Dedication to Mortimer.'

Dr. A. To be praised along with such a writer, I think an abuse.

Mr. W. The world thinks far otherwise of that wonderful genius, Churchill; but you, Doctor, have sacrificed private friendship at the altar of politics. After many years' mutual intercourse of good offices, you broke every tie of friendship with me on no pretence but a suspicion, for you did not ask for proof, of my having abused your country, *that* country I have for years together heard you inveigh against, in the bitterest terms, for *nastiness and nationality*.

Dr. A. I only did it in joke, Sir; you did it with bitterness; but it was *my* country.

Mr. W. No man has abused England so much as Shakspeare, or France so much as Voltaire; yet they remain the favourites of two great nations, conscious of their own superiority. Were you, Doctor, attacked by me in any one instance? Was not the most friendly correspondence carried on with you the whole time, till you broke it off by a letter, in 1763, in which you declared to me, that you could not with honour associate with one who had distinguished himself by abusing your country, and that you remained *with all due sincerity?* I remember *that* was the strange phrase.

Dr. A. You never answered that letter, Sir.

Mr. W. What answer could I give, Doctor? You had put a period to the intercourse between us. I still continued to our common friends to speak of you in terms of respect, while you were grossly abusing me. You said to Boswell, Millar, and others, "I hope there is a hell, that Wilkes may lie in it."

Dr. A. In a passion I might say so. People do not often speak their minds in a passion.

Mr. W. I thought they generally did, Doctor.

Dr. A. I was thoroughly provoked, although I still acknowledge my great pecuniary obligations to you— although, I dare say, I could have got the money elsewhere.

Mr. W. I was always happy to render you every service in my power; and I little imagined a liberal mind, like yours, could have been worked up by designing men to write me such a letter in answer to an affectionate one I sent you, on the prospect of your return.

Dr. A. I was happier with you than any man in the world for a great many years, and complimented you not a little in the *Day,* and you did not write to me for a year and a half after that.

Mr. W. Your memory does not serve you faithfully, Doctor. In three or four months at farthest, you had two or three letters from me together, on your return to the head-quarters of the army. I am abused in *Dies* for that publication, and the manner, both of which you approved.

Dr. A. I did so.

Mr. W. I was abused at first, I am told, in the manuscript of *Dies* for having sold the copy, and put the money in my pocket; but that charge was suppressed in the printed letter.

Dr. A. I know nothing of that, and will do you justice.

Mr. W. Will you call upon Mr. D——, our common friend, your countryman, and ask him what he thinks of your conduct to me, if it has not been wholly unjustifiable?

Dr. A. Have I your leave to ask Mr. Woodfall in your name about the letters?

Mr. W. I have already told you, Doctor, what directions he has from me. Take four-and-twenty hours to consider what you have to do, and let me know the result.

Dr. A. I am sorry to have taken up so much of your time, Sir.

Mr. W. It stands in no need of an apology, Doctor. I am glad to see you. Good morrow.

N.B.—These minutes were taken down the same afternoon, and sent to a friend.

Dr. Armstrong's last publication was his 'Medical Essays,' which appeared in 1773. In this he complains of the little attention that had been paid to him, while so many other physicians of inferior abilities had risen to fame and fortune, forgetting that his own indolence and levity, and not the fickleness or want of discernment of the public, occasioned the neglect. A large portion of his time was spent at Slaughter's coffee-house, in St. Martin's lane, where he took his meals, and where messages for him were ordinarily directed to be addressed. He died on 7th September, 1779, and left, it is said, three thousand pounds, which his prudence and good management had enabled him to collect. He left his fortune by his will to his three nieces, the daughters of his brother Dr. George Armstrong; who, after having been an apothecary for several years at Hampstead, at length obtained a diploma constituting him doctor in medicine. Settling in London, he was appointed physician to a dispensary for the benefit of poor infants, opened at a house taken for him by the subscribers in Soho square. To aid the design, he published a small treatise on the diseases of children, in which he was supposed to have been assisted by his brother John. The dispensary, however, did not succeed, and the doctor died some years after in obscurity. Armstrong possessed a glowing imagination and a lively fancy, chastened, at times, by the guidance of a sound judgment, and a well regulated taste. Of his 'Art of Preserving Health,' Dr. Aikin, in his Critical Essay prefixed to Cadell and Davis' edition of his works published in 1796, says, "The manner of Armstrong is distinguished by its simplicity, by a free use of words which owe their strength to their plainness, by the rejection of ambitious ornaments, and a near approach to common phraseology. His sentences are generally short and easy, his sense clear and obvious. The full extent of his conceptions is taken in at the first glance, and there are no lofty mysteries to be unravelled by repeated perusal. What keeps his language from being altogether prosaic, is the vigour of his sentiments. He thinks boldly, feels strongly, and therefore expresses himself poetically. Where the subject sinks, his style sinks with it; but he has for the most part excluded topics incapable either of vivid description or of the oratory of sentiment. He had from nature a musical ear, whence his lines are never harsh, and are usually melodious, though apparently without much study to render them smooth. Perhaps he has not been careful enough to avoid the monotony of making several successive lines close with a rest or pause in the sense. On the whole, it may not be too much to assert, that no writer in blank verse can be found more free from stiffness and affectation, more energetic without harshness, and more dignified without formality." In Thomson's ' Castle of Indolence,' to which he contributed four stanzas, at the conclusion of the first part, describing the diseases incidental to sloth, he is depicted as the shy and splenetic personage who " quite detested talk." The following is the stanza:

" With him was sometimes joined in silent walk,
    (Profoundly silent, for they never spoke)
One shyer still, who quite detested talk;
    Oft stung by spleen, at once away he broke,
To groves of pine and broad o'ershadowing oak,
    There, inly thrilled, he wandered all alone,
And on himself his pensive fury wroke:
    Nor never uttered word, save, when first shone
The glittering star of eve—' Thank heaven! the day is done!'"

A portrait of Dr. Armstrong is here given, taken from an engraving by Fisher from a painting by Sir Joshua Reynolds.

A list of Dr. Armstrong's works is subjoined.

An Essay for abridging the study of Medicine; to which is added, A Dialogue between Hygeia, Mercury, and Pluto; relating to the Practice of Physic, as it is managed by a certain illustrious Society, as also an Epistle from Usbech, the Persian, to Joshua Ward, Esq. Lond. 1735, 8vo, (anon).

Synopsis of the history and cure of the Venereal Disease. Lond. 1737, 8vo.

The Economy of Love. Lond. 1737, 8vo.

Art of preserving Health, a poem. Lond. 1744, 4to, 1745, 8vo., numerous editions, with a critical essay, by Dr. Aikin, 12mo.

Benevolence, a poem. 1751, fol. An excellent production.

Taste, an epistle to a young Critic. 1753. A pretty successful imitation of Pope.

Sketches, or Essays on various subjects. 1758.

Day, a poem. 1761.

Miscellanies, containing the art of preserving Health. Lond. 1770, 2 vols. 12mo.

A short ramble through some parts of France and Italy, by Lancelot Temple. Lond. 1771, 8vo.

Medical Essays. Lond. 1773. 4to. These treat of Theory, Medicine, Instruments of Physic, Fevers, Blisterings, Cordials, Ventilation, Bathing, Lodging, &c., and, lastly, Gout and Rheumatism.

An Essay on Topic Medicines. Ed. Med. Ess. ii. p. 36. 1733.

ARMSTRONG, John, a miscellaneous writer, was born at Leith in 1771, and educated at the college of Edinburgh, where he took the degree of M.A. During his attendance at the university he published a volume of ' Juvenile Poems,' some of which possessed considerable merit. The same volume contained an ' Essay on the Means of Punishing and Preventing Crimes.' For this essay he had, in January 1789, a few months before, received the gold prize medal, given by the Edinburgh Pantheon Society for the best specimen of prose composition. Some time previous to this he had entered himself at the divinity hall, and had gone through the greater part of the exercises necessary to qualify him to become a preacher in the Church of Scotland. In 1790 he repaired to London, and supported himself by writing for the daily papers. In 1791 he published a collection of ' Sonnets from Shakspeare.' He also preached occasionally, and was rising in reputation, when he was cut off, in 1797, in the 26th year of his age.

The following is a list of his works:

Juvenile Poems; with remarks on Poetry, and a dissertation on the best method of Punishing and Preventing Crimes. Lond. 1780, 12mo.

Confidential Letters from the Sorrows of Werter. Lond. 1799, 12mo.

Sonnets from Shakspeare. Lond. 1791, 8vo.

———

ARNOT, a surname derived from the lands of Arnot in the county of Fife. In Sibbald's List of the heritors of Fifeshire, published in 1710, we find the names, as landholders of that county, of Arnot of that ilk, Arnot of Woodmiln, Arnot of Balkaithlie, Arnot of Balcormo, Arnot of Chapel-Kettle, Arnot of Freeland, Arnot of Lumwhat, and Arnot of Berryhole. Sir John Arnot of Berwick, of the family of Arnot, was provost of Edinburgh, and treasurer depute to King James the Sixth. The lands of Chapel, in the parish of Kettle, have long belonged to a family of the name of Arnot. Upon the last day of December 1558, James, commendator of the priory of St. Andrews, disponed the church lands called Chapel-Kettle to John Arnot and his heirs, declaring that he and his progenitors had been possessors of these lands past the memory of man. [*Sibbald's History of Fife*, p. 385.]

Sir Michael Arnot of Arnot, in the county of Perth, the descendant of a very ancient Fifeshire family, designated of that ilk so early as the 12th century, was created a baronet by Charles the First, 27th July 1629. His son and heir, Sir David Arnot, second baronet, was member of the Scots parliament for Kinross, in 1689. He was the father of Sir John Arnot, the third baronet, who, having devoted himself early to a military life, was appointed, in 1727, adjutant-general of Scotland. In 1735 he was promoted to the rank of brigadier-general, and in 1739 to that of major-general. He died 4th June 1750, a lieutenant-general. His eldest son, Sir John Arnot, fourth baronet, was succeeded by his son Sir William Arnot, fifth baronet, lieutenant-colonel of the Queen's regiment of dragoon guards, who died in 1782, leaving a son, Sir William Arnot, sixth and last baronet. The title is now extinct.—*Burke's Extinct and Dormant Baronetages.*

In Perthshire there was a family of the name of Arnot of Benchill, who for a long time were provosts of Perth.

ARNOT, HUGO, an antiquarian writer and local historian, was the son of a merchant and shipowner in Leith, where he was born on the 8th December 1749. His own name was Pollock, but on the death of his mother, December 5, 1773, at her house in Fifeshire, he changed it to Arnot, on obtaining, through her right, the estate of Balcormo in Fife. He was educated for the law, and in December 1772 he was admitted a member of the faculty of advocates, under the name of 'Hugo Arnot, Esq. of Balcormo.' Having in his fifteenth year caught a severe cold, he was ever after afflicted with painful asthma, which reduced him almost to a skeleton, and which any exertion always aggravated. In 1776 he published at London in 12mo, 'An Essay on Nothing,' a discourse delivered in the Edinburgh Speculative Society, which was favourably received. Of that society Mr. Arnot was admitted a member January 3, 1770, and, besides the Essay on Nothing, he delivered others on the following subjects: The Com-

parative Happiness of the Polished and Barbarous State; Whether a man would be most happy in retiring from or continuing in business after making a competent fortune; Foundation of the Inequality among Mankind; Literary Property; Nature and end of Punishments; and the Necessity of Mankind living in Society, and the advantages of it, which was his valedictory essay. [*Hist. of Speculative Society*, p. 99.] In 1779 appeared his 'History of Edinburgh,' one vol. 4to, a work of much research. He was prevented, however, from deriving much pecuniary benefit from it, by a piratical edition having been printed at Dublin, and sent over to Edinburgh and sold at a cheap rate. Taking a strong interest in local matters, he afterwards published various pamphlets and essays of a temporary nature; and his exertions in promoting the improvements then in progress in Edinburgh, were rewarded by the freedom of the city being conferred upon him by the magistrates. From his great local influence he is said to have been able to protract the erection of the South Bridge of Edinburgh for ten years, by his opposition to the proposed tax upon carts to defray the expense. He was also instrumental in preventing the formation of the spacious road called Leith Walk for some years, on account of the putting on a toll, which, however, was done, and not removed till about 1837. In 1785 came out his 'Collection of celebrated Criminal Trials in Scotland, from 1536 to 1784, with Historical and Critical Remarks,' one vol. 4to, published by subscription. In December 1784 he issued an advertisement of the work, with the following notice appended to it, from which it would appear that he and the Edinburgh booksellers were not on the best of terms: "Mr. Arnot printed, a few days ago, a prospectus of the work that the public might form some idea of its nature, and he sent it to be hung up in the principal booksellers in town; but they have thought proper to refuse, in a body, to allow the prospectus and subscription papers to hang in their shops. The prospectus will, therefore, be seen at the Royal Exchange Coffee house, Exchange Coffee house, Princes street Coffee house, and Messrs. Corri and Sutherland's Music shop, Edinburgh, and Gibb's Coffee house, Leith." The work is curious of its kind, but is not so full nor so valuable as Pitcairn's collection of Criminal Trials, a more recent publication. Mr. Arnot died on 20th November 1786, aged 37, and was interred in South Leith church-yard, in a piece of ground presented to him before his death by the magistrates of his native town. For several weeks previous to his death he regularly visited his appointed burial-place, to observe the progress of some masons whom he had employed to wall it in, and frequently expressed a fear that he would die before they should have completed his work. Mr. Arnot was of great height, and extraordinary thinness. The following is a full-length portrait of him as he appeared in the dress of his time taken by Kay. He is represented giving alms to a beggar, a sly piece of satire on the part of the artist.

His person altogether was so remarkable that it was the source of many jests and witticisms. It is related that the Honourable Henry Erskine meeting him once while engaged eating a dried haddock or spelding, complimented him " on looking so like his meat!" Discussing with the same wit on the disposition of the Deity to pardon the sins of the flesh, and on Hugo expressing his hope of forgiveness, Erskine impromptued,—

" I've searched the whole Scriptures, and texts I find none
  Extending God's mercy *to skin and to bone*."

He himself was reputed to be a humorist in his way. One day, when suffering severely from his complaint, he was annoyed by the bawling of a man selling sand on the street. "The rascal," said the unhappy asthmatic, "he spends as much breath in a minute as would serve me for a month!" In his professional character he was no less singular. He would not undertake a case, unless thoroughly convinced of its justice. Once when a cause was offered him, of the merits of which he had a very bad opinion, he asked the person employing him, " Pray, Sir, what do you suppose me to be?" "Why," answered the client, "I understand you to be a lawyer!" "I thought," said Arnot, sternly, "you took me for a scoundrel!" and dismissed the litigant with indignation. Various stories are told of his intrepidity of mind in early life. One of these was his riding to the end of the pier of Leith on a spirited horse, on a stormy day, when the waves were dashing over the pier so furiously as to impress every onlooker with the belief that he could not fail to be swept into the sea. Leith pier, it must be remarked, was then neither so extended nor so well bulwarked as it is now, and consequently this feat was one of great danger. Another was his accepting the challenge of an anonymous enemy who took offence at one of his political pamphlets, and wrote to him to meet him in the King's Park at a particular time and place, to answer for his statements. Mr. Arnot repaired to the spot at the appointed hour, and waited for some time, but no antagonist came forward. His purpose in going might not have been to expose his person in a duel, but to ascertain who was his unknown challenger. Though recorded as a proof of his intrepidity, we do not see in this occurrence any striking mark of moral courage. A sensible man would have paid no attention to such a letter, which appears to have been intended merely as a hoax. Of a nervous and irritable disposition, he was guilty of many eccentricities which rendered him one of the most remarkable local characters of his time. Among other anecdotes the following is related of him, which does not say much for his urbanity or neighbourly feeling. He was in the habit of ringing his bell with a violence which much annoyed an old maiden lady, in a weak state of health, who resided on the floor above him. Of this annoyance she frequently complained, but without effect. At length, wearied with her constant messages, he gave her to understand that he should cease to use it in future; but in the belief that her importunities proceeded from mere querulousness, instead of ringing the bell as usual, he fired off a loaded pistol, whenever he desired the attendance of his servant, to the great alarm of the invalid upstairs, who now as earnestly besought the restitution of the bell, as she had before requested its discontinuance. He left eight children. His grandson, Dr. David Boswell Reid, the author of 'Elements of Chemistry,' acquired a high character as teacher of practical chemistry in the university of Edinburgh. Hugo Arnot figures as a principal personage in Kay's Edinburgh Portraits, in which some amusing anecdotes of his peculiarities may be found.

ARRAN, earl of, one of the secondary titles of the duke of Hamilton, [see HAMILTON, duke of,] derived from the island of that name in the frith of Clyde. In Gaelic it is pronounced *Arrinn*, that is, 'the island of sharp pinnacles,' from, according to Dr. Macleod, *Ar*, 'a land' or 'country,' and *rinn*, 'sharp points;' an etymology far more satisfactory than that of *Ar-fhin*, 'the land,' or 'the field of Fion,' (Fingal); or from *Aran*, 'bread,' as denoting extraordinary fertility, which is by no means a characteristic of this island. The title of earl of Arran was first conferred on Sir Thomas Boyd, eldest son of Robert lord Boyd, [see KILMARNOCK, earl of,] in April 1467, on his marriage with the Princess Mary, eldest daughter of James the Second. He was attainted and forfeited in 1469, and died soon after. The princess married, a second time, in 1474, James, first lord Hamilton, to whom she had been betrothed in 1454, and their son James was, in August 1503, created earl of Arran. The title was afterwards bestowed on Captain James Stewart of Bothwellmuir, the second son of Andrew, lord Ochiltree, [see OCHILTREE, lord,] whose mother Lady Margaret Hamilton, was the only child of James first earl of Arran, by his first wife Beatrice Drummond. He entered the army of the states of Holland, and served some years against the Spaniards. On his return to Scotland in 1579, he obtained the favour of James the Sixth, who, a few days after his appearance at court, appointed him a gentleman of his bedchamber, a privy councillor, captain of his guard, and tutor to the third earl of Arran of the Hamilton family, who by a shameful abuse of law had been imprisoned by order of the regent Morton, and was afterwards cognosced as an idiot. It was on the accusation of the king's new favourite, Capt. Stewart, that the earl of Morton was tried, convicted, and beheaded, for being accessary to the death of Lord Darnley. For five years he possessed the whole power of the government, and in 1584 was appointed lord high chancellor and lieutenant of the kingdom. In 1581 he obtained from the king a grant of the baronies of Hamilton and Kinniel, and the other estates of the Hamilton family. In October of the same year, under the pretence that he was the lawful heir of the family, and that the children of the third marriage of the first earl of Arran were illegitimate, he was created earl of Arran, which dignity he held, along with the

estates, until his disgrace in 1585, when they were restored to the true owner. About the end of 1596, as he was riding homeward through Symington, near Douglas in Lanarkshire, he was unexpectedly attacked by Sir James Douglas of Parkhead, nephew of the regent Morton, who, in revenge for the death of his uncle, killed him on the spot. His body was exposed to dogs and swine, and his head being cut off was carried on the point of a lance, in triumph through the country. He married, 6th July 1581, Lady Elizabeth Stewart, eldest daughter of John, fourth earl of Athol, who had been twice previously married, and by her had Sir James Stewart of Killeith, Lord Ochiltree, [see OCHILTREE, Lord,] and another son.

ARRAN, earl of, is also an Irish title, created in 1762, and possessed by a family of the name of Gore, properly earl of the ARRAN Islands in Galway.

ARRAN, EARL of, see HAMILTON, James.

ARTHUR, a surname derived from *Art-uir*, signifying the chief or great man; hence the renowned Welsh prince, King Arthur, whose achievements have formed the subject of so much romantic fiction, and whose name has been traditionally given to various places in Scotland, as well as in England and Wales. "It cannot easily be discovered," says Stoddart, "why several mountains in Scotland take their name from the Welsh prince, Arthur, of whom no other traces remain in this country; but it appears that they have been traditionally considered as places of sovereignty. Thus it is said that Ben Arthur (a lofty mountain-crag in the wilds of Glencroe, Argyleshire), being, at one period, the most elevated and conspicuous of the mountains in the domain of the Campbells, the heir to that chieftainship was obliged to seat himself on its loftiest peak, a task of some difficulty and danger, which, if he neglected, his lands went to the next relation sufficiently adventurous." Arthur's Seat in the immediate neighbourhood of Edinburgh is said to have taken its name from King Arthur having surveyed the country from its summit, previous to the eleventh battle which he fought against the Saxons, in the sixth century, and which, according to Whittaker, was decided on the castle-hill of Edinburgh. Pinkerton says that the name arose from the tournaments held near it, as did Arthur's round-table at Stirling, Arthur being quite popular in the centuries of chivalry and romance, [*Enquiry into the History of Scotland*, vol. i. p. 77, note]; but there cannot be a question that the name of Arthur's Seat, as applied to the height immediately beside the palace of Holyrood, the residence of Scotland's later kings, meant no more than the hill of the chief or sovereign of the whole country, without any reference at all to King Arthur of Welsh history. The same may be said of all the other places in Scotland to which his name has been given, and of which Chalmers in his Caledonia [vol. i. p. 244] has collected many notices. Arthur's fountain in the parish of Crawford, Clydesdale, is referred to in a grant made in 1239 by David de Lindsey to the monks of Newbottle, of the lands of Brother-alwyn in that district, as being bounded on the west, "*a fonte Arthuri usque ad summitatem montis.*" [*Cart. Newbottle*, No. 148.] This, however, may only mean the fountain of the chief or great man of the district. The Welsh poets assign a palace to Arthur among the northern Britons at Penryn ryoneth, corresponding to Dumbarton castle, which, as appears from a parliamentary record of the reign of David the Second in 1367, was, long before, named *Castrum Arthuri*. But this might mean only the castle or fort of the chief or sovereign. The romantic castle of Stirling was equally, during the middle ages, supposed to have been the festive scene of Arthur's round table. "*Rex Arthurus*," says William of Worcester, in his Itinerary, p. 311, "*custodiebat le round-table in castro de Styrlyng, aliter, Snowdon-west-castell.*" Sir David Lindsay, in his 'Complaint' of the Papingo, makes her take leave of Stirling castle thus:

> "Adew, fair Snawdoun, with thy touris hie,
> Thy chapell royall, park, and tabill round."

In Neilston parish, Renfrewshire, there are three places of the name of Arthur-lee. The ancient monument of Arthur's Oven, or 'Oon,' on the Carron, which was demolished many years ago, was known by that name as early as the reign of Alexander the Third, if not earlier. Arthur's Seat near Edinburgh is not the only hill which bears the name. Not far from the top of Loch Long, that separates Argyle and Dumbarton, there is a conical hill also called Arthur's Seat, which is likewise the name given to a rock, on the north side of the hill of Dunbarrow in the parish of Dunnichen, Forfarshire. In the parish of Cupar-Angus, Perthshire, there is a standing stone called the Stone of Arthur; near it is a gentleman's seat called Arthur-stone, and not far from it is a farm named Arthur's fold. At Meigle, in the same vicinity, some antique and curious monuments in the churchyard are associated by tradition with the name of the fabulous King Arthur's faithless queen, Vanora, Guenevra, or Ginevra. Arthur is, besides, the apparent founder of a numerous clan, whose antiquity is proverbial among the Highlanders.

ARTHUR, ARCHIBALD, professor of moral philosophy in the university of Glasgow, eldest son of Andrew Arthur, a farmer, was born at Abbot's-Inch, Renfrewshire, September 6, 1744. He was taught Latin at the grammar school of Paisley, and studied for the ministry at Glasgow college, where, when yet a student, he lectured on church history for a whole session, during the absence of the professor, to the great satisfaction and improvement of the class. In October 1767 he was licensed as a preacher of the Church of Scotland, and soon after became chaplain to the university of Glasgow, and assistant to the Rev. Dr. Craig, one of the clergymen of that city. Becoming also librarian to the university, he compiled the catalogue of that library. In 1780 he was appointed assistant and successor to the venerable Dr. Reid, professor of moral philosophy, who died in 1796. Mr. Arthur taught the class fifteen years as assistant, and only held the chair as professor for one session, as he died on 14th June 1797. In 1803, Professor Richardson, of the same university, published a part of Arthur's lectures, under the title of 'Discourses on Theological and Literary Subjects,' 8vo, with a sketch of his life and character.

ASTON, lord, a title in the peerage of Scotland, now extinct, possessed by a noble family of the same name, which originally belonged to the county of Stafford in England, the progenitor of which was Randal or Ranulph de Astona, who lived in the reign of Edward the First. His descendant, Sir Edward Aston of Tixall, in the reign of Queen Elizabeth, possessed estates of the value of ten thousand a-year, in the counties of Stafford, Derby, Leicester, and Warwick. He married Anne, only daughter of Sir Thomas Lucy of Charlecot, and died in 1598. His eldest son, Sir Walter Aston, at the coronation of James the First of England, was honoured with the order of the Bath, and in 1611 he was created a baronet. In 1622 he was employed to negociate a marriage between Charles, prince of Wales, afterwards Charles the First, and the Infanta of Spain; and, in requital for his services upon that occasion, he was elevated to the peerage 28th November 1627, as Lord Aston of Forfar. He married Gertrude, only daughter of Sir Thomas Sadler of Standon, son of the celebrated Sir Ralph Sadler, and died in 1689. He supported Michael Drayton the poet for many years, and his seat of Tixall is noticed in his 'Polyolbion.' At his investiture as knight of the Bath in 1603, Drayton, who has dedicated several of his poems to this Lord Aston, acted as one of his esquires. The title became extinct on 21st January 1845, on the death without issue of the Rev. Walter Hutchinson-Aston, ninth baron Aston, a clergyman of the church of England, vicar of Tardebigg, Worcestershire, and of Tamworth, Warwickshire. The motto of the family was "*Numini et Patriæ Asto.*" The title does not appear on the Union Roll; but the eighth baron Aston, the father of the last lord, was recognised as a peer by George the Third.

ATHOL, ATHOLL, or ATHOLE, earls of, an ancient title, formerly possessed by the royal family of Scotland, subsequently in right of marriage by Thomas de Galloway and his son, and after him by David de Hastings, afterwards by the Strathbogie family, then after being held by a Campbell and a Douglas, it was conferred on a scion of the royal house of Stewart, and through a second creation in the house of Stewart, it came latterly to be possessed by a branch of the noble family of Murray. It is the name of a mountainous and romantic district in the north of Perthshire, which, from a remote period, has preserved its boundaries unaltered. It was the original patrimony of the family which gave kings to Scotland from Duncan to Alexander the Third; and it is the earliest district in Scotland mentioned in history. The name signifies 'pleasant land,' and Blair of Athol, its principal valley, 'the field or vale of Athol.' "Its chief interest, says Skene, "arises from the strong presumption which exists that the family which gave a long line of kings to Scotland, from the eleventh to the fourteenth century, took their origin from this district, to which they can be traced before the marriage of their ancestor with the daughter of Malcolm the Second raised them to the throne." [*History of the Highlanders*, vol. ii. p. 127.] When Thorfinn, the Norwegian earl of Orkney, conquered the north of Scotland, in the early part of the eleventh century, the only portion of the territory of the Northern Picts which remained unsubdued was the district of Athol and part of Argyle. The lord of the Isles had been slain in an unsuccessful attempt to preserve his insular dominions, and the king of the Scots, with the whole of his nobility, had also fallen in the short but bloody campaign which preceded the Norwegian conquest. In their disastrous condition the Scots had recourse to Duncan, the son of Crinan, abbot of Dunkeld, by Beatrice, the daughter of Malcolm the Second, the last Scottish king. Duncan came to the vacant throne in 1034, but after a reign of six years, he was slain in an attempt to recover the northern districts from the Norwegians, and his sons were driven out by Macbeth, who for a time ruled over the south, whilst

L

the Norwegians possessed the north of Scotland. After the overthrow of Macbeth, 5th December, 1056, and the establishment of Malcolm Canmore on the throne, the Lowlands of Scotland were, according to the Saxon polity, divided into earldoms, all of which were granted to the different members of the royal family. These earldoms consisted of the country inhabited by the Scots, with the addition of the district of Athol; and from this circumstance it has, not unreasonably, been presumed that Athol was the original possession of this royal race. This is further confirmed by the designation which early Scottish historians apply to Crinan, the father of Duncan. Besides being abbot of Dunkeld, he is styled by Fordun, "*Abthanus de Dull ac Seneschallus Insularum*" (Abthane of Dull and steward of the Isles). Pinkerton has denied that such a title as Abthane was ever known or heard of; but Mr. Skene has most conclusively shown, not only that there was such a title as Abthane in Scotland, but that the very title of Abthane of Dull, which is the name of a district in Athol, existed until comparatively a late period. [*Skene's History of the Highlanders*, vol. ii. part 2, chap. 5.] See ABTHANE, *ante*, p. 16.

By King Edgar, the whole of Athol, except Breadalbane, was erected into an earldom, and conferred upon his cousin Madach, the son of King Donald Bane. Madach married a daughter of Haco, earl of Orkney. He was a witness to the foundation charter of Alexander the First, of the monastery of Scone, in 1114, and he was himself afterwards a benefactor to the abbey. On the death of Madach towards the end of the reign of David the First, the earldom of Athol was obtained by Malcolm the son of Duncan, the eldest son of Malcolm Canmore, by Ingioborge, the widow of Thorfinn, earl of Orkney, whose descendants were excluded from the throne by that king's younger sons. The earldom was thus bestowed on Malcolm, "either," Skene says, "because the exclusion of that family from the throne could not deprive them of the original property of the family, to which they were entitled to succeed, or as a compensation for the loss of the crown." [*Hist. of Highlanders*, vol. ii. p. 139.] His son Malcolm, the third earl of Athol, gave in pure alms to the monks of Scone the church of Logen Mabed, with four chapels thereunto belonging, and to the abbey of Dunfermline the tithes of the church of Moulin. He also made a donation to the priory of St. Andrews of the patronage of the church of Dull. His son Henry succeeded to the earldom, and on his death, in the beginning of the thirteenth century, his granddaughters, by his eldest son who predeceased him, carried it into the families of Galloway and Hastings.

The eldest of these granddaughters (erroneously stated by Douglas in his Peerage to have been the daughters of Earl Henry) married Alan de Lundin, Ostiarius Regis, who in her right became fifth earl of Athol, and who died without issue. Her next sister, Isabel, married Thomas de Gallovidia, the brother of Alan lord of Galloway, and in her right became sixth earl of Athol. He died in 1231. His son Patrick, seventh earl of Athol, was the youth who overthrew W. Bisset at a tournament on the English borders, and was murdered at Haddington in 1242 (see *ante*, life of Alexander II., p. 75). Fernelith, the youngest of Earl Henry's granddaughters, succeeded her nephew, Earl Patrick, as countess of Athol. She married David de Hastings, an Anglo-Norman, descended from the steward of William the Conqueror, and he, in her right, became the eighth earl. He was one of the guarantees of the treaty of peace between Alexander the Second and Henry the Third in 1244. [See *ante*, p. 77.] In 1268 he accompanied other Scottish barons in an expedition to the Holy Land, and died at Tunis the following year. His

daughter Adda married John de Strathbogie, who in her right became ninth earl of Athol. The grandfather of this John of Strathbogie, Duncan earl of Fife, had obtained the lands of Strathbogie, in Aberdeenshire, from King William the Lion. He settled them on his third son, David, who assumed his name from these lands, and was the father of the eighth earl of Athol. The son of the latter, David de Strathbogie, became the tenth earl of Athol, and was the father of John, eleventh earl, who was one of the chief associates of Robert the Bruce, and assisted at his coronation at Scone, 27th March, 1306. He fought on Bruce's side at Methven, and on his discomfiture accompanied him during his disastrous flight. After the surrender of the castle of Kildrummy the same year, he was seized by the forces of Edward in attempting to escape by sea, and conducted to London. Being condemned to death in Westminster Hall, 7th November 1306, he was executed the same day, on a gallows thirty feet higher than ordinary, in consequence of his royal descent.

The earldom of Athol was then forfeited and bestowed on Ralph de Monthermer, styled earl of Gloucester, who, however, relinquished his title to it for 5,000 merks, in favour of David de Strathbogie, son of the deceased earl. This David, the twelfth earl, had from King Robert the Bruce, the office of high constable of Scotland, as appears from a charter of that monarch 26th February 1312, where he is so designated. Two years after, however, he revolted against Bruce, whereupon his office of high constable was given to Gilbert de la Haye, and Athol's estates in Scotland were forfeited. He married Joan, daughter of John Cumyn of Badenoch, killed by Bruce at Dumfries in 1306, with whom he got great estates in England. He died in 1327, leaving a son, David, who was *styled* thirteenth earl of Athol.

Along with other forfeited Scottish barons this David accompanied Edward Baliol into Scotland in 1332, and had a considerable share in achieving the victory over the Scots at Dupplin, 12th August of that year. He was now restored to his paternal inheritance and title. In 1334 Edward Baliol bestowed on him the whole estates of the steward of Scotland; but the same year, the earl of Moray, regent of Scotland, compelled him to surrender, when he swore allegiance to David the Second, the lawful king. Being in consequence denounced as a rebel by Edward the Third, he was fain, on the invasion of Scotland by that monarch in July 1335, to agree to a treaty of peace, and make his submission to Edward, on which he was again received into favour with the English king, and had the office of governor of Scotland conferred upon him under Baliol, when he acted very insolently and tyrannically towards all the adherents of the family of Bruce. Having been appointed commander of the English forces in the north, with three thousand men he proceeded to lay siege to the castle of Kildrummy, the asylum of the royalists; but was surprised in the forest of Kilblane by the earl of March, Sir William Douglas of Liddesdale, and Sir Andrew Moray of Bothwell, at the head of eleven hundred men. Athol's troops, panic-struck, fled and dispersed; the earl, finding himself abandoned, disdained quarter, and was slain 30th November, 1335, in the 28th year of his age. He left a son, David, *styled* fourteenth earl of Athol, who was only three years of age at the time of his father's death. He accompanied Edward the Black Prince into France in 1356, and was in the subsequent expeditions to Gascony. He died 10th October 1375, leaving two daughters.

When the Celtic earls of Athol became extinct, says Skene, and, in consequence, the subordinate clans in the district of Athol assumed independence, the principal part of that district was in the possession of the clan Donnachie or the Robertsons. [*History of the Highlanders*, vol. ii. pp 139, 140.] Skene states in a note that the peerage writers have been more than usually inaccurate in their account of the earldom of Athol. From its origin down to the fourteenth century, " there is," he says, " scarcely a single step in the genealogy correctly given."

On the forfeiture of David, the twelfth earl, his estates were granted to Sir Niel Campbell of Lochow, and Mary his spouse, sister to King Robert the Bruce, and Sir John Campbell of Moulin, their second son ; and the latter was created earl of Athol. This appears from a charter of King David the Second to Robert Lord Erskine, of the customs of Dundee and third part of Pettarache in Forfarshire, which some time pertained to John Campbell, earl of Athol, as well as from a charter granted by the latter to Roger de Mortimer of the lands of Billandre. He was killed in the battle of Halidon-hill, 19th July 1333, without issue, whereby the title reverted to the crown.

The next possessor of the title of earl of Athol was William Douglas, eldest son of Sir James Douglas of Laudon, ancestor of the earls of Morton. Not long after the death of the above-mentioned John Campbell he had the earldom conferred upon him, but the precise date is unknown. On the 16th February 1341 he resigned his title by charter in favour of Robert, great steward of Scotland, and on the latter's accession to the throne in February 1371, under the name of Robert the Second, it became vested in the royal family. Walter Stewart, the second son of that monarch by his second wife, Euphemia Ross, was the next earl. He was at first earl of Caithness, but afterwards had the earldom of Athol, being so designed, 5th June, 1403, in letters of safe-conduct by King Henry the Fourth, allowing him to pass into his dominions as far as St. Thomas of Canterbury, with a retinue of a hundred persons. He had a charter from his brother Robert duke of Albany, governor of Scotland, of the barony of Cortachy in Forfarshire 22d September 1409. On the 10th April 1421 he obtained a safe-conduct to England, to arrange as to the restoration to liberty of his nephew James the First, which he was very instrumental in accomplishing. He sat as one of the jury on the trial of his nephew Murdoch, duke of Albany, and his sons, in 1424. [See *ante*, p. 41.] The king conferred upon him the office of great justiciary of Scotland, and also gave him the county palatine of Strathern for his life, 22d July 1427. Nearly ten years after this he engaged in the conspiracy of his kinsman Sir Robert Graham against James the First, one of the objects of which was the placing of the crown on the head of Sir Robert Stewart of Athol, the earl's grandson. The king was cruelly assassinated in the Blackfriars monastery at Perth by the three conspirators, 20th February 1437. The murderers were apprehended, and put to death at Edinburgh with horrible tortures, in the following April. Before being beheaded, Athol was set upon the pillory, and his head encircled with a redhot iron crown, on which was inscribed " The king of traitors." His titles and extensive estates were forfeited.

The title of earl of Athol was conferred, about 1457, on Sir John Stewart of Balveny, the eldest son of Sir James Stewart, the Black Knight of Lorn, and the queen Joanna, dowager of James the First, who had chosen him for her second husband. The earl of Athol's father, the Black Knight of Lorn, was the third son of Sir John Stewart of Lorn and Innermeath, descended from Sir James Stewart, fourth son of Sir John Stewart of Bonkill, who was second son of Alexander, high steward of Scotland. This earl of Athol was, with the earl of Crawford, appointed in 1475 to the command of the armament employed in suppressing the rebellion of the

earl of Ross, on which occasion he assumed the motto, still borne by the Athol family, of " Furth fortune and fill the fetters," and had a grant of many lands that had belonged to that nobleman, on his resignation of the earldom of Ross and the lands of Kintyre and Knapdale. He also acted a prominent part in the attempt made in 1480 to reduce to obedience Angus of the Isles, the illegitimate son of the Lord of the Isles, the new title of the earl of Ross. Some time after the battle of the Bloody Bay, fought in that year in the Isle of Mull between the Island factions, in which Angus was victorious, occurred the event known in history as the ' Raid of Athol.' The earl crossing privately to Islay had carried off the infant son of Angus, called *Donald Dubh*, or the Black, whom he placed in the hands of his maternal grandfather the earl of Argyle. Angus immediately summoned his adherents and sailed to the neighbourhood of Inverlochy, where he left his galleys, and with a chosen body of Island warriors made a rapid and secret march into the district of Athol, which he ravaged with fire and sword. The earl and his countess took refuge in the chapel of St. Bride, to which sanctuary many of the country people likewise fled with their most valuable effects. The chapel, however, was violated by Angus and his followers, who, loaded with plunder, returned to Lochaber, carrying with them the earl and countess of Athol as prisoners. In the voyage from Lochaber many of his galleys sunk, and much of his plunder was lost in a dreadful storm which he encountered. Believing this to be a judgment from heaven for the violation of the chapel of St. Bride, he was touched with fear and remorse, and voluntarily liberated his prisoners, without procuring what seems to have been the principal object of his *raid* into Athol, the recovery of his son. He even performed an ignominious penance in the chapel which he had so lately desecrated.

In 1488 the earl of Athol had a principal command in the army of James III. against his son and the rebel lords, for which, on the death of that monarch, he was imprisoned in the castle of Dunbar. He died 19th September 1512. By his first wife, Lady Margaret Douglas, only daughter of Archibald, fifth earl of Douglas, duke of Touraine, the widow of the eighth earl of Douglas and the wife of the ninth earl, her marriage with whom after his rebellion in 1455 was annulled, he had two daughters. By his second wife, Lady Eleonora Sinclair, daughter of William earl of Orkney and Caithness, he had two sons and nine daughters. John, the elder son, second earl of Athol, of this new creation, did not enjoy the title one year, being killed at Flodden 9th September, 1513. His son John, the third earl, was famous for his great hospitality and princely style of living. Pitscottie minutely describes a grand hunting match and sumptuous entertainment given by him to King James the Fifth and his mother and the French ambassador, in 1529. He died in 1542, and was succeeded by his son John, fourth earl of Athol. In the parliament of 1560, with the Lords Borthwick and Somerville he strongly opposed the Reformation, saying they would believe as their fathers had done before them. Being afterwards constituted lord high chancellor of Scotland, he was sworn into office at Stirling, 29th March 1577. He opposed the measures of the regent Morton, and took up arms to rescue the king from his power, but by the mediation of Bowes the English ambassador, an accommodation took place, in August 1578. At a grand entertainment given by Morton, at Stirling, to the leaders of the opposite party, in token of reconcilement, 20th April 1579, Athol, the chancellor, was taken ill, and died four days afterwards, not without strong suspicions of his having been poisoned. He was twice married ; the second time to Margaret, third daughter of Malcolm third lord Fleming, great chamberlain of Scotland, widow of Robert master of Montrose, killed at Pinkie, 1547, and of Thomas master of Erskine, son of John earl of Mar. During her lifetime it was the general belief that this countess of Athol possessed the powers of sorcery, and it is said that when Queen Mary was confined with James the Sixth, the countess cast all the pains of childbirth upon Lady Rires. If so, it must have been by some unknown species of mesmerism. Their son, John, fifth earl of Athol, was sworn a privy councillor in 1590, and died at Perth, 28th August 1595, without issue male, when the title reverted to the crown. He married Lady Mary Ruthven, second daughter of William first earl of Gowrie, by whom he had four daughters. His countess afterwards became the second wife of John lord Innermeath, created earl of Athol by James the Sixth, in 1596. Lady Dorothea Stewart, the eldest daughter of John the fifth earl and this lady, married William, second earl of Tullibardine, and was the mother of John, created earl of Athol, the first of the Murray family who possessed that title, as afterwards mentioned. Lady Mary, the second daughter, married James, earl of Athol, the son of her stepfather, Lord Innermeath, and he dying without male issue, the earldom again reverted to the crown. [See INNERMEATH, Lord.]

ATHOL, duke of, a title possessed by a branch of the ancient family of Murray. The progenitor of the Murray family in Scotland was a Flemish settler in the reign of David the First, of the name of Freskin, who obtained the lands of Strathbrock in Linlithgowshire, now called Brocks or Broxburn. A rebellion having broken out in Moray in the year 1130, he is supposed to have assisted in quelling it, and was rewarded with a large tract of land in the lowlands of Moray, where his descendants settled, and in consequence assumed the name of de Moravia. From Walter de Moravia descended the Morays, lords of Bothwell, the Morays of Abercairney (see MURRAY, surname of), and Sir William de Moravia, who acquired the lands of Tullibardine, an estate in the lower part of Perthshire, with his wife Adda, daughter of Malise, seneschal of Strathern, as appears by charters dated in 1282 and 1284.

His son, Sir Andrew Murray of Tullibardine, who succeeded him, was an adherent of Edward Baliol, and contributed greatly to the decisive victory gained by the latter at Dupplin in August 1332, by fixing a stake in a ford in the river Earn, through which his army marched and attacked the Scots. He was taken prisoner at Perth about two months afterwards, and immediately put to death for his adherence to Baliol. His descendant, Sir William Murray of Tullibardine, succeeded to the estates of his family in 1446. He was sheriff of Perthshire, and in 1458, one of the lords named for the administration of justice, who were of the king's daily council. He married Margaret, daughter of Sir John Colquhoun of Luss, great chamberlain of Scotland, by whom he had a numerous issue. According to tradition they had seventeen sons, from whom a great many families of the name of Murray are descended. In a curious document entitled "The Declaration of George Halley, in Ochterarder, concerning the Laird of Tullibardine's seventeen sons—1710," it is stated that they "lived all to be men, and that they waited all one day upon their father at Stirling, to attend the king, with each of them one servant, and their father two. This happening shortly after an act was made by King James the Fifth, discharging any persons to travel with great numbers of attendants besides their own family, and having challenged the laird of Tullibardine for breaking the said act, he answered he brought only his own sons, with their necessary attendants; with which the king was so well pleased that he gave

them small lands in heritage." The ancient Scottish song, "Cromlet's Lilt," was written on the supposed inconstancy of Miss Helen Murray, commonly called "Fair Helen of Ardoch," granddaughter of Murray of Strewan, one of the seventeen sons of Tullibardine. She was courted by young Chisholm of Cromleck who, during his absence in France, imposed upon by the false representations of a treacherous friend, believed that she was faithless to him, and wrote the affecting ballad called Cromlet's or Cromleck's lilt. The lady's father, Stirling of Ardoch, had by his wife, Margaret Murray, a family of no less than thirty-one children, of whom fair Helen was one. It is said that James the Sixth, when passing from Perth to Stirling in 1617, paid a visit to Helen's mother, the Lady Ardoch, who was then a widow. Her children were all dressed and drawn up on the lawn to receive his majesty. On seeing them the king said, 'Madam, how many are there of them?' 'Sire,' she jocosely answered, 'I only want your help to make out the *twa* chalders!' a chalder contains sixteen bolls. The king laughed heartily at the joke, and afterwards ate a collop sitting on a stone in the close. The youngest son of this extraordinary family, commonly called the *Tutor* of Ardoch, died, in 1715, at the advanced age of one hundred and eleven.

The eldest of Tullibardine's seventeen sons, Sir William Murray of Tullibardine, had, with other issue, William, his successor, and Sir Andrew Murray, ancestor of the viscounts Stormont. (See STORMONT.) His great-grandson, Sir William Murray of Tullibardine, was a zealous promoter of the Reformation in Scotland; and in 1567, at Carberry-hill, he accepted the gauntlet of defiance to single combat thrown down by the earl of Bothwell, but the latter objected to him as being of inferior rank, as he did also to Tullibardine's brother, James Murray of Purdorvis, for the same reason. His sister Annabella married the earl of Mar, afterwards regent, and was the governess of the infant king, James the Sixth. He himself married in 1547 Lady Agnes Graham, third daughter of William second earl of Montrose. On the death of his brother-in-law, the earl of Mar, in 1572, he and Sir Alexander Erskine of Gogar were appointed governors of the young king and joint keepers of the castle of Stirling, where his majesty resided, and he discharged the office with the applause of the whole kingdom till 1578. George Halley, in the curious document already quoted, says that "Sir William Murray of Tullibardine having broke Argyle's face with the hilt of his sword, in king James the Sixth's presence, was obliged to leave the kingdom. Afterwards, the king's mails and slaughter cows were not paid, neither could any subject in the realm be able to compel those who were bound to pay them; upon which the king cried out—'O, if I had Will. Murray again, he would soon get my mails and slaughter cows;' to which one standing by replied—'That if his majesty would not take Sir William Murray's life, he might return shortly.' The king answered, 'He would be loath to take his life, for he had not another subject like him!' Upon which promise Sir William Murray returned, and got a commission from the king to go to the north, and lift up the mails and the cows, which he speedily did, to the great satisfaction of the king, so that immediately after he was made lord comptroller." This office he obtained in 1565.

His eldest son, Sir John Murray, the twelfth feudal baron of Tullibardine, was brought up with King James, who, in 1592, constituted him his master of the household. He was afterwards sworn a member of his privy council, and knighted, and on 25th April 1604 King James raised him to the peerage by the title of Lord Murray of Tullibardine. On 10th July 1606 he was created earl of Tullibardine. His lordship married Catherine, fourth daughter of David second lord Drummond, and died in 1609.

His eldest son, William, second earl of Tullibardine, was the means of rescuing James the Sixth from the earl of Gowrie and his brother at Perth on the 5th August 1600, for which service the hereditary sheriffship of Perth, which had belonged to the earl of Gowrie, was bestowed on him. He married, as has been stated, the lady Dorothea Stewart, daughter of the 5th earl of Athol of the Stewart family, who died in 1595, and on the death in 1625 of James, second earl of Athol, son of John sixth lord Innermeath, created earl of Athol by James the Sixth, he petitioned King Charles the First for the earldom of Athol, as his countess was the eldest daughter and heir of line of Earl John, of the family of Innermeath, which had become extinct in the male line. The king received the petition graciously, and gave his royal word that it should be done,—thereby a recognition on the part of the Crown of the right of the heir female to an ancient peerage, of which the constitution was unknown. The earl accordingly surrendered the title of earl of Tullibardine into the king's hands, 1st April 1626, to be conferred on his brother Sir Patrick Murray, as a separate dignity, but before the patents could be expeded, his lordship died the same year. His son John, however, obtained in February 1629 the title of earl of Athol, and thus became the first earl of the Murray branch, and the earldom of Tullibardine was at the same time granted to Sir Patrick. This earl of Athol was a zealous royalist, and joined the association formed by the earl of Montrose for the king, at Cumbernauld, in January 1641. He died in June 1642. His eldest son John, second earl of Athol of the Murray family, also faithfully adhered to Charles the First, and was excepted by Cromwell out of his act of grace and indemnity, 12th April 1654, when he was only about nineteen years of age. At the restoration, he was sworn a privy councillor, obtained a charter of the hereditary office of sheriff of Fife, and in 1663 was appointed justice-general of Scotland. In 1670 he was constituted captain of the king's guards, in 1672 keeper of the privy seal, and 14th January 1673, an extraordinary lord of session. In 1670 he succeeded to the earldom of Tullibardine on the death of James fourth earl of the new creation, and was created marquis of Athol in 1676. He increased the power of his family by his marriage with Lady Amelia Sophia Stanley, third daughter of the seventh earl of Derby, beheaded for his loyalty 15th October 1651. Through her mother, Charlotte de la Tremouille, daughter of Claude de la Tremouille, duke of Thouars and prince of Palmont, she was related in blood to the emperor of Germany, the kings of France and Spain, the prince of Orange, the duke of Savoy, and most of the principal families of Europe; and by her the family of Athol acquired the seignory of the Isle of Man, and also large property in that island.

In 1678, on the irruption into the western shires of the Highland host, the marquis of Athol joined the duke of Hamilton in opposition to the duke of Lauderdale, in consequence of which he was deprived of his office of justice-general, but retained his other places. He was instrumental in suppressing Ar-

gyle's invasion in 1685. Notwithstanding his conspicuous loyalty in the reigns of Charles the Second and his brother James, he promoted the Revolution, and went to London in 1689, to wait on the prince of Orange, but was disappointed in his expectations of preferment under the new government. William, though related to the marchioness, did not receive him cordially, and in consequence he joined the Jacobite party. At the convention of the Scottish estates, 14th March 1689, he was put in nomination as president by the adherents of King James. The Whigs on the other hand proposed the duke of Hamilton, and the latter was elected by a majority of fifteen votes. When the viscount of Dundee proceeded into the Highlands for the purpose of trying the chance of a battle, the defence of the castle of Blair Athol, belonging to the marquis, was the means of occasioning the battle of Killiecrankie, in the same year. This strong fortress, which commands the most important pass in the Northern Highlands, had already been the scene of remarkable events in the previous civil wars. In 1644 the marquis of Montrose had possessed himself of it, and was here joined by a large body of the Athol Highlanders, to whose bravery he was indebted for the victory at Tippermuir. In the troubles of 1653 it was taken by storm by Colonel Daniel, one of Cromwell's officers, who, unable to remove a magazine of provisions lodged there, destroyed it by powder. In 1689 it had been taken possession of by Stewart of Ballechan, the marquis of Athol's chamberlain, who refused to deliver it up to Lord Murray, the marquis's son, as he was supposed to favour the Revolution party, Stewart declaring that he held it for King James, by order of his lieutenant-general. Lord Murray had summoned his father's vassals to join him, and about twelve hundred assembled, but no entreaties could prevail on them to declare in favour of the government of King William. They intimated that if he would join Dundee they would follow him to a man, but if he refused they all would leave him. His lordship remonstrated with them, and even threatened them with his vengeance if they abandoned him, when, setting his threats at defiance, they ran to the river Banovy in the neighbourhood of Blair castle, and filling their bonnets with water, drank King James's health, and left his standard. Dundee knew the importance of preserving Blair castle, and with his usual expedition he joined the garrison. A few days afterwards, however, the battle of Killiecrankie took place, when he was slain in the moment of victory. The following is a view of Blair castle:

The last siege which Blair castle sustained was in March 1746, when it was gallantly defended by Sir Andrew Agnew, against a party of the Pretender's forces, who retired from before it a few weeks preceding the battle of Culloden. As soon as peace was restored, a considerable part of the castle was reduced in height, and the inside most magnificently furnished. The marquis continued in the opposition for the remainder of his life. He died 6th May 1703 His second son, Lord Charles, was created first earl of Dunmore, and his fourth son, Lord William, was created first Lord Nairn.

His eldest son John, the second marquis, and first duke, of Athol, designated Lord John Murray, was one of the commissioners for inquiring into the massacre of Glencoe in 1693. By King William he was appointed in 1695 one of the principal secretaries of state for Scotland. He was created a peer in his father's lifetime, by the title of earl of Tullibardine, viscount of Glenalmond, and Lord Murray, for life, by patent dated 27th July 1696, and in April 1703 he was appointed lord privy seal. On the 30th July of that year, immediately after his father's death, he was created duke of Athol, by Queen Anne, and invested with the order of the Thistle. Having, the same year, introduced the act of security into the Scottish parliament, the duke of Queensberry and the other ministers, greatly displeased, formed a plan to ruin him, by means of Simon Fraser of Beaufort. Fraser had fled to France some years before, to elude a sentence of death pronounced against him in absence, by the court of justiciary, for an alleged rape on the person of Lady Amelia Murray, dowager Lady Lovat, and sister of the duke of Athol, but returning to Scotland in 1703, as the agent of the exiled family, he, after intriguing with the duke of Queensberry, then at the head of the government party in Scotland, revealed the existence of a Jacobite conspiracy, in which the dukes of Hamilton and Athol, as well as others, were deeply involved. Fraser was Athol's bitter enemy [see FRASER, SIMON, twelfth Lord Lovat], and the whole pretended plot having been brought to light by Ferguson, celebrated as the plotter [see FERGUSON, Robert], with whom Fraser had had some communication in London, he immediately acquainted the duke with the discovery he had made. Athol at once laid the matter before the queen, who had been previously apprised of the alleged conspiracy by the duke of Queensberry. The latter being called upon for an explanation, excused himself by saying that when Fraser came to Scotland he had received a written communication from him, to the effect that he could make important discoveries, relative to designs against the queen's government, in proof of which he delivered him a letter from the queen dowager, the widow of James the Seventh, at St. Germains, addressed to L—— M——, which initials Fraser stated were meant for Lord Murray, the former title of the duke of Athol, and that, after seeing him, he (Queensberry) had given him a protection in Scotland, and procured a pass for him in England, to enable him to follow out further discoveries. The English house of peers took the subject up warmly, and passed strong resolutions regarding the supposed conspiracy, for the purpose of clearing Queensberry; but nothing farther was done in the matter. The effect, however, was to incense Athol against the government, and so zealous was he against the Union that he is said to have had six thousand Highland followers ready to oppose it. This did not prevent him, however, from pocketing one thousand pounds of the equivalent money sent down, nominally to satisfy such claims of damage as might arise out of the Union, but in reality given in many instances as a bribe. At the beginning of the session of the Scots parliament in which the Union was carried, the duke was appointed commissioner, as Lockart in-

forms us, in place of the duke of Queensberry, the latter wishing to ascertain the state of public feeling before he ventured himself to face the difficulties of the time, "and therefore he sent the duke of Athol down as commissioner; using him as the monkey did the cat, in pulling out the hot roasted chestnuts." [*Lockart's Memoirs*, p. 139.] His grace died 14th November, 1724. He was twice married; first to Catherine, daughter of the duke of Hamilton, by whom he had six sons and a daughter, and secondly to Mary, daughter of William lord Ross, by whom he had three sons and a daughter. His eldest son, John marquis of Tullibardine, died in 1709. His second son William, who succeeded his brother, was the marquis of Tullibardine who acted the prominent part in both the Scottish rebellions of last century, which is recorded in history. He was one of the first that joined the earl of Mar in 1715, for which he was attainted for high treason, and the family honours were settled by parliament on his next brother James. Another brother, Lord Charles Murray, a cornet of horse, also engaged in the rebellion of 1715, and had the command of a regiment. Upon the march into England he kept at the head of his men on foot in the Highland dress. After the surrender of Preston, his lordship being amongst the prisoners, was tried by a court martial as a deserter, and sentenced to be shot, but received a pardon through the interest of his friends, and died in 1720. The marquis of Tullibardine had escaped to the continent, but returned to Scotland with the Spanish forces, in 1719, and with a younger brother, Lord George Murray, afterwards commander-in-chief of the Pretender's army, was in the battle of the pass of Glenshiel, in the district of Kintail, Ross-shire, in June of that year, where Lord George was wounded. After the defeat at Glenshiel, the marquis escaped a second time to the continent, and lived twenty-six years in exile. In 1745 he accompanied Prince Charles Edward to Scotland, and landed with him at Borodaile 25th July. He was styled duke of Athol by the Jacobites. On the 19th August he unfurled the prince's standard at Glenfinnan, and supported by a man on each side, held the staff while he proclaimed the Chevalier de St. George as king, and read the commission appointing his son Charles prince regent. After the battle of Culloden he fled to the westward, intending to embark for the isle of Mull, but being unable, from the bad state of his health, to bear the fatigue of travelling under concealment, he surrendered, on the 27th April, 1746, to Mr. Buchanan of Drummakill, a Stirlingshire gentleman. Being conveyed to London, he was committed to the Tower, where he died on the 9th July following.

James the second duke of Athol was the third son of the first duke. He succeeded to the dukedom on the death of his father, in November 1724, in the lifetime of his elder brother William, attainted by parliament. Being maternal great-grandson of James seventh earl of Derby, upon the death of the tenth earl of that line, he claimed and was allowed the English barony of Strange, which had been conferred on Lord Derby, by writ of summons, in 1628. His grace was married, first to Jean, sister of Sir John Frederick, bart. by whom he had a son and two daughters; secondly to Jane, daughter of John Drummond of Megginch, who had no issue. The latter was the heroine of Dr. Austen's song of 'For lack of gold she's left me, O!' She was betrothed to that gentleman, a physician in Edinburgh, when the Duke of Athol saw her, and falling in love with her made proposals of marriage, which were accepted; and, as Burns says, she jilted the doctor. Having survived her first husband, she married a second time, Lord Adam Gordon. Dr. Austen, on his part, although in his song he says

"No cruel fair shall ever move
    My injured heart again to love,"

married, in 1754, the Hon. Anne Sempill, by whom he had a numerous family.

The son and the eldest daughter of the second duke of Athol died young. Charlotte, his youngest daughter, succeeded on his death, which took place in 1764, to the barony of Strange and the sovereignty of the Isle of Man. She married her cousin, John Murray, Esq., eldest son of Lord George Murray, fifth son of the first duke, and the celebrated generalissimo of the forces of the Pretender in 1745, [see MURRAY, Lord George.] Though Lord George was attainted by parliament for his share in the rebellion, his son was allowed to succeed his uncle and father-in-law as third duke, and in 1765 he and his duchess disposed of their sovereignty of the Isle of Man to the British government, for seventy thousand pounds, reserving, however, their landed interest in the island, with the patronage of the bishopric and other ecclesiastical benefices, on payment of the annual sum of one hundred and one pounds fifteen shillings and eleven pence, and rendering two falcons to the kings and queens of England upon the days of their coronation. His grace, who had five sons and two daughters, died 5th November, 1774, and was succeeded by his eldest son John, fourth duke, who in 1786 was created Earl Strange and Baron Murray of Stanley, in the peerage of the United kingdom. He died in 1830. His second son, Lord George Murray, was bishop of St. David's, whose eldest son became bishop of Rochester. His fifth son, Lord Charles Murray, dean of Bocking in Essex, having married Alice, daughter of George Mitford, Esq., and heiress of her great uncle, Gawen Aynsley, assumed the surname of Aynsley. The fourth duke was succeeded by his eldest son John, who was for many years a recluse, and died single 14th September, 1846. His next brother James, a major-general in the army, was created a peer of the United kingdom, as baron Glenlyon of Glenlyon, in the county of Perth, 9th July, 1821. He married, in May 1810, Emily Frances, second daughter of the duke of Northumberland, and by her he had two sons and two daughters. He died in 1837. His eldest son, George Augustus Frederick John, Lord Glenlyon, became, on the death of his uncle in 1846, sixth duke of Athol. In 1853, knight of the Thistle; married, with issue.

ATKINS, ETKINS, AITKENS, or AIKEN, JAMES, bishop of Galloway, was born at Kirkwall, about the year 1613. He was the son of Henry Atkens or Aiken, sheriff and commissary of Orkney. He commenced his studies at the university of Edinburgh, and completed them at Oxford in 1638. On his return to Scotland, that year, he was appointed chaplain to James, marquis of Hamilton, his majesty's high commissioner to the General Assembly, in which situation he behaved so well that on the marquis' return to England he obtained for him from the king a presentation to the church of Birsa in Orkney. In the beginning of 1650, on the landing of the marquis of Montrose in that stewartry, Dr. Atkins was appointed by the presbytery to draw up a declaration of loyalty and allegiance to Charles the Second, which, with their consent and approbation, was published. For this step the whole presbytery was deposed by the General Assembly, while Atkins was excommunicated for holding correspondence with the marquis. An act of council was also passed for his apprehension; but receiving private notice thereof from his relative, Sir Archibald Primrose, clerk of council, afterwards lord register, he fled into Holland. In 1653 he returned to Scotland, and quietly resided with his family in Edinburgh, till the king's restoration in 1660, when he accompanied Dr. Sydserf, bishop of Galloway, the only surviving prelate in Scotland, to London to congratulate his majesty; at which time, he was presented by the bishop of Winchester to the rectory of Winfrith in Dorsetshire. In 1677 he was consecrated bishop of Moray; and in 1680 he was translated to the see of Galloway, when, on account of his age, he received a dispensation to reside in Edinburgh, where he died of an apoplectic stroke, 28th October 1687, aged 74 years, and was buried in the church of the Greyfriars in that city. He showed himself very zealous in opposing the taking off the penal laws.—*Keith's Scottish Bishops.*

ATKINSON, THOMAS, a pleasing poet and miscellaneous writer, was born at Glasgow about the year 1801. He is said to have been the illegitimate son of a butcher of that city. After receiving his education, he was apprenticed to Mr. Turnbull, bookseller, Trongate, on whose death he entered into business, in partnership with Mr. David Robertson. From boyhood he was a writer of poetry, prose sketches, and essays; and among other things brought out by him were, 'The Sextuple Alliance,' and 'The Chameleon.' Three successive volumes of the latter were published annually, containing his own pieces exclusively. He was also sole editor and author of 'The Ant,' a weekly periodical, and an extensive contributor to 'The Western Luminary,' 'The Emmet,' and other local publications. His writings are distinguished by taste and fancy, and he was indefatigable in producing them. His talents for speaking were also of a superior order, and he took every opportunity of displaying his powers of oratory. At the general election, after the passing of the Reform Bill, Mr. Atkinson, who was a keen reformer, started as a candidate for the Stirling burghs, in opposition to Lord Dalmeny, who was returned. Being naturally of a delicate constitution, his exertions on this occasion brought on a decline; and when seized with advanced symptoms of consumption, he disposed of his business, his books, and his furniture, and sailed for Barbadoes, but died on the passage on the 10th October 1833, in the 32d year of his age. He was buried at sea in an oaken coffin, which he had taken with him! He left an annuity to his mother, and a sum, after accumulation, to be applied in building an Atkinsonian Hall in Glasgow for scientific purposes. His relatives erected a monument to his memory in the necropolis of his native city.

AUCHINLECK, a surname derived from lands of that name. Auch, sometimes ach, its diminutive auchin and augmentative avoch, occurs frequently alone, as also in composition, in names of lands. It implies an elevation, but in a relative sense only. In valley lands near the mouths of rivers, where the plane is intersected by channels of deep watercourses, the auchin or haughs are the separated and higher portions of that plane; as the Haughs of Cromdale in the valley of the Spey; and being heavy clays, are generally very fertile. On hill-slopes auchin or haughs are more level portions or banks; as Auchinross or Rosehaugh in Avoch, Ross-shire. The augmentative avoch refers to continuity as well as elevation; as in the parish of that name, where a deep alluvial soil is furrowed into a high parallel flat ridge of some miles long by dividing streams. The plural is Auchen, frequently corrupted into Auchens. These and their genitives Auchie—augh-i and Auchenie, occur as surnames, from lands so called. They both enter into topographical combinations, as Auchendenny, Auchen-den-i, haughs of the den,—abbreviated into Denny, also a surname,—whose undulating lands are cut through by deep dens or stream beds; Craig-al-achie, the rock of the haugh or ach, through which the Spey has cleft a passage for itself; and others of similar formation. Aughter, augh-ter, is applied to the upper and higher portions of river basins where the affluents are numerous and their bed valleys wide and deep worn. It means high lands, but in a sense not identical with mountainous. The aughter in Aughterarder is derived from the dividing ridge, or plane of the original bed of the basin, lying between the valleys of the Ruthven and the Earn. Aughter, sometimes Ochter, having in composition given names to baronies, has, again, become a part of various surnames. Augh, or och, is the Gothic root of the German Hoch, and under this form is found in Continental topography wherever the Gothic races held rule. It becomes Hock in English topography. It has been claimed as Gaelic, and is certainly used by a Gaelic-speaking population as a descriptive name in regions now inhabited by them. But their explanations of its meaning are unsatisfactory, and having been introduced into the parochial statistical accounts, are followed in works on topography, so that auch is rendered a field, a height, or a ridge, as appears to suit the locality. Leck or Lyke is the Gothic word for dead, as in Lykewake, the watch of the dead, Cromlech, the circle of the dead, and in this word is applied

in the sense of barren, sterile, as in the dead sea. The barony of that name in Ayrshire is an upland flat lying between the valleys of the waters of Ayr and Lugar, which flow in parallel directions so closely approximating to each other that in sixteen miles of length it has never more than two of breadth, with a moss in a great part of its centre. Lech, Lach, or Lake, is sometimes duplicated with the Latin mort, as Mortlech, in Aboyne, the sterile land; Mortlach, in Moray, the place of battle; and its genitive Leckie is also a surname.

The Gaelic definition, "field of the flagstones," is simply absurd. There is not a flagstone in the parish or barony; and the name was bestowed before the subdivision of land into fields was known. The name is often pronounced and sometimes written Affleck.

The lands of Auchinleck in the parish of Monikie, Forfarshire, appear to have given origin to the surname at an early period. Two rivulets running parallel in deep dens through a valley at a level of 300 feet, yet near the sea, leave between them a flat auchin or elevated stripe on which stands the old tower or castle of Affleck, somewhat more than a mile from the parish church, a beautiful specimen of its class, entire although long uninhabited, and since 1746 has been used for purposes connected with agriculture. It still serves as a mark for mariners. These lands were bestowed by charter from David I. The office of armour-bearer to the Lindsays, earls of Crawford, was hereditary in the family of Auchinleck of that ilk. [Lives of the Lindsays, vol. i. p. 114, note.] They became the property of a family of the name of Reid, which was attainted for being engaged in the rebellion of 1745. The castle and a large part of the estates were then purchased by Mr. James Yeaman, one of the bailies of Dundee, from the representatives of whose descendant, they were acquired by Mr. Graham of Kincaldrum, in whose possession they still remain. In the year 1733, Thomas Reid of Auchinleck, presented a silver communion cup to the kirk-session of Dundee, as recorded in letters of gold on the session-house wall of that time.

The lands of Auchinleck, in Ayrshire, are known to have given a surname to their proprietors so early as the 13th century. In 1300, the laird of Auchinleck accompanied Sir William Wallace to Glasgow from Ayr, when he attacked and slew Earl Percy. [See WALLACE, Sir William.] The Chartulary of Paisley records a donation from Sir John de Auchinleck, in 1385, of twenty shillings yearly to the abbot and convent of that house, as a compensation for having mutilated the person of one of the monks. Thomas Boswell, a younger son of Boswell of Balmuto in Fife, having married one of the daughters and co-heiress of Sir John Auchinleck of that ilk, received in 1504 a grant of these lands from James the Fourth. This Thomas Boswell, who fell at Flodden, was the ancestor of the present possessor. The family of Boswell of Auchinleck has acquired celebrity in several of its members. [See BOSWELL, surname of.] There was another family of Auchinleck in Perthshire, designed of Balmanno, an Auchinleck having married the heiress of Balmanno of that ilk.

AUCHMUTY, or auch-moot-i, augh or haugh of moot or judgment, a surname derived from lands in the parish of Newburn, anciently called Drumeldry, (Drum, hill, eldry elderi or alderi, of the wise men or elders) Fifeshire, once belonging to an old family styled Auchmoutie of that ilk. The estate of Drumeldry, now the property of Thomas Calderwood Durham, Esq. of Largo, and Lawhill, now called Hallhill, the residence of Charles Halket Craigie, Esq., at one time formed part of the barony of Auchmoutie. In 1600 Capt. Auchmuty, a descendant of the ancient Fifeshire house of Auchmuty, settled at Brianstown, county of Longford, Ireland, and his posterity, now named Achmuty, still possess that estate. A branch of the Brianstown family, who continue to spell their name Auchmuty, are the proprietors of Kilmore House in the county of Roscommon. The name is not a very common one, but uncouth as it may sound in the ears of our English neighbours, it has been rendered familiar by the deeds of Major-general Sir Samuel B. Auchmuty, C. B., who in 1807 distinguished himself in the reduction of Monte Video, on the river Plate.

AUCHTERLONY, the surname of an ancient Forfarshire family, who formerly possessed the barony of Kelly in the parish of Arbirlot. Rather more than two miles west of Arbroath, on the edge of a precipice, at the side of the river Elliot, are the ruins of the castle of Kelly, otherwise Auchterlony. The first proprietor of Kelly noticed in history was Roger de Moubray, an adherent of Edward the First of England, who, in the distribution of the estates of the Scottish barons opposed to his pretensions as lord paramount of Scotland, bestowed these lands upon him. In 1321, Moubray was declared a traitor, and his barony forfeited. Kelly was then conferred on the steward of Scotland, the son-in-law of Bruce. In the reign of Robert the Second we find Alexander Auchterlony designed of Kelly. This Alexander Auchterlony married Janet, daughter of Sir William Maule of Panmure, knight, and got with her the lands of Greenford, in the same parish. It would seem that the barony of Kelly had passed from him or his successor, for it is recorded that William Auchterlony acquired Kelly in the year 1444, and from that date till 1630 it remained in possession of the family of Auchterlony. At the Reformation the chief of the Auchterlonies, according to tradition, was very active in the destruction of the abbey of Arbroath. Being indebted to the abbey steward, at the head of three hundred men he attacked the abbey, and setting fire to it, burnt all evidence of a claim against him. Among the witnesses to a charter of a donation to the hospital at Dundee, dated 2d May 1587, appears the name of David Auchterlony dom. ae Kelly, who is supposed to have been either the incendiary or his son. Kelly now belongs to Lord Panmure, and the ancient family of Auchterlony is represented by John Auchterlony of Guynd, Esq.—See OCHTERLONY.

AVANDALE, Lord, a title conferred by James the Second on Andrew Stewart, the eldest of the seven illegitimate sons of Sir James Stewart, called James the Gross, fourth son of Murdoch, duke of Albany, and the only one who escaped the vengeance of James the First, when his father and three brothers were ruthlessly cut off by that monarch. On their imprisonment he had flown to arms, assaulted and burnt the town of Dumbarton, and killed Sir John Stewart, the king's uncle, who held the castle with thirty-two men. He afterwards took refuge in Ireland, where he formed a connection with a lady of the family of Macdonald, by whom he had seven sons, and a daughter, Matilda, married to Sir William Edmonstone of Duntreath. These children are supposed on their father's death to have been adopted by Murdoch's widow, the duchess Isabella, countess of Lennox, to bear her company in her castle on the small island of Inchmurrin on Lochlomond, where her latter years were spent in retirement; as his name and that of three of his brothers, Murdoch, Arthur, and Robert Stewarts of Albany, appear as witnesses to charters granted by the duchess Isabella as countess of Lennox, betwixt 1440 and 1451. [*Napier's History of*

the Partition of the Lennox, pp. 18—20.] King James the Second, touched perhaps with regret for the ruin which his father had caused Duke Murdoch's family, honoured the eldest of his illegitimate grandsons with peculiar marks of regard and affection. He placed him at one of the English universities, and on his return to Scotland, after his education had been completed, appointed him a gentleman of his bedchamber, and knighted him. In 1456 he bestowed on him the barony of Avandale or Evandale in Lanarkshire, which had been forfeited by the last earl of Douglas in 1455, and in 1457 created him Lord Avandale [*Ibid*, p. 45]. Before the 1st of March, 1459, the new peer had superseded George fourth earl of Angus, as warden of the marches, and in 1460, on the accession of James the Third, he was chosen lord-chancellor of Scotland, an office which he held for twenty-two years, with the high distinction of precedence next to the princes of royal blood. He was one of the lords of the regency, and in a charter of King James the Third, in 1465, he is styled guardian of the king. In 1468 he was sent ambassador to Denmark to treat of a marriage between James the Third and the princess Margaret of Denmark, which was happily accomplished. On the 4th May 1471, he had a life-rent grant, under the great seal, of the whole earldom of Lennox, which had been in non-entry from the year 1425, when Earl Duncan, the father of the duchess Isabella, was beheaded, though it had never been forfeited, as erroneously stated by Douglas in his Peerage, and other writers. To fortify himself in this grant, he obtained letters of legitimation under the great seal, of date 28th August 1472, to himself and two of his brothers, Arthur and Walter, by which a right of general succession was thrown open to them. These letters were repeated on the 17th April 1479, and on the 18th of the same month he had a charter of the lordship of Avandale. In 1482, when the king's brother, the duke of Albany, with the assistance of Edward the Fourth of England, invaded Scotland, Lord Avandale and many other noblemen who had been till then the most loyal supporters of the crown, abandoned the sovereign who had heaped upon him wealth and honours, and after the king had been conveyed prisoner to Edinburgh castle, he as chancellor, with the archbishop of St. Andrews, the bishop of Dunkeld, and the earl of Argyle, entered into a bond, dated 2d August of that year, for the protection and indemnity of Albany. The noblemen who sign this deed declare that they and the other nobles of the realm " sall cause our soverane lord frely to gif and grant " to the duke of Albany " all his landis, heritagis, strenthis, houses, and offices quhilk he possessit the day of his last parting furth of the realm of Scotland." [*Fœdera*, b. xii. p. 160.] To punish his ingratitude, the king, before the 25th of the same month of August, deprived him of the chancellorship, which he had held so long, and bestowed it on John Laing, bishop of Glasgow. This took place before the siege of Edinburgh castle, which occurred 29th September 1482, and not after that event, as Mr. Tytler, in his history, records it, and could not therefore have been in consequence of Albany's partial success, as Tytler says it was. [*See Napier's History of the Partition of the Lennox*, p. 68, *note*.] Albany was soon received into favour, and in the following December appointed lieutenant-general of the kingdom, but in 1484 the Albany party was completely crushed. Although not restored to the chancellorship, Lord Avandale appears to have regained the confidence of the king, and in 1484 he was one of the commissioners sent to France to renew the ancient league with that crown. He was also one of the plenipotentiaries who concluded the pacification with King Richard the Third at Nottingham, 21st September of that year. His name appears as one of the witnesses to a charter of James the Third, dated 11th March 1487. He continued to possess the lands of the earldom of Lennox till his death in 1488. He left no issue, whereby the title for the time became extinct.

The title of Lord Avandale was next bestowed on his nephew, Andrew Stewart, second son of his younger brother, Walter Stewart of Morphie, in the county of Kincardine, sixth son of Sir James the Gross. The mother of the second Lord Avandale was Elizabeth, daughter of Arnot of Arnot, in the county of Fife. Crawford (*Officers of State*, p. 39) says that Alexander Stewart, the eldest son of Walter Stewart of Morphie, was, in 1503, created Lord Avandale by solemn investiture in parliament, but this is a mistake, as it would appear that the said Alexander Stewart died before 1500, and that he was succeeded in the estate of Avandale and other lands by his immediate younger brother Andrew above mentioned, second Lord Avandale. [*Douglas.*] By his wife Margaret, daughter of Sir John Kennedy of Blairquhan in Ayrshire, had three sons and three daughters. Andrew, the eldest son, succeeded as third Lord Avandale. Henry, the second son, on marrying the queen dowager, was created Lord Methven. [See METHVEN, Lord.] The third son, Sir James Stewart of Beath, was the ancestor of the earl of Moray. [See MORAY, earl of.]

The third Lord Avandale was governor of the castle of Dumbarton, and held the office of groom of the stole to King James the Fourth. In 1534, he transferred the barony of Avandale and the lands of Coldstream to Sir James Hamilton of Fynnart, in exchange for the barony of Ochiltree in Ayrshire, and in consequence of this exchange, on the 15th March 1543, the earl of Arran, governor of the kingdom, with consent of parliament, ordained that Andrew lord Avandale should in future be styled Lord Stewart of Ochiltree. By his wife, Lady Margaret Hamilton, only child of James, first earl of Arran, he had a son, Andrew Stewart, who became second lord Ochiltree. [See OCHILTREE, Lord.]

AVENEL, a surname now scarcely known, except in the pages of romance. Like Umfraville, de Morville, and others, it was once borne by high and powerful barons, whose descendants, if any now exist, have long ceased to be called by the name of their progenitors. Among the Anglo-Norman knights introduced into Scotland by David the First, was Robert Avenel, who, in reward of military services, received Upper and Lower Eskdale, and flourished during the reigns of Malcolm the Fourth and William the Lion, whose charters he witnessed. He officiated as Justiciary of Lothian for a short time after the accession of William, in 1165. His latter years were spent in the monastery of Melrose, to which he granted a large portion of his estates, and where he died in 1185. His son and heir, Gervase, confirmed the grant. Roger Avenel, the successor of Gervase, had a serious dispute with the monks regarding the game on the lands. The king, Alexander the Second, at his request interfered, and "found that the monks were entitled to the soil, but not to the game, which belonged to the Avenels, as lords of the manor." For several generations the Avenels continued among the most powerful families on the Borders; and in the Tales of the 'Monastery,' and the 'Abbot,' they have been introduced with singular success by Sir Walter Scott. The family of Avenel merged, like many others, in an heiress, who married Henry, the son of Henry de Graham of Abercorn and Dalkeith, and the property of the Avenels thus passed into other families.

AYMOUTH, baron of, in the Scottish peerage, a title be-

stowed on the great duke of Marlborough in 1682, as Baron Churchill of Aymouth, or Eyemouth, in Berwickshire, although he had no connexion with that place. The title became extinct on his death in 1722.

AYTON, or AITON, a surname derived from the village or Eytown, now called Ayton, in Berwickshire, which seems to have taken its name, anciently written Eytun and Eitun, from the water of Eye, that, rising among the Lammermuir hills, flows into the sea at Eyemouth. The etymology of the word is ' the town on the river.'

The family of Ayton were descended from Gilbert de Vesci, an Anglo-Norman knight, who, settling in Scotland shortly after the Conquest, obtained the lands of Ayton in Berwickshire, and adopted the name of the lands as his family name. About the year 1166 Helias and Dolfinus de Eitun attested a charter of Waldeve, earl of Dunbar. Stephanus de Eyton appears as witness to a charter " *de quieta clamatione de terra de Swintona*," granted by his son, Earl Patrick, who died in 1232. In the reign of William the Lion, Helias, Mauricius, and Adam de Eitun are among the witnesses to a donation of David de Quixwood to the lazaret or hospital of lepers at Auldcambus. In 1250 Adam de Eiton granted to Henry de Lamberton three tofts of land with houses in Eyemouth. In 1331, Adam, the prior of Coldingham, acknowledged a grant made to him of land for the site of a mill near the bridge of Ayton, by Adam, the son of William de Ayton. Robert de Ayton was among the number of the Scots slain at the battle of Nesbit-moor, 22d June 1402.

The principal family ended in an heiress, who, in the reign of James the Third, married George Home, a son of the house of Home, who thus acquired the original lands of Ayton. By charter of date 29th November 1472, the greater part of the lands of Ayton, with those of Whitfield, were granted to George Home, son of Sir Alexander Home of Dunglass, who thus became ancestor of the Homes of Ayton.

History mentions the baronial castle of Ayton, on the banks of the Eye, founded by the Norman baron de Vesci, which was taken by the earl of Surrey in 1498, but no vestiges of it now remain. The modern mansion-house of Ayton, built upon its site, was destroyed by fire in 1834.

A branch of the Berwickshire Aytons settled in the county of Fife, and Skene imputes a Gaelic origin to the name. "The Pictish Chronicle," he says, "in mentioning the foundation of the church of Abernethy, describes the boundaries of the territory ceded to the Culdees by the Pictish king as having been ' *a lapide in Apurfeit usque ad lapidem juxta Cairful, id est Lethfoss, et inde in altum usque ad Athan.*' It is a remarkable fact that the same places are still known by these names, although slightly corrupted into those of Apurfarg, Carpow, and *Ayton*, and that the words are unquestionably Gaelic." [*Skene's Highlanders of Scotland*, vol. i. p. 76.]

In 1507, James the Fourth disponed the west half of the lands of Denmuir, or Nether Denmuir, in the parish of Abdie, Fifeshire, to Andrew Ayton, captain of the castle of Stirling, a son of the family of Ayton of Ayton, in Berwickshire, "pro bono et fideli servitio." He was the uncle of the heiress of Ayton above mentioned, and in consequence of the original lands of Ayton having passed, by her marriage, to the house of Home, he obtained a new charter of the lands of Nether Denmuir, in which they were named Ayton, and the Fifeshire branch of the family were afterwards styled Ayton of Ayton.

Sir John Ayton of that ilk left two sons, Robert and Andrew. Robert, the eldest, succeeded to the estates of his uncle Robert, Lord Colville of Ochiltree, and in consequence, assumed the name of Colville, being styled Robert Colville of Craigflower. The second son, Andrew, was a merchant in Glasgow, of which city he became lord provost. He built a large house, surrounded by a garden, near the High Street of Glasgow, the site of which, now occupied by public works, is still called Ayton court.

About the commencement of the eighteenth century the lands of Ayton in Fife were acquired by Patrick Murray, Esq., second son of Sir Patrick Murray, the second baronet of Ochtertyre, and they still continue in the possession of his descendant.

The Aytons of Inchdairnie, in the parish of Kinglassie, are understood to be the lineal descendants of the Anglo-Norman de Vescis, who settled in Berwickshire. Inchdairnie has, for a long period, been the property of the Aytons. Of this family was Major-general Roger Ayton of Inchdairnie, who died about 1810. His eldest son, John Ayton, was served Ayton of Ayton in 1829. Another son, James Ayton, Esq., advocate, stood candidate for the representation of the city of Edinburgh, some years ago.

Towards the end of the seventeenth century the lands of Kippoo, in the parish of Kingsbarns, were sold by the representative of the family of John Philp, burgess in Cupar, to whom they belonged, to Sir John Ayton, younger son of Ayton of Ayton, who was gentleman of the bed-chamber and usher of the black rod to Charles the Second. He was succeeded in them, in 1700, by his grandson, John Ayton of Kinaldie. To the latter family Sir Robert Ayton, the subject of the following notice, belonged.

AYTON, SIR ROBERT, an accomplished poet, a younger son of Andrew Ayton of Kinaldie, Fifeshire, was born there in 1570, and studied at St. Leonard's college, St. Andrews, where he took the degree of master of arts in 1588. He afterwards went to France, where he resided for some time. In 1603 he addressed from Paris an elegant panegyric, in Latin verse, to King James the Sixth, on his accession to the crown of England, which was printed at Paris the same year. On his appearance at court he was knighted, and appointed one of the gentlemen of the bedchamber, and private secretary to the queen. He was also, subsequently, secretary to Henrietta Maria, queen of Charles I. About 1609 he was sent by James as ambassador to the emperor of Germany, with the king's 'Apology for the Oath of Allegiance,' which he had dedicated to all the crowned heads of Europe. He was highly esteemed by all the men of genius and poets of his time, and Ben Jonson took pride in informing Drummond of Hawthornden, that "Sir Robert Ayton loved him dearly." He died at London in March 1638, and was buried in the south aisle of the choir of Westminster Abbey, where a handsome monument was erected by his nephew, David Ayton of Kinaldie, to his memory.

A representation of it is given in Smith's *Iconographia Scotica*, with his bust in the centre, of which the following is a woodcut:

The following is the inscription on his monument:

Clarissmi omnigenaq. virtvte et ervditione, præsertim Poesi ornatissmi eqvitis, Domini Roberti Aitoni, ex antiqva et illvstri gente Aitona, ad Castrvm Kinnadinvm apvd Scotos, orivndi, qvi a Serenissmo R. Jacobo in Cvbicvla Interiora admissvs, in Germaniam ad Imperatore, Imperiiq. Principes cvm libello Regio, Regiæ avthoritatis vindice, Legatvs, ac primvm Annæ, demvm Mariæ, serenissmis Britanniarvm Reginis ab epistolis, consiliis et libellis supplicibvs, nec non Xenodochio Stæ Catherinæ præfectvs. Anima Creatori Reddita, hic depositis mortalibvs exvviis secvndvm Redemptoris adventvm expectat.

Carolvm linqvens, repetit Parentem
Et valedicens Mariæ, revisit
Annam et Avlai decvs, alto Olympi
Mvtat Honore.
Hoc devoti gratiq. animi
Testimonium optimo Patrvo
Jo. Aitonvs M L P.

Obiit Cœlebs in Regia Albavla
Non sine maximo Honore omnivm
Lvctv et Mœrore, Ætat. svæ LXVIII.
Salvt. Hvmanæ M.DCXXXVIII.
MVSARVM DECVS HIC, PATRLÆQ. AVLÆQ. DOMIQVE ET FORIS EXEMPLAR SED NON IMITABILE HONESTI.

At the top is, Decerptæ Dabvnt Odorem, the motto of the Aytons.

His English poems are few in number. They are remarkable for their purity of style and delicacy of fancy. The following lyric is accounted one of his best pieces:

ON WOMAN'S INCONSTANCY.

I lov'd thee once, I'll love no more,
  Thine be the grief as is the blame;
Thou art not what thou wast before,
  What reason I should be the same?
      He that can love unlov'd again,
      Hath better store of love than brain:
God send me love my debts to pay,
While unthrifts fool their love away.

Nothing could have my love o'erthrown,
  If thou hadst still continued mine;
Yea, if thou hadst remain'd thy own,
  I might perchance have yet been thine.
      But thou thy freedom did recall,
      That if thou might elsewhere enthral;
And then how could I but disdain
A captive's captive to remain?

When new desires had conquer'd thee,
  And changed the object of thy will,
It had been lethargy in me,
  Not constancy to love thee still.
      Yea, it had been a sin to go
      And prostitute affection so,
Since we are taught no prayers to say
To such as must to others pray.

Yet do thou glory in thy choice,
  Thy choice of his good fortune boast;
I'll neither grieve nor yet rejoice,
  To see him gain what I have lost:
      The height of my disdain shall be,
      To laugh at him, to blush for thee;
To love thee still, but go no more,
A begging to a beggar's door.

In a different style are the following stanzas prefixed to his *Basia sive Strena Cal. Jan.* Lond. 1605, 4to. They are addressed "To the most worshipful and worthy Sir James Hay, Gentleman of his Majesty's bedchamber."

When Janus' keys unlocks the gates above,
  And throws more age on our sublunar lands,
I sacrifice with flames of fervent love
  These hecatombs of kisses to thy hands.
Their worth is small, but thy deserts are such,
They'll pass in worth, if once thy shrine they touch.

Laugh but on them, and then they will compare
  With all the harvest of th' Arabian fields,

With all the pride of that perfumed air
  Which winged troops of musked Zephyrs yields,
When with their breath they embalm the Elysian plain,
And make the flow'rs reflect those scents again.

Yea, they will be more sweet in their conceit
  Than Venus' kisses spent on Adon's wounds,
Than those wherewith pale Cynthia did entreat
  The lovely shepherd of the Latmian bounds,
And more than those which Jove's ambrosial mouth
Prodigalized upon the Trojan youth.

I know they cannot such acceptance find,
  If rigour censure their uncourtly frame;
But thou art courteous, and wilt call to mind
  Th' excuse which shields both me and them from blame;
My Muse was but a novice into this,
And, being virgin, scarce well taught to kiss.

A panegyrical sonnet by Ayton occurs among 'The Poetical Essays of Alexander Craige, Scotobritane,' sig. F. 3. London 1604, 4to. [*Irving's Scottish Poets*, vol. ii. p. 300, *note*.] A beautiful song, commencing, "I do confess thou'rt smooth and fair," printed anonymously in Lawes's 'Ayres and Dialogues,' 1659, and rendered into Scotch by Burns without improving it, has been attributed to Sir Robert Ayton, but without any other ground than that "in purity of language, elegance, and tenderness, it resembles his undoubted lyrics." In 'Watson's Collection of Scottish poems,' 1706-11, several of Ayton's pieces are inserted together with his name, but the poem mentioned appears without it, separate from those that are stated to be his. John Aubrey styles Ayton "one of the best poets of his time." According to Dempster, he also wrote Greek and French verses. Several of his Latin poems are preserved in the 'Delitiæ Poetarum Scotorum,' printed in 1637 at Amsterdam.—*Bannatyne Miscellany.*—The following is a list of his works:

Ad Jacobum VI. Britanniarum Regem, Angliam petentem, Panegyris, p. 40. inter Delitias Poetarum Scotorum, edit. ab Arturo Johnstono. Amst. 1637, 8vo.

Basia, sive Strena ad Jacobum Hayum, Equitem illustrissimum, p. 54.

Lessus in Funere Raphaelis Thorei, Medici, et Poetæ præstantissimi, Londoni peste extincti, p. 61. ibid.

Carina Caro, p. 63. ib.

De Proditione Pulverea, quæ incidet in diem Martis, p. 65. ib.

Gratiarum Actio, cum in privatum Cubiculum admitteretur. p. 66. ibid.

Epigrammata Varia, ib.

In Obitum Ducis Buckingamii, à Filtono cultro extincti, MDCXXVIII. p. 74. ibid.